THE NATIONAL HISTORY OF FRANCE

EDITED BY

FR. FUNCK-BRENTANO

WITH AN INTRODUCTION BY J. E. C. BODLEY

THE CENTURY OF THE
RENAISSANCE

THE NATIONAL HISTORY OF FRANCE

THE CENTURY OF THE RENAISSANCE

[CROWNED BY THE ACADÉMIE DES
SCIENCES MORALES ET POLITIQUES]

BY

LOUIS BATIFFOL

AUTHOR OF "THE DUCHESSE DE CHEVREUSE"

TRANSLATED FROM THE FRENCH BY

ELSIE FINNIMORE BUCKLEY

WITH AN INTRODUCTION BY

JOHN EDWARD COURTENAY BODLEY

CORRESPONDING MEMBER OF THE INSTITUTE OF FRANCE

LONDON

WILLIAM HEINEMANN

London: William Heinemann, 1916

INTRODUCTION

By JOHN EDWARD COURTENAY BODLEY

CORRESPONDING MEMBER OF THE INSTITUTE OF FRANCE

FOR the keener enjoyment of life there is no pursuit so profitable and so easy as the familiar study of French history. It does not require that special education which enables the few to find consolation at times of trouble in the ancient classics, where Greek tragedy makes sublime the depths of human woe, or where the brighter scepticism of Horace dispels for a sunny hour the darkest clouds of dejection. Apart from such favoured amateurs of distraction there are very many cultivated English people who, in their desultory or regular reading, like to understand allusions, and who have a sense of missed enjoyment when a name of place or person conveys to them no distinct idea.

To comprehend every allusion met with in general literature and to recognize every name would need, if not the whole sum of human knowledge, at least a portion so large that it would be more conveniently lodged in an encyclopædia than in the memory of man or woman. But it is astonishing what an extensive and enlivening light is thrown on ordinary reading by a knowledge of the history of France. This has always been the experience of English readers in their perusal of fiction and of memoirs, of political and of philosophical works. It is more than ever apparent in the present war-time, when every morning brings a list of places in France where things have happened, which when details are known, may for ever after be associated in many a British home with proud sorrow or pathetic rejoicing.

The part of France which is now the scene of war is a relatively small tract of that country. There is many a province—Touraine, Burgundy, Provence—richer in traditions of the past. Yet this north-eastern region, which includes populous industrial districts of unromantic aspect as well as rural expanses of mountain, forest, and vineyard, has more historical associations on its soil than the whole of Great Britain —our comparative poverty in that respect being chiefly due to our insular immunity from invasion. Not that all the annals of north-eastern France are those of siege and battle, as we shall see if we pass in review some of the place-names which to-day are of warlike sound to English ears. From a survey of this limited portion of France, which happens to be of peculiar interest to us just now, we shall gain some idea of the wealth of associations which abound on the whole of French territory for those who enjoy a knowledge of the history of France.

In one of the recurring periods of war which desolated this region, when Louis XIV had so many feats of arms to celebrate that he founded the Academy of Inscriptions to invent devices for his medals and triumphal arches, not a few of the inscriptions so composed relate to towns on either side of the present frontier, the names of which are sadly familiar in England to-day. " Ypris captis " and " Atrebatum liberatum," engraved on fine examples of the medallist's art, show that, in the days of *la guerre en dentelles*, Ypres was taken and Arras relieved without the barbarous havoc which before our eyes has irreparably wrecked noble monuments which even then were the ancient pride of Flanders and of Artois.

In these war-frequented provinces the memory of a hundred battles and sieges in different ages is revived in the names of places where the forces of England and France have resisted a common foe. At Compiègne the Tour de la Pucelle recalls Joan of Arc captured by the Burgundian army and delivered to her executioner, Cauchon, bishop of Beauvais. The stately collegiate church of Saint Quentin witnessed the deadly assault when Coligny and his Huguenots were overcome, and Philip II of Spain vowed to build the Escorial in gridiron shape, in honour of the martyrdom of St. Lawrence, under whose invocation the Catholics won the day. The cathedral-crowned mountain of Laon stands above the fateful plain where Napoleon, in his last struggle in France, might have won a victory to save him from

vi

INTRODUCTION

Fontainebleau and Elba, if Marmont had only come up sooner from Berry-au-Bac—that ferry on the river Aisne well-known to all who pore over the war-maps of to-day.

While battle scenes such as these make the invaded French provinces of unusual interest to the student of military history, they are rich in associations which can charm the imagination away from memories of warfare. Herein lies a signal advantage of a familiar knowledge of the history of France. The names of places in the dry official *communiqués* of the war need no longer be associated solely with heroic and tragic conflicts. As we scan them the brilliant procession of the annals of France defiles before us, illustrating every element and phase of human intelligence and emotion, as expressed in romantic adventure, in ambitious statecraft, in religious controversy, in philosophic and popular movement—all recorded, in poetry and in prose, in that noble tongue which reflects the genius of the people, who, since their language attained its perfection, have never lost their proud position in Europe, in spite of harsh vicissitudes.

Take, for instance, the little town of Albert on the blood-stained road from Amiens to Arras. Its name, often mentioned in the dispatches, had its origin in events from which modern France may be said to have sprung. It was once called Ancre, after the rapid tributary of the Somme which flows thereby ; and when Louis XIII was a boy, Concini, the Italian favourite of the Queen-mother, became Maréchal and Marquis d'Ancre, and governor of Picardy. The young king also had a favourite, his falconer, Albert de Luynes, who had Concini slain on the drawbridge of the Louvre and inherited the Marquisate, which, as the name of Ancre had become odious, was henceforth called Albert. It was out of the disorders caused by the government of the two favourites that Richelieu arose and moulded the future destinies of France.

Then there is Cambrai, the witness of wars for a thousand years, yet endowed with gentler associations, such as those which cling to the remains of the archiepiscopal palace where Fénelon solaced his exile from the Court by writing *Télémaque*—not imagining, as Voltaire said, how superior was the pastime of his banishment to his controversial works on quietism. At the far

INTRODUCTION

limit of the invaded territory where the German advance was turned, stands another city, Meaux, which had much to do with those same controversies ; for it was there that the mystical Mme. Guyon was interned until she retracted her doctrines before Bossuet, who lies in the cathedral made famous by his eloquence. It has now a new title to fame, since the first anniversary of the battle of the Marne was celebrated at its high altar under circumstances not anticipated by the Eagle of Meaux, when mass was sung by a gallant lieutenant on leave from active service, who in civil life was a Jesuit father.

Thence each town and village on the line of the German retreat is full of old memories. Away to the right is Sainte Ménehould, where Postmaster Drouet changed the course of the Revolution and the history of Europe by his chance recognition of Louis XVI and the Queen trying to escape from France through the Argonne woodlands. Westward from here is Reims, where German barbarians showed that there are even worse enemies of noble architecture than restoring architects, who had already ravaged the superb cathedral. Amid the memorials of coronation pageants it is rarely remembered that under its shadow La Fontaine, till he found his own vocation, studied for the priesthood, coming from another ancient town on the line of retreat, Château Thierry, where, by the Marne, he kept company with *Maître Corbeau* and *Petit Poisson*, whose descendants have watched the flight of German airships or felt the shock of spattering shells.

Northward hence is all that bombardment has left of Soissons, whither Louis XIV used to send noble Protestant maidens to be converted to the Catholic faith in the Benedictine Abbey of Our Lady. This brings us again near Compiègne, where Louis le Grand in different mood set up a glittering camp as a spectacle for Mme. de Maintenon. Here too is the site of another camp which Napoleon pitched—for once in his life with peaceful intent—to grace his first meeting with his bride, Marie Louise, when Berthier, who had married her by proxy, brought her to France as tribute from vanquished Austria. Here on the edge of the forest is the frigid château of Louis XV, which was warmed into boisterous life by the other Napoleon, who held his gay court there when Mexico was giving premoni-

viii

tions of Sedan, and Galliffet, a hero of both fatal campaigns, led the imperial revels.

This beautiful woodland country is now associated in many English hearts with a rare episode in the grim, underground war of trenches ; for it was here that British cavalry was able to charge the enemy in the open. To one who for many a year wandered at leisure through the exquisite region which stretches from the confines of Île de France and Picardy to the undulating plains of the Brie and the vineyards of Champagne, it is difficult to realize that such pleasant scenes, which had lost all trace of ancient battles, should now be dotted with little crosses which mark the resting-places of hundreds of brave young Englishmen who were the light and joy of their distant homes. When one drove on a summer morning through the forest, where Pierrefonds rises among the trees like a fairy palace, and met with peasants on their way to market at Villers-Cotterets ; or at the Fête-Dieu passed a procession of rustic maidens crossing the fields to a village by the Marne ; or among the autumn tints heard " le son du cor, le soir, au fond des bois," which rallied a joyous troop cantering along grass-rides after the stag or the wild boar—how little one thought that

> *Every turf beneath their feet*
> *Shall be a soldier's sepulchre*

—a sepulchre in which lie side by side stalwart young English heroes in khaki and gallant little red-legged soldiers of the French army, united in fraternal sleep, never anticipated by the warriors of old who passed this way, from Joan of Arc to Napoleon.

Of all the picturesque towns hereabout, whose names have now pathetic significance in many an English home, Villers-Cotterets is perhaps most suggestive of historical reminiscence, for a particular reason. Noyon, embowered in fruit blossom in the spring, has the austere tradition of Calvin, descended from a race of bargemen who lived upon the Oise ; and the less austere memory of its bishops, such as Clermont-Tonnerre with his heraldic fancies still traced on a fragment of the palace, and his Gallican presumption which moved him to refer to the Pope as " Monsieur de Rome." Senlis, sad victim of German savages, who murdered its mayor and left it in ruins, was so desirable that Saint-Simon records how the son of the Grand Condé envied his family the governorship of this royal town—"Monsieur le Prince muguetoit fort le gouvernement de Senlis." Yet Villers-Cotterets, though its church, unlike those of Noyon and Senlis, was never a cathedral, and though its château, a faded memorial of the most magnificent of royal builders, François I, has been put to base uses, has an importance in the romance of French history which none of its neighbours can approach. For here Dumas Père was born; and having died during the invasion of 1870 he was brought back to his birthplace by his illustrious son when the Germans had departed, and he lies by the side of his parents beneath the great trees of the cemetery at Villers-Cotterets.

Whatever inaccuracies flowed from his rapid pen in describing unfamiliar scenes, Dumas' works relating to his native region are better than any guide-book. There is scarcely a town or village of north-eastern France touched by the present war which he has not illustrated. Many of the itineraries traced in his novels read like passages from the letters of English officers at the front, whose mention of place-names has escaped the censor. Take the last youthful adventure of the Mousquetaires when they were riding down Milady to her doom. From Béthune (where they had found the red-mantled headsman), they rode in silence through the village of Festubert, past the woods of Richebourg, to Herlies. Just before Fromelles a storm broke, and then on their right, by a lightning flash, they saw the village of Erquinghem, and at midnight, the moon, rising behind Armentières, lit up the scene of the drama on the banks of the Lys. This is pure romance; but when Dumas enters the domain of history we find similar enumeration of places which we all know by name too well. Twenty years later, when the son of Athos was on his way to join the staff of Condé, just before the battle of Lens, "the little troop followed the road to Cambrin, where they expected to find the Prince. But he had retired to La Bassée, having been informed that the enemy would cross the Lys at Estaires. Misled by this information the Prince had withdrawn his forces from Béthune and had concentrated between Vieille Chapelle and La Ventie." What

x

INTRODUCTION

memories and associations the dozen names in those two passages evoke in the minds of many an English family which has known the anguish of suspense while waiting for news from the front.

A score of similar passages, relating to places where English soldiers have fought and died in the present campaign, are at hand from Dangeau, Saint-Simon, Voltaire, and other orthodox historians who wrote not long after the events which they described. But Dumas is chosen for a special reason. To him a very large number of English people of the last three generations owed the only notions they possessed of French history, and many of them were first tempted by his fascinating pages to study the authentic annals of France, a knowledge of which doubles the enjoyment of his romances by enabling his readers to reconstitute the scenes while verifying their accuracy. Indeed with such a knowledge we may sometimes find that the history of France in its unadorned details is more romantic than any romance founded upon it. Thus, in *Vingt Ans Après* Dumas wrote retrospectively, in a moment of exaggerated restraint, that Concini, whose career we have noted, was prosaically hanged ; the bare truth being that the favourite of Marie de Médicis was shot by the captain of the guard beneath the portcullis of the Louvre amid picturesque surroundings of melodrama.

After all, professional historians are often more inaccurate than Dumas ever was. When he placed the sale of Charles I by the Scots in the month of the King's execution, he made a milder error than did Lord Morley of Blackburn, the author of several works of serious merit on French history, when in a debate on the Parliament Bill he told the House of Lords that the " Day of Dupes "—on which Richelieu foiled an intrigue of the Queen-mother in 1630—was an episode of the Revolution in 1789, when " the aristocrats, as they were called, surrendered their rights."

More pertinent to our subject than the Minister's mistake was the failure of the Lords to detect it. The force of his didactic warning lay in the allusion to the French Revolution which had swept away another nobility, and his words offered a twofold opening for retort—first that the " Day of Dupes " was 159 years before the Revolution ; and second, that when the French nobility did surrender their privileges on a famous day of 1789, those rights had no analogy whatever with the powers of the House of Lords. While a moderate knowledge of the capital events of French history would have furnished an effective reply, no one moved—neither the peers by inheritance; nor the bishops, some of whom still merit their consecrated epithet of " well-learned " ; nor even the lords of the new plutocracy, who earned the purchase-money of their peerages after enjoying the advantages of " a good modern education," which being innocent of the ancient humanities ought to include the rudiments of modern history.

While the incident indicates the utility of an acquaintance with French history, and the limitations of educated Englishmen in that pleasant field of knowledge, there is no doubt about the keen interest which our cultivated classes take in the literature of France. Though a large number of English people read the French language as easily as their own, there is a considerable demand for good translations of memoirs and historical works among those who are too indolent or too diffident to read the French originals. For such the systematic study of French history is not easy if they seek pleasure in their reading. There is no lack of English works on various periods of French history, and among them are a certain number of valuable monographs, well written by conscientious workers who have gone to original sources for their material. None the less it must be confessed that the majority of English books on the history of France are ill-made and unattractive. It is to be hoped that we have left behind the age when anything was considered good enough for a handbook of modern European history—as Matthew Arnold complained when his son, by the rule of Balliol, had to read for a low " class " in the History-school, from second-rate manuals produced by second-rate minds, instead of learning thoroughly the Plato and the Tacitus set for the old Pass-degree. Yet even now the compilation of books on French history for the use of candidates for honours at the Universities is sometimes confided to writers so incompetent that their confused pages show that they have not mastered even the elements of the French language.

However good may be a monograph which deals with a single period or movement, it fails to give the reader who has little previous acquaintance with the subject, a general view

xii

of the history of a nation which will make him feel at home in any of its epochs and with its chief characters. It would be a very great labour for an Englishman to write a general history of France. Ten years of incessant toil would not suffice for it, and however well equipped the writer, the result would certainly not justify his trouble. The English reader, therefore, who would have that general view of French history which, as was said in the first words of this preface, will make his outlook on the world more agreeable, must find it in a French work, either in its original form or in a translation.

It is to be hoped that the history of France, which is here presented in an English translation, will fulfil that purpose. The *National History of France*—which in its original version is entitled " *L'histoire de France racontée à tous* "—in form and volume stands between Duruy's excellent abridgement and the exhaustive *Histoire de France, depuis les origines, jusqu'à la Révolution*, edited by M. Lavisse. For a complete survey of French history there is no work more useful than that of Victor Duruy, Minister of Education under the Second Empire, and under the Third Republic the successor of Mignet, a more academic historian, at the French Academy. The industrious Duruy's manual is a marvel of compression and of lucid narrative, but is perhaps too concise to be read with pleasure in a translation. On a different plan is the more recent work, edited by M. Lavisse, each section of which, written by an expert, is an invaluable guide for the special student—such as that masterpiece of attractive erudition *Les Premiers Capétiens* by the lamented Achille Luchaire. But this series of big volumes is perhaps too long for general readers.

The National History of France is planned on the same model —but on a smaller scale. It is written for a more numerous though not a less cultivated class of readers. The serious student will find in it a scientific exposition of the development of France from the period when it first became a homogeneous nation down to the lifetime of old people whom some of us have known. The reader who looks for artistic or romantic diversion will meet with many a page, drawn from contemporary memoirs or correspondence, which illustrates the manners, the social conditions, the intellectual achievement of successive generations of the French.

INTRODUCTION

Each volume of this history has been written by an author whose ability has been recognized by competent French authorities, and all of them but one are " Laureates " of the Institute of France. The Institute, with the five Academies composing it, holds vast revenues to distribute for the encouragement of every branch of human intelligence. About £18,000 of these funds are dispensed each year in prizes for recently published books. Many of the prizes awarded by the Académie Française and the Académie des Sciences Morales are for works on history, and often an historian who has won fame and a seat in one or both of those companies found his first incentive when he carried off a prize together with the title of " Laureate of the Institute."

Those who fear that criticism in France is going the way that George Meredith thought it had taken in England when he wrote, " I have seen many reviews, not one criticism of my books," should look at the reports of the academicians who recommend the awards of these prizes. Hidden away in the official *Bulletins*, they are sometimes fine examples of that critical faculty which is inborn in most Frenchmen, and a prize-winner often feels that, with a substantial recompense, he has received a stimulating criticism which if heeded will add to the value of his future work. A history book " crowned " by the Institute is sure to be a sound piece of work, sometimes the first-fruits of a promising career, sometimes a masterpiece of mature talent ; for historians as eminent as Albert Sorel and Albert Vandal (*nulli flebiliores quam mihi*) have been glad to submit their work to an academic prize tribunal. While poets and novelists have sometimes revolted against the taste of the French Academy, complaint is rarely heard of the judgment of the Institute of France in appraising historical work.

The Institute thus fulfils the traditional functions of academies in maintaining a certain standard of excellence; it also out of its wealth aids promising writers to persevere in their work, relieved from that care which often dogs unremunerated literary labour. One reason for the rarity we have noted of good English monographs on French history is the cost of their production. An eager student spends time and money in exploring foreign archives, and on his researches writes a book of real value. If he is urged to continue his work he will reply

xiv

INTRODUCTION

that he cannot afford it, as the only material result of his labour
is a debt to his publisher. Many an English author of such
unrequited work would in France be aided in his difficult years
by the substantial encouragement of academic prizes. The well-
meaning people who periodically conceive the idea of starting
in England an Academy on the French model should bear in
mind that even if they could possess the unattainable authority
of tradition for performing academic functions, they would still
need rich endowments to make their influence effective.

M. Louis Batiffol's history of the age of the Renaissance in
France, which forms this volume, was awarded the *Prix Perret*
by the Académie des Sciences Morales et Politiques. The
report of M. Welschinger, recommending that award, is an
admirable example of the judicious criticism which, as has been
observed, academicians bestow on the books submitted to their
examination. M. Welschinger is a patriotic Alsatian, who for
five-and-forty years has been longing for the day—perhaps
nearly in sight—when his birthplace and the scenes of his
youth may be once more united to France. This loyal patriot
is also an accomplished writer of French history in its most
attractive guise, whose work had won the highest academic
recompenses before he was called to a seat in the Palais Mazarin.
His report on M. Batiffol's work is one of those which shows
what an advantage writers enjoy in France to have their early
efforts reviewed and analysed by distinguished veterans who
have won fame in their own paths of literature.

The National History of France when complete will have as
its first part a volume on the Middle Ages by M. Funck-Brentano,
the editor of the series, the other books, in their order of publication, being *The Century of the Renaissance*, by M. Louis Batiffol ;
The Great Century (Le Grand Siècle), by M. Jacques Boulenger ;
The Eighteenth Century, by M. Casimir Stryienski ; *The Revolution*, by M. Louis Madelin ; and *The Consulate and the Empire*,
by the same author.

Pending the publication of the volume on the Middle Ages,
the English reader need have no reason to regret that his study of
French history begins at a later period. For it was only with the
Renaissance that the territory which we know as France became
a nation, and took its place on the map of Europe in a shape not

b   xv far removed from its present contour—though each subsequent century has seen considerable adjustments of its frontier, which have not yet come to an end. It was during the Renaissance that the French language developed its present form. Until then French was a language which in its relation with modern French may, in an unscientific way, be compared with the language of Wyclif's Bible in its relation with the English of the Authorized Version. Just when that period was ending " Enfin Malherbe vint "—as Boileau wrote to a later generation—and, doing for poetry what Calvin, Amyot, La Boétie and Montaigne had already done for prose, with them gave to the newly-formed nation the noble language which more than any other element has contributed to the greatness of France.

Our narrative begins before either of those writers was born, in 1483, with the death of Louis XI at Plessis-le-Tours, and it is a good starting-point for the English student of the modern history of France. He must bear in mind the importance of the reign of Louis XI, who, coming after the Hundred Years' War, carried on the work of the unification of France with results more definitive than those produced by the expulsion of the English when Joan of Arc inspired the idea of nationality. The Burgundian domain of Charles the Bold was only a small part of his annexations, when he crushed the feudal territorial houses and out of their ruins began the building of the absolute French monarchy on the double basis of unity of government and unity of territory. In 1483 it was only thirty years since the taking of Constantinople by the Turks, and the invention of printing. As Hume says, writing of two years later, " We have at last reached the dawn of civility and science." The Renaissance was in full progress ; but it was so young that it was only in 1483 that two lives began which in different ways affected the course of one of its greatest movements—Martin Luther and Catherine of Arragon being born in that year.

M. Batiffol is a skilful guide through that most important century of human progress which spans the interval between the Middle Ages and modern civilization. It is a confused epoch of French history, a period of contradictory movements and currents, in which the nation was only beginning to discover its destiny. The author instead of subjective dissertations on the origins of events and movements, gives us a series of vivid pictures and portraits, chiefly taken from contemporary records, and the result is an animated narrative which cannot fail to impress the memory and charm the imagination of the reader.

After the sinister and forcible figure of Louis XI, his young son, Charles VIII (1483–1498) and his cousin, the virtuous Louis XII (1498–1515), are somewhat pale shadows. France, becoming a united nation, was prosperous, but the importance of territorial unity was not yet understood. The lure of Italy tempted these kings and their immediate successors to try to extend their domain beyond the Alps, instead of consolidating the conquests of Louis XI, which were so little valued that Artois and Franche Comté were ceded in their vain efforts to annex Italian provinces. Their failure was a blessing for French nationality, and the main result of the Italian campaigns was the importation to France of the artistic spirit of the Renaissance. How much France owed to the Italian Renaissance is discussed in these pages. Even if the debt is smaller than usually estimated, as M. Batiffol argues, the Italian artists brought to France by François I (1515–1547) undoubtedly had a great influence on the native genius. In popular tradition that king was a magnificent voluptuary, the munificent patron of artists and of poets. Yet as one reads the fascinating story of his reign one wonders how he found the time to hold a brilliant court and to adorn France with sumptuous monuments of domestic architecture, which taking the place of the fortified feudal castles, seem to have been planned at leisure for the enjoyment of luxurious peace. If one studied his reign in an old-fashioned history dealing only with public events and international relations, he would seem to be a warrior king passing from Italian battlefields to Spanish prisons, the rival or the captive of the Emperor Charles V, instead of the builder of Fontainebleau and Chambord, the patron of Clément Marot, Jean Goujon and Philibert Delorme.

The shorter reign of his son Henri II (1547–1559), who had little taste for art, was associated with two women. There was his wife Catherine de Médicis, destined to play a great part when she became Queen-mother; and there was his *amie* Diane de Poictiers, whose cipher, still seen on the walls of Chenonceaux intertwined with that of Henri, suggests the romantic union of two young lives to console a king whose childhood was saddened

INTRODUCTION

by captivity in Spain as a hostage for his father, and who was married to an unattractive wife. In these pages it is written that when Henri II succeeded at the age of twenty-nine, Diane was nearly fifty and was the pious companion of the royal couple, under whose influence the King was an affectionate husband—an edifying version of the royal romance.

While such sidelights on history are instructive and entertaining, the great undercurrent of French history in the sixteenth century must not be ignored. While the spirit of reform was transforming the civilized world in art, letters, philosophy, and religion, there was no such movement affecting the system of government in France. The Renaissance consolidated the absolute powers of the monarchy, and from the reign of François I the *ancien régime* may be said to have begun. This is an important fact to be noted by the student who follows the history of France, in the volumes which will succeed this, through the seventeenth century, early in which the policy of Richelieu under Louis XIII leads to the absolute reign of Louis XIV, and through the eighteenth century, in which the excesses of absolute monarchy lead to the catastrophe of 1792. In the sixteenth century, whatever the feeling in the nation about the character of the sovereign, whatever the controversy about the succession to the Crown, whatever the religious test to which the King had to submit, there is no aspiration, no movement towards popular government.

After Henri II came the turbulent reigns of his three sons : François II (1559–1560) who died at seventeen, the tragic boy-husband of Mary Queen of Scots ; Charles IX (1560–1574), who was a king at nine ; Henri III (1574–1589), an effeminate prodigal, the extravagances of whose Court began that disarray of the public finances which was never permanently repaired till it ended two centuries later in the Revolution, of which it was the chief determining cause. In these reigns the Reformation took a dramatic form. It had begun under François I, when Clément Marot, leaving his madrigals, rhymed a Huguenot version of the Psalms—as did the author of *Comus* in the next century, under dissimilar circumstances. Among the Protestants were the greatest names of France—La Rochefoucauld, Grammont, Condé, Rohan, La Trémouille. But the time had not yet come for Protestantism to be withstood as a power

xviii

within the State. The *imperium in imperio* which was resisted by the last of the Valois kings was the catholic League, headed by the Guises, a family of unbounded ambition, which had intended to rule France by Mary Queen of Scots, whose mother was a Guise; and when the death of her husband sent her back to Scotland, the clan devoted its power and ability to obtain the supremacy by other means. The story is graphically told in these pages, how Catherine de Médicis, who had encouraged one of her sons, Charles IX, to countenance the Protestant massacre of St. Bartholemew, abetted his brother Henri III to wage war on the catholic League and to have Henri de Guise murdered before his eyes at the Château of Blois.

With Henri IV (1589–1610) the crown of France fell to the Bourbon family, which was the last line of French kings. The reign which began with civil war and anarchy became pacific when Henri of Navarre abjured the Protestantism of which he was the champion and embraced the religion of the majority of his subjects. In becoming a Catholic the King did not adopt the inflexible policy of his new faith. By the Edict of Nantes he established liberty of conscience in matters religious, and by thus proclaiming the modern principle of toleration he illustrated his reign by a definitive rupture with the Middle Ages. Among the Protestants he chose the wisest of all his counsellors, Sully, whose re-organization of the disordered national finances established the prosperity of France on so firm a basis that it took three long reigns of prodigality to undo all his good work.

With the end of the reign of Henri IV this volume closes. It leaves France consolidated as a nation, enjoying temporary peace and a more solid prosperity, after long years of warfare at home and abroad. In that period of frequent civil war, in which the king was constantly in conflict with part of the nation, we have noted that the issue to be decided was never the power of the Crown or the monarchical principle. Another point, not less important, is to be observed. In the civil wars of this age which were known as the Wars of Religion, the forces opposed to the doctrines and claims of Rome were little influenced by that rationalistic " free-thought " which later became the chief factor in the opposition of the French nation to the Roman Church. In the Reformation epoch the struggle was between Catholic believers and Protestant believers. The execution of Etienne Dolet, who held heretical opinions which happened to be atheistic, was an almost isolated case having no connexion with any great intellectual movement such as was to come.

When Henri IV died in 1610 the French language as we have seen had attained its classical form ; but the great masters who were soon to give expression to it were as yet unborn, excepting one or two, such as Descartes, who was fourteen, and Corneille, six years old. In respect of national literature England was in advance of France, for in 1610 Shakespeare had nearly completed his work. But in the age which was then dawning, France after a tardy start was to surpass its neighbour for a time in the splendour of its literature. The new period was so abundant and illustrious in intellectual achievement that it has been called by posterity the *Grand Siècle*.

The boundaries of the *Grand Siècle* are not unanimously defined. Some make it co-terminous with the reign of Louis XIV (1643–1715). Others extend it to the Regency (1715–1723), under which such great writers as Saint Simon, Le Sage and Montesquieu did some of their work. M. Jacques Boulenger in the second part of the English edition of this history, considers the reigns of Louis XIII and Louis XIV to constitute the *Grand Siècle*. There is good reason for including in it the reign of Louis XIII (1610–1643), which in politics saw the whole career of Richelieu and in literature the finest dramas of Pierre Corneille.

In commenting upon this and the other volumes of the series no attempt will be made to give a summary of the events recorded in them, which are probably familiar to the majority of the readers of this work. But for those who are commencing their study of French history it may be useful to take a rapid view of some of the movements which mark the periods extending from the end of the Renaissance to the French Revolution.

The reign of Louis XIII was the reign of Richelieu, who, having been the spokesman of the clergy at the meeting of the States General when the King was a boy of thirteen, became Minister two years later. It was owing to the outgrowth of Richelieu's policy that the representatives of the nation never met again till 1789. Although the Third Estate made some revendication of the rights of the commons, it was not with them that Richelieu joined issue. He had to deal with the great nobles, still tenacious of their old feudal rights, who again and again revolted against the practical application of his theory that all the political power of the nation should be vested in the King. Many of the nobles were Protestants and utilized the privileges of association, granted to the Huguenots by Henri IV, to set up a State within the State. Richelieu crushed the Protestants and the nobles too, whether Huguenot or Catholic. He died six months before Louis XIII, leaving the monarchy in a position of absolute power, such as the most masterful of the Valois kings had never contemplated.

Richelieu's twofold work, the investiture of the sovereign with absolute power, the abuses of which led to the Revolution, and its corollary, the centralization of government, which still is the basis of the French administrative system, had one rapid result. The feudal aristocracy, with its localized influence, was transformed into a *noblesse de cour* which established itself in the royal precincts, and out of this arose French polite society, which soon became the most brilliant that the world has ever seen. During the reign of Louis XIII and the minority of his son the Hôtel de Rambouillet and the rival salons became the centre of all that was most distinguished by birth or intelligence, and Cardinal Richelieu had in 1635 founded the French Academy, thus securing the support of men of letters to further his policy. Henceforth French history in its minutest detail may be studied in most attractive form. For the age of Memoirs had arrived, and the use which has been made of them in M. Boulenger's and the following volumes should tempt many readers to find inexhaustible delight in the originals. They will not fail to be so tempted by M. Boulenger's narrative—which is as easy to read as a romance— in order to make more intimate acquaintance with some of the makers of the *Grand Siècle*, of whom only a passing glimpse can be given in his attractive pages.

Louis XIV was not five years old when he began his reign, and during his minority the policy of Richelieu was continued by his successor the Sicilian Mazarin, for whom the greater Cardinal had obtained a red hat, and to whom the Queen-Regent, Anne of Austria, gave her affection as well as her confidence. The story of the long reign of Louis XIV is in one sense the chronicle of his Court, for the people counted only as so many millions of human beings capable of being taxed. For this, before another century ended, the monarchy had to pay the supreme penalty. Meanwhile the civil strife which disturbed the minority of Louis XIV did not shake the ever growing royal authority. When the *Parlement*, which was not a representative body but a corporation of magistrates with quasi-legislative powers, resisted the King's government, and when this movement developed into the first war of the Fronde, the leaders on both sides professed their devotion to the person and to the office of the King—in contrast to what had happened in England in that year 1649. So on Mazarin's death, when Louis was twenty-three, all was prepared for his absolute autocracy, and he was trained and ready to exercise it. Other kings of France had reigned with unlimited powers; but Louis XIV established absolute monarchy as a divine theory.

This being accepted by his subjects, so far as they had any voice in the matter, there arose out of the absolute prerogatives of the King a sentiment corresponding to what later on was called patriotism. The word in its French form is not found in the Dictionary of the Academy until the next century, for it did not exist in the *Grand Siècle*, the sentiment as yet being inspired not by the *patrie* and the soil of France, but by the person and the office of the King. The glories of France, in war and in peace, show how strong that devotion was. The highest exponents of the genius of the nation, in every branch of human intelligence and action, were proud of the monarch who encouraged it, and who with their co-operation, added to the national patrimony not only rich territories, but a greater glory than that of conquest—the intellectual supremacy of France and of the French language.

When Louis XIV, his minority ended, took the government into his own hands, the genius of France which illustrated the seventeenth century was already in full development. In letters the work of Pascal, in art the work of Lesueur and Poussin was done. But that posterity was not wrong in giving the name of " the age of Louis XIV " to the most brilliant period of the seventeenth century is shown by a very incomplete list of those who served him or who enjoyed his protection : La Rochefoucauld, Molière, La Fontaine, Bossuet, Boileau, Racine in letters ; in art, Lebrun and Mansard ; in war Turenne, Condé, Louvois ;

INTRODUCTION

in civil and financial administration Colbert. After Colbert's death in 1683 the glory began to fade, though the reign had still thirty-two years to run. War and the King's extravagance, notably in the building of Versailles and other royal palaces, brought dire distress upon the people, owing to the unjust incidence of taxation. Two years after the death of Colbert, who began to re-organize on a sound basis the finances of France and founded its industrial prosperity, Louis XIV revoked the Edict of Nantes. It was the greatest blunder of his reign. The intolerant act, which gave religious monopoly to the Catholic Church, was one of the causes of the philosophic movement in the next century hostile to all religion. It was also economically disastrous, as the persecution of the Protestants swept out of France the industry, the intelligence and the wealth of a large community. This folly was committed when the King had fallen under the influence of Mme. de Maintenon. Had she died and had the great financier lived to direct his master, the reign of Louis XIV perhaps would have been as solidly glorious as it was on the surface, and the monarchy might have avoided the Revolution, which Mirabeau said at its outset was the result of "two centuries of depredation and brigandage."

While the brilliant Court, which insatiably swallowed up the resources of the nation, had, with its social authority, high influence in the domain of art and letters, the nobles composing it had no political power. This point, already mentioned in this preface, cannot be too clearly borne in mind by the English student of French history, who is apt to suppose that there was some analogy between the attributes of the French nobility and the English peerage. The reign of Louis XIV was so long that it covered several entire epochs of English history, in which the relative positions of the Crown and the Estates of the Realm were settled. It began in the year that Hampden fell, when Charles I was fighting for the right divine to tax his subjects. It did not end until England, by Act of Parliament, had imported the Hanoverian dynasty, and George I was reigning under statutory limitations. During the reign of Louis XIV, which had strengthened his absolute prerogatives, our two Revolutions had so settled the British Constitution that the monarchy was subordinate to the Parliament, of which the House of Lords had legislative powers similar to those of the House of Commons.

INTRODUCTION

In England the hereditary nobility was a very limited body enjoying immense political power which descended solely to the eldest sons of peers, without any " privileges " in the French sense of the term.   In France the nobility was an ever growing multitude which enjoyed immense fiscal immunities inherited by all their male descendants, without any political power, which was entirely vested in the King.   The nobles served in the army and had most of the rich prizes of the Church ; but they were so excluded from the government of the country that almost all the great administrative and judicial posts fell to members of the *bourgeoisie*—some of whom were ennobled and added to the crowd of privileged persons.   The privileges of the French nobility were mainly fiscal, and their exemption from the ever increasing burden of taxation caused it to fall on the part of the nation least able to bear it.

The foregoing is not a digression.   It is a necessary exposition of what was at the background of French history in the generations preceding the Revolution.   In the third volume of this series—*The Eighteenth Century*, by M. Casimir Stryienski— the author quotes Voltaire's well known observations, made during his exile in our country, on the advantages of the British Constitution.   " Over here a man is not exempt from paying certain taxes because he is a noble or a priest. . . . The English nation is the only one in the world which has succeeded in limiting the power of the Kings by resisting them. . . . If in England there were only one religion there would be danger of it becoming a despotism : if there were only two they would cut one another's throats ; but as there are thirty they live in peace and happiness."   The last proposition is somewhat exaggerated, though the others are of sober truth.   They were written at the time when the English Constitution, based on a parliamentary system which was in the hands of a governing class, was perfection in the eyes of philosophers whose admiration of it made it the envy of the civilized world.   Such sentiments it ceased to inspire when the representative system became democratic and imitations of it were set up in every corner of the globe.   At all events Voltaire's remarks sum up the condition of things which undermined the brilliant surface of the French monarchy in its last days—the unjust incidence of taxation ; the unlimited prerogative of the royal power ; the monopoly of religion held by one Church.

INTRODUCTION

M. Stryienski, the author of this interesting study of the eighteenth century, though not a Frenchman by origin, is so proficient a master of French history and of the French language that three of his works, including this volume, have been " crowned " by the Institute of France—a distinction of special significance when conferred on a foreigner. Seventy-four years of the eighteenth century are covered by this volume—from the accession of Louis XV in 1715 to the meeting of the States General in 1789, when the march of the deputies through the streets of Versailles to the solemn service before the opening session was likened to the funeral procession of the monarchy. M. Stryienski does not make excessive allusion to the dark undercurrents of national life which were rushing along to the flood of revolution ; nor does he show himself too sensible to the charm of that society which, wilfully unconscious of the rising flood, maintained its gracious brilliancy until it was overwhelmed.

The history of the eighteenth century in France affects attentive students of the declining years of the monarchy in different ways, according to their temperament. By those who judge an epoch not by the general prosperity of the people who lived in it, but by the amount of happiness its products have given to later generations, the eighteenth century, with all its abuses, cannot be deplored without insincerity. For it was those very abuses, arising out of the extravagances of a luxurious and powerful Court, which left for posterity the enjoyment of a profusion of works of art, destined to give refined pleasure to mankind so long as beauty can inspire the most delicate joys of the human senses. After the Renaissance, when France began to take delight in the creations of art revealed to her by the campaigns of her kings in Italy ; after the *Grand Siècle* under the pompous yet noble authority of Louis XIV, who ordained a system, emanating from the King, in which every group of workers, including artists, should have its assigned function in the State in order to enhance the august splendours of the monarchy ; after these epochs, the eighteenth century, in spite of the continued influence of the Royal Academy founded by Louis XIV, is a period of freedom and spontaneity in art which represented all that was most gracious in the society soon to be swept away. In one branch of art alone, that of painting, a mere enumeration of the names of a few of the masters shows that the irregularities of the Regent and of Louis XV, and the light-hearted frivolity of Marie Antoinette, before the evil days drew nigh, were not without compensation. In portraiture there were Rigaud, Largillière, Nattier and Drouais; among decorative painters Van Loo, Boucher and Fragonard; among the painters of *fêtes galantes*, Watteau, Pater and Lancret; among painters of more familiar scenes, Chardin and Greuze. In this list there are, perhaps, no names of the highest rank such as those of Velasquez or of the chief masters of the Italian Renaissance. Yet the world would be poorer without their memorials of the age in which they lived. It is likely that the present generation, in more than one democracy, will see public misery not less acute than that suffered by the people in the latter days of the French monarchy. If it befalls us it will be found that its causes are some of those which were at the root of the distress in France in the eighteenth century—ruinous war, improvident statesmanship, extravagant finance in peace-time. But our posterity will not be consoled with the heritage of exquisite works of art reflecting a brilliant society which brought to perfection the relations of human intercourse.

Without referring to the other branches of French art we should note that in the eighteenth century literature and art did not go hand in hand. While the prevailing characteristic of French painting was an unrestrained love of lightness and grace, the general tendency of literature was profoundly serious—not solemn or austere, for there is little solemnity in the fine sarcasm of the *Lettres Persanes* or austerity in the bitter raillery of the *Ingénu*. There are exceptions, such as the comedies of Marivaux, which re-echo the graceful trifling of the age; but the great names in letters, which fill the period, are Montesquieu, Voltaire and Rousseau. Never before or since have writers had such influence on the opinion and the destinies of a nation.

If Louis XV had not been a fool as well as a profligate, if he had been advised by ministers of the intelligence of Colbert, and had followed their advice, the people, receiving a due share of the wealth of their rich country, would have remained the indifferent and contented spectators and subjects of the absolute government. But the public misery was so profound under the ever-growing burden of inequitable taxation that the philosophers, continuing the studies of social conditions begun by La

xxvi

INTRODUCTION

Bruyère, Fénelon, and others under Louis XIV, first created a public opinion which had not hitherto existed in France, and then guided it to demand full inquiry into the causes of the ills which oppressed the nation. The circles about the Court did not oppose the new ideas. The salons and boudoirs which inspired the graceful masterpieces of artists, became the meeting-places of philosophers, dilettante and serious, of both sexes, who discussed the *Esprit des Lois*, the *Dictionnaire Philosophique* and the *Contrat Social*, little thinking that the application of the doctrines contained in them was about to sweep out of existence their brilliant society.

Every school of thought and intelligence encouraged the revolt, from the authors of the *Encyclopædia*—in which the whole range of the sciences was expounded in a manner hostile to the existing social order and to religion—to Beaumarchais, whose *Mariage de Figaro*, played at the Français in 1785, was the final expression before the Revolution of the hatred and contempt of the commons for the privileged classes of society and for the institutions from which the privileged alone derived any profit. So it came about that the chaos in all departments of the State, the defective judicial and administrative organization, the financial disarray, the plunder of public money and the crushing incidence of taxation on the lower classes—all this combined with military disasters abroad, in which France lost her finest oversea possessions, and with religious persecution at home, aided the philosophic precursors of the Revolution to stir up the people to overthrow the power which had made France a nation. Even though Louis XVI had been a wise man, he came too late to save the absolute monarchy, though he might have saved his own head.

Then came the Revolution. If any one is capable of writing a brief summary of the ten years between the election of the Deputies of the States-General and Bonaparte's *coup d'état* of Brumaire, 1799, it is not the author of this Introduction. M. Madelin, who contributes to this series the section on the *Revolution*, apologizes for having attempted to do it in a closely printed volume of 600 pages in the French edition. Every year brings to light a mass of new documents on the period, in such abundance that Reviews and Societies have been founded for the purpose of studying them. Moreover, the Revolution is not a " *bloc*," as M. Clemenceau argued in 1891 when he opposed the representation of Sardou's *Thermidor* at the Français, on the ground that nothing should be played at a state-subventioned theatre which held up to reprobation any part of the Revolution from which the Republic claimed its origin. In the words of the lamented Albert Vandal, quoted in the Preface to this volume: "The Revolution, far from being a '*bloc*' is perhaps the most complex phenomenon that ever existed, a phenomenon essentially manifold in its causes, its elements, its movements, its consequences." M. Madelin has done his work well, as might be expected from a historian whose shorter monographs have shown great promise. With this volume he won the *Grand Prix Gobert* of the French Academy. That distinction, which is the blue riband of history-prizes, puts him in the same category with Albert Sorel, Albert Vandal and Thureau-Dangin, among historians who have died in recent years, and with M. Henri Welschinger and M. Pierre de la Gorce, who are happily still with us. The bibliographies at the end of each chapter are a testimony to M. Madelin's thoroughness. If any student of French history first masters the text and then sets to work to examine every authority named in the bibliographies he will acquire a knowledge of the French Revolution such as no Englishman ever possessed. But he must be prepared to devote at least ten years of his life exclusively to the task.

M. Madelin has another volume nearly ready on the *Consulate and the Empire*, the publication of which has been delayed by the war, and it will be added to the English series. The Revolution had not run its course when General Bonaparte returned from Egypt to drive out of power and place the lawyers and the other politicians, who had brought France to the brink of ruin and were reviving all the extravagant vices of the ancient monarchy with none of its dignity and traditions. The history of the reconstruction of France by Napoleon— whose mission it was to repair the disintegrating mischief perpetrated by the so-called representatives of the people, before the ambitious conqueror had got the better of the statesman and the organiser, — is full of lessons for the coming generation.

J. E. C. BODLEY

December 12, 1915

CONTENTS

CHAPTER I

THE "SMOKE AND GLORY" OF ITALY:
CHARLES VIII. LOUIS XII.

Charles VIII, 1483–1498 : the Regency of Anne de Beaujeu ;
States-General of 1484 ; Rebellion of the Duke of Orleans and the
Mad War ; Battle of Saint-Aubin du Cormier ; Treaty of Sablé,
1488. Marriage of Charles VIII and Anne of Brittany, 1491.
Charles VIII's personal government : characters of Charles VIII
and Anne of Brittany. The Italian War : the rights over Naples ;
the crossing of Italy, 1494 ; entry into Naples, 1495 ; the retreat,
Battle of Fornovo, 1495. Death of Charles VIII, 1498. Louis XII,
1498–1515 : Cardinal Georges d'Amboise ; marriage of the King
with Anne of Brittany, 1499. Conquest of the State of Milan, 1500,
and of Naples, 1501. Conflict with Spain, the defeats of Seminara
and Cerignola, evacuation of Naples. The trial of Marshal de Gié,
1504. The League of Cambray against Venice, 1508 ; the victory
of Agnadello, 1509. Pope Julius II and the Holy Alliance against
Louis XII, 1511 : Battle of Ravenna, 1512 ; evacuation of Italy.
Louis XII at Blois : death of Anne of Brittany, 1514, and of
Louis XII, 1515.

WHEN, on August 30, 1483, the old King, Louis XI,
passed away in the solitude of the Château du
Plessis, near Tours, the prince, his son, who
succeeded him under the title of Charles VIII, was a child
of thirteen, and a puny, delicate boy into the bargain.
Charles VIII, His father, anxious about his health, had arranged
1483–1498. for him to be brought up at Amboise, a place
beautifully situated on the banks of the Loire within
a stone's throw of the forest. Here he had confided him
to the care of Jean Bourré, an accountant, and Étienne
de Vesc, a sheriff.* The child had been a difficult one to rear ;

* Sheriff is perhaps the nearest English equivalent for the French *bailli*,
a term used in the north of France, whilst a similar official in the south
was called *sénéchal*.—[Tr.]

he had a large head and a feeble body, and his guardians had humoured his health in every way and taught him nothing. They had merely encouraged him to take physical exercise—hunting above all—in order to develop his body. The King, though inspired by no very great affection for his son—for there were but few he loved—was nevertheless full of solicitude on his behalf. He used to write frequently to Jean Bourré to ask for news and to give advice. The child's chief amusement consisted in reading the *Grandes Chroniques de France* and romances of chivalry.

The question as to who should govern the kingdom when he was dead was one which had not escaped Louis XI. Queen **Regency of** Charlotte, his wife, he passed over as incom-**Anne de** petent, and rested all his hopes upon his daughter **Beaujeu.** Anne. It is true she was only twenty-two, but " she was a proud woman and as shrewd as any, the very image in every way of King Louis, her father," says Brantôme, who had heard a great deal about her from his grandmother. Louis XI had married Anne when she was quite young to Pierre de Beaujeu, a wealthy man twenty-one years her senior. He was a younger son of the House of Bourbon, rich in lands, influential, and of royal birth. Louis had grown fond of this son-in-law, who was a good, quiet man, "sweet-tempered and humble," and had gradually allowed him to help him in the government, showing him every mark of confidence and initiating him into all his business. When he felt that death was approaching, Louis XI went to Amboise on purpose to tell his son, the Dauphin, that when he was no more he must obey Pierre de Beaujeu, and on his death-bed he explained to the latter that he left the new King under his guardianship. Whereupon he breathed his last without leaving any other will.

Pierre de Beaujeu found himself in a difficult situation. His position was ill-defined. He was not regent, as in another year the little prince, Charles VIII, would be fourteen, an age at which, in accordance with tradition, he would attain his majority. Moreover, his guardianship had only been conferred upon him by the late King by word of mouth, unratified by any authentic act. He felt extremely uneasy. But he had an intelligent

2

and imperious woman at his side. Contemporary writers are not very friendly towards Anne de Beaujeu. They describe her as " full of dissimulation and a great hypocrite," " shrewd " it is true, but " very vindictive, and a regular little mischief-maker." The Venetian ambassador adds that she was extremely miserly, " that she would do anything for money and regarded the glory of God as little as the honour of the Crown." However that may be, she was essentially a " masterful woman " and led her husband with great firmness and decision.

The difficulties of the situation were such as to cause considerable anxiety. Louis XI's government had been so harsh **Difficulties** towards all concerned that reactionary outbursts **of Govern-** were to be feared. In order to forestall these, **ment.** the Beaujeus hastened to sacrifice the officials who had been most deeply compromised in the late King's service. Olivier le Daim was sentenced to be hanged. They cancelled taxes that were overdue, lowered the *taille*, reduced the army, opened the prisons, and gave back goods that had been confiscated. These measures apparently met with success.

The most pressing problem, however, was connected with the nobility. There was a certain number of persons who were redoubtable on account of their wealth, power, and authority, and whose discontent would entail the worst possible consequences. First and foremost among these were: the heir presumptive to the throne after the weakling Charles VIII, a young prince of twenty-one, frivolous, impetuous, and restless, " with a small head in which there was not room for many brains," a second cousin, Louis, Duke of Orleans, grandson of a brother of Charles VI; then the eldest Beaujeu, the Duke of Bourbon; René, Duke of Lorraine; Francis II, Duke of Brittany; Alain d'Albret, a southern nobleman; Dunois, the son of the famous Orleans bastard of the same name, who afterwards helped his great friend, the Duke of Orleans, and organized his rebellions; and many others. How would all these people regard or acquiesce in the exceptional position enjoyed by the Beaujeus?

In order to conciliate them the Beaujeus tried heaping favours on their heads. Pierre and Anne formed a council of

3

twelve to carry on the government, at the head of which they placed the Duke of Orleans, whom they also made Governor of l'Ile de France, Champagne and la Brie. They appointed the Duke of Bourbon Constable, Lieutenant-General to the King and Governor of Languedoc, and they made Dunois Governor of Dauphiny. Their plan proved abortive, for they learned that the Duke of Orleans regarded their dominant position as intolerable and had made up his mind to demand their downfall. Thereupon they decided to summon the States-General in order that their powers might be confirmed by the representatives of the nation.

In doing this they set to work very cleverly. Wherever they could they nominated their own candidates. They decreed that members should be indiscriminately elected by the three estates of the realm, the clergy, the nobility and the people, instead of having separate members for each order, and they issued a dazzling programme of which the essential feature was to be a reduction of taxes.

On January 15, 1484, the States-General solemnly assembled at Tours, in the great hall of the Archbishop's palace. It was **States-General** chiefly composed of honest but somewhat timid **of 1484.** individuals who were uncertain as to their duties and not very sure of their rights, but who at all events had plenty to say. They made contradictory statements and few among them were of the same opinion. The Duke of Orleans had his followers, and Anne had her partisans to whom she gave instructions. A struggle at once ensued. The Duke's friends asserted that from time immemorial the heir presumptive to the throne had been the guardian of a king who was still a minor. The other side retorted that as Charles VIII would attain his majority in a few weeks it was useless to discuss the matter. The States admitted the truth of this. They thereupon debated the question of the composition of the King's council, or rather the question as to who should nominate the members of the council. The nobles, with the Duke of Orleans at their head, demanded this right. Anne de Beaujeu had the States informed that she proposed granting this privilege to the Assembly. The States refused. Each member gave expression to his own opinion and some confusion followed. Thereupon Philippe Pot, Sire de la Roche, one of the members for Burgundy, who was one of Anne's supporters, and the King's chamberlain and private tutor, made a long speech. He enunciated some bold theories, asserting that if authority were put in the hands of princes, anarchy would be the result. He gave utterance to ideas which have a very modern ring : " The State belongs to the people ; " " in the beginning the sovereign people created kings ; " " sovereignty cannot belong to a prince who only exists by the will of the people." He maintained with great eloquence that as the Assembly was superior to the King, it had only to issue its orders. His audience listened attentively and applauded him, but did not dare to carry his principles into practice. In the end they decided to entrust themselves " to the good pleasure of the King and the said lords and princes and the council " ; which seemingly amounted to answering one question by another, but in reality left matters exactly where they stood. The Assembly added that they desired to be convoked every other year. The next day they found the hall dismantled, the hangings taken down and the benches removed. They understood and took their departure. Pierre and Anne de Beaujeu remained masters of the situation.

The Duke of Orleans was extremely angry and entertained the extraordinary notion of kidnapping Charles VIII. Unfortunately for his designs Anne was warned in time and hastened to place the young King in safety behind the solid walls of Montargis. Upon being found out, the Duke of Orleans cast aside his mask. He went to Brittany, a semi-independent grand-duchy of France, and invited its Duke, Francis II, who detested the Beaujeu government, to join with him in driving out Anne. He also found supporters among the nobility— the Count of Angoulême, the Duke of Alençon and Dunois. Anne, for her part, was energetic and resolute. She mustered **The** her troops, stripped Orleans and Dunois of **" Mad War."** their offices and functions, and marched boldly against them in the direction of Évreux and Verneuil, where they were encamped. Orleans took flight. Brittany was not moving a finger to help him. He capitulated, was granted pardon and resumed his seat on the council. Thus ended the first act of what was known as the " Mad War."

The second was not slow to follow and its result was no less disastrous. Hunted, surrounded, and blockaded at Beaugency, the Duke of Orleans and Dunois were obliged to capitulate. This time Dunois was exiled to Piedmont.

The third and final act followed in 1486. Dunois, who had returned from exile, had taken up the negotiations with Brittany on behalf of his friend, and had extended them to Lorraine. He won over the King of Navarre to his cause, as well as the Sire d'Albret and the Counts of Angoulême, Nevers, and Comminges. With their help he formed a league and matters began to assume a serious aspect. Anne de Beaujeu acted with her usual decision. The first step to take was to rout her enemies in the south before the rest could be rallied. She marched against them and broke their lines everywhere. D'Angoulême, d'Albret, and Comminges, taken unawares and put to confusion, laid down their arms. She thereupon sent three bodies of troops against Brittany under the command of the Comte de Montpensier, the Comte de Saint-André and Louis de Trémoïlle, a clever young general of twenty-seven, full of promise. The first campaign, which was fought in 1487, was unsuccessful. In the following year La Trémoïlle was made commander-in-chief over 16,000 men. He captured Ancenis and Fougères, and at Saint-Aubin du Cormier came into contact with the Duke of Orleans, who was lying in wait for him with 6000 foot, 2400 horse, and a number of cannon. A sharp fight took place. Orleans was beaten and made prisoner. By this time, however, Anne was tired of pardoning him. She had her dangerous cousin imprisoned in the depths of a strong tower at Bourges, where, at last reduced to subjection, he lay for three years lamenting his fate.

The Duke of Brittany then sued for peace. This was granted him at Sablé on harsh and humiliating terms. His heir was a daughter, the celebrated Anne of Brittany. By the Peace of Sablé, Francis II was bound not to give her in marriage without permission from the King of France, and he was also forced to pay all the expenses of the war. Francis II

6

was so deeply affected that he died. The question which now assumed important proportions was the marriage of his daughter.

The aspirants to her hand were both numerous and formidable. First and foremost were foreigners, and, among **Marriage of** these, the Archduke Maximilian of Austria, the **Charles VIII.** son of the Emperor Frederick III. Maximilian's first wife had been Mary of Burgundy, a daughter of Charles the Bold. She had died leaving him with two children, one of them a girl Margaret, who had been betrothed to Charles VIII and even sent to the French Court. Her father sighed after the brilliant heritage of Charles the Bold, upon part of which Louis XI had laid hands. If he married Anne of Brittany, in spite of the difference of age between them, he would be master of Brittany and hold France in a vice. The other suitors were Alain d'Albret; the Duke of Buckingham, whose suit was backed by the King of England; Don Juan, the heir to the thrones of Aragon and Castille; and several others. In the face of the dangers which any one of these combinations afforded, Anne de Beaujeu resolutely decided to arrange a marriage between the precious heiress and Charles VIII, an arrangement which would solve all difficulties. Unfortunately the news suddenly reached her that Anne of Brittany was about to marry Maximilian. Those who surrounded the person of the young princess had arranged this in accordance with the dying wishes of her father. The French Court was furious. An energetic protest was drawn up against this violation of the Treaty of Sablé, and between 30,000 and 40,000 men were dispatched to ask the Duchess of Brittany to give up Maximilian and accept the hand of Charles VIII. The French troops laid siege to Nantes and the Duchess was faced by the alternative of either marrying the Archduke and being driven out of Brittany, or accepting the King of France and retaining her lands. Anne had no choice. She gave way and the contract of marriage was signed on December 13, 1491, in the great hall of Langeais castle. The wedding followed, celebrated with great pomp, and the new queen was crowned at Saint-Denis.

Charles VIII was now twenty-one and was showing signs

of wishing to govern the kingdom himself. Anne of Brittany was seventeen and seemed a self-willed young lady whom it would not be easy to manage. The Beaujeus realized that their public part was at an end. They retired gradually, and little by little relinquished their hold on the reins of government. The Duke of Bourbon, the head of their family, had just died without issue, leaving them vast possessions. They withdrew into the background. They had, on the whole, ruled the kingdom with firmness and decision, solved difficulties skilfully, and come safely out of perilous situations. Louis XI had done well in making them the guardians of his son.

The young King who now took upon himself the government of his kingdom was far from being a brilliant youth. He **Character of** was short and terribly thin, with an enormous **Charles VIII.** head. The portrait of him found on Pollajuolo's curious terra-cotta in the museum at Florence and a miniature in a manuscript in the Bibliothèque Nationale, both depict him with large goggle eyes, a huge prominent nose, a vulgar, thick-lipped mouth with a loose underlip, and a short chin upon which sprouted a sparse red beard. He was certainly ugly. Zachariah Contarini, the Venetian, declared that he was " misshapen." His appearance stamped him as a mediocre, ill-balanced individual. Physically he was a degenerate. He indulged in strange tastes, soaking himself with insufferably pungent perfumes and loading his fingers with numberless rings. He was either silent or spoke but rarely. He was a prey to nervous, twitching movements to which his jerky signature bears witness. He was, in short, an altogether misbegotten creature. His letters, which have been published, have been cited as proofs of his intelligence. But these letters were the work of secretaries. Stress has been laid upon the manner in which he entered into personal negotiations with foreign ambassadors. These ambassadors, however, declare that he saw no one himself but referred everybody to some member of his council. Della Casa, the Florentine, calls him " a fool, guided by the first comer " ; Contarini adds, " In body as in spirit he is of little worth." There are, indeed, many facts which point to his being but a poor specimen of royalty.

8

His wife, the little Duchess of Brittany, had a very different personality, and was greatly his superior, though she, too, **Character of** was not beautiful. She was small, flat-chested **Anne of** and thin, and was even lame in one leg, an infirmity **Brittany.** she managed to hide by means of pattens. Her face was rather long and colourless, with a short nose, and too large a mouth. But, as Brantôme says, she was " a shrewd Brittany woman," alert, fiendishly clever, prudent, and above all, self-willed to the point of obstinacy ; when she wanted a thing, she wanted it with her whole heart and soul. She was well educated and knew Greek and Latin, and she prided herself upon patronizing poets and granting them pensions. She possessed artistic tastes and had quantities of wrought gold and silver ornaments made for her, as well as tapestries and pictures. She gave commissions for manuscripts adorned with miniatures, which rank among the most beautiful creations of their kind that France possesses. She also had quantities of chased gold and silver plate, trinkets and stuffs, for her domain of Brittany brought her vast wealth. She and Catherine de' Medici were the richest of all the Queens of France. Anne had two entirely different sides to her nature. She could be a simple little native of Brittany, dressed for ordinary occasions in a modest black costume, her head covered with the hood characteristic of her country, also black, with a white coif on the top, a woman with an eye to the main chance, severe, and even miserly. But she could also be a proud princess, who kept no count of her fine dresses in cloth of gold lined with ermine, and who on feast days covered her person with glistening jewels and distributed her largesse sumptuously both to Church and poor. Throughout her life she remained a true Brittany woman at heart. She was worshipped in her Duchy where she always came open-handed. At Amboise she had a permanent bodyguard of a hundred Breton nobles, and a band of native singers and musicians who soothed her spirit with songs of her own land. As she was richer than Charles VIII and had done him the honour of embellishing Amboise with beautiful hangings, Oriental carpets, and artistic furniture, she insisted upon living a fairly independent life. She was surrounded by a brilliant

9

court and had thirty or forty maids-of-honour. Though she was very jealous she did not interfere in her husband's affairs, but allowed him to rule the kingdom as he pleased.

Charles carried on his government in a peculiar fashion. This boy of twenty-one who, according to Comines, " was **Charles VIII's** a mere fledgling," indulged in an extraordinary **dreams of** dream of conquest. It was his great wish to **conquest.** march on Constantinople, drive out the infidel Turk, and place upon his own head the imperial crown of Constantine. Undertaken by a powerful prince the scheme would have been an audacious one ; but conceived as it was by a sick boy it was merely the figment of a disordered imagination. However, there was one tangible fact which gave some substance to the dream. The right of the Kings of France to lay claim to the throne of Naples was destined to put Charles VIII on the high road to Greece and Constantinople.

Two hundred years had gone by since a brother of St. Louis, Charles, Count of Anjou and Provence, had set forth at his own risk and peril to carve out a kingdom for himself in the south of Italy. His success was short-lived. In 1282 the Sicilians revolted, massacres took place, and Spanish princes of the House of Aragon came over, drove out the Angevins, and for two hundred years remained undisturbed masters of Naples. But the Counts of Anjou and Provence on their return to France had jealously preserved their pretensions to the kingdom they had once held. In 1420, Alfonso V, another prince of Aragon, crossed the sea and seized the ill-fated kingdom, because its Queen, Juana II, who had no children, had adopted René of Anjou, an Angevin prince. On July 10, 1480, René of Anjou, the last Count of Anjou and Provence and pseudo-king of Naples, surnamed "good King René" died, leaving no direct heir. In his will he bequeathed Anjou to the King of France, the counties of Maine and Provence and the famous rights to Naples to a nephew, Charles, Comte du Maine, on condition that the latter at his death should leave his entire heritage to the King of France. Charles du Maine died on December 11, 1481, and Louis XI thus found himself possessed of all the lands and rights of the House of Anjou. Louis XI

10

was a practical man. He seized all the territory offered him; but in the shadowy rights connected with a distant land, which he would need men and money to win, he took not the smallest interest. His daughter, Anne de Beaujeu, who inherited his ideas, held these rights of so little account that she was on the point of handing them over to René II, Duke of Lorraine, a relative of the Angevins. A stray chance, however, was destined to revive their memory in the breast of the romantic successor of the most matter-of-fact and astute of mediæval monarchs.

Italy at this time consisted of a mosaic of independent states of varying sizes, each one jealous of its neighbour and constantly at war one with the other. Those amongst them who felt themselves too weak, would call in foreign Powers to help them, such as the Emperor of Germany, the King of Spain and the King of France. The King of Spain was far away; the Emperor of Germany, trammelled by the semi-federated constitution of the Holy Roman Empire, had his hands tied. The King of France alone was in a position to help. Louis XI had frequently been asked to act as mediator, and France had thus entered into relations with Italy. At this juncture the reigning Duke of Milan was Gian Galeazzo Maria Sforza, a young man of somewhat delicate health, who had succeeded his father under the guardianship of his mother, Bona of Savoy, a sister of Louis XI's wife, Charlotte, and therefore aunt to Charles VIII. Bona was a woman of scant intelligence "with but little sense." Her brother-in-law, Ludovico Sforza, surnamed

Ludovico Sforza. the Moor on account of his dark complexion, seized the reigns of government and made up his mind to usurp the throne of his nephew. The existing portraits of Ludovico the Moor and especially the picture by Zenale in the Brera Museum at Milan, do not give us a very engaging idea of this man. They depict him with regular features, straight unflinching gaze and the close-shut thin lips of a man whose thoughts are veiled. His face was inscrutable and untrustworthy, with a disingenuous glance, whilst his head was that of a shady attorney, deficient in courage and in scruple, if not in intelligence, with feelings entirely self-centred or base. The plan he had conceived was not easy to carry out. The chief obstacles in his path were the

11

claims of Charles VIII, the cousin of the Duke whom he wished to dethrone, and of the latter's father-in-law, Alfonso of Calabria, the eldest son of King Ferrante of Naples. Ludovico could think of no better plan for ridding himself of these two foes than that of setting them at war with each other.

He forthwith dispatched ambassadors to Amboise with instructions to bribe Charles VIII's most powerful counsellors and imbue the King of France with the desire of making good his rights over Naples. Amongst these counsellors the most important were Étienne de Vesc, the ex-sheriff of Meaux, who had been made sheriff of Beaucaire and whose influence was all powerful with the King; a priest named Guillaume Briçonnet, whom Charles VIII had raised to the bishopric of Saint Malo, and Jean de Baudricourt, Marshal d'Esquerdes. The two first mentioned were the real masters. They accepted large sums from Ludovico, as is conclusively proved by documents found in the archives of Milan. According to Comines they were also dazzled by seductive hopes. Étienne de Vesc was told that in Italy he would win territories and titles and Briçonnet was promised a cardinal's hat. The four men were hand in glove. Étienne de Vesc was the most determined of them all, and Charles VIII, for his part, entered stoutly upon the adventure. Certain Neapolitan nobles, who had fled their country on account of the brutal behaviour of their King, urged him to undertake the expedition. King Ferrante of Naples, a big man with a fat, bestial face, and hard pitiless expression, had carried on his government entirely by violence; he had massacred, betrayed, and imprisoned right and left. Étienne de Vesc had learned treatises drawn up, proving the legality of the French King's rights over Naples and Sicily, and preparations were made forthwith.

When the news of this enterprise was made known, it was regarded as ridiculous by every one in France. Not a single **Charles VIII** voice was raised in its favour and the opposition **decides to** to it became exceedingly active. But Charles VIII **invade Italy.** stood his ground. Ludovico the Moor was delighted and swore that Charles and all his council together "did not make up half a wise man between them;" but when Charles came down into Italy, he added, "It

12

is I who brought him here, and I shall lead him yet further afield!" However it was not long before he himself met with grave difficulties.

A commission, consisting of the King's four counsellors and Comines, was nominated to prepare for the "enterprise" as it was called. They decided that 500,000 to 600,000 ducats must be set aside, that the people must be taxed to the extent of 800,000 ducats, that 24 ships, 12 galleons and 50 galleys must be chartered at Genoa and elsewhere, for the transport of the main body of the army, consisting of 10,400 men, and that a force of 41,900 must be levied. Steps were immediately taken to raise these numbers

The expedition also required the help of diplomacy. An envoy, Perron de Baschi, was dispatched to Italy to see how the land lay. The Italians were alarmed. The advent of this foreign King and his army boded but little good in their eyes. Ludovico the Moor began to grow uneasy. A treaty of alliance was made between France and the Duke of Milan, in which Ludovico succeeded in having his name inserted. The Republic of Venice sent evasive answers. Piero de' Medici gave expression to vague protestations of good will from Florence. In Rome, Pope Alexander VI confined himself to generalities. Ferrante, for his part, was getting under arms. But at all events the neutrality of the various States had been secured.

Lastly, before leaving France, Charles VIII made all the arrangements necessary for his absence. He confided the **Treaties with** regency to Pierre de Bourbon and handed over **England,** the various departments of government to trust- **Spain, and** worthy individuals. With the view of preventing **Austria.** the Kings of England and Spain, or Maximilian of Austria, from seizing upon some pretext to profit by his absence in order to attack his frontiers, he made treaties with them. For the sum of 745,000 golden crowns the King of England bound himself by the Treaty of Étaples of November 3, 1492, not to interfere. An old story was revived of a loan of 300,000 golden crowns made by France to Aragon as a surety for which France had occupied Cerdagne and Roussillon. By the Treaty of Barcelona, of January 3, 1493, Charles VIII agreed to cancel the debt and give up the

13

security in return for the neutrality of Aragon. Maximilian had entered a claim for the return of the provinces which he had given his daughter, Margaret of Austria, as a dowry, before she had been sent home to him by Charles VIII upon his marriage with Anne of Brittany. By the terms of the Treaty of Senlis, Charles VIII gave back Franche-Comté and Artois to Maximilian. Thus did the King of France relinquish the substance for the shadow!

When these arrangements had been made, Charles VIII set forth. His army, which had been laboriously concentrated, marched on ahead, divided into two bodies. The **Charles VIII enters Italy.** land army was under the command of Gilbert de Montpensier; the troops destined for embarkation were placed under the Duke of Orleans, who had been released from prison and had made his peace with the King. The Col di Genevra was crossed, the baggage being carried by mules. But no sooner had the troops left the mountains behind them, than they discovered that they were already short of money. Charles VIII, however, received a friendly welcome from the Duke and Duchess of Savoy, from whom he borrowed 12,000 ducats, and at Asti he fell in with Ludovico the Moor, from whom he extracted 60,000 ducats. King Ferrante of Naples, terrified by the storm that was about to break over his head, had tried to raise troops and collect thirty galleys. He had sent envoy after envoy far and wide to seek allies. His overtures, however, had been coldly received. To the court of Charles VIII he had dispatched ambassadors charged to bribe the French King's counsellors. They had been conducted back to the frontier. Ferrante, maddened by this, died of rage. His son, Alfonso of Calabria, who succeeded him, inherited all his cruelty without his talents. He dispatched his brother, Frederick, to Genoa, with orders to attack the French troops as they embarked. Frederick landed at Rapallo, near Genoa, with 4000 men, whom the Duke of Orleans speedily attacked with his Swiss troops and routed. This first French victory caused a great stir.

Charles VIII, after a mild attack of small-pox, renewed his march. The forces that followed him felt no enthusiasm for the enterprise. They found the weather hot and the wine sour.

14

As Comines says, "They firmly believed that the King would go no farther." The State of Milan was crossed without difficulty (October, 1494). At Milan Charles paid a visit to his cousin Gian Galeazzo Maria, whom he found laid up in bed, very weak and ill, and then marched on to Placentia. He advanced with an escort of 7000 cavalry and forty cannon, followed by a throng of vehicles. Sometimes he drove, sometimes he rode on horseback, dressed invariably in black. The whole of the French army collected at Placentia, presenting to the astonished eyes of the Italians a motley and barbarous crowd. They were, according to Sanuto: "A haughty people, full of courage and spirit, who had enormous wide slippers on their feet, very long stirrups, top boots coming up over their greaves, large hats on their heads, and short coats with long sleeves." The Italians were greatly incensed.

The next step was to enter Tuscany. At Florence, the ruling city of the district, the people were quite willing to **Charles VIII at Florence.** receive Charles VIII. But Piero de' Medici, whose wealthy relatives had succeeded in abolishing the republic, would not give his consent. The Dominican monk, Girolamo Savonarola, who was an eloquent preacher and a stirring apostle of the people, had, in his sermons, long been condemning the pagan corruption of manners. "You will be punished ! " he warned the Florentines. "There cometh a man who in a few weeks will overrun Italy without drawing the sword, and fortresses shall fall before him " ! The attitude of Savonarola lent strength to the feelings of the populace. Charles VIII advanced and crossed the Apennines. Piero de' Medici, caught between two fires, came to him and offered to allow him to cross Tuscany on condition that the French King secured him in his ruler-ship of Florence. Charles VIII accepted his terms and borrowed 200,000 ducats from him. The Florentines, however, rose up in fury against Piero de' Medici and sacked his house. Charles VIII marched forward to Lucca and Pisa, and finally reached Florence on November 17. He was accorded a magnificent reception, in spite of two heavy showers which forced the clergy, in their gold-embroidered vestments, to retreat. The streets were strewn with sand and adorned with hangings ;

the bells pealed and crowds of people hailed him. The Italians were astonished at the sight of the great drums and small fifes of the French troops ; they were filled with admiration by their beautiful gilt halberds, and the archers of the guard, with their ' *hoquetons*,' or mantles, covered with gold lace, looked like noblemen in their eyes. Charles VIII, however, mounted on his black horse, with his gilded armour, his jacket of gold brocade, his full blue cloak and his white hat covered with black plumes and surmounted by the royal crown, seemed to them insignificant. Meanwhile, Gian Galeazzo Maria had died in Milan. Ludovico at once had himself proclaimed Duke of Milan, after having bought the consent of the Emperor of Germany with a sum of money. Charles VIII was taken entirely by surprise, but he was so deeply involved in his undertaking, that he was obliged to make the best of a bad business, and bow to circumstances over which he had no control.

His sojourn in Florence proved a pitiful affair. The Florentines, irritated by the King's awkwardness, showed themselves hostile. Charles VIII prevailed upon them to allow Piero de' Medici to return as a private citizen. Some scuffles took place, and at last the people paid Charles VIII 120,000 gold ducats and requested him to take his departure, which he did on November 28.

He now had to cross the Papal States. Alexander VI, who had but little love for the House of Aragon, was never-
Charles VIII in Rome. theless still less in favour of the King of France as a neighbour in Naples. On being asked whether he would allow Charles VIII to cross his territory or not, he was at a loss to know what answer to give. Mechanically, he took measures to fortify himself and then sent to beg the King not to come. Finally, moved by a sudden impulse, he summoned the Neapolitan Duke of Calabria to Rome with 5000 infantry and fifty-five squadrons. The French immediately made a rapid advance. Gilbert de Montpensier galloped with his cavalry right up to the walls of Rome. At this moment a piece of the city walls fell in, an occurrence which the Pope regarded as a sign from heaven for him to yield. The Duke of Calabria was asked to evacuate Rome, whose gates were thrown open for 1500 French soldiers to march

16

through the streets on December 27. Charles VIII arrived on the 31st by night, without making any show. The Pope had shut himself up in the Vatican, thinking that the French wished to depose him. He was meditating hurling a bull of major excommunication against the King of France when, upon further reflection, he decided to come to terms and granted him a free passage and stores, together with Civita Vecchia and Ostia. Alexander VI and Charles now became extremely friendly. Briçonnet obtained his Cardinal's hat and the King, after staying at the Vatican and receiving a solemn blessing from the Pope on January 28, took his departure.

Meanwhile, Alfonso of Naples, terrified, and realizing that his subjects were irreconcilably hostile to him, had abdicated **Entry into Naples, 1495.** in favour of his son Ferrante II. The populace of Naples had risen up with shouts of " *Francia* " and Ferrante had only just had time to shut himself up in the Castel dell' Uovo while his faithful friend Pescara held Castel Nuovo. The vanguard of the French army advanced apace and Marshal de Gié, with forty horse, took one of the city gates amid the cheers of the crowd. Charles VIII reached Poggio Reale, the country seat of the Kings of Naples, whither Neapolitan envoys were sent to congratulate him. At this point Ferrante fled to the island of Ischia and from thence to Messina, and the Castel dell' Uovo, also surrendered to Charles VIII, who had ridden into the city on February 12, with ninety horse and found himself master of Naples. In a few days the provinces on all sides offered to submit. The conquest had been achieved, accomplished by magic, as in a dream, without resistance and without effort.

Charles VIII was enchanted. He sent accounts of his victories to France, and had them all printed and distributed in the form of " bulletins of the Grand Army," one of the first examples of an " inspired " press. He then set to work to organize his new kingdom, confirming privileges, lowering the taxes, appointing magistrates and governors, and distributing rewards all round. Étienne de Vesc was given two Duchies, d'Aubigny was made a Marquis, lands were divided amongst his archers and officers, and the Duke of Montpensier was made Lieutenant-General and Viceroy of the kingdom. After this

Charles VIII sought diversion ; he organized jousts and festivals, and gave himself up to amusement, whilst his army drank and revelled beneath soft and pleasant skies.

But he had a rude awakening. The Italian States roused themselves from the stupor into which the rapid conquest of **Retreat of** the kingdom of Naples had cast them. They **Charles VIII.** realized that they were all threatened, and joining together decided to form a league against the dangerous victor, calling in the help of the Emperor and the King of Spain. On April 1, 1495, in the cabinet of the Doge, at Venice, a league was formed including the Pope, the Emperor, the King of Spain, Ludovico the Moor—who was now anxious to defend himself against Charles VIII—and Venice. The King of France was indignant. He flew into a passion, exclaiming that it was a scandalous shame. Nevertheless, the allies continued to arm, and there was no time to be lost. It was imperative for Charles VIII to reach the French frontier as quickly as possible if he wished to avoid being cut off from the Alps. The French fleet had not been of much use since the victory at Rapallo, and the Duke of Orleans had even gone so far as to shut himself up in Asti. Charles VIII summoned his ships to Naples to take away part of the artillery and the booty, and then, after having indulged in a childish notion of having himself crowned King of Naples, and making a solemn entry into the city, clothed in the purple robes of emperor, and holding the imperial orb in his hand, he set forth on his return journey, leaving 12,000 men behind him under the command of Montpensier.

He took the same route by which he had come. The Pope did not wait to receive him but took flight, and ambassadors were sent by Florence to implore Charles VIII not to pass through that city. The king was irritated by this, but made direct for Pisa and began crossing the Apennines.

The allies were lying in wait for him on the other side of the mountains. They had 40,000 men under the command **Battle of** of Francesco di Gonzaga, Marquis of Mantua, **Fornovo, 1495.** who had sent on his vanguard as far as Fornovo, on the Ceno, at the foot of the hills. Charles VIII had only 10,000 men. The rest were either in garrison, or dispersed

18

and lost. He met with great difficulty in crossing the passes, for it was the end of June and the heat was stifling. The cannon, fourteen huge pieces, had to be dragged along by the Swiss guards. On June 30 the French army took up its position round Fornovo, and on July 6 the two armies met. It was raining, the cannon boomed, the troops charged with lances lowered and a furious hand to hand fight took place. At this juncture the baggage convoy of the French army was seen advancing on the left. The allies jumped to the conclusion that the baggage, which was said to contain much booty, was going to slip through their fingers. Many of them made a rush for it. The lines wavered and the French seized the opportunity to break through. In a short time, thanks to the inefficiency of the Italian soldiery, the enemy was routed.

With the road thus cleared before him, Charles VIII pressed forward as quickly as possible. In a week he reached Placentia amid tropical heat. He passed the town without entering it, marched by Alessandria, and on July 15 reached Asti. Meanwhile all his work at Naples had fallen to pieces. King Ferrante re-entered the town amid the acclamations of the same populace which had saluted Charles VIII with cheers, and the whole kingdom returned to its former allegiance. Gilbert de Montpensier at first shut himself up in Castel Nuovo. He afterwards took flight, collected 10,000 men, which were all that remained of the French army, and was besieged at Atella. On July 20 he capitulated and four months later died of fever, a prisoner in the hands of Ferrante. No sign remained of the fleeting conquest of Naples ; and Charles VIII recrossed the Alps.

What had he gained by this enterprise, which according to Comines, had not proved ill-omened from the beginning merely
Futility of the Expedition. " because the expedition had been guided by God, and owed but little to the good sense of its leaders " ? He had gained nothing—"nothing but glory and smoke," says the same writer. It is asserted that the French, wonder-struck, discovered Italy and brought back the Renaissance with them. Contemporary writers, however, prove that this crowd of rough men-at-arms crossed Italy with their eyes shut. The poets Octavien de Saint Gelais and André de la Vigne, in their *Vergier*

d'honneur which is a record of the expedition, describe only the merrymaking. At Pavia, Comines and Gaguin, it is true, noticed a Charterhouse " built of marble with a doorway in alabaster." But that was all ! The thing which struck Charles VIII most in Florence was a menagerie of lions. He visited Rome, and the Vatican, where his cicerone was Burchard, the master of ceremonies. In his *Diarium,* the latter has left us a description of this visit. Charles VIII, it seems, found nothing to admire ! Naples alone made any impression on him. He wrote that he was particularly struck by the gardens and the ceilings of the houses. He was anxious to take back workmen with him and engaged about twenty men, joiners, tailors, and " scent-makers " as well as masons, painters, and sculptors. The only certain fact we know about these workmen is that one of them, Pacello de Mercoliano, introduced Italian gardens at Amboise and Blois. Charles VIII had additions made to Amboise both before and after the expedition ; and further, it is difficult to tell what was due to him and what to Louis XII. It is, consequently, hard to see what impetus the expedition against Naples gave to the progress of the arts in France.

The remainder of his reign was short and sad. It was only possible for sickly children to spring from a father so unhealthy **Death of** as Charles VIII. He had two children, the elder **Charles VIII,** of whom was named Charles Orland. But they **1498.** both died on his return from Italy. He did not seem to feel their loss and " his mourning was but short-lived." He was not destined to survive them long. On April 7, 1498, on the " eve of Palm Sunday," the King left the Queen's room at Amboise about twelve or one o'clock in the day, accompanied by his wife, to go and watch a game of tennis in the castle moat. He went through a gallery, called " Haquelebac's Gallery " after some Swiss guard. The door happened to be out of order and he struck his forehead against it. In spite of this, however, he went and watched the players, and remained a long time talking and chatting. Suddenly about two o'clock he fell back in a faint. They laid him down on a mattress, where he remained till eleven o'clock at night, surrounded by a crowd of frightened

20

people, hurrying to and fro. Three times he seemed to be coming round and spoke a few words. But at eleven o'clock he breathed his last. The real reason of his death is uncertain, as also whether or not the blow he gave himself was in any way responsible for his end. Comines speaks of a "catarrh or apoplexy," probably a cerebral lesion. He was twenty-eight when he died. He was given magnificent obsequies, which lasted a month and cost 45,000 francs.

The Duke of Orleans, who succeeded him as Louis XII, was a man of thirty-six. He was a second cousin of Louis XI **Louis XII,** through his father the poet, Charles of Orleans, **1498–1515.** his grandfather Louis of Orleans, who was assassinated in the Rue Barbette, and his ancestor Charles V. Years had brought him discretion. He again was not handsome ; he was thin, with a pronounced stoop, a bony face and a long nose. He had the feeble health of an old man's son, as his father was well advanced in years when he was born, and throughout his life he remained a valetudinarian. He had been brought up to love physical exercise. According to Saint Gelais he was a good rider and hunter, a skilled wrestler and a fine tennis player. He was a marvellous archer and withal, if tradition is to be believed, a hearty eater and heavy drinker. He was, moreover, a charming man, with an elegant, easy carriage, "sweet-tempered, gracious, and benign." He was always amiable and good-natured with everybody, obliging, anxious not to give offence, easy to get on with, and open-handed. His manner was "urbane and frank " ; he was, in short, endowed with an altogether sympathetic nature, which he inherited from his mother, Mary of Cleves, who was the best of creatures and the most modest of women. He had been brought up at Blois, his birthplace, which he loved to the end of his days, surrounded by all the wealth and luxury that ample means could afford—for his family was extremely rich. This circumstance gave him the distinction of a gentleman of birth and breeding, of which the elder branch of the family could no longer boast.

Such were the qualities which made Louis XII so popular, that throughout the centuries he has preserved the reputation of a good king. The masses loved him for his kindness and his sense of justice, and considered themselves happy under his rule. As a matter of fact, this well-being was due to the exceptional prosperity enjoyed by France at the end of the fifteenth and the beginning of the sixteenth century, a condition to be attributed to complicated economic causes generally prevalent at the time, for which Louis XII was in no way personally responsible. He merely reaped the fruit of this auspicious state of affairs. For his policy, with its perpetual wars and consequent ruinous expenditure, ought to have made him a hated monarch. But his country's good fortune saved his reputation by allowing him to meet his expenses without over-burdening the people, and his own attractive personality did the rest.

The levity of mind of which he had been accused in his youth by Louis XI and Anne de Beaujeu, covered a substratum of somewhat mediocre intelligence. His policy was never skilful and his lack of aptitude for statecraft lent an undue importance to his counsellors.

The principal and most celebrated of these was Cardinal Georges d'Amboise. The son of a former chamberlain of **Cardinal** Charles VII and Louis XI, he had been destined **Georges** for the Church, and at the age of fourteen had **d'Amboise.** been appointed Bishop of Montauban. At Court he made the acquaintance of the future King Louis XII, who was his junior by three years, and the two young men formed an intimate friendship which was to last throughout their lives. From Montauban, Georges d'Amboise was raised to the bishopric of Narbonne, and after that he became Archbishop of Rouen. On his accession, Louis XII made him his minister. He was a sweet-tempered man of refined demeanour, prudent, fat, and bald, somewhat heavy and slow of comprehension, but diligent and loyal. Louis XII placed the utmost confidence in him. He comprised in his person "the whole government of the king and of France." He was endowed with a sense of economy and of justice, the two virtues which stood highest in the estimation of the people who used to exclaim familiarly : " Leave it to Georges ! " He had a love of magnificence ; was himself responsible for several buildings, and spurred on Louis XII to follow his example.

Only two faults marred his character. He was too anxious to push forward his own family, his brothers and his nephews; and he was over-ambitious. He had set his heart upon becoming Pope, an aspiration which proved a source of great vexation to his country. But, like his master, he profited by the extraordinary prosperity of the masses at this time and consequently left behind him the reputation of having been a better minister than he really was.

The other counsellors were men of well-balanced minds, used to the conduct of affairs of State—Chancellor Guy **Louis XII's** de Rochefort; Marshal de Gié; Louis de la **advisers.** Trémoïlle; Canon Étienne Poncher; Florimond Robertet, and Imbert de Batarnay, Admiral de Graville. Louis de la Trémoïlle was the man who had beaten the Duke of Orleans at the Battle of Saint Aubin du Cormier, and he felt somewhat nervous when the new King ascended the throne. His fears, however, were set at rest by Louis XII's amiable reception of him. Étienne Poncher, who afterwards became Bishop of Paris, was a learned and extremely eloquent divine and a virile personality, endowed with sound judgment; whilst Florimond Robertet, "Florimond the good" as he was called, the son of a humble Montbrison family, who was destined, on the death of Georges d'Amboise, to take the whole weight of the government on his shoulders, was a zealous administrator and a precise and conscientious worker—the prototype and model of all secretaries of State, whose forerunner he was.

As soon as Louis XII became King he set to work to calm the fears of all who had reason to tremble at his accession. "It is not becoming or honourable to a King of France," he was fond of saying, "to avenge the quarrels of a Duke of Orleans." He made it known that he would introduce no changes either in things or persons. He was most considerate to all with whom he came in contact, and everybody thought him perfect. Anne of Brittany, above all, who was weighed down with grief, had nothing but praise to bestow on his behaviour towards her. He was extremely attentive to her. By the terms of her marriage contract with Charles VIII, she was bound, in the case of being left a widow, to marry her husband's successor.

Louis XII was not forgetful of this. He realized that he would derive three advantages from such a marriage ; he would keep Brittany ; he would marry a princess with whom he had long been secretly in love ; and he would have to repudiate his own wife, who was ugly and had no children and towards whom he felt utterly indifferent. He made this the first duty of his reign.

Jeanne de France, the wife of Louis XII, was a daughter of Louis XI. She was a woman with masculine features—to **Annulment of Louis XII's first marriage.** judge by her death-mask in the Louvre—lean and ungraceful, "short, dark, round-shouldered" and lame into the bargain. The match had been arranged by Louis XI to suit his convenience, and he had had the couple married when they were mere children. The Duke of Orleans, who was but eleven years old at the time, had wept and refused to do as he was bid. The old king had then threatened to make " a monk or a priest " of him, and he had been obliged to give way. But the young prince never developed any feeling of affection for his wife. As soon as he had decided to marry Anne of Brittany, Louis XII's first step was to get his former marriage annulled by the Papal Court. The Chair of St. Peter was occupied at this time by Alexander VI, the famous Borgia. Georges d'Amboise had an interview with the pontiff's sinister son, Cæsar Borgia, and they agreed to terms together. The grounds for annulling the marriage were based upon eight canonical objections—the youth of the parties, their consanguinity, the absent of consent on their part, &c. The suit ended favourably and, as a reward for his pains, Louis XII granted Cæsar Borgia the County of Valentinois, which he raised to the rank of a Duchy, and a pension of 20,000 pounds. In return for this Cæsar brought a Cardinal's hat to Paris for Georges d'Amboise. Jeanne de France conducted her defence with dignity and firmness. Public sympathy was on her side and Louis XII did not show to advantage. The judges, however, naturally returned a verdict in favour of the annulment, which was thereupon decreed. The unfortunate Jeanne, who was consoled by visions, humbly accepted the will of God. She retired to Bourges, where she founded the Order of the

Annunciation, and in 1505 she died there in obscurity, unnoticed by the world, but locally regarded as a saint.

Anne of Brittany accepted Louis XII. Having loved Charles VIII, she was also ready to love her new husband. She had tasted of the sweets of royalty and did **Marriage of** not care to return to the rank of a mere duchess. **Louis XII and** The marriage was celebrated at Nantes, in **Anne of** January 1499. "The shrewd Brittany woman," **Brittany,** as Louis XII used playfully to call her, took care **1449.** to make a stipulation that if she died without issue, Brittany should not fall into the hands of the King of France, but should remain in her own family. The newly married couple took up their abode in the castle of Blois and, to judge by their mutual tenderness and their devotion and loyalty to each other, they must have been a model couple.

This first act of the new reign was followed by another far graver in its results. Louis XII conceived the desire of invading Italy to conquer the Duchy of Milan. **Louis XII's** There was no immediate connexion between **schemes of** this enterprise and that of Charles VIII. The **Conquest.** motives which led up to it and the end in view were alike different. Whilst it was not quite so mad as Charles' scheme for the conquest of Constantinople *via* Naples, Louis XII's project was none the less extremely impolitic. As Étienne Poncher, who was violently opposed to the idea, maintained at the king's council-board, Louis XII would have done far better to turn his attention towards " fixing the boundaries " of his own kingdom. For years Louis XII squandered men and money in trying to keep this precarious conquest. He became involved in an interminable and tedious series of international complications which were constantly breaking out afresh, and in the end merely resulted in his final evacuation of Italy ! Few reigns afford the spectacle of a policy so vain, supported by so many futile efforts. The council, or rather Georges d'Amboise in the council, upheld and encouraged the king. The fact that during the French occupation of Milan, Georges d'Amboise tried by every means in his power to have himself elected Pope, seems to point to

25

the true reason of Louis XII's persistency in maintaining his rights over the Duchy of Milan.

These rights were derived from his grandmother, Valentina Visconti, daughter of Gian Galeazzo Visconti, the first Duke of Milan, and wife of that Louis of Orleans who was murdered by John the Fearless. As the line of Gian Galeazzo had become extinct, the descendants of Valentina should by right have been lords of Milan. But during the fifteenth century the princes of the House of Orleans had either been prisoners in London, or else were too young to assert themselves, and the Sforzas, who were condottieri, had seized their lands. All the House of Orleans had managed to keep was the county of Asti, in Piedmont, which had been Valentina's dowry. Louis XII made up his mind to claim his rights, which had been in abeyance for fifty years, ever since 1447. Louis XII may not have avenged his wrongs as Duke of Orleans on private individuals, but he was thoroughly mediocre in his policy and used his people's money to support a cause which concerned his dukedom, but was of no interest to the nation at large.

The council, obliged to follow his lead, prepared for the venture. Negotiations were entered into with foreign Powers to secure their neutrality. Venice was approached **Conquest of Milan.** with a view to an alliance and the Swiss for a supply of soldiers. Cæsar Borgia was flattered in order to win over the Pope. The scandalous Ludovico Sforza, who was universally hated on account of his knavery, was abandoned by all. By July, 1499, the French army was ready. The three generals in command, Gian Giacomo Trivulzio, Louis de Luxembourg, Lord of Ligny, and Stuart d'Aubigny crossed the Alps with 13,000 foot, 6000 horse and fifty-eight cannon. They seized upon the strongholds one by one. Alessandria was captured by assault and brutally sacked. Isolated and betrayed on every hand, Ludovico packed up his treasure in carts and fled to Como. Thence he crossed the Alps, where he had to hide in a grotto, and finally took refuge at Innsbruck with the Emperor Maximilian, the strangest and most changeable personality of his time. The State of Milan was now in the hands of Louis XII. A leisurely march of twenty days had been sufficient to ensure its occupation. Meanwhile, on the

26

east, Venice, the ally of the French, was laying hands upon the whole of the Cremona district, as far as the Adda, a task much to her liking. Delighted by his conquests, Louis XII decided to pay his new territories a visit. He was given a magnificent reception everywhere. He feasted, granted audiences to ambassadors from every corner of Italy who came to bow before the conqueror, and lent some of his French troops to Cæsar Borgia, for the conquest of the towns of Imola, Forli, and Pesaro, which belonged to the relatives of Ludovico, and with which Cæsar proposed to create a small independent principality for himself.

However, when he returned to France to take into his arms the little daughter, Claude, who had just been born to him, everything changed in Milan. Trivulzio, whom he left behind in command, committed several blunders, and caused great discontent by his " haughty swashbuckler airs." The French soldiery, moreover, were brutal. Ludovico sent emissaries to sound the country and succeeded in raising a band of 20,000 Italian, Swiss, and German adventurers, at whose head he crossed the frontier into Milan. The people, fickle as ever, declared themselves in his favour. On January 25, 1500, Milan revolted and Trivulzio, who escaped death by the skin of his teeth, took flight. Ludovico entered Milan in triumph, and thus— the usual fate of such achievements—a conquest gained with ease fell to pieces at a touch. The French evacuated the territory under great difficulties and retreated to the foot of the Alps.

Loss of Milan.

Louis XII, however, was determined to regain his possessions. A fresh army crossed the Alps under the command of Louis de la Trémoïlle, who was accompanied by Georges d'Amboise. Ludovico marched with 30,000 men to meet the French force, which he encountered at Novara on April 8, 1500. Unfortunately for him his mercenaries were not to be relied upon. They had no desire to enter into a serious conflict and their pay was overdue. Some refused to move, others deserted, and the remainder were utterly routed. Ludovico, who was obliged to disguise himself as a German foot-soldier, was recognized and taken prisoner. But this time his fate was sealed. La Trémoïlle

Re-conquest of Milan.

treated him with courtesy, invited him to dinner and tried to console him by talking of the " King's clemency." But the unfortunate man was destined for the remainder of his life to pay a heavy price for his brief spell of glory and good-fortune. Whilst Cardinal d'Amboise entered Milan and in solemn state promised to forgive the inhabitants who begged for mercy, Ludovico was conducted by an escort of two hundred archers to Lyons. He entered the town through serried ranks of curious and hostile citizens who lined the streets on either side. Mounted on a mule and clad in a black camlet cloak, he presented an impressive figure with his tall frame, his long white hair and his cold calm glance. Louis XII refused to receive him and had him imprisoned first at Pierre-Encise, afterwards at Lys-Saint-Georges in Berry, and finally at Loches in " a vaulted underground chamber " secured by iron bars, where he is believed to have died about 1510.

It was left to Georges d'Amboise to reorganize the State of Milan. He had appointed as governor one of his nephews, Charles d'Amboise, Lord of Chaumont-sur-Loire, a man, who though still very young, was already Lord High Steward of France. He was a mild, benevolent youth, who succeeded very well in his new office. As a sign of good will the Pope nominated Georges d'Amboise his legate in France, an extremely important position, which practically amounted to making him Vice-Pope.

Louis XII, delighted by his success and having whetted his appetite for conquest, now conceived the notion of extending his possessions in Italy. With this object in view, and with the traditional claims of the French kings over Naples as his pretext, he revived the schemes of Charles VIII with regard to that state. His predecessor's failure had taught him nothing ; he may, perhaps, have been spurred on by the desire of d'Amboise to get nearer Rome.

With the sole object of avoiding a dispute with the King of Spain, should the latter challenge his right to the coveted kingdom, Louis XII thought it wise to make a friendly division of territory between himself and his possible rival. By the Treaty of Granada it was decided that Spain should have Calabria and

Treaty of Granada.

Apulia, and that France should take the rest—extremely vague terms. Thus the most dangerous adversary was satisfied and Italy was humoured by the suggestion that Louis XII did not aspire to be the sole conqueror of Naples. These precautions, however, were destined to recoil upon their author.

A French army set forth on the march in May 1501, under the command of Stuart d'Aubigny. Cardinal d'Amboise went

Conquest of Naples, 1501. on ahead and Cæsar Borgia, also eager for a share in the spoil, led the rear-guard. Once again the expedition proved a mere military parade. The French entered Rome on June 25, where they received the Pope's blessing and good wishes which, however, were not as sincere as they might have been. The French and Spaniards from opposite sides made a simultaneous invasion of Naples, whose king, Frederick, unable to offer any resistance, shut up his troops in some of the towns. The latter surrendered at the first summons. Capua, alone, was carried by assault on July 25 and was mercilessly pillaged, whilst its inhabitants were put to the sword. Frederick, in terror, capitulated and left the country in tears " with his disconsolate wife and children stripped of their patrimony." He retreated to France where he was promised a pension of 50,000 pounds. Upon his departure the Spaniards and the French each took the share of territory allotted them by the terms of the Treaty of Granada. The Spaniards were under the command of Gonzalo di Cordova, a soldier of great valour, a skilled general and a cold, calm man of remarkable ability, who, moreover, had a larger army at his back than the French.

Contingencies which should have been foreseen naturally followed. As the Treaty of Granada had not clearly defined

Conflict with Spain. the exact limits of the possessions to be divided between the two kings, disputes arose. Louis XII had appointed Louis of Nemours governor and viceroy of Naples. Gonzalo di Cordova was impatient. He solved the difficulties at issue by abruptly seizing the places in dispute and driving out the French garrisons. Relations between the two governors grew increasingly strained and bitter, and eventually Gonzalo broke off all communication with Nemours. Gradually a state of war was established,

29

and Louis XII, who had divided the state of Naples with Spain in order to avoid a conflict, found that he had only succeeded in provoking it.

He sent reinforcements, 2000 Swiss and 10,000 Gascons. The King of Spain did likewise—2500 Germans and 10,000 Spaniards. On April 21, 1503, a battle took **Battles of** place at Seminara. The French were under the **Seminara and** command of Stuart d'Aubigny. Gonzalo di **Cerignola,** **1503.** Cordova routed him completely, and, after killing 2000 of his men, summoned the soldiers from all the garrisons and marched against the Duke of Nemours, whom he caught at Cerignola. Nemours was beaten and slain and the disaster of the French army was complete. At that very moment Louis XII was holding negotiations with the King of Spain; but to this Gonzalo paid no heed. "This is the second time he has deceived me ! " the King of France exclaimed indignantly of Ferdinand the Catholic. When this remark reached the latter's ears, however, he merely retorted : "He lies, the sot ! I have deceived him ten times over ! "

Instead of learning wisdom by this cruel lesson Louis XII merely became more determined than ever, and sent out a fresh relay of 11,000 men to Naples. Alexander VI had just died under dramatic circumstances, possibly poisoned by the drugged food he had himself intended for others. Georges d'Amboise hastened to the conclave in order, if possible, to have himself nominated Pope. He had done all he could to prepare the way for this, but he was doomed to disappointment. Pius III was elected and, on his death three weeks later, he was succeeded by Giuliano della Rovere, who became the famous pontiff, Julius II, the patron of the arts and the Mæcenas of his time, and withal a fiery, bellicose, and martial personage.

The 11,000 men sent out to Naples dragged out a miserable existence. Their chiefs were quarrelling, they were de- cimated by plague, and the weather was abomin- **Evacuation of** able. Hounded down by the able Gonzalo di **Naples, 1504.** Cordova, they were gradually demolished, and finally, on January 1, 1504, they laid down their arms at Gaëta. It was during the course of these daily combats that a knight, whose name rings through the centuries as an example

30

of courage, tenacity, vigour, and heroism—the famous Bayard
—won great renown. Among other feats of valour his defence
of the bridge at Garigliano has remained famous to this day.

Louis XII, who was very sensitive, was filled with consternation at the news of this fresh disaster. In fact he made
himself quite ill over it. His health had long
Ill-health of Louis XII. been delicate and he grew visibly thinner, weaker,
and more exhausted. So feeble did he become
that he seemed on the point of death, and the people about
him were filled with anxiety. Anne of Brittany, alarmed for
her own future, thought it her duty to take precautions. As
Louis XII had no son, the heir to the throne was a distant
cousin, Francis, Count of Angoulême, the future Francis I,
a young man who had been brought up at Amboise by his
mother, Louise of Savoy, an extremely strong-minded woman,
and his tutor, Pierre de Rohan, Marshal de Gié. Anne and
Louise very naturally detested each other and the two
households of Amboise and Blois were divided by feelings
of the deepest antipathy. Anne of Brittany, who was anxious,
in the event of the King's death, at once to make good her
escape to her own Duchy, out of the menacing clutches of Louise
of Savoy and her minions, hastened to pack all her belongings
at Blois—furniture, tapestries, and works of art—into boats,
and dispatched them down the Loire to Nantes. Marshal de
Gié, who had summoned troops to the side of the Count of
Angoulême, and was making preparations for the new reign
which he believed to be imminent, played her the trick of
seizing this convoy, and the rumour was spread abroad that
he was actually planning the arrest of Anne the moment she
was left a widow. But at this juncture Louis XII surprised
the whole world by recovering from his malady. The Queen,
however, whose haughty Breton spirit had been severely
wounded by what had occurred, demanded the
Trial of Marshal de Gié, 1504. immediate arrest and trial of Marshal de Gié for
high treason. Louis XII was greatly distressed
by this, as he would fain have avoided placing
an old servant of the Crown and a personal friend of long
standing in such a lamentable predicament. The Queen,
however, stood her ground, and he was obliged to give way.

The trial of Marshal de Gié formed one of the most important events in the reign of Louis XII. It stirred public opinion deeply, and its progress was watched by the people with passionate interest. It dragged on for a long time. As the Parliament of Paris seemed favourable to the accused, whom they restored to temporary liberty, Anne had the Parisian court disqualified—she paid the enormous costs of the proceedings in order to make sure of her revenge—and the trial was thereupon handed over to the Parliament of Toulouse, whose reputation for severity was notorious. The judges, however, could or would only convict the prisoner of having slightly overstepped the limits of his authority, and made a few wrongful exactions. Gié was sentenced to be deprived of the tutorship of the Count of Angoulême, to be suspended for five years from the rank of Marshal, and to be exiled from Court, which he was not to approach within a radius of ten miles. He retired to his magnificent seat, the Château du Verger, where he died in 1513, and Georges d'Amboise was popularly accused of having supported Anne of Brittany, from fear and jealousy of his rivalry.

After his first illness in 1504 Louis XII had a relapse in 1505 which proved quite as serious. But he once again recovered, to the great joy of his subjects, who were devoted to their excellent, kindly, and sympathetic monarch. During the hours of his convalescence the King pondered over many things, amongst others the question of his will. He also came to the conclusion that it was sheer folly to persist in the Neapolitan

Betrothal of the Princess Claude. enterprise. It was at this juncture, moreover, that he made up his mind to give his beloved daughter, Claude, whom he worshipped and who was "his only treasure and solace in this world," in marriage to his cousin and heir presumptive, the Count of Angoulême, in order that she might be Queen of France and keep Brittany in the possession of that country. His council, to whom he communicated his plan, gave it their approval, but Anne of Brittany, who could not bear any mention of the House of Angoulême, had to be won over. It was her desire to marry her daughter to some archduke, who would place her upon the imperial throne of Germany and thus preserve

32

for Brittany some sort of independence, which she would lose if she were constantly bound to France. As she advanced in years "the shrewd Brittany woman" became ever more obstinate, over-bearing, and self-sufficient. She only gave vague answers to the entreaties which assailed her from every quarter. Louis XII grew anxious. He wanted a more formal understanding, and pressure was brought to bear upon the Queen to come to some definite decision. In obedience to secret orders from the King, deputations from various towns came to him at Tours, and assembling in a suppliant mass, solemnly begged him to proceed to the betrothal of Claude and Francis. At the sight of their sovereign sitting in his arm-chair, bowed with sickness, pale and thin, and holding himself up with difficulty, the worthy envoys began to weep and called him the " father of his people." In accordance with a pre-arranged plan, the council, upon being consulted, returned a favourable reply. The King declared the petition just and reasonable, and gave his royal word that the betrothal should take place forthwith. Anne of Brittany thus had her hand forced. The betrothal followed and the whole kingdom indulged in great rejoicings. But Italy, alas, was destined to cast a gloom over it once more !

A proud and haughty city, selfish and cynical, who from the inaccessible fastnesses of her great lagoons seemed to look **The League of** forth with disdainful eyes upon the rest of the **Cambray, 1508.** world, the Republic of Venice was held in detestation by the other States of Italy. She had carved out for herself a fairly wide domain in the peninsula by filching from the Emperor territory to the north near the Alps, from the Pope lands to the south near the Apennines, and on the east, towards the Adda, by encroachments on the State of Milan. The chief sufferer from these amputations was Julius II, who made up his mind to form a league against Venice with the object of forcing her to give back the lands she had stolen. He sent invitations to Louis XII, the Emperor Maximilian, the King of Spain and the King of England to join him. Louis XII, to whom the deceit, treachery, and violence of the Republic were described, gave his consent. Spain and England, neither of whom had much to gain or lose, also acquiesced, and the allies formed at Cambray the League which bears that name (1508). It was decided to send an army against Venice. But whose army? Clearly Louis XII was the only signatory who was in a position to carry out any efficacious military stroke. In vain did the faithful Étienne Poncher raise his voice in the council against any such futile and suicidal policy, pointing out that the other allies were useless, and that Louis XII would be exerting himself for their benefit alone, merely to be betrayed by them in the end. Georges d'Amboise was enthusiastically in favour of the expedition, for some reason which is not very clear, and war was declared against Venice.

A French army of some 40,000 men was collected in the State of Milan under the command of Chaumont d'Amboise.

Battle of Agnadello, 1509. The Venetians placed a similar number in the field, headed by Petigliano and Alviane. Louis XII rode forth on horseback to watch his troops cross the Adda with drums beating. The two armies met at Agnadello on May 14, 1509. In spite of the fact that the advance on the hostile forces had been carried out somewhat clumsily, the attack was made in perfect order, and notwithstanding the deadly fire of the Venetian artillery, which ravaged the French columns, the latter, in a vigorous onslaught, broke through the ranks of their adversaries and put them to flight. It was a brilliant victory. Julius II seized the opportnuity to get back Ravenna, Faënza, and Imola from Venice. The Emperor Maximilian, anxious to have a share of the spoil, appropriated Vicenza, Padua, Verona, and Treviso, whilst Louis XII occupied the Ghiara d'Adda, Brescia, Cremona and Bergamo. Thereupon the incident was regarded as closed. The King of France disbanded his army, which was already decimated by pestilence and overcome by the excessive heat. The Pope, who had got what he wanted, made overtures of peace to the Venetians and offered to absolve them from the excommunication which he had hurled against them, a proposal which, like sensible people, they hastened to accept. And thus, after having formed a league against Venice, in order to make Louis XII enter the field, Julius II withdrew from it the moment he had obtained all he could from it. The ever-

34

changing, restless Maximilian, for his part, had also made good his escape.

The Venetians, however, raised another army, and at last, when it was too late, Louis XII realized that Étienne Poncher had been right and that the whole weight of the conflict was destined to fall on his shoulders alone. His friend, Cardinal d'Amboise, had died on May 25, 1510, of some internal complaint aggravated by gout. He was only fifty at the time of his death, and his loss was a great sorrow to the King.

The Pope, instead of being an ally, was now neutral, and it was not long before this attitude was changed to one of avowed hostility. He declared, whether sincerely or not, that the ambition of the King of France was a menace to Italy, which stood in danger of a general invasion by this foreigner, and preached the necessity of a Holy War. Louis XII's entreaties and threats were alike vain; the bellicose pontiff in alliance with Venice prepared for hostilities. The King of France tried the expedient of summoning a Council of the French Church to meet at Tours, in order to implore the Pope to put an end to this sacrilegious conflict, but the Pope turned a deaf ear to all their remonstrances. Europe was terrified at the idea of a war against the sovereign pontiff, and Anne of Brittany, who was extremely pious, was in a state of consternation. Something had to be done. The Marquis of Mantua, the commander-in-chief of the papal forces, who had been given the title of Gonfalonier of the Church, was advancing in the direction of Ferrara, attacking and seizing places on his march. Chaumont d'Amboise, thereupon mobilized his troops, retook the conquered towns, and marched upon Bologna, the headquarters of Julius II. The news that the Venetian army was advancing on his rear obliged him to fall back. Thereupon the Pope excommunicated Chaumont and came in person to lay siege to the little town of Mirandola. As he was making his exit from Bologna, he was surprised by an ambuscade and almost captured by Bayard, with the result that " he shook with fever the whole day from the great alarm he had felt." Aged as he was, however, he was to be seen riding out on horseback to superintend the attack on Mirandola, giving orders as to the position of the batteries

Holy Alliance against Louis XII, 1511.

and inspecting the outposts. As soon as a breach had been made the town surrendered, and Julius II entered in state through a gap in the walls.

On the death of Chaumont d'Amboise, the French army was placed under the command of Gaston de Foix, Duke of Nemours, **Battle of** a young prince of twenty who had already won **Ravenna,** distinction by great valour. Louis XII sent out **1512.** reinforcements and the French once more took the offensive. After the capture of Bologna they offered to make peace with the Pope, but the latter, who was a prey to " obstinacy, hatred, and contempt," refused to come to terms. He fled to Rome, where he joined forces with the Aragonese princes of Naples, and then marched back upon Gaston de Foix, who, with 18,000 infantry, 1600 men-at-arms, and eighty cannon was prepared to offer him a stout resistance. The two armies met at Ravenna (1512) where a hotly contested fight took place. Finally " the clerics and Spaniards " as they were called, were worsted, but, unfortunately, in a final charge of minor importance, Gaston, carried away by his temerity, was wounded in the side by a lance and killed. The victory was a brilliant one, but it had been bought at a heavy price. La Palice then took over the command of the French troops.

To make matters worse this victory bore no fruit. On the contrary, it was the signal for complete disaster. After **Evacuation** complicated negotiations, the Venetians, who **of Italy.** declared that the King of France must be driven out once and for all, succeeded in rousing the interest of the Swiss, of Maximilian, and of the King of England in the fate of Italy. The League of Cambray was thus turned against Louis XII. Three armies marched forth against La Palice, who, realizing the impossibility of showing fight in such circumstances, did not even attempt to hold his ground, but beat a retreat, evacuating everything, including the city and State of Milan. In a few short days that costly and hard-won conquest crumbled away and Maximilian Sforza, a son of Ludovico Sforza, who had been brought to light, ascended the ducal throne of his father.

Julius II was triumphant. He excommunicated the King

of France and placed his kingdom under an interdict. This
time Louis XII realized that he was beaten. Anne of
France and Brittany now proposed to her husband that she
the Papacy. should approach the Pope in person. Harrowed
by the conflict which the King persisted in sustaining
against the sovereign pontiff, she had, after giving birth
to another child who did not live, remained in a state of
pining sickness and depression. Her health was giving way
and preoccupations for the future filled her mind. In
spite of the betrothal of her daughter Claude to Francis
of Angoulême, she still nursed the hope of marrying her to the
Austrian Archduke, a plan which peace alone would allow her
to set on foot. She accordingly offered her services to bring
pressure to bear upon Julius II. Weary of the whole matter,
Louis XII allowed her to have her way. Julius II was immovable. However, seized by a slow fever, he died on
January 21, 1513, at the age of seventy. He was succeeded
by a young cardinal of thirty-seven, Giovanni de' Medici, who
became the celebrated Leo X, a more amenable character
with whom to carry on negotiations. At first he declared
that he would remain neutral, but agreed to receive Claude
de Seyssel and Claude de Forbin, Louis XII's ambassadors,
at Rome. His next step was to annul the decrees against
the King of France. In the direction of the Holy City the
horizon was clearing.

But elsewhere it remained dark and lowering. Henry VIII,
King of England, had landed in France with an army, and
Difficulties meeting the French force at Guinegate, had
with England, routed it so completely that the vanquished
Austria, and troops had fled in hot haste and were obliged
Switzerland. to bear the shame of hearing the encounter dubbed
the Battle of Spurs. Louis XII hastened to Amiens to
guard the frontier. But the Emperor, on his side, was
threatening to invade Burgundy, and the Swiss were making
a deliberate attack. It was a critical and anxious moment.
Fortunately for the King of France the difficulty solved itself
owing to the lack of unity among the enemy. The Swiss consented to retire, upon securing a treaty signed by La Trémoïlle,
the terms of which were so onerous for Louis XII that he

subsequently refused to ratify it. But the essential point had been gained, inasmuch as the Swiss had left the country. Maximilian, as usual, vanished into space. Henry VIII, angry at his desertion, also retreated, and Louis XII finally made peace with him. The Pope showed himself disposed to restore tranquillity to Italy on condition that the King of France renounced all claims upon the State of Milan. Louis XII was obliged to reconcile himself to the distasteful idea, but asked, in return, to be allowed to give that state as a dowry to his second daughter Renée, whom he proposed to marry to a son of the King of Spain. The King of Spain, thus allowed to share the spoils, became reconciled with France. Matters gradually calmed down, and peace was at last restored at the cost of the final shipwreck of all Louis XII's plans of conquest in Italy.

The poor King went into melancholy retirement at Blois, the home in which he had spent the first happy years of his

Louis XII at Blois. life, and in which he was now to pass his last sad hours, the old house " beneath whose roof his mother and father had dwelt, his birthplace and the citadel of Kings! " As he could not endure the old feudal manor house, a massive and imposing edifice, the original comfortless and gloomy fortress, he had had the east wing pulled down and rebuilt in the new style. It was the fashion among the great folk of this period to raise buildings of regular appearance well open to the sun, instead of shutting themselves up, as they had done before, inside the dark towers of defence characteristic of the castles of the fifteenth century. With their high roofs gilt at the extremities, dormer windows encased in graceful sculpture, pierced galleries, window-frames with mouldings simple but suitable in design, the whole still in the Gothic style with gables and rosettes, after the manner of the old cathedrals, but novel in virtue of the high artistic taste displayed, the new buildings were eminently pleasing to the eye. Pierre de Rohan, Marshal de Gié, had built the Château du Verger; Georges d'Amboise, who loved magnificence, was responsible for the Courts of Justice at Rouen, as well as the Archbishop's Palace and the Château Gaillon, one of the most remarkable monuments of the period, admirable alike for the elegance and variety of its structure. At his instigation Louis XII

38

had also added the Court of the Exchequer to the Law Courts in the French capital and carried on the constructions at Amboise begun by Charles VIII. Blois was built on a similar principle, and the Louis XII wing is a charming edifice, thoroughly French in its taste, its proportions, its restraint and the sobriety of its decoration. The names of some of the workmen have been discovered, but the architect remains unknown to this day. It is possible that he never existed, and that master masons of the district, who were accustomed to the building of similar structures in those parts, carried out a particularly finished and skilful piece of work for the King. Louis XII might possibly have reconstructed the whole of Blois Castle in the same style had not time and means failed him. His emblem, a porcupine with bristling quills, with the device *Cominus ac eminus* " from far and near " (an allusion to the belief of the time that the porcupine shoots out its quills in self-defence) marks the buildings for which this prince was responsible.

And here in the " new dwelling " of Blois, as it was called, Loius XII passed his last days in the company of Queen Anne, in loving and peaceful unity. As in the time of Charles VIII the rich Brittany heiress had adorned the royal home with her works of art. On its walls she had hung rich " storied " tapestries. The great hall had a hanging representing the Fall of Troy ; in the " King's Dining-room " was one called " The Battle of Formigny." The room of the little Princess Claude was adorned with pastoral scenes, " little inscriptions " and tiny figures. In the Queen's room were illustrations of tales and battles ; in the bedroom extraordinary birds and beasts from foreign climes. Everywhere she placed a profusion of furniture and draperies, cloth of gold mantelpiece-covers, beds " hung with cloth of gold " and adorned with canopies of crimson or white damask ; silver chandeliers supported by silver chains ; red and yellow taffetas curtains ; sideboards draped with cloth of gold ; stools to sit upon covered in velvet or " checkers ; " " carved and gilded chairs from Italy." The floors were covered by carpets " so thickly woven that the boards were entirely hidden," and a glow of luxury prevailed beneath the thick low beams, a scintillating play of gold and colour set in a frame of intimate peace.

Here Anne of Brittany dwelt surrounded by her ladies-in-waiting, working at her distaff or sewing, whilst a secretary read aloud from the pages of romance or history, or a poet—some favourite or pensioner of hers, such as Jean Marot or Jean Meschinot—recited verses, to which she listened more because it was the fashion than because she liked them, for she was not a particularly good judge of literature. Or else, some court jester, like Triboulet, a misshapen creature, with goggle eyes, big nose and narrow brow, would entertain them with his insolent quips and buffooneries. All the denizens of the royal Court, ladies-in-waiting, maids-of-honour, squires and knights, surrounded her with respectful attention. She had the cold imposing presence of a great lady, but as soon as she was addressed, her sweetness and kindliness at once aroused sympathy. People were struck by her goodness and left her bewitched by her charm. The populace—or at all events that of France, if not the Bretons, whose hearts she had won by her liberality—only knew her self-willed character and her rancorous spirit, and she was but little loved by them. The ministers were frequently irritated by her dictatorial airs and by the commands which she took upon herself to send them with the high-handed comment : " Unknown to the King." " Be patient," Louis XII would observe with a smile, when they came to him with complaints about her. But her immediate circle adored her.

Death came to her swiftly. Ever since the birth of her last child, the poor woman had been failing. Persistent weak-**Death of** ness had been wearing away her strength as if **Anne of** some mysterious malady were gradually under-**Brittany, 1514.** mining her. There was some talk of gravel. On December 31, 1513, she was seized with fever, and ten days later, on January 9, 1514, she died. She was only thirty-eight, and her loss was the occasion of universal mourning. The whole Court was in tears ; even the people were moved and talked of nothing but the "noble lady's" generosity, and the King, for his part, was in the depths of despair. Rarely in the course of history has the death of a Queen been the cause of such wide-spread grief. She was buried with great solemnity at Saint Denis. A long funeral

40

procession accompanied her remains on their way from Blois to Paris, and the crowds of sorrowing people who thronged round it bore witness to the mourning in which the whole nation was plunged.

The greatness of his grief made Louis XII leave Blois, which had now become odious to him on account of the memories **Marriage of** it revived. He went to Saint-Germain-en-**the Princess** Laye, another old mediæval castle, and to **Claude.** Vincennes, thoroughly depressed and indifferent to everything, for he had received a blow from which he was destined never to recover. It was pointed out to him that as he had no heir except the young Count of Angoulême, it was now perhaps time to consummate the marriage of that prince with his daughter, Claude, as at present the couple were merely betrothed. He accepted the advice without demur, and the ceremony took place in the deepest gloom in the chapel of Saint-Germain (still in existence) on May 18, 1514. The congregation was all in black and the bride was in tears.

Those who surrounded Louis XII, arguing that as he was only fifty-two, an age at which it is possible for a man to marry **Louis XII's** again and have children, and thinking that the **Marriage with** creation of a new home would rouse the King **Henry VIII's** from the fatal grief which overwhelmed him, **Sister.** conceived the idea of a third marriage for him. The King of Aragon, who at this juncture was doing his best to secure a settled peace between England and France, suggested that this should be sealed by a marriage between Louis XII and Henry VIII's sister, Mary, a strapping young Englishwoman, a "*haquenée*" as the disapproving populace dubbed her. Henry VIII gave his consent, and Louis XII, worn and feeble, and moved, perhaps, by some vague desire of having an heir, or of escaping from his melancholy, gave way. The marriage was celebrated without pomp or show of any kind.

But the King's health was ruined. He grew daily thinner and more delicate; broken down by grief and sickness, his constitution had lost all power of resistance. His young Queen, full of delight at her new greatness, insisted upon making Louis XII lead a life of gaiety. The poor King found himself obliged to change all his habits. He had to go to **Death of** bed late, eat a great deal at all sorts of hours, **Louis XII,** and also, as Fleurange l'Aventureux says in his **1515.** *Mémoires,* act the part of the "loving spouse to his wife." He was seized by a violent attack of fever aggravated by dysentery, and on January 1, 1515, he passed away in the Hôtel des Tournelles in Paris, leaving the throne of France as a New Year's gift to his successor.

SOURCES. The very important work by H. Hauser, *Les' Sources de l'histoire de France, XVIᵉ siècle*, 1906 ; *Lettres de Charles VIII*, ed. Pélicier and B. de Mandrot, 1898 ; Octavien de Saint Gelais and André de la Vigne, *Le Vergier d'honneur* in Godefroy's *Hist. de Charles VIII*, 1684 ; Robert Gaguin, *Compendium de origine et gestis Francorum*, 1586 ; Comines, *Mémoires*, ed. B. de Mandrot, 1901 ; Brantôme, *Œuvres complètes*, ed. Lalanne ; Marino Sanuto, *Diarii*, vol. i to xxvi, 1879 ; Burchard, *Diarium*, ed. Thuasne, 1883 ; J. Masselin, *Journal des États généraux en 1484*, 1835 ; Jean d'Auton, *Chronique de Louis XII*, ed. Maulde la Clavière, 1889 ; Claude de Seyssel, *Hist. singulière du roi Louis XII* in Th. Godefroy's *Hist. de Louis XII*, 1615 ; Fleurange l'Aventureux, *Mémoires*, ed. Michaud and Poujoulat ; *Histoire du gentil seigneur de Bayart par le Loyal Serviteur*, ed. Roman 1878 ; *Procédures politiques du règne de Louis XII, ed* De Maulde, 1885 ; *Lettres de Louis XII et du cardinal d'Amboise*, 1712.

WORKS. Du Cherrier, *Histoire de Charles VIII*, 1871 ; P. Pélicier, *Essai sur le gouvernement de la dame de Beaujeu*, 1882 ; Fr. Delaborde, *Expédition de Charles VIII en Italie*, 1888 ; P. van der Haeghen, *Examen du droit de Charles VIII sur Naples* (*Rev. hist.* 1885) ; Müntz, *La Renaissance en Italie et en France à l'époque de Charles VIII*, 1885 ; De Boislisle, *Notice biographique et historique sur Étienne de Vesc* (*Annulaire-bullet. de la Soc. de l'hist. de France*, 1878–1883) ; De Maulde, *Histoire de Louis XII*, 1889 ; Le Roux de Lincy, *Vie de la Reine Anne de Bretagne*, 1860 ; and *Détails sur la vie privée d'Anne de Bretagne*, 1850 ; Legendre, *Vie du cardinal d'Amboise*, 1725 ; L.-G. Pélissier, *Louis XII et Ludovic Sforza*, 1896 ; Kohler, *Les Suisses dans les guerres d'Italie de 1506 à 1512*, 1897.

CHAPTER II

THE KING AND THE EMPEROR

Francis I, 1515–1547. Conquest of the Duchy of Milan and the victory of Marignano, 1515 ; the Concordat of Bologna, 1516. Candidature of Francis I for the Imperial Throne ; election of Charles V, 1519. Conflict between the King of France and the Emperor. Interview with Henry VIII on the Field of the Cloth of Gold, 1520. The hostilities of 1521 ; defeat of Lautrec in Italy at the Bicocca, 1522. Constable Bourbon's treachery, 1523. Defeat of Bonnivet in Italy at Rebecco and Romagnano, 1524 ; invasion of Provence by Charles V and his retreat. Descent of Francis I into Italy and the disaster of Pavia, 1525. The captivity of the King of France and the Treaty of Madrid, 1526. The Holy League of Cognac. Sack of Rome by the Emperor's soldiers under Charles of Bourbon, 1527. Peace of Cambray, 1529. Fresh preparations for war on the part of Francis I and his alliance with the Turks. Re-opening of hostilities, 1535. Second invasion of Provence by Charles V and his retreat, 1536. Truce of Monçon, 1537 ; fresh rupture, 1544 ; descent into Italy and victory of the Duc d'Enghien at Cerisola. Treaty of Crépy, 1544. Death of Francis I, 1547.

> De sa beauté il est blanc et vermeil
> Les cheveux bruns, de grande et belle taille ;
> En terre il est, comme au ciel le soleil.
> Hardi, vaillant, sage et preux en bataille ;
> Il est bénin, doux, humble en sa grandeur,
> Fort et puissant, et plein de patience.*

THIS portrait of Francis I, drawn by his charming sister, Margaret of Navarre, is on the whole accurate. He was very tall and strong, with broad, powerful shoulders —though rather thin in the leg—his face was broad and massive,

---

* White and rose is he in his loveliness,
   With his brown hair and stature fair and tall ;
   As the sun in the heavens, he seems on earth ;
   Bold, full of valour and most skilled in war,
   Humble and sweetly kind despite his strength ;
   Steadfast endurance his and kingly power.

43

the features fine enough, though the nose was somewhat too aquiline ; his hair showed black upon a white skin and **Francis I,** his expression was frank and straightforward. **1515–1547.** Altogether the new king of twenty who succeeded the gaunt and cadaverous Louis XII deserved his predecessor's compliment when the latter exclaimed, " What a fine young gallant ! " He was above all a fascinating young prince, full of life and spirits, vigorous, imprudent, frivolous, lavish, and witty. All with whom he came in contact were delighted with him, he scattered money right and left without a thought, he was chivalrous, generous and full of the joy of life—a true Frenchman with the best qualities and the worst faults of his race. " All our work is useless, " Louis XII used to say, shaking his head, " that great youngster will spoil it all ! "

Francis had been brought up at Cognac and at Amboise by two women who worshipped him—his mother, Louise of **Education of** Savoy and his sister Margaret, who was his **Francis I.** senior by two years. Louise of Savoy, whose husband, Charles of Angoulême, had died and left her a widow at the age of eighteen, had surrounded her son during the time of his tutelage with all the joys that an easygoing and inexperienced character could provide. The child had been the pride of her heart and she had spoilt him. In the kindly atmosphere of Louise's little Court, surrounded by art, poetry and festivals, the young prince had developed his gracious and light-hearted nature. His sister, Margaret, had played no small part in his education. Herself extremely bright, intelligent and well-read,—" no bread-and-butter-miss," according to Brantôme—witty, not a very great stickler for morality, with an extremely independent spirit, but otherwise a superior woman worthy of respect, she had surrounded her brother, who was the passion of her life, with tender devotion. In this atmosphere of affection Francis grew up. He was allowed to do exactly as he pleased. Twenty times over, carried away during some violent exploit while hunting or riding, he narrowly escaped death. He studied little or not at all, read romances of chivalry, led the gay life of a rich young man, wrote verses, had adventures and came into power with

44

everything calculated to make him a magnificent monarch, a Mæcenas of taste, and a thoroughly bad politician. With his mother and sister he always remained on very good terms, and he was also extremely fond of his wife, Claude, the daughter of Louis XII. She was a good, modest and sensible woman, not uncomely in face, but short and fat and slightly lame. In theory, if not in practice, Francis was faithful to this " good lady of honest and upright life," and when, in 1524, after bearing him seven children, she died, worn out with travail, at the age of twenty-five, his grief was sincere. Queen Claude is now remembered only on account of the plums that bear her name.

One day when Francis was talking with his friends at Amboise, he amused himself by listening to their jesting enum-
Advisers of eration of the Crown offices it would be the dream
Francis I. of their ambition to fill. As soon as he became King, the first step he took was to gratify each man's desire. Arthur de Gouffier, Sieur de Boissy, was made Lord High Steward of France, and his brother, Bonnivet, High Admiral, whilst Anne de Montmorency was destined to become Constable. Naturally generous, Francis distributed money and honours with a lavish hand. His mother was given the Duchy of Anjou and Maine ; his brother-in-law, the Duke of Alençon, Margaret's husband, was made Duke of Berry and Governor of Normandy. Charles of Bourbon received the sword of Constable and the Governorship of Languedoc, whilst Lautrec and La Palice were appointed Marshals of France. The post of Chancellor was vacant, and to fill this he summoned Antoine Duprat, the first President of the Parliament of Paris— the man who was destined to act such an important part as his adviser !

For this young and vigorous monarch, light-hearted and full of fire, the glory of some military campaign was absolutely
Invasion of essential. There was no need to seek far for a
Milan. cause. As Louis XII's heir through his wife Claude, and consequently possessing rights over that perpetual bone of contention the State of Milan, Francis I had only to make good his claim, sword in hand, at the expense of Maximilian Sforza, Duke of Milan. It was a brilliant moment.

A formidable army was raised, consisting of 30,000 foot, 10,000 horse and seventy-two cannon. The whole of the youth of France hastened to join the standards; princes and soldiers of renown wished to share in the enterprise, and, in the summer of 1515, the French host crossed the Alps by the steep and arduous pass of Largentière, surrounded by incredible difficulties, which it seemed impossible for any army ever to overcome, leading their horses by the bridle, dragging along the cannon, and blowing up rocks. The Swiss, who were in the pay of Duke Maximilian, retreated beneath the walls of Milan, and

Battle of Marignano, 1515. Francis I took up his position close by at Marignano, a place which he was to make famous by a brilliant victory. The attack was made by chance, and arose out of a scuffle between some scouts. Matthäus Schinner, Bishop of Sion, a fiery prelate who detested the French, stirred up the Swiss. He had the tocsin rung and the drum beaten, with the result that on September 13, at about four o'clock in the afternoon, the Swiss battalions, to the sound of the cornets of Uri, Unterwalden and Schwiz, headed by Schinner, mounted on a Spanish jennet, marched out against the French army. The latter were in an unfavourable position, drawn up in lines on the road between Milan and Marignano. They could only meet the onslaught of the enemy, who were charging with lowered pikes, by a series of partial counter-attacks. Bourbon and La Palice retaliated with their men-at-arms, whilst Francis I made a charge with 600 horse to defend his artillery which was in danger. At nightfall the battle was undecided, and both sides remained as they were. But before day had dawned, the King of France, who had spent the night leaning against a gun carriage, succeeded in collecting his forces into a single body, with Bourbon on the right, Alençon on the left, and the cannon forming a battery in the centre. Eight thousand Swiss advanced, but were held in check by the artillery. Whilst Alençon's lines were wavering on one side, Bourbon held firm on the other, and Francis I made a vigorous onslaught with all his cavalry, routing and hewing down the Swiss, who took to flight. The young King, flushed with victory, had himself dubbed a knight by Bayard on the field of battle. The State of Milan

46

was won, and Duke Maximilian consented, in consideration of a yearly pension, to abandon his territory and retire to France.

This was a glorious dawn for the new reign. The victory filled Francis I with joy and hope. The long chain of defeats Concordat of and misfortunes which were to follow were des-Bologna, 1516. tined to give the lie to these first favourable auspices ! But, for the moment, everything smiled upon the victor. The Pope, who had made common cause with the Duke of Milan, terrified by the news of Marignano, now wished to make peace. Francis I was quite ready to negotiate, and a magnificent meeting took place between the two sovereigns at Bologna. The young King had an escort of 1200 men-at-arms and 6000 lansquenets, whilst the Pope was surrounded by thirty cardinals. Francis I and Leo X vied with each other in amenities. They ate their meals together and took part in grand ceremonies. Whilst the terms of the treaty were under discussion, Leo X pointed out to the King that, by the clauses of a pragmatic sanction dating from the reign of Charles VII, France enjoyed the privilege of electing her archbishops, bishops and abbots ; that a certain right, called the right of annats, by which the Pope appropriated for one year the revenues of a see on the appointment of a new bishop, had been abolished ; and that the Holy Chair had no jurisdiction over ecclesiastical cases in France. The Pope maintained that he could not allow the validity of this pragmatic sanction, which was heretical and a menace to his privileges. Its revocation was the price he demanded for a cessation of hostilities. Francis I and his counsellors discovered a *via media* by signing a convention in virtue of which the archbishops, bishops and abbots should in future be appointed by the King. This was the chief clause. A few vague words were added on the subject of the third point and nothing at all was said about the second. The convention was signed and became the celebrated Concordat of 1516, which gave the Church of France over to the King's nomination. The Parliaments offered a lively opposition. The treaty during the course of centuries, was destined to produce very different results from any that could have been foreseen by the contemporaries of Leo X !

Francis I returned to France surrounded by a halo of glory.

47

He was the most conspicuous monarch in Europe and the most
fortunate. No hope seemed too great for him to nurse.
The question of the moment was the forthcoming election of
an Emperor in Germany. Francis I considered himself great
Candidature of enough to stand as a candidate and make an
Francis I for attempt to win this crown. Never in the whole
the Imperial course of history, since the days of the old
Throne. Roman Emperors or of Charlemagne, would any
prince have been so great as he. He made his preparations
and entered upon the adventure which was destined to bring
about the disasters of his own life and the gravest complications for his country !

A vast amorphous body, the German Empire was made up
of an infinite number of small semi-independent and federated
Rivalry of States. In accordance with ancient custom, the
Charles V. Emperor was elected at Frankfort by seven
electors—the Archbishops of Mainz, Cologne and Treves, the
King of Bohemia, the Duke of Saxony, the Count Palatine
and the Margrave of Brandenburg. The electors chose an
Emperor before the death of his predecessor, and whilst
waiting to ascend the throne, the heir presumptive took the
title of King of the Romans. Now Maximilian, the reigning
Emperor, had his own candidate—his grandson Charles, the
future Charles V ! In order to understand the mosaic of territory
which Charles V had to rule, it must be borne in mind that his
grandfather, the Emperor Maximilian, had married Mary of
Burgundy, daughter of Charles the Bold, from whom the family
inherited Burgundy and Flanders ; and that his father, the
Archduke Philip the Fair, who died in 1506, had married Joanna
the Mad, the daughter of Ferdinand, King of Aragon, and
Isabella, Queen of Castille. From this source Charles V inherited Spain and Naples. Accordingly it was the lord of
Spain, Flanders and Naples that the Emperor Maximilian
wished to make Emperor of Germany. Francis I, in proposing
to solicit the votes of the imperial electors, not only dreamed
of securing the overlordship of all Europe for himself, but was
also inspired by the legitimate desire of preventing the creation
of such a monarchy for another's advantage. Had he been wiser,
the King of France would have realized the danger of facing

48

the countries concerned with the choice of two dangers, of which, whether rightly or wrongly, they were bound to consider his election the graver. In order to checkmate the grandson of Maximilian he should have sought out some inoffensive candidate. But this he did not see. He threw himself into the electoral campaign. The adversary whom he was attacking was destined, by his character, to be the most implacable agent of the drama which was beginning.

Charles V, who was born in 1500, at the dawn of the new century, offered a complete contrast to Francis I. He was of medium height and pale complexion, with a pinched aquiline nose obstructed by adenoids. His eyes were grey, and his ugly chin was so excessively prominent that it obliged him to keep his mouth perpetually open—a characteristic known as a prognathous jaw, and, according to doctors, a sign of incipient degeneracy. Altogether he was far from handsome, though, if we may judge by Titian's portrait of him, he had an air of distinction. He was a cold, calm person, who spoke but little, and was neither amiable nor open-hearted, but perfectly self-possessed, calculating, judicious and decided—a man who took a long time to make up his mind, and when he had once done so never changed it, but was absolutely ruthless and frigid in his tenacity of purpose. His look was that of one who never lost his head, and was embarrassing as revealing a nature formidable in its superior self-mastery and inexorable will. To crown all, he was miserly. Francis I, full of exuberance and spirit, wore his heart on his sleeve ; Charles V was reserved and self-contained. The King of France, openhanded and pleasure-loving, conducted affairs of State with a light-hearted superficiality, whilst his adversary, a man of shrewd administrative gifts, hating hunting and amusement of any kind, gave himself up studiously to serious matters. Francis I's nervous, enthusiastic, unreliable nature met in Charles V a cool, evenly balanced mind, obstinacy and subtlety of judgment. Even if their political positions had not forced them into enmity they would never, as Queen Margaret pointed out to the Venetian ambassador, Giustiniano, have understood each other. They were made to hate each other to the death !

Contrast between Charles V and Francis I.

D   49

From 1516 onwards, Francis I sent envoys to Germany to buy over the electors. He instructed them to promise anything **Manœuvres** that might be asked—matrimonial alliances, **of Francis I.** pensions, or sums of money. A policy of barefaced trafficking was the result. Two of the electors distinguished themselves by their greed—Joachim, Margrave of Brandenburg and his brother, the Archbishop of Mainz. They consented to sell themselves. The Archbishop of Treves and the Count Palatine followed their example, thus securing Francis I four votes—the majority! At the same time, the King of France won over various other personages from different localities to his cause, among them Franz von Sickingen, a bold and extremely popular soldier from the Rhineland, a man of superior intellect and a friend of Ulrich von Hutten, the man of letters attached to the little archiepiscopal court of Mainz. He was a warrior who could summon a host of lansquenets to muster about his fortress of Ebernburg near Kreuznach and terrorize the surrounding country. Franz paid a visit to Amboise, where he was loaded with costly gifts and given a pension.

Charles of Austria, from the depths of his Spanish kingdom, learnt what was happening and immediately warned his grand- **Counter-** father. Maximilian replied that they must outdo **manœuvres** Francis I in bribery. Had his grandson any **of Charles V.** money? Hampered though he was by grave difficulties caused by subjects who detested the Flemish advisers of their King, a poor man still, and lacking in authority on account of his youth, Charles nevertheless succeeded in raising a loan of 300,000 ducats, which he forwarded to Maximilian. The old Emperor, who had not the slightest intention of spending a farthing of his own money, sent word that the sum was too small and borrowed 30,000 gold florins from the banking house of Fugger on account of the King of Spain. The latter thereupon found means to send a further instalment of 100,000 gold ducats, and the work was set on foot. In response to extremely tempting offers, Joachim of Brandenburg and his brother of Mainz decided to abandon Francis I. The Count Palatine was no less easy to win over, whilst the King of Bohemia and the Archbishop of Cologne had already been secured. Charles now possessed five votes, but the transaction had cost 514,000 gold florins without counting promises for the conferring of privileges, rights, &c. Maximilian sent in the bill to his grandson with the addition of 50,000 gold florins for his own petty personal expenses ! He then summoned the electors ; but on January 12, 1519, this strange person breathed his last !

Francis I, however, was not to be discouraged. He sent fresh envoys to Germany, some of them official ambassadors, **Election of** such as Jean d'Albret, Bonnivet, and President **Charles V, 1519.** Guillart, and others as secret agents. It was now a question of winning back the electors by means of fresh inducements. " If it is necessary," exclaimed Francis I, " I will spend three millions in order to be Emperor ! " He wrote plainly and crudely enough : " I want the Margrave Joachim to be glutted to surfeit ! "—and his bribes were increased. Charles, on his side, also raised his prices and the contest became so hotly disputed, feverish, and implacable, that its like had not been seen for many a long day. Brandenburg, the Count Palatine and the Archbishops of Mainz and Cologne, greedy and cynical, consented to return to the King of France, on exorbitant terms. But as soon as Armestorff, the envoy of Charles of Austria, arrived upon the scene, they admitted the state of affairs, and added that for an increase of 100,000 florins, they would go over to his side. Armestorff succeeded in beating them down to somewhat less than 100,000 florins, and they accordingly kept their word to support him. Francis I thereupon sent off 400,000 crowns packed up in leather bags and collected some troops to intimidate them. But as a matter of fact, when the electors met at Frankfort on June 18, 1519, nobody felt sure of anything. They entered into discussions, and brought forward many reasons to prove the danger for Germany which the choice of the King of France would entail, and finally, Charles of Austria was elected without much difficulty. Francis I was at Poissy when the news of his defeat was brought to him on July 3. He bore the disappointment without flinching, and in public even congratulated himself upon his escape from the responsibilities of the German Empire. He had no idea that he had just made an irreconcilable enemy, and that Charles V would never forgive him for having tried to rob him of a crown which had been in his family for eighty years !

But a conflict between these two monarchs was inevitable ! Charles V, who hemmed in France with his territories, was a **Conflict between** source of perpetual menace. Moreover, pretexts **Francis I and** for quarrels were ready to hand. The Emperor, **Charles V.** as the heir of Charles the Bold, laid claim to Burgundy, which had been seized by Louis XI. France demanded the restitution to Henri d'Albret of the Kingdom of Navarre, which Ferdinand the Catholic had appropriated ; whilst in Italy Charles V would certainly desire the expulsion of the French from the State of Milan ; and the French, on their side, would endeavour to drive out the Spaniards from Naples. It would have been a miracle if the collision had been avoided at a time when wars were waged for the merest trifles.

Before coming to blows in an encounter which they felt would be decisive, both rivals endeavoured to win over the **Negotiations** two sovereigns of Europe whose alliance would **of both with** be most useful—the Pope and Henry VIII, King **the Pope and** of England. The same process was repeated as **Henry VIII.** in the case of the electors—it was a question as to which would make the highest bids. Francis I promised Leo X half the Kingdom of Naples as soon as he had conquered it ; Charles V consented to give up Parma, Placentia, and Ferrara, and talked of driving the French out of Milan and putting an Italian, a Sforza, in their place. The Pope considered the Emperor's offer the safer of the two and entered into a secret treaty with him. The negotiations with Henry VIII were even more mortifying. It was necessary to have an understanding with England, in order to prevent Henry VIII from making an attack upon the north of France whilst Francis I was fighting his Italian battles. Francis I accordingly proposed a meeting with the English King between Calais and Ardres, to which the latter gave his consent—an acceptance which resulted in the celebrated interview of the Field of the Cloth of Gold. But as soon as Charles V heard of the project he immediately set sail from Spain, and hastening to London

52

in five days, promised Henry VIII that if Spain were victorious
he would hand over several French provinces to him; then
turning to Cardinal Wolsey, the all-powerful minister to whose
advice the King always lent a ready ear, he offered him the
Triple Crown. When Henry VIII disembarked at Calais to
meet Francis I he had already been won over by the astute
and crafty Emperor!

What a melancholy and humiliating spectacle the magnificent pageant of the Field of the Cloth of Gold was destined
The Field of   to present, since its negative result had been
the Cloth of   decided even before it took place! Francis I
Gold, 1520.   wished to dazzle Henry VIII by the sight of
matchless luxury and splendour. He came with a gorgeous
escort of 5172 people and 2865 horses. All the Court was
present, including the Queens, Louise and Claude, the King's
sister Margaret, four cardinals, and all the princes and nobility
of the realm. Near Ardres he pitched his camp, consisting
of 300 tents covered with cloth of gold and silver and
lined inside with velvet and silk. Above the King's tent,
which was also of cloth of gold, was erected a golden statue
of St. Michael. The whole presented the spectacle of a glistening
mass of gold. In order not to be outdone Henry VIII was
obliged to put up a little palace of wood also covered with velvet
and silk, and adorned with Arras tapestries. The interview
took place with great solemnity on June 7. The two Kings
rode out to meet each other mounted upon horses caparisoned
with gold and silver; their clothes were glistening with pearls,
diamonds, emeralds, and rubies; their velvet caps, covered
with precious stones, were adorned with huge white plumes,
whilst their attendants, dressed in suits of gold and silver,
surrounded them on prancing steeds. The two Kings, preceded
by their Constables carrying huge drawn swords, rode down
towards each other from opposite slopes and met in front of a
pavilion situated in the middle of the little plain of Valdoré.
They saluted and kissed each other whilst still on horseback
and then, dismounting and linking arms, they entered the
pavilion followed only by their chief advisers, Wolsey and
Bonnivet respectively. The interview was most cordial. The
conversation lasted a long time, but Henry VIII evaded any

idea of a definite engagement whilst assuring Francis I of his good will and friendship. For five and twenty days the two monarchs exchanged an uninterrupted series of festivals, dinners, tournaments, and jousts held in vast lists surrounded by elegant stands in which the ladies of the two Courts had seats. Francis I proved himself an adept in games, whilst Henry VIII showed great vigour. The athletic strength of the English King and his solid sporting qualities were objects of universal admiration. He even challenged Francis I in joke to wrestle a bout with him and seized him round the waist with his muscular hands. But his opponent, with a twist of his leg, sent him flying, and it was necessary to interfere between them in order to put a stop to an incident which would have ended in a scene. When they finally bade each other farewell they exchanged words of friendship and no more. On leaving Francis I, Henry VIII went straight to Gravelines to meet Charles V, who was awaiting him, and concluded his understanding with the Emperor.

Whether he had been deceived or not, Francis I made up his mind not to postpone his attack upon the Emperor. Circumstances chanced to be propitious. In Spain, **Hostilities of 1521.** where Charles V was struggling with money difficulties, the people, exasperated by constant demands for taxes, were in a state of rebellion. In Germany, the dawn of Lutheranism was causing a profound upheaval, and the Emperor had his vast and too widely scattered dominions badly in hand. In the spring of 1521, André de Foix, Sieur de Lesparre, crossed the Pyrenees with 8000 infantry and seized Navarre without meeting with any resistance except at Pampeluna, where one of the defenders, a nobleman of Guipuzcoa, had his leg broken. This man was none other than Ignatius Loyola, and the wound he received on this occasion was destined to play an important part in the history of the foundation of the Jesuit Order ! When Charles V heard of this act of aggression he was delighted, and exclaimed, " The King of France wishes to make me greater than I am. In a little while either I shall be an extremely poor Emperor, or he will be a poor King of France ! " The Duke of Najera, his representative in Navarre, collected 12,000 men and 2000 horse and attacking Lesparre, routed his army and took him prisoner. The Emperor's prophecy was beginning to be fulfilled.

Charles V immediately went to Flanders with the intention of himself leading an attack upon the French frontier from that quarter. He also set on foot a movement in Italy. The King of France mobilized three armies; he sent Lautrec with some troops to Milan, Bonnivet with 6000 lansquenets to the Pyrenees, and marched in person to the north with a force of 26,000 infantry, 1500 men-at-arms, and twelve cannon to the relief of Bayard who, shut up in Mézières, was holding his own vigorously against the Count of Nassau and Franz von Sickingen, the latter of whom had taken service under the Emperor. He put these two generals to flight and presently near Valenciennes fell in with Charles V, who had entrenched himself behind the Scheldt. Francis I might have offered him battle; but he did not dare to attack him, and allowed him to escape. The favourable opportunity he thus missed was never offered to him again.

From this moment everything turned against Francis I. In Italy, Lautrec was attacked by an army of 20,000 men under **Battle of the** Prospero Colonna. Deserted by his Swiss mer-**Bicocca, 1522.** cenaries, because, owing to lack of funds, he had not been able to pay them, and with the Milanese in a state of rebellion against his brutalities, he was obliged to evacuate the country. Francis I entrusted him with another army with which he tried to win back Milan, but the Emperor's general attacked him at the Bicocca. He might have held his own in triumph had not the Swiss, who had not been paid, once again insisted upon either fighting or being discharged. Lautrec consented to fight on April 27, 1522. He was worsted and the Swiss disbanded themselves, whereupon he retreated to France, leaving the valley of the Po in the hands of the Imperialists.

This proved one of the first disastrous moments of the reign of Francis I. Henry VIII informed him of his alliance **Treachery of** with Charles V, and broke off all relations with **Constable** him. The Pope and the Venetians followed the **Bourbon, 1523.** example of the English King, and Francis I found himself with the whole of Europe against him. He met the blast with calm dignity and lofty resignation. " All Europe is in league against me," he proudly informed the Parliament of Paris; "Well, I will face all Europe!" And he prepared a great army which he proposed to lead in person into Italy. Why, like his predecessors, was he so enamoured of those unfortunate Italian provinces which it was impossible to hold, when he ought to have turned his attention to the north from which he was presently to be attacked? The only explanation that can be found for this obstinacy is afforded by the fact that he had definite rights over Milan which he did not possess elsewhere. But, to crown his ill-luck, when the whole of Christendom was against him, Francis I found himself betrayed by the most powerful man in his own kingdom. His cousin, Charles, Duke of Bourbon, a high Crown official and Constable of France, went over to the enemy!

This act of treason caused a profound sensation. The effect produced was due not so much to the results of the act, which

Bourbon's grievance against Francis I. were not so grave as they might have been, as to the moral conditions which had brought it to pass. Feminine animosities have wrongly been mixed up in the affair, which in itself was, relatively speaking, simple enough. Charles of Bourbon, a man of thirty-three, thin and bony-faced, with a narrow receding brow, close-cropped beard, and a restless, troubled and discontented expression—if we may judge by Titian's portrait of him—did not inspire confidence by his appearance. He was somewhat feeble in character. He was the head of the powerful House of Bourbon, which traced its descent from Saint Louis and was destined to ascend the throne at the end of the century in the person of Henry IV. He himself belonged to the younger branch, the Montpensiers, but had united all the rich lands of his family by marrying the sole heiress of the elder branch—Suzanne de Bourbon, the daughter of Pierre, Duke of Bourbon, and Anne de Beaujeu. But the latter, ever prudent and far-sighted, had made it a condition of the marriage settlement that if Suzanne died without issue, her property should revert to the Crown. Charles, who was the greatest landed noble of France, was well treated by the Court. He was made Chamberlain, Governor of Languedoc, and Constable. He frequently entertained Francis I at his residence at Moulins, giving magni-

Pompérant. After numerous dramatic adventures, he reached the eastern frontier, where he was welcomed by the Emperor and given a post in his army with the prospect of being made Lieutenant-General of the force in Italy destined to fight against the King of France! Francis I gave orders for all the property of the fugitive to be seized, but offered to restore it if the Constable would consent to return. Bourbon replied that it was too late! This treachery caused a profound agitation among the public.

In these circumstances it was wiser for Francis I not to cross the Alps. Moreover all his frontiers were being attacked simultaneously. The enemy's scouts had reached Compiègne and terrified the Parisians who had been obliged to prepare for defence. The indecision of the allies, however, saved France.

Battles of Rebecco and Romagnano, 1524.

Henry VIII did not advance; the Flemish army fell back; and in the south the Spaniards made an unsuccessful attack on Bayonne and beat a retreat; with the result that the year 1523 had a less dangerous ending than there had been reason to fear. The King then turned his attention to Italy, whither he ordered Bonnivet to march with 25,000 foot and 1500 men-at-arms against Prospero Colonna, a man who was destined on his death to be replaced to some extent by Lannoy, Viceroy of Naples, but even more conspicuously by Bourbon. The Imperialists were stronger than the French, and Bonnivet was driven from the banks of the Ticino as the result of the battle of Rebecco. He retreated towards the Alps in order to effect a junction with the Swiss mercenaries he was expecting, but was attacked once more at Romagnano on the Sesia and again defeated. It was during the course of this retreat that Bayard, who was in command of the rearguard, was shot in the back by an arquebuse and mortally wounded. He was laid on the ground at the foot of a tree. Bourbon, who chanced to be passing by at the moment, expressed his sorrow at seeing him in such a grievous state and assured him of his pity. The fearless and faultless knight—*le chevalier sans peur et sans reproche*—answered in melancholy accents: "There is nothing to pity in me, for I am dying the death of an honourable man. But I pity you for serving against your King, your country, and your plighted word!" Bonnivet then recrossed the Alps.

At this juncture the Imperialists, on the suggestion of Bourbon, crossed the mountains in their turn and invaded **The Imperial-** Provence (June, 1524). Their object was to **ists invade** take Marseilles and then to march through **Provence.** Lyons to Paris, where Henry VIII was to meet them in order to be crowned King of France. Marseilles, however, was well stocked with food and ammunition, and was admirably defended by its citizens, who fought with invincible courage. The project failed. Bourbon's troops,— mercenaries raised from many sources and difficult to keep in hand—after several wearisome and futile attacks, announced that they had had enough. Bourbon was obliged to give up the campaign and return to the valley of the Po. No invasion of France from that quarter ever succeeded.

This seemed to Francis I to afford a favourable opportunity for returning to the plan he had formed two years previously, and marching in person into Italy at the head of a large army, to repeat his success at Marignano. He had faith in his star and believed that victory was assured. When once he had conquered Milan he would go even as far as Naples! Former reverses had taught him nothing. He regarded the vindication of his rights merely as a means for attacking Charles V, for the legal aspect of his case seemed for the moment to have supplanted any abstract notion of conquest. The catastrophe of Pavia and the imprisonment which was to follow were to prove a rude awakening from his dreams!

In October, 1524, he crossed the Alps with 30,000 infantry and 1500 lancers under the command of his oldest and most **Francis I** experienced generals. The Imperialists were **invades Italy.** terrified and melted away at his approach. He entered Milan. In Pavia only 6000 men held their ground, and he marched to lay siege to the city. For three months he blockaded it, hoping to starve out the defenders. Meanwhile, however, Lannoy and Bourbon were marching to its relief with 20,000 infantry, 700 men-at-arms, and 500 light cavalry. The two armies met in January, 1525. For three weeks they faced each other, but at last the Imperialists, threatened by the desertion of their troops *en masse*, owing to lack of funds for paying them—the Grisons and the Italians had already abandoned the King of France—decided to give battle. They accordingly opened the attack beneath the walls **Battle of** of Pavia on the night of February 24, reaching **Pavia, 1525.** the left flank of the French army through a large park, surrounded by high walls, in which stood the castle of Mirabello. The French wheeled to the right in order to face their assailants, and the artillery, under the command of Galiot de Genouillac, opened fire. For a moment, the Imperialists, surprised by this counter-movement, wavered. But Pescara, one of the leaders, urged them on to the attack. Francis I made a vigorous sally at the head of his nobles and two free companies. But on his flank and in his rear, Pescara was cutting his way through with his Spaniards. The right wing of the French army was demoralized; it wavered and broke. The centre, in its turn, was routed, and the Swiss, who were held in reserve in the second echelon, seeing the confusion in the centre, fled without striking a blow. The whole of the French army was routed. Francis I and his nobles were left unsupported, fighting with the courage of despair. Rather than take flight the chivalrous King of France made up his mind to meet his death. He continued his charge like a madman. One by one his brave nobles fell about him—a hecatomb of the best blood in France : the aged La Trémoïlle, Marshal la Palice, Marshal de Foix, Admiral Bonnivet, the Lord High Steward and the Master of the Horse. Recognizing the King, the enemy's soldiers endeavoured to capture him. At length the unfortunate monarch's horse fell; his foes rushed upon him and M. de Pompérant, Bourbon's friend, tried to make Francis I give up his sword, which, however, he would only consent to surrender to the Viceroy Lannoy. All was over !

It was a fearful disaster ! In two short hours the French army had been dispersed, 10,000 men had fallen, high Crown **Capture of** officials and illustrious subjects lay scattered on **Francis I.** the field of battle or had been taken prisoners. The King of Navarre, the Count of Saint-Paul, and Marshal Anne de Montmorency had fallen into the hands of the enemy. The Duke of Alençon, the King's brother-in-law,

alone had escaped—but he died of shame two months later !
Francis I was taken away in the darkness of the evening and
shut up in the fortress of Pizzighettone under a guard of 200
men-at-arms and 1200 infantry commanded by a Spaniard
named Alarcón.   A letter which he wrote to his mother, Louise
of Savoy, to inform her of the full extent of the disaster is still
in existence.   In it he said : " Of all I possessed only my
honour and my life are saved."

Francis I and his country were indeed in a terrible plight !
The eldest of the captive King's children was but eight years
old ! Louise of Savoy, who was made Regent, had not a
regiment, a general, or a crown piece for the defence of the
State ! If France was not conquered and dismembered at
this juncture she owed it to the incompetence which divided
her foes against themselves.

Charles V was at Madrid when he received the extraordinary
and unexpected news of his decisive victory ! He maintained
his usual imperturbability, however, and when it was suggested
that he should celebrate his triumph by some magnificent
festival, he refused.   With perfect calmness he went to a service
to return thanks to the Almighty for his success, and took part
in a thanksgiving procession, after which he deliberated upon
his future course of action.   Bourbon wished him to invade the
conquered country without delay, have Henry VIII crowned
at Saint-Denis, and divide the spoils.   Henry VIII, on his side,
laid claim to France, though he consented to hand over Burgundy, Provence, and Languedoc to the Emperor, whilst the
Duke of Bourbon was to have Dauphiny and the whole of his
ancient heritage.   If this claim were considered too exorbitant
he would be content with the provinces which had once belonged
to England : Normandy, Gascony, Guyenne, Anjou, Poitou
and Maine, with Brittany thrown in.

Two courses of action were proposed in Charles V's council.
Either the downfall of Francis I must be compassed and his
Demands of   ruin completed once for all, or peace must be
Charles V.   made with him on terms more or less acceptable
to all concerned. Gattinara, the Chancellor, who supported
the latter alternative, held his ground firmly, pointing out
that Henry VIII's proposals were degrading to a fallen foe,

and that, moreover, their realization would make the King of England far too formidable. Charles V agreed, and a discussion ensued as to the conditions which should be imposed upon Francis I. They were extremely harsh ! The King of France was to renounce all his rights in Italy, both in Milan and in Naples ; he was to give back the territories of Charles the Bold which had been unlawfully seized by Louis XI, including Burgundy and a number of seigniories ; he was solemnly to abjure any right of suzerainty over Flanders and Artois, a privilege humiliating to Charles V, inasmuch as it made him a vassal of the King of France ; and, lastly, he was to give back to Charles of Bourbon all his possessions with the addition of Provence. Henry VIII was to receive compensation. In order to make this treaty more binding it was to be ratified by the States General and as soon as the King of France found himself thus obviously crippled, he was to make an alliance with the Emperor, and accompany the latter on a campaign he was meditating against the Turks, with the object of checking the Mussulman invasion which had become serious in the valley of the Danube. If Francis I refused, his country would be occupied.

These conditions were conveyed, not to Francis I himself, but to Louise of Savoy. In spite of the gravity of the situation, **Louise of** Louise had kept her head. With the help of **Savoy, Regent.** Florimond Robertet, the clever Secretary of State, and Chancellor Duprat, she had taken active measures to put the country in a state of defence. In this task she had been backed by all. Nobody tried to turn the condition of affairs to account or to make trouble. The Parliament of Paris had organized a defence of the capital. In Normandy, the clergy, the nobility and the towns had combined to offer resistance to any invasion and to maintain order. The Regent on going to Lyons had succeeded in raising a small army, and the paralysis that had seized the country when the blow had first fallen was followed by a growth of confidence and a firmer hope for better things. When Charles V's envoy presented himself to Louise of Savoy in order to make known to her his master's conditions, she answered resolutely that the State was in a position to defend itself, and that she would not yield an inch of territory !

Francis I, shut up in the prison of Pizzighettone, passed through contradictory phases of depression and careless levity. **Francis I. a captive at Pizzighettone.** He had dressed himself in clothes of ashen grey and had written Charles V letters of doubtful dignity, in which he begged him to be generous and not drive him to extremity, but on the contrary to make a friend of him rather than force him to despair. " You may be certain," he assured him humbly, " that instead of a useless prisoner you will make a king your slave for all time ! " After an entreaty of this kind he would play tennis or write verses which he sent to his mistress, the fair Mademoiselle d'Heilly, and snatch a few hours of gaiety in spite of the fact that, although treated with all possible respect, he was closely watched and not allowed the smallest liberty. Charles V had him informed of the conditions he had sent to Louise of Savoy. Francis I received them with a gesture of unutterable weariness and replied that the terms were " extremely hard," but that he left the task of discussing them to his mother, the Regent. As far as he was concerned he was ready to renounce all right over Italy, Milan, Naples, Artois and Flanders ; he would give Bourbon back his territories with the addition of Provence, and pay Henry VIII compensation. About Burgundy he said nothing. Louise of Savoy considered these concessions excessive, whilst Charles V was of opinion that they were inadequate.

Francis I then thought that if he could see the Emperor and speak to him personally he might perhaps find it easier **Francis I. a captive in Spain.** to secure terms which negotiations carried on at a distance through intermediaries armed with insufficient authority would never wring from him. He begged his custodians—Alarcón, Lannoy, Viceroy of Naples, Pescara and Antonio de Leiva—to take him to Spain. They had received orders from Charles V that after an imprisonment of three months at Pizzighettone, the captive King was to be removed to Naples. To this Francis I objected violently, as the climate of Naples did not agree with him. Lannoy, a kindly, temperate man, who wished to see matters settled and an honourable peace concluded, suddenly, without consulting any one, not even the Emperor, took the step of putting the French King on board ship and sailing for Spain. He landed at Barcelona on June 19, 1525, and announced his arrival by a letter to Charles V, who was in Toledo. Charles was furious, but the Viceroy of Naples succeeded in assuaging his wrath. It was decided that Francis I should be shut up in Madrid in the tower known as the Alcazar. The captive's journey across Spain was made the occasion for demonstrations of respect and esteem which the unfortunate man had little expected. He was everywhere received with the deepest sympathy and speeches were addressed to him as he stood beneath a canopy. He made his entries on horseback surrounded by troops, his dignity, in reality so gravely impaired, affording a sad contrast to his actual position as a prisoner kept constantly under surveillance. He was even allowed to hunt, attend bull-fights, and watch festivities held in his honour. But his mind was tortured by the knowledge that Charles V absolutely refused to see him, and after a journey upon which he had been surrounded by consoling attentions, his awakening in the prison of the Alcazar was indeed a rude one. The Alcazar was a lofty tower in Madrid with thick walls rising a hundred feet above the ground; it looked out upon the dry bed of the Manzanares and the vast barren plain of Castille beyond. The room in which he was lodged was small and bare, and sparsely furnished with a bed, a table, and some chests. Hangings adorned with the fleur-de-lys had to be brought from France in order to cover and lend a little brightness to the dismal walls. The only window, which was barred, opened from an embrasure in the walls so deep that it had been possible to make a separate room of it by glazing it on the inside. Such was the place in which the unfortunate prince was doomed to spend long months of imprisonment without distractions or outdoor exercise of any kind. A bodyguard of arquebusiers guarded him below.

Negotiations were re-opened, but they were long and painful. Louise of Savoy had sent Jean de Selve, the First President of
Prolonged the Parliament of Paris, and François de Tournon,
negotiations. Archbishop of Embrun, to discuss matters on behalf of the Government. They had instructions to renounce all rights over Italy and the suzerainty of Artois and

E   65

Flanders; they were at liberty to consider a proposal of marriage between Francis I, whose wife Claude was now dead, and Eleonora, the sister of Charles V and widow of the King of Portugal. If necessary a money ransom might be paid for the King's release ; but on the subject of Burgundy no concession was to be made. Charles V refused to accept a ransom, and on the question of Burgundy he remained firm. Nothing on earth would move him. It was his property and he considered himself extremely moderate in not laying claim to all that was his due. In vain did the two ambassadors discuss, reason, and plead with him. The Emperor, who was still at Toledo with his council, refused to yield. The negotiations had to be suspended, as it was impossible to come to an understanding on such a basis.

At one moment it seemed likely that a diversion might be caused which would change the face of affairs. Henry VIII, hurt by the fact that Charles V was paying no heed to him and his interests, accused the Emperor of ingratitude and arrogance. Louise of Savoy profited by the occasion to ask him to make peace in return for a sum of money of which she knew he was for the moment urgently in need. Henry VIII promptly accepted. In Italy, moreover, the Italians were beginning to think that Charles V was growing too dangerously powerful and feared that he would entertain the ambition of making himself absolute master of the peninsula and dominating them. They accordingly combined. Louise of Savoy was clever enough to suggest that they should come to an understanding with her as well. She was ready to renounce all French claims in Italy; her only stipulation was that she should be allowed to put Francesco Sforza on the throne of Milan. It was merely a question of driving out the Imperialists. The Italians welcomed these terms which the Pope, Venice, and Florence signed. The Pope even went so far as to offer to place Pescara, Charles V's general, on the throne of Naples and have him crowned King, thus depriving the Emperor of one of his best soldiers. But moved by scruples of loyalty and honour Pescara refused, and at the same time sent a warning to Charles V. The danger, as he pointed out, was extremely great. The bribe which he had refused might be accepted by another, in which case the

Emperor would find himself involved in inextricable difficulties ! The whole of Italy was declaring against him, and it would be better, continued Pescara, to come to terms with Francis I, and accede to his original proposals even at the cost of Burgundy, than to tempt fortune. Louise of Savoy and her son awaited his decision with anxiety. The Emperor replied that his decision was unalterable, and absolutely refused to yield an inch !

Deprived of the physical exercise necessary for a vigorous and active prince, and above all of the slightest hope of **Illness of** ever seeing the end of a confinement which had **Francis I.** become intolerable, Francis I fell ill under the crushing effects of these repeated disappointments and his long captivity. He was seized with fever. He realized that he was in danger and in a few days the disease secured a disquieting hold over him and reduced him to a state of prostration. On September 18, 1525, after a period of three weeks, he became unconscious and was thought to be dying. The Emperor was seriously alarmed, and realizing, moreover, that if his prisoner were to die, he would lose his case, hurriedly rode to the scene bringing with him the best doctors he could find. He arrived at Madrid in hot haste one evening at nine o'clock. Lannoy and Marshal de Montmorency received him at the Alcazar, and the latter, bearing a lighted torch, led the way up to the sick man's chamber. Charles V showed the utmost affection. He kissed Francis I, assuring him that there was no need for him to torment himself, as everything could be arranged between them, and telling him that his first duty was to get well. The French King's devoted sister, Margaret, had been summoned from France, and by travelling two stages at a time she managed to arrive at Madrid on September 20. Charles V went to meet her at the bottom of the stairs in the Alcazar. She was in tears. He kissed her and endeavoured to console her, then conducted her to her brother and returned to Toledo, ordering public prayers to be offered on the King's behalf.

Francis, however, seemed to grow worse. For three days he was unconscious and the doctors declared that there was **Recovery of** no hope. Margaret, in despair, had mass cele-**Francis I.** brated in the invalid's room by the Archbishop of Embrun. When at the elevation of the host the celebrant held it out towards Francis I for adoration, the King, to the surprise of every one, half opened his eyes. They tried to make him receive the communion, and he managed to take half a wafer, of which Margaret consumed the remaining portion. It is possible that some abscess had just burst, but contemporary accounts of the nature of his illness are rather obscure. From that time forward the King improved, though he remained extremely feeble. But his strength seemed to return from day to day and finally he was out of danger.

An attempt was made to profit by the presence of Margaret to make the princess re-open the negotiations with Charles V **Charles V and** and thus turn to account the good will of which **Margaret of** the Emperor had just given evidence. On **Navarre.** October 3 Margaret went to Toledo, where she was courteously received by Charles V, who came to meet her and conducted her to the house he had had prepared for her. On the following day they had a long conversation of two hours alone together. But Margaret found her host as inexorable as ever. She proposed a marriage between her brother and Eleonora, with the stipulation that the bride should receive Burgundy as a dowry from the hands of the Emperor, an arrangement which would imply that the King of France had renounced his ancient rights over that province, but held it, in actual fact, by virtue of a freshly conferred privilege. Charles V refused. She then suggested that the Parliament of Paris should decide the question at issue. Again the Emperor refused. Moreover he insisted upon every one of the conditions he had already demanded—the renunciation of Italy and Flanders, the re-installation of Bourbon in the whole of his territory, with the addition of Provence, and the promise that, once peace was made, Francis I should accompany the Emperor against the Turks. He considered himself generous in not demanding a ransom. Margaret had failed ! There was nothing more to be done, and on October 13 she left Toledo.

In a fit of temper caused by the Emperor's inflexible animosity and the barren result of the conciliatory feeling he had displayed during his illness, Francis I made a desperate resolve. He decided to abdicate and thus leave merely a worthless prisoner in the hands of his adversary. He accordingly abdicated in favour of the Dauphin. This step terrified the Emperor's counsellors, who advised their sovereign to give in. Pescara reiterated his warnings about the dangerous state of Italy. Louis de Bruges, Sieur of Praet, Charles V's ambassador in France, wrote saying that it would be wiser not to insist upon all his terms. Charles V turned a deaf ear to everybody. The abdication left him cold. Its only result was that as he no longer had a King of France in his hands, he seemed disposed to make his prisoner's captivity less strict.

Francis I thereupon tried to make his escape. He had a negro to wait upon him and keep up his fire. This man was **Francis I tries** bribed, and it was arranged that the King should **to escape.** change clothes with him, blacken his face and one evening at dusk take flight. Relays of horses were to be held in readiness. But, unfortunately, a valet, who had a grudge against Montmorency for having once taken him to task, betrayed the whole plot, with the result that the King was more closely watched.

Meanwhile, in France, Louise of Savoy, seeing month after month pass by without bringing any solution, began to lose **The Treaty** heart. It was impossible for the kingdom to **of Madrid,** remain indefinitely without a master. The King's **1526.** presence was becoming more and more urgent; and she herself felt she had not the strength to assume the unlimited responsibilities of government indefinitely. What was the point at issue? After all, the whole quarrel was over the matter of a single province. Was the destiny of all France to hang upon one province? Would not the evils entailed be far greater than the loss of a mere duchy? Had not John the Good sacrificed far more in order to regain his liberty? Louise eventually made up her mind to give in and to renounce Burgundy, and sent Chabot de Brion to Madrid to make known her resolve. Francis I, whose courage had completely ebbed, bowed his head to the inevitable, and the French plenipotentiaries, the Archbishop of Embrun, Jean de Selve, and Chabot de Brion met the Spanish envoys Lannoy, Ugo de Moncada and Jean Lallemand in conclave. Francis I insisted upon marrying Eleonora. She had been promised

69

to Charles of Bourbon and the latter was angry at the demand. In order to solve the difficulty Charles V asked the young widow her opinion on the subject and she replied that she would prefer to be Queen of France. Gattinara, the imperial Chancellor, moved that, pending the actual surrender of Burgundy, Francis I should be kept prisoner. Whereupon the latter offered to give his two sons as hostages for his word, a proposal accepted by Charles V. The final clause of this grievous treaty was completed on December 19, and by it a stipulation was made that the King of France should have the agreement ratified by the States-General and the various Parliaments of the country within four months. January 14 was fixed for the solemn signing of the treaty.

On the evening before this day Francis I assembled in his room at the fortress all the French plenipotentiaries—the President de Selve, the Archbishop of Embrun, and Chabot de Brion, together with Marshal de Montmorency, the Provost of Paris, who happened to be on the spot, and his own private secretary. In firm accents he declared to them that his action of the morrow had been wrung from him by force. He protested against this use of force and considered that it annulled the obligations demanded of him in advance, for these obligations were a menace to the rights of the Crown, prejudicial to the interests of his country, and injurious to his honour. The Emperor was making exorbitant demands upon him which it was impossible for him to fulfil. He was yielding from necessity, but he called upon God and every one present to witness that inasmuch as he was not a free man he regarded the promises he was about to make as non-existent, null and void.

On the following day, after mass had been celebrated by the Archbishop of Embrun, both parties signed the treaty. Signing of Charles V, who did not trouble to attend in person, the Treaty. was represented by the Spanish plenipotentiaries. Francis I swore upon the Gospels to keep the treaty and the French negotiators in their turn likewise took the oath. Only on February 11, after an interval of almost a month, did the Emperor ratify it. The betrothal of the King of France to Eleonora was solemnized, but he was kept in prison to await the arrival of his sons to take his place. The utmost

70

he was allowed was a certain freedom to go to mass, but even on these occasions he was always strictly guarded. At length Charles V decided to pay his fallen foe a visit. He came dressed in black velvet with an escort of 250 horsemen, and Francis I went to meet him on the bridge of the Manzanares mounted upon a richly caparisoned mule. The interview between the two princes was conducted with great courtesy. They supped together and had a long conversation. On February 16, upon the King expressing a desire to see his bride elect, the two monarchs went to the castle of Illescas, near Toledo, where the princess was staying. Francis I was exceedingly amiable. A festival was given at which Eleonora performed a Spanish dance with much grace, and finally, on February 19, the King and the Emperor bade each other adieu, the latter in order to go to Seville for his marriage with the Infanta of Portugal, and Francis I, who had at last been given leave to depart, to make his way to the French frontier, where he was to regain his liberty. Before parting, however, Charles V was seized with qualms of doubt. "Give me your word," he said to Francis I, "that you will faithfully fulfil your pledges." "I swear to you that I will keep my word," the King replied. They then saluted each other and parted.

On February 21 Francis finally turned his back upon Madrid and the dismal fortress in which for six long months **Release of** he had suffered so much physical and moral **Francis I.** agony. Another month was required to reach the frontier. He was still closely guarded and infinite pains were taken to ensure that the King should be replaced by his sons at a meeting-place on the Bidassoa between Hendaye and Fontarabia. Here Louise of Savoy had sent the little princes of eight and a half and seven years old respectively—the latter the future King Henry II—in the care of Lautrec. On March 17 at seven o'clock in the morning, in the presence of two bodies of troops representing France and Spain, who occupied either bank, the King and his sons, borne in two boats containing an equal number of rowers and passengers, were exchanged in the middle of the river on crossing an empty landing-stage which had been erected in the water. As he placed his foot on French soil Francis I exclaimed: "I am a King again!" He then mounted his horse and rode quickly to Bayonne where in the great church of the city he returned a solemn thanksgiving to the Almighty.

Up to this moment the clauses of the treaty had been kept secret. They were now made public, and their extreme character aroused universal indignation. In Italy, over which the document in question proclaimed the Emperor's hegemony, the voice of discontent was unanimous. The Pope gave vent to the opinion that there was no ground for regarding as valid an agreement which had been extracted under constraint, an agreement; moreover, which placed the King of Spain "upon the throne of Christendom." Henry VIII was of the same mind, whilst in France the general outburst of fury reached its height. States, Parliaments, and nobility all raised a concert of vehement protestation.

Francis I, by the terms of the treaty, had bound himself to ratify it the moment he was free. He did nothing of the **Francis I.** kind, however, and when the imperial ambassador **repudiates the** came to remind him of this obligation, he evaded **Treaty.** the question by giving dilatory answers and excusing himself on the ground that opposition was breaking out in every quarter and that it was necessary for him at least to consult the States of Burgundy, the province chiefly affected. Charles V, who was extremely busy, sent Lannoy to the King of France to insist upon his keeping his word and to bring home to him the argument that as he was an absolute monarch it was unnecessary for him to pay any attention to the arguments of his subjects. Lannoy reached Cognac, where Francis I arrived on May 8. On May 10, accompanied by the ordinary ambassador, Louis de Praet, he was given an audience before the King's council, at which he was officially informed, without much beating about the bush, by the French Chancellor, Duprat, in the name of the Government, that it was impossible to separate Burgundy from France. Then Francis I, in his turn, addressed them, and declared that inasmuch as his word had been wrested from him in Madrid at a moment when he had no freedom whatever, his promise was null and void, and that he consequently regarded himself as free from all obligation. Nevertheless, he was desirous of

72

living in peace and concord with the Emperor, and apart from this matter, counted upon fulfilling all such clauses of the treaty as allowed of fulfilment.   Charles V's envoys made no reply. They merely bowed and withdrew.   Francis I without further delay profited by the terror with which the menacing spectre of " a monarchy of all Christendom " inspired the Italians,

The Holy League of Cognac. to join an alliance formed under the ægis of Pope Clement VII—the Holy League of Cognac. And the allies thereupon prepared for war.

Charles V was in Seville, where his marriage with the Infanta of Portugal had just taken place, when he received the news of these events.   So the Treaty of Madrid had been repudiated and torn in two, and Italy stirred up against him !   It was a violent blow.   After securing so fair a prospect, to lose all in this way !   The English ambassador wrote to his master that the Emperor " remained in retirement plunged in silence, often ·spending three or four consecutive hours alone with his own thoughts."   Charles V now had to start afresh from the very beginning.   He had hoped to turn his attention to Germany, where Lutheranism was spreading, and the advance of the Turks was threatening; but he was now forced to return to Italy.   He gave orders for the French King's sons to be put into strict confinement.   The little princes were shamefully treated by the brutal soldiers to whom they were entrusted. They were dragged from one fortress to another, imprisoned behind barred windows in dark bare rooms, cut off from all French society, miserably clad, and were altogether pitiable to behold.

The Papal forces, together with those of Venice and the other confederates, began to concentrate in Italy.   The Pope informed the Emperor of the existence of the Holy League, and the French ambassador, Jean de Calvimont, President of the Parliament of Bordeaux, was sent with a similar mission from Francis I. He demanded from Charles V the renunciation of Burgundy and the return of the French princes upon payment of a ransom. " Your master," replied Charles V to Calvimont, " has deceived me.   I shall never again trust his word.   His behaviour is not that of a knight and a gentleman ! "   The children he refused to give up at any price.   Nevertheless he endeavoured to

73

turn aside the blast by separating the Italians from Francis I. He made persistent overtures to Clement VII, using all manner of inducements and threats. But in vain. The menace of imperial domination was too great. And meanwhile the excesses of his representatives in Italy were making matters worse for his cause.

In Rome, Ugo di Moncada, the imperial delegate, had come to an understanding with the Colonna family, who were at enmity with the Pope. These latter raised a tumult which degenerated into frightful disorder, during which the Vatican was carried by assault, pillaged and sacked. The Pope was obliged to seek refuge in the Castle of St. Angelo where they forced him to sign an agreement to withdraw from the League. This event aroused the indignation of Europe, and Charles V himself was extremely annoyed by an escapade which was a scandalous act of barbarism. It was not, moreover, destined to be unique of its kind.

The Emperor had sent Charles of Bourbon to the north of Italy to take over the command of an army which was being **Sack of Rome by the Imperialists, 1527.** raised there by recruiting mercenaries from all quarters—Italy, Spain, and Germany—a violent mob of hirelings inspired by no faith and governed by no law. Bourbon made for central Italy, but he had no money, and his soldiers, seething with discontent, were demanding their pay. Moreover a perpetual downfall of rain was soaking these miserable and frenzied desperadoes, who had neither clothes, shoes, nor provisions. They were in a constant state of mutiny and Bourbon barely escaped with his life. In order to calm them he was foolish enough to dazzle their eyes by the prospect of towns to be sacked, and even breathed the name of Rome. With one accord the imperial army, beside themselves at the idea, insisted upon marching on Rome against the Pope, who had rejoined the League. There was no help for it, and Bourbon grimly faced the inevitable. He made a rush through the valley of the Arno, and on Monday, May 6, 1527, the imperial hordes attacked the Eternal City in the Borgo quarter. As he was attempting to scale the walls Charles of Bourbon was mortally wounded by a bullet. He was carried to a neighbouring chapel where

74

he just had time to make his confession and receive the sacrament before he died. The Borgo was captured and after it the rest of the city. A week of horrible carnage followed. The Lutheran lansquenets threw off all restraint; murder, arson, and sacrilege were rife. Over 4000 people were put to the sword. The Pope, who had shut himself up in the Castle of St. Angelo, capitulated together with thirteen cardinals, and was kept a prisoner in the hands of Alarcón, the Spanish captain who had once had charge of Francis I. Happy the Emperor who had had both the Pope and the King of France prisoners in his power! The sack of Rome, however, caused universal horror throughout Christendom, and when, by command of Francis I, Lautrec descended upon Italy with an army of 40,000 men for the deliverance of the Pope, he was everywhere greeted with acclamations of joy.

But alas! Lautrec's new campaign was doomed, like its predecessors, to a disastrous termination. After winning back the valley of the Po from the Imperialists without striking a blow, Lautrec marched upon Rome. Charles V, by a bold stroke of policy, ordered the Sovereign Pontiff to be liberated upon payment of a ransom of 368,000 crowns. A French herald at arms was thereupon dispatched to Spain to make an official declaration of war against the Emperor. Charles V received him sitting upon his throne and surrounded by all his Court, when with profound solemnity he replied that as the King of France had broken his faith he was a " coward " and that if he wished to "gainsay the same he would prove it to him man to man." This was a challenge. When the herald returned to France with this reply Francis I also sat upon his throne surrounded by all his Court, and with equal solemnity gave audience to the Spanish ambassador, Granvelle. Reminding him of the terms of the insult which Charles V had hurled at him, he charged Granvelle to tell his master that " he lied in his throat " and to challenge him to a duel. A contest in the lists between these two monarchs would have provided a strange epilogue indeed to the drama! But although the Emperor retorted that his adversary was himself a " liar " and consented to meet him on the Bidassoa, the duel was never fought. Minor obstacles were raised, but, as a matter of fact, neither side was really anxious for it to take place.

Meanwhile Lautrec pushed forward in Italy, occupied the Papal States, and conquered the Kingdom of Naples without **The French** encountering much resistance. He laid siege **driven from** to the city itself, and might have succeeded in **Italy.** capturing it, as the sea was in the hands of one of the cleverest and most famous admirals of the day— the Genoese Andrea Doria, who had for some time been in the service of Francis I. Unfortunately the latter had offended him by various ill-considered acts and irritated him by injudicious threats, with the result that Doria, deeply mortified, had gone over to the Emperor. Naples was re-victualled and put in a position to hold out against a siege, and the French army, as usual, gradually melted away, decimated by plague, famine, and lack of funds. Lautrec himself fell ill and died and the remnant of his troops—less than 10,000 men—took their departure and wandered about until they were made prisoners in Aversa. This fresh attempt had resulted in utter failure and the whole of Italy remained in the hands of the Emperor.

Louise of Savoy then attempted to use her influence in order to make peace between her son and Charles V. The contest **The Peace of** had now dragged on for eight years, and there **Cambray, 1529.** must surely be some means of putting an end to it. She approached the Emperor's aunt, the Archduchess Margaret, who was Governor of the Netherlands, and the latter consented to do her best. The two princesses settled the basis upon which a settlement could be reached. The terms were the same as before. France was to renounce all right over Italy, Flanders, and Artois, but Margaret was begged to induce Charles V to give up Burgundy. Twenty times over the negotiations were almost broken off, but, by dint of patience, the Archduchess succeeded in convincing her imperial nephew that the wisest course was to give up the province of Burgundy, which France would never, on any consideration, consent to relinquish, and remain the undisputed master of Italy, which would otherwise be constantly rising up against him. Charles V, with infinite difficulty, was at last induced to consent. He agreed to give back the French King's sons for a ransom of two million gold crowns. The two princesses had held their discussions at Cambray, and the peace was accordingly named the Peace of Cambray or the "Ladies' Peace" after its authors. It was signed on August 3, 1529. When the little princes returned from Spain and described the treatment they had received, Francis I was furious. His children's sufferings, together with the remembrance of all he had himself endured at Madrid, left in his breast an invincible hatred for his implacable foe. He signed the peace, but only whilst awaiting an opportunity for making a war of revenge. The events which had taken place, wrote the Venetian ambassador, Giustiniano, had so "roused the hatred of the King and exasperated him that he never mentioned these matters without showing violent anger and an unquenchable thirst for vengeance."

But on this occasion Francis I meant to take his time. He would make his preparations slowly and to good purpose. It was, moreover, necessary to give his kingdom a breathing-space. He entered upon a long campaign of diplomacy calculated to place the Emperor gradually in a position of political isolation. French envoys were sent to solicit the various Italian states, the Pope, and the King of England; they found the ground well prepared. The imperial omnipotence which overshadowed Europe was a veritable nightmare to all who had reason to fear they might become its victims. Clement VII, especially, and his cardinals, who had terrified recollections of the sack of Rome, were ready for any alliance against their hated adversary. So friendly were they that a marriage was even arranged between Francis I's son, the future King Henry II, and a distant cousin of the Pope, Catherine, Duchess of Urbino. This Catherine was none other than the famous Catherine de' Medici, daughter of Lorenzo de' Medici, who at this time was but thirteen years old, the same age as the young prince to whom she was betrothed. An interview took place at Marseilles between Clement VII and Francis I, at which the latter kept recurring to the ever-vexed question of the Duchy of Milan, with the result that the Pope gave his consent to the King's re-conquest of the lost province.

Francis I. makes fresh preparations for war.

An interview also took place with Henry VIII, and in return for a sum of money that self-seeking and greedy monarch consented to follow any line of policy desired. Thus the alliance was set on a firm basis.

This time Francis I went even further, and attempted to win the support of the German princes who were hostile **French alliance with the Protestants and Turks.** to the Emperor. In the midst of the struggles occasioned by the growth of Lutheranism, the German princes who upheld the new doctrines had been obliged in 1530 to form a league at Schmalkalden in order to defend themselves against the designs of Charles V and the Catholic princes. His Most Christian Majesty, however, had the boldness to propose making common cause with them. They accepted. And why not? since the theologians had explained to Francis I that "natural right and the canons of the Church allowed a man to make use of any means of defence" if he were gravely menaced. By virtue of this principle Francis I went even further and had recourse to the Turks themselves—a daring innovation! For the first time the Sultan entered the concert of European Powers. Francis I dispatched Rincon to Constantinople in order to see how the land lay. In 1534 Khair Eddin Barbarossa, a Turkish admiral, came on a mission to France, and in 1535 a second French ambassador, La Forest, presented himself at the Court of the Grand Turk, Solyman. This act laid the foundations of a connexion destined to last to this day. Europe was taken by surprise. "The French people," wrote one of the Italian ambassadors, "consider this alliance as shameful as it really is" . . . "an ignominious blot." An unconscious feeling having sprung up that a balance of power was necessary in Europe, the use of any efficacious means to this end, regardless of anything but political expediency, seems to have been accepted as its corollary.

In addition to political innovations the government of Francis I made various alterations in military matters. Under the old system of recruiting, a captain was entrusted with the charge of raising a force of 300 men whom he might have to take anywhere, frequently to foreign lands. On July 24, 1534, following the ancient Roman system, seven legions of infantry were created, each containing six companies of 1000 men. These seven legions were appointed respectively to each of the seven provinces of Normandy, Burgundy, Languedoc, Brittany, Picardy, Dauphiny, and Guyenne. This made a sum total of 42,000 infantry, of which 30,000 were armed with pikes and halberds, and the rest with arquebuses, forming the nucleus of the old French regiments.

When everything was ready, the death in 1535 of Francesco Sforza, Duke of Milan, afforded Francis I a pretext for taking **Re-opening of** up arms against the Emperor once more. He **hostilities,** laid claim to Milan, and when Charles III, Duke **1535.** of Savoy, raised difficulties, he began operations by occupying Savoy and Piedmont, which were invaded by Admiral Chabot de Brion. Charles V had not failed to realize as soon as the Peace of Cambray was signed, that the war had merely been interrupted. He had been informed of his adversary's diplomatic campaigns and the success which attended them, and, profoundly irritated, had also made military preparations. He faced the war resolutely, and with 50,000 men crossed the Alps in 1536 and invaded Provence, determined to capture Marseilles. The French army which had been told off to keep him in check, had been placed under the command of Anne de Montmorency, a prudent and cautious soldier. He avoided an encounter with the imperial forces, and systematically laid bare the whole country before the invader, burying the corn and wine and destroying the mills, so that when the Emperor's army advanced it found no food. Aix was pillaged, but Marseilles, Arles, and Tarascon, strongly fortified and armed, and with an ample supply of provisions and soldiers, awaited the enemy. Charles V hurled himself upon these barriers, whilst Montmorency kept watching over him from the Rhone. The Emperor attempted the impossible in trying to take Marseilles, which held out against him. His army was dying of hunger and crumbling away. After a campaign of two months, during the whole of which Montmorency remained immovable in his camp at La Durance, Charles V decided to beat a miserable retreat to Italy without having accomplished anything.

Things then dragged on in a state of impotence and general lassitude on both sides. Anne de Montmorency, put on his **Truce of Monçon, 1537.** mettle by the success of his defensive tactics, forced the Pas de Suse by a brilliant attack in which he was accompanied by the Dauphin, Henry. But on November 16, 1537, the two adversaries, unable to accomplish anything, signed a three months' truce at Monçon on the basis of the *statu quo*. What was it possible for either side to do ? It was arranged that an interview should take place between the Emperor, the Pope, and the King of France, at which an attempt would be made once more to restore peace. But at the meeting in 1538 it was admitted that it was impossible to agree upon any definite plan. A fresh truce was signed, this time for ten years, by the terms of which Francis was temporarily to keep Savoy and the Emperor Milan, and a short lull followed upon the preceding period of hatred and hostility.

The lull, indeed, was of such a nature that when, in the following year the people of Ghent rebelled against their sovereign, and Charles V, in difficulties about reaching Flanders, ventured to ask Francis I to allow him to cross France, the latter gave permission with alacrity. By his orders the detested monarch was everywhere given a cordial and sumptuous reception, showing how perfectly the French could practise the chivalrous virtue of courteous hospitality. At Bordeaux, Poitiers, Châtellerault, Blois, and Orleans there was a constant succession of triumphal arches, speech-making, and festivities of all sorts. In a spirit of bravado directed against his anxious counsellors who predicted terrible disasters, the Emperor was accompanied by an escort of only 20 or 25 nobles and 50 horsemen. He made his entry into Paris with great magnificence, and was lodged at the Louvre, from which he attended a series of banquets and jousts. He was thus enabled to reach Flanders without difficulty. The French people had received him with smiles and gracious words, but in their hearts three wounds still remained unhealed : the remembrance of the hardships of Madrid, the fear of the Emperor's overpowering influence in Europe, and regret for the loss of Milan.

THE KING AND THE EMPEROR

Consequently when, five years later, in 1544, Rincon and Fregose, two French ambassadors, were treacherously murdered **Fresh rupture,** on the banks of the Po by some of the Emperor's **1544.** soldiers, Francis I profited by the occasion once more to break with his hated enemy and attack him. A young prince, the Duc d'Enghien, the brother of Antoine de **Battle of** Bourbon, King of Navarre, and uncle of the future **Cerisola.** Henry IV, was placed at the head of an army which crossed the Alps and on April 14, 1544, gained a brilliant victory at Cerisola over the Emperor's general Del Guasto. Every student of history is familiar with the spirited account given by Monluc, who was with the French forces, of how he was sent to France to ask leave to give battle, and the difficulty he had in gaining the consent of the Council, in spite of his southern fire and eloquence which fascinated Francis I ; also with his description of that magnificent feat of arms. After a few abortive attempts to open a campaign on the northern and southern frontiers, in Picardy and Lorraine, the two monarchs concluded a fresh peace—the Peace of Soissons **Treaty of** or Crépy-en-Valois—by the terms of which Charles, **Crépy, 1544.** Duke of Angoulême, the King's second son, was to marry a niece of the Emperor's, who was to have Milan for her dowry, while the Duke of Savoy was to regain his territories the day the son of Francis I entered Milan as its sovereign.

During this last conflict the fickle Henry VIII had declared for Charles V. It was, therefore, necessary to fight him, and a few attempts were made in the north both by land and sea. The French forces crossed the Channel and made a descent upon the Isle of Wight ; on land a few encounters took place. But Henry VIII finally made a treaty at Ardres by which, in return for 800,000 crowns, he gave up Boulogne and its territory. Everybody was thoroughly tired out.

Henry VIII did not long survive this last episode. His death, which was rather sudden, took place in 1547. The **Death of** disappearance of a man who was more or less **Francis I, 1547.** his contemporary gave Francis I a profound shock, and he followed him to the grave in the same year, at the age of fifty-three. He died discouraged and over-

CENTURY OF THE RENAISSANCE

whelmed by a reign of thirty-two years, which had counted more hours of misery than moments of happiness, and had left bitter memories of a series of disasters more permanent in their effects than any joys and satisfactions, at least in the domain of politics.

SOURCES. *Catalogue des actes de François Ier*, 1887 onwards ; Martin du Bellay, *Mémoires*, ed. Michaud and Poujoulat ; Louise de Savoie, *Journal*, same edition ; *Comptes de Louise de Savoie et de Marguerite d'Angoulême*, ed. A. Lefranc, 1905 ; Marguerite d'Angoulême, *Lettres*, ed. Genin, 1841 and 1842 ; *Journal de Jean Barillon, secrétaire du chancelier Duprat*, ed. de Vaissière, 1897 ; *Journal d'un bourgeois de Paris sous le règne de François Ier*, ed. Lalanne, 1854 ; *Chronique du roi François Ier de ce nom*, ed. Guiffrey, 1860 ; Monluc, *Commentaires et lettres*, ed. de Ruble, 1864 ; Brantôme, *Œuvres complètes*, ed. Lalanne ; *Captivité du roi François Ier*, ed. A. Champollion-Figeac ; Tommaseo, *Relations des ambassadeurs vénitiens*, 1838 ; Alberi, *Relazzioni degli ambasciatori veneti al senato*, 1839.

WORKS. R. de Maulde, *Louise de Savoie et François Ier*, 1895 ; De Lescure, *François Ier*, 1878 ; P. Paris, *Études sur François Ier*, 1885 ; B. Zeller, *Claude de France*, 1892 ; Mignet, *Rivalité de François Ier et de Charles Quint*, 1875 ; Baumgarten, *Geschichte Karls V*, 1885 ; A. Lebey, *Le connétable de Bourbon*, 1904 ; A. de Barral, *Le camp du Drap d'or*, 1879 ; Gachard, *La captivité de François Ier et le traité de Madrid*, 1860 ; Jacqueton, *La politique extérieure de Louise de Savoie*, 1892 ; Decrue, *Anne de Montmorency grand maître et connétable de France*, 1885 ; A. Spont, *Marignan et l'organisation militaire sous François Ier* (Rev. des quest. hist., 1899).

82

CHAPTER III

THE COURT OF FRANCIS I

Francis I towards the end of his reign, the King and the man; his mother, Louise of Savoy; his sister, Margaret of Navarre; his Queens, Claude and Eleonora; Madame de Chateaubriant; the Duchess d'Etampes; the King's children; his counsellors—Montmorency, Admiral d'Annebaut, Cardinal de Tournon. The constitution and the officials of the King's household. Court gatherings, balls, festivals, and jousts. The King's journeys. The luxury of Francis I and of his courtiers; his financial extravagance and one of its victims : Semblançay. Francis I's love of art and letters. The personal nature of the literature of the day—Clément Marot, Margaret of Navarre, Rabelais, Dolet. Francis I's encouragement of learned men; the library of Fontainebleau, the *Collège de France*. The arts, the Renaissance; evolution of French art; its precursors—Jean Fouquet, Bourdichon, Perréal, Colombe. Gradual change in architecture—Amboise, Blois; great buildings of Francis I, Chambord, Madrid, Fontainebleau; Italian decorative work, Il Rosso, Primaticcio, Benvenuto Cellini; the Fontainebleau School.

IN the print-room of the Bibliothèque Nationale there is a curious chalk drawing dating from the time of Jean Clouet which gives a portrait of Francis I towards the end of his life. It shows the King considerably aged, although he was but fifty-three. His features are drawn with years

Francis I. towards the end of his reign. and obvious fatigue; beneath his grey beard his mouth is compressed and bitter, as though he had lost all illusions; his gaze is sad, his eye dull, and the whole picture conveys the impression of a man weighed down by the disappointments of life, disenchanted, and painfully resigned. And, indeed, if we consider the political history of the period, few reigns in the annals of France—except that of John the Good—record such lamentable disasters as the defeat of Pavia and the captivity in Madrid, few witnessed such an interminable succession of unfortunate wars, constantly repeated complications, and mortifying diplomatic failures. Nevertheless, the reign of Francis I preserves its reputation as a brilliant epoch in the history of France—a reputation due to the character and tastes of the King, and to all he did for the cause of art and letters.

Marino Cavalli, the Venetian ambassador, who arrived at the French court in 1546, a few months before the death of Francis I, sent his government an account of the impression produced upon him when he saw the King. His description is extremely minute. Francis I, who was still tall and upright and apparently strong, possessed the measured and noble dignity of gesture which long years of public life and the weight of maturity confer upon a man. He was impressive, extremely majestic, and regal. Like Louis XIV, he would have been recognizable anywhere by his stately appearance. Robust, inured to fatigue, indefatigable in riding, hunting, and travelling, a large eater, a heavy drinker, and an even better sleeper, he appeared to enjoy excellent health. The allegations about some serious disease that consumed him seem never to have been substantiated. He merely suffered from an abscess which formed and burst every year, a symptom which the doctors regarded as favourable, inasmuch as it " purged his humours." And, indeed, in 1547, the abscess did not make its appearance, with the result that Francis I died rather suddenly. He was, moreover, a dandy. Invariably well-dressed himself, he set the fashion for all. There was even a certain studied refinement and affectation in his attire. He would only wear costumes trimmed with lace and embroidery and covered with precious stones. His doublets were of gold tissue, with an opening showing a shirt of fine linen edged with rare lace ; and he had rich clothes innumerable.

He was above all a charming talker. Full of life and gaiety, and cordial with everybody, his spirits and good temper were
Character of   the life and soul of every party. Without having
Francis I.   read much or studied methodically, he, nevertheless, knew something of everything and his varied and inexhaustible store of knowledge astonished his listeners. Whether he were discussing war, painting, literature, languages,

geography, hunting, physical exercise or agriculture, he had accurate knowledge and sensible ideas on every subject. " Not only artists might profit from his conversation," wrote Thomas Hubert of Liège, who, in 1535 accompanied the Elector Palatine on a visit to Paris, " but gardeners and labourers as well." His memory was so good that he could discuss the genealogies of the gentry, of which he knew every particular, just as he remembered every noble in his kingdom. With soldiers he talked about strategy, the management of armies, artillery, and commissariat ; and astounded them by the precision and clarity of his ideas. When they expressed their surprise, the King would laugh and say it was perfectly true that he knew the right thing to do, but that he had no idea of how to apply his conceptions, or rather, he could not trouble to try, and had unfortunately never discovered the person who could carry them out for him. Finally, with men of learning. he loved to discuss philosophy, books, and manuscripts, and by a curious anomaly, it was perhaps this kind of conversation which best pleased this monarch, who was essentially an aris-tocrat and a typical representative of an amiable though fundamentally frivolous race. As a matter of fact, he was endowed with an inquisitive mind, and possessed the gift of picking up information by making those who knew a subject talk about it. He was extremely adaptable and endowed, in addition, with good sense and judgment ; " there was," according to Cavalli, " no subject, whether it were a branch of knowledge or one of the arts, upon which his arguments were not very much to the point, or on which he could not express quite as confident an opinion as anyone who was a specialist in the matter." No other King of France, not even excepting Henry IV, whom in certain respects he so closely resembled, was able to confer greater charm and distinction upon his banquets and Court gatherings, great or small.

But taking him all in all, Francis I was nothing more than a man of pleasure. If, in his youth, he had had such a fondness for rough and dangerous games that twenty times over he had run the risk of being killed ; if he had had somewhat savage tastes, as shown by the fact that he made a bull and three lions fight in the moat of Amboise ; if, as the spoilt son of a rich family he had amused himself with such follies as masquerading with boon-companions, and as the *Journal d'un Bourgeois de Paris* relates, " going about the town and into sundry houses for pleasure and amusement " and committing Heaven alone knows what excesses " which the people bore with a bad grace " ; in his old age he certainly preserved a marked love of dissipation. Hunting, festivals, conversations, constant journeys, dress and the collection of beautiful things all engrossed a mind which gradually became incapable of applying itself for any length of time to serious matters. In spite of his good judgment and knowledge this lack of concentration made Francis I a frivolous man.

This frivolity was chiefly displayed in matters connected with his government. He hated affairs of State, and his duties as a King were a regular nightmare to him which he preferred to discuss as little as possible. Easy to approach, good-natured and simple, he accepted any idea suggested by his advisers, in order to have done with the matter as quickly as possible. His sister, Queen Margaret, frequently complained of this to the ambassador Giustiniano, more especially when she thought of Charles V, the King's jealous, reserved, and calculating foe ! But fortunately, in really momentous cases, Francis I claimed his right to decide for himself, and in such circumstances, he even assumed a peremptory tone of authority. The good side to this levity of character was his utter inability to bear a grudge. He found it easy to forgive and forget. Its bad side was responsible for a foolish policy which may have given him scope for proving his gallantry and spirit, two qualities he certainly possessed, but attested his lack of subtlety and skill, which would have been of far greater use to him. It is possible that the feminine influences which had been exercised upon him from his childhood upwards, and in his maturity assumed such undue importance, were to some extent responsible for this frivolity of mind.

Of the women who influenced him the first and foremost was certainly his mother, Louise of Savoy. The historians of
Louise of the seventeenth century who had to tell the story
Savoy. of Charles of Bourbon after his family had ascended the throne of France, were anxious to offer some sort

of excuse for his treachery. They accordingly vilify Louise of Savoy and represent her as a splenetic, avaricious creature, moved by base feelings of resentment, and ready to sacrifice anybody and everybody to her disappointment at not being able to find a second husband. The fact that she was grasping when her interests were at stake is certainly beyond dispute, but that she was base in character is doubtful. She was proud of her son, upon whom she lavished her whole affection, and she adored him too much to be able to guide him aright. The part she played during his captivity at Madrid was both dignified, intelligent, and resolute, and the high esteem in which Francis I held her is proved by the letters he wrote her. When this slim, pallid woman died on September 22, 1513, at the age of fifty-six, she was universally regretted and the melancholy epitaph, " Here lieth the body of one whose soul hath been raised to glory," &c., which the King, her son, wrote for her tomb, seemed justified in the eyes of the whole world.

The woman who, after his mother, influenced Francis most, was his sister " Madame Marguerite d'Orléans " as she was **Margaret of** called, the charming Queen of Navarre, who, **Navarre.** after the death of her first husband, the Duke of Alençon, following upon the battle of Pavia, contracted on January 31, 1527, a loveless marriage with Henri d'Albret, King of Navarre. She bore him a daughter, Jeanne d'Albret, who became the mother of Henry IV. This clever, intelligent woman, so kindly and gracious, so good, so sweet, so charitable, so incapable of despising anyone, whose mind was open to every idea, who loved to talk with learned men and who wrote tales, comedies, pastorals, songs, and verses— *Marguerites de la Marguerite*—also idolized the spoilt brother— who called her his darling—far too much to attempt to correct his faults. " Don't talk to me about her," was Francis I's reply to a man who was denouncing his sister's Lutheran tendencies, " she loves me far too much ; she will believe only what I believe ! " . . . And, indeed, she believed and desired everything her brother wished. This attitude of admiring approval—or at all events in cases where she actually disapproved, her inability to hazard a remonstrance—made this

brilliant, though somewhat indolent princess but a poor instrument in the hands of those who wished her to make the
King more businesslike and serious. It is possible that in
her heart of hearts she was herself ashamed of her weakness,
and the marigold * her favourite flower, which she chose as her
emblem, may have been a symbol of the secret anxiety of her
mind !

The influence of the two Queens, Francis I's first and second
wives, was negligible. The first, Claude, who died at the age

Wives of Francis I. of twenty-five, was too young to have any weight
with him ; whilst the second, Eleonora, the sister
of Charles V, was married from motives of political expediency.
She had no children by the King and lived apart, somewhat
lonely and isolated, though she had a numerous Court of
her own. She remained a stranger to the end, without
influence, appearing but rarely, and playing no active part of
any kind.

The King's mistresses, on the other hand, filled a much more
important position. Francis I enjoys the reputation of having

His mistresses : Anne de Graville. been one of the gayest and most fickle monarchs
who ever reigned in France. But this is an
exaggeration. In his youth he may, perhaps,
have shown himself both ardent and volatile in his affections,
but he only had three real passions, lasting moreover throughout
his life, which is saying a good deal. The first and least important was the love inspired by Anne de Graville, one of Anne
of Brittany's maids-of-honour. She was a fair, delicate girl,
intelligent and graceful, and very attractive with her dark eyes,
broad forehead, small mouth and pink complexion. The
romance did not last long, for one fine day Anne eloped with
her cousin Pierre de Balzac d'Entraigues. The couple were
subsequently married and given a dowry, and the union proved
extremely fruitful.

The second *liaison* was more serious. Françoise de Foix
was the sister of two great soldiers of that family of Foix which

Madame de Chateaubriant. was to be found on every battlefield of the period—
Odet de Foix, Vicomte de Lautrec, who received
twenty wounds at Ravenna, and André de Foix, Seigneur

* In French, *souci*, which also means care.

de Lesparre, who was blinded by a gun-shot. She had married in 1509 a Breton nobleman, Jean de Laval, Sire de Chateaubriant. She was a tall, strong woman, dark, massive and of ample proportions. She wrote poetry more remarkable for quantity than for delicacy, though she had a cultivated mind. But she was a coquette by disposition, with but little distinction, lacking in reserve, and indifferent to her husband. The King's preference for her dated from his return from Marignano in 1516. Their relations proved tempestuous. They exchanged reams of poetry—it was the fashion of the period to write verse—and quarrelled a good deal, for she was lively, high-handed, and jealous, whilst he was gay and careless. She became somewhat of a nuisance, and Marot in composing her epitaph later on, had good reason to say : " Here lieth in nothingness one who once was all-triumphant." The Countess of Chateaubriant was supplanted about 1523 by the Duchess of Étampes, who was in every respect her opposite.

Anne de Pisseleu, demoiselle d'Heilly, who afterwards became Duchess of Étampes, was, in 1523, a fair, pale young **The Duchess** girl of seventeen, charming, distinguished, slight **of Étampes.** and graceful. She was maid-of-honour to Louise of Savoy, and was as gentle and reserved as her predecessor had been bold and outspoken. Francis I remarked her among his mother's elegant little band of maids-of-honour, and though he hid his passion, Louise of Savoy and Margaret were not deceived. At the time of the King's departure for Pavia, the Court knew nothing, but all was revealed on his return. Her rival, Madame de Chateaubriant, was beside herself with rage. She gave way to ungovernable fury and kept calling Anne d'Heilly a " fuzzy-haired chit." Francis I was obliged to inform the Countess that all was over between them, and give her her dismissal. This he did in a letter in verse in which he compared her to a " rabid beast."

> *Liken'd to a rabid beast she was sent*
> *With the flocks in the meadows to pasture !*

wrote Queen Margaret ironically. The King's new passion, which was destined to last for four and twenty years, until the day of his death, won for him a faithful and intelligent devotion, a dainty, witty, affectionate, and serene mistress. On the death of Louise of Savoy, Madame d'Étampes was appointed governess to the King's daughters, Margaret and Madeleine, who were ten and seven years old respectively—a signal testimony of esteem and affection. In 1534, when she was twenty-eight, she married Jean de Brosse, Count of Penthièvre. The King conferred upon the newly wedded pair the county of Étampes, which after two years, he raised to the rank of a duchy.

It was chiefly in the company of this group of women that Francis I passed his life. He rarely left them, for he delighted in their society, and made them accompany him on his various journeys.

But his daughters must be included in the list. By his wife, Claude, he had six children—three sons, Francis, Henry, and **Children of** Charles, and three daughters, Louise, Madeleine **Francis I.** and Margaret. The eldest of the three boys died rather suddenly in 1536, as the result of drinking a glass of very cold water immediately after taking violent exercise. The third, the Duke of Orleans, fell a victim in 1545, at the age of twenty-three, to some epidemic caught near Abbeville ; whilst the second, Henry, was destined to become Henry II. Of the three daughters, Louise died when she was just betrothed ; Madeleine became Queen of Scotland ; and Margaret was still at home with her father at the time of his death. She was then twenty-two. Francis I had not been able to arrange a match for her, though she was intelligent and gifted like her aunt, and knew Latin, Greek, and Italian. She was a charming girl of whom her father was extremely fond, and she gave the finishing touch to the pleasant circle which surrounded and entertained the King.

As a result of the indifference of a King who gave himself up to social life and an existence of constant enjoyment and **Advisers of** pleasure, the advisers of Francis I who enjoyed **Francis I.** their master's favour assumed an extremely important position. At the beginning of his reign the King had four or five favourites—his old friends Bonnivet, Brion, Montchenu, and Montmorency. After his brilliant campaign against Charles V, Montmorency took the lead and was seconded in the government by Admiral Chabot de Brion and the Chancellor Poyet. But these three men did not agree. Montmorency and Poyet hated Brion. They compassed his downfall, drove him from office, and made him stand his trial. Montmorency, however, in his turn, was disgraced, when the policy of remaining on good terms with the Emperor, which he had advocated, proved a failure. Poyet shared in his fall. Towards the end of his life, Francis I placed his whole trust in Admiral Claude d'Annebaut, a good soldier, and an extremely honourable and worthy man who was afflicted with a slight stammer; and Cardinal de Tournon. He saw everything through their eyes, transferred all cares of State to their shoulders, and approved of anything they did. " The King," wrote the Venetian ambassador, " no longer comes to any decision or gives any reply without hearing their advice. In everything he listens to their counsels and if ever—a contingency which but rarely occurs—an answer is given to some ambassador, or a concession made that has not been approved by these two advisers, he revokes or modifies it." And thus, in his dislike for affairs of State, having found two administrators to whom he could commit the whole care of government, Francis I was free to give himself up to the life of his choice—a life of Court festivities, pleasure, and travel.

The Court of Francis I was the earliest of those royal gatherings of lords and ladies who were always elegantly dressed, Court of always *en fête*, and who, with their air of perFrancis I. petual enjoyment, their love of display, brilliance, and splendour remained for so long the highest achievement of social life. The actual constitution of the Court, with its functions and its offices, had existed for some time. It had been gradually formed during the centuries of the Middle Ages, and was destined to last, without many changes or fresh additions, till the reign of Louis XIV and even Louis XVI. By giving a special position to women, by arousing in the breasts of all a love for magnificent personal adornment, and by multiplying Court gatherings, Francis I gave life, as it were, to this setting, and endowed it with that character of stateliness, richness, and elegance which reached its apogee in the time of Louis XIV. "A court without ladies," wrote Brantôme, "is a garden without flowers." Women shone with particular

91

brilliance under Francis I, but in addition, a lavish supply of attendants, officials, and "servants" surrounded the King with a vast retinue that increased his dignity and added lustre to his prestige. Let us make a rapid survey of this gallery.

Under the direction of the master of the King's household, Boissy, who was succeeded by Montmorency, the various **Officials of** attendants in this royal hierarchy were as follows : **his Royal** first, the Chamberlain, who had charge of the **Household.** King's bedchamber ; four Gentlemen of the Bedchamber, afterwards called the First Lords-in-waiting, who each served for a quarter, that is to say three months at a time, never leaving the King. They had twelve Pages of the Bedchamber under them ; a bevy of Lords of the Bedchamber, varying in number from twenty to fifty-four, supported these four. Then came some twenty stewards— also nobles—whose charge was to see to the material wants of the King's life, especially the food. They had under them for the practical accomplishment of their duties about thirty pantlers, five-and-twenty cup-bearers, and fifteen carvers. Everything connected with secretarial work, correspondence, and State documents, belonged to a department consisting of seven private secretaries, among them the famous family of Robertet, including François, one of the King's godsons, and Jean, all of whom owed their posts to their ancestor Florimond. A certain Nicolas de Neuville was also of this number. He was the first of the interminable series of royal and State secretaries of the same name, who afterwards assumed that of Villeroy, and for three hundred years, handed on from father to son, so to speak, the right to fill posts in the royal household. The pages of Francis I, called *enfants d'honneur*, were about thirty in number. Upon them devolved innumerable small offices, such as fetching the King anything he might happen to want, and above all adorning Court receptions by their youthful beauty and handsome silver livery.

Then there was the royal chapel with its Grand Chaplain, who was a cardinal; the Master of the Oratory, who was a **The Royal** bishop ; the King's confessor, who was a Domi- **Chapel.** nican ; fifty royal chaplains, from whom Francis I chose the bishops whom the Concordat of Bologna gave him the right to appoint to the dioceses of the kingdom; and lastly seven ordinary chaplains and seven lay chapel attendants.

Below these were a host of officials of lower rank who fulfilled subordinate duties, chiefly " servants "—four Ushers of the Bedchamber, who were personages in their way ; from twenty to forty Grooms of the Chamber ; this title was not confined to those who fulfilled the actual duties but was also conferred upon persons the King desired to honour, such as Clément Marot and François Budé, and carried with it an annual pension of 240 pounds ; a Master of the Robes, two cloak-bearers, seven choristers, seven doctors, seven surgeons, four barbers, one librarian, eight to twelve handicraftsmen, eight clerks of the kitchen and eight ushers of the audience-room.

The kitchens required a large staff which was divided into two sections : those who prepared the King's meals—*la* *The kitchens.* *cuisine bouche*—and those who were responsible for the food of the rest of the court—*la cuisine commun.* Each of these kitchens had four chefs and six under-cooks, together with a whole array of soup-cooks, roasters, sauce-makers, pastry-cooks, scullions, kitchen-boys and cellar-men, without counting assistants. There was, besides, in addition to all this, a whole crowd of functionaries of various kinds, the inevitable retinue of a great Court, fruiterers, butchers, upholsterers, farriers, musicians—players of tambourines, fifes, cornets, and other instruments—pursers, &c. &c.

The stable formed a department in itself ruled by the Master of the Horse, Galiot de Genouillac, who had under *The stables.* his orders twenty-five Equerries, all men of good family, superintending a host of coachmen and grooms. For, indeed, Francis I required a huge stable to meet all the necessities of his constant journeyings with his Court and household !

Yet another department was formed by the hunting staff, which was no less numerous. There was the Captain of the *The hunt.* Toils with a hundred archers, whose duty it was to arrange the toils used for enclosing certain parts of the forest ; the game was beaten into this enclosure and then shot. There were also fifty waggoners, twelve huntsmen, and numerous kennel attendants ; over a hundred dogs and bloodhounds ; as well as the falconry with its three hundred falcons, in the charge of fifty sub-falconers and fifty nobles under the command of the Grand Falconer, René de Cossé.

The two Queens, the Queen of France and the Queen of Navarre, and the princes had their separate households, forming satellites to the King's household ; if not quite so magnificent, these had at least as many grades. The Queens, moreover, had ladies-in-waiting. By an irony of fate one of Queen Claude's ladies was none other than Madame de Chateaubriant ! Of ladies-in-waiting proper, Claude had fifteen and Margaret ten ; of maids-of-honour, called *filles demoiselles*, there were sixteen for the former and eight for the latter. The King's daughters had nineteen ladies-in-waiting, three of whom were governesses, not to mention numberless lady's maids, &c.

To the persons of the King's sons were attached two tutors, five chancellors, ten stewards, three gentlemen, fourteen pages and a whole host of servants similar to those in the King's household.

This rapid survey would not be complete without mention of the King's guards, consisting of four hundred archers of the guard, of whom three hundred were French and the rest Scotch— the origin of the bodyguard ; the hundred Swiss, halberdiers clad in the royal livery ; and the two hundred gentlemen " each of whom carried on his shoulder a staff decorated with a falcon's beak "—dressed in suits of various colours that added splendour to the Court ceremonies by a display of gorgeous uniforms.

These ceremonies must be pictured with all the splendour conferred upon them by the costumes of cloth of gold and silver **Court** so dear to the heart of Francis I, standing out **gatherings.** in relief against the background of black, white, and tan provided by the royal liveries. As a matter of fact Francis I had some difficulty in finding a mansion in Paris suitable for such display. He would not live in the Louvre, a square, dark, inconvenient old fortress, obstructed in the middle by a huge keep, which shut out the light from the rooms and made them sombre and gloomy. The Louvre was used solely as a prison and treasure-house. Francis preferred Les Tournelles, near the Bastille, which consisted of an agglomeration of ill-assorted buildings of various periods and styles, packed with small rooms and courtyards, possessing but little accommodation. Or failing this he stayed at the Palace, where the Parliament used to sit. This contained a huge hall, called the procurators' hall, divided into two Gothic naves, and adorned with statues of painted and carved wood, representing all the kings of France. It was, indeed, the finest room in Paris, and here Francis I generally held his receptions, when the walls would be hung with tapestries. If the occasion were that of a solemn audience granted to some ambassador, a platform adorned with hangings was raised near the marble table at the end of the hall, and upon this platform was placed the King's seat, or, as it was called at that period the King's "Chair of State." If a banquet was to be given or an evening ball, the hall was lighted by innumerable candles, "glowing wax lights hanging in the form of a cross from the roof." Against the background of sumptuous tapestries, beneath the flood of light falling from the vaulted roof, the golden dresses of the lords and ladies of the court gleamed and scintillated. Francis I also held receptions in the bishop's palace behind Notre Dame ; and gave banquets in the court of the Bastille, when all the walls were hung with tapestry adorned with garlands of ivy and illuminated by twelve hundred torches. These were called festivals "of the burning torch" and the banquet would be followed by a ball. But besides dinners and balls, the chief amusement of the courtiers consisted of the jousts which were held in front of the Hôtel des Tournelles, when tapestry-covered stands were put up in which elegantly dressed ladies took their seats, whilst their cavaliers clad from head to foot in the inlaid armour, of which France still possesses some wonderful specimens, would hold contests of skill, vigour, and endurance. Twice a week Francis I loved to assemble his Court at some joyous and brilliant gathering, a custom, however, which was partly a matter of policy. For his daughter-in-law Catherine de' Medici, in later years once wrote to Charles IX, "I have heard your grandfather, Francis I, say that to live peaceably with the French and have them love their King, he must keep them amused for two days in the week, for that otherwise they would find themselves more dangerous employment."

As a matter of fact the King never stayed very long in Paris, or indeed, anywhere else. He was so changeable that **Journeys of** he was perpetually on the move and constantly **Francis I.** travelling. He would stay a fortnight at most in one place and then suddenly go off somewhere else. His whole Court was obliged to follow him, a tremendous cortège demanding a vast transport system. Benvenuto Cellini writes in his *Memoirs* that twelve thousand horses were required, or, if the whole Court were present, eighteen thousand, to convey all these people about ! According to Soranzo, the entire train consisted of six thousand who rode on horseback, and twelve thousand pedestrians. Now life was not very agreeable during these extraordinary peregrinations. If the caravan arrived in the evening at some place where there were only a few houses or none at all, it was necessary to make a camp, and pitch tents and canvas huts. According to Cellini, who suffered a great deal under these circumstances, it was something like a " gypsy " camp ! Every one had to undergo hardship of some description. The King alone apparently did not suffer in any way from the consequences of this unstable manner of life. He wanted for nothing. He had upholsterers, called *reposteros*, who went on ahead to arrange his lodging for the night. They put up his bed—for all the furniture of his room was carried about—" went about the fields spreading tapestries, cleaning thick carpets for the floor of his room (Oriental rugs) and clothes for him to wear." His table lacked nothing but was served with everything he could possibly desire. " Whether he is in a village, in a forest or at the assembly," writes Brantôme, " he is treated as though he were in Paris." Charles V, on his journey across France, was astonished by all these arrangements. But the Court grumbled and wrangled. The nobility were ruined by these expensive journeys, upon which everything was excessively costly, whilst the foreign ambassadors, who were obliged to accompany the King on his travels, never ceased to complain bitterly. Whilst creating the first Court of modern times, Francis I still preserved the wandering spirit of his vagrant Capet predecessors.

This restless existence also proved extremely costly for the King himself. Expenditure, however, was a matter **Extravagance** to which he never paid the smallest heed. Francis **of Francis I.** I was one of the French Kings who squandered most money, in an exceedingly magnificent way, no doubt, but with no care or consideration of any sort.

He carried this extravagance into every department of life. He adored luxury for its own sake. We have already pointed out that as an arbiter of elegance, he set the fashion; and the fashion, in his time was extremely expensive. Everything that Francis I wore was of gold. The numerous trinkets with which he delighted to cover his person were all of gold, as well as his spurs, his mirrors, and the buttons and hooks on his clothes. The mule he rode had a saddle-cloth adorned with gold, a bridle of silk studded with gold, and gold buttons on its trappings. His clothes were of cloth of gold, embroidered and edged with gold, like sacerdotal vestments. He covered his fingers with rings of diamonds and rubies. His underclothing was made of the finest Flanders linen and his shirts, embroidered with black silk, were kept in scented Russia leather cases. The common objects of everyday use about him, his inkstands, flagons, candlesticks, plate, his rebec (the musical instrument upon which he played) and his desk were all of silver. He had endless elegant sable and martin furs, whilst the sheath of his sword was of white velvet. One year his tailors' bill amounted to 15,600 pounds.

His Court was obliged to follow his example. On days of grand ceremonies, the two hundred lords of the guard wore **Extravagance** cloth of gold, whilst the King appeared all in **of the Court.** white, in cloth of silver, with the Chancellor of France at his side dressed in his robes of State with a scarlet mantle. The Pages and Grooms were also in white, partly velvet, partly cloth of silver, whilst the courtiers were obliged to outshine each other in magnificence and splendour and spend their last farthing on their clothes. The public, though filled with admiration, nevertheless ridiculed all this display, and the morality plays acted at the Place Maubert made mock of the noble lords "who carried their estates on their backs."

But this extravagance was most ruinous of all to the King

himself. At any other period in the history of France but this, when the public revenue was very large, the misery caused by this lavish expenditure would have been extremely great. It is not easy to arrive at the exact figures, for, as we shall see, the accounts were not very strictly kept. The regular revenue seems to have been about three million gold crowns. On paper the expenditure seemed to balance this. The estimate for the King's expenditure was as follows : 50,000 crowns for dress, presents and current expenses ; 50,000 crowns for his petty pleasures ; 200,000 for the upkeep of the guards ; 70,000 for the Queen and her household ; 300,000 for the Dauphin ; 40,000 for sport. But as a matter of fact as Francis I made presents and gave commissions without either reflexion or reserve, the list of expenses increased indefinitely. Costly wars, pensions paid to foreigners, and sums handed over to the King of England, helped to widen the breach, and it is impossible to find out how much the reign of Francis I cost. As early as 1518 the deficit amounted to 1,261,203 pounds. Every possible means for getting money was used. Loans were perpetually raised from all sources—the towns, the clergy, and French and foreign bankers; the Hôtel de Ville fund was invented, the first experiment in Government loans from the public ; property was alienated, all manner of expedients were employed, duties were raised, and offices were negotiated for money. It was a miracle that the Government did not become bankrupt. But so great was the prosperity of the country that the people paid without over-much grumbling, inspiring a certain Italian ambassador with admiration of their submissiveness. At his death, moreover, Francis I managed to leave over two millions in gold in his coffers ! But one man, at least, was doomed to fall a victim to the disorder which reigned in the King's finances —and this was Semblançay. The history of Semblançay provides a typical example of the King's carelessness and frivolity in his extravagances, and throws light upon the organization and method of administration of the period.

It has been asserted that Semblançay's fall was due to Louise of Savoy who prevented him from forwarding to Semblançay. Lautrec, then fighting in Italy, a certain sum of money which the latter demanded. She is said to have done this in order to have her revenge on Lautrec, with whom she was in love, for his coldness towards her, and was thus responsible for the defeat of that unfortunate general at the Bicocca. But this story is a mere fabrication. Jacques de Beaune de Semblançay was an old servant of the Crown, who had grown white in the administration of the finances. He was the son of a plain merchant of Tours, and had been in turn Treasurer to Anne of Brittany, General (Receiver-General) of Languedoc in 1495, and of Langue d'oïl in 1509 ; in 1518 he became a sort of Superintendent of Public Finance with " charge, cognizance, and administration of the business and handling of all our finances " to quote the words of the royal act. He managed the King's money and also the private fortune of Louise of Savoy, and was an important functionary. Unfortunately for a man in his position, though he was clever, he had no method, and his book-keeping left much to be desired. When Francis I's extravagances got the royal exchequer into debt and it became necessary to use various expedients to replenish it, the complicated treasury transactions ended by compromising Semblançay's administration. But he did not trouble about the matter, and, moreover, whether rightly or wrongly, he was under the impression that Louise of Savoy meant her own private fortune to come to the rescue in extremity when the royal exchequer was exhausted. He availed himself of this permission, which was, as a matter of fact, admissible in principle. The result was dire confusion. When the money required was about to be dispatched to Lautrec it was found that the treasury owed to the account of Louise of Savoy a sum equivalent to that destined to cross the mountains, and instead of reaching Italy it remained in the coffers of the King's mother. The raising of loans, alienations of property, sales of public offices and various devices of a similar nature, were the result. But the chaos in the public finances only increased. In 1522 the deficit was 2,500,000 pounds. The King, not so much alarmed at his own lavish expenditure as irritated by the perpetual embarrassment of his finances, according to Semblançay, suddenly realized that Semblançay himself was extremely rich—that every day he seemed to grow more and more opulent, and that he was constantly buying huge estates, building castles, and displaying the possession of a strangely large fortune. Filled with mistrust and suspicion the King demanded to see his " Superintendent's " accounts. The latter gave evasive replies. Francis I and Louise of Savoy, however, insisted, and returned again and again to the charge. At last the King, tired out by Semblançay's delay and subterfuges, appointed a Commission to examine and audit the accounts. After many evasions, Semblançay produced his books. The Commission examined them and pronounced them to be in order. Matters consequently remained as they were. Two years passed, when it chanced that one of Semblançay's clerks was sent to prison for some offence. Out of revenge the man confessed that his master had made him and others of his fellow-clerks produce false entries, antedated memoranda, and sham receipts—in short, that Semblançay had bribed and corrupted his employees to falsify the accounts which had been submitted to the commission. Francis I was furious, and decided to take criminal proceedings against the Superintendent. Semblançay was cross-examined, confronted by the evidence and tried, with the result that he was found guilty of theft, fraud, malversation, and abuse of confidence, and was sentenced to be hanged and to have all his property confiscated. The judges, under the impression that the King would not have the sentence executed, were inexorable. But Francis I carried it out. The sight of the old man—Semblançay was seventy-five—whose life had been so enviable, going to the scaffold at Montfaucon, was indeed lamentable. He met his death on August 11, 1527, with constancy and courage. Maillart, the governor of the criminal department of the Châtelet, who conducted him, trembled more than the doomed man. As Marot said :

> Et Semblançay fut si ferme vieillard
> Que l'on cuidoit au vrai qu'il menât pendre
> A Montfaucon le lieutenant Maillart.*

Such was the revenge or ransom demanded by the magnificence of the Court !

* So dauntless was the aged Semblançay
That one had deemed Lieutenant Maillart went
Led forth by him to hang at Montfaucon.

THE COURT OF FRANCIS I

Of all Francis I's financial extravagance nothing connected with his festivals and merrymakings has left a trace behind. All that remains is a half-obliterated memory of them. But to the glory of this monarch a part, and that not the least part, of the result of his lavishness has survived : his patronage of letters, to which the Collège de France even now bears witness, and his love of art, attested by the castles built by him and still existing.

The interest which Francis I took in literature and in art was certainly due to some extent, as in the case of the Italian **Francis I's love** art-patrons of his time, to a desire to appear **of Art and** great and generous by an intelligent appreciation **Letters.** of artists. But unlike Louis XIV, he was actuated by something deeper than the idea of making his reign illustrious by the glory shed upon it by men of letters, painters, architects, and sculptors. Francis I had a disinterested personal love of beautiful things. Brought up as he had been, surrounded by the delicate luxury of works of art, he preserved throughout his life a marked predilection for everything elegant in shape or form. He had taste, and took pleasure in inspiring creations of beauty, in following their progress to completion, and correcting their defects. It was not, therefore, merely as a rich and extravagant man, who gave endless commissions and allowed artists to produce works without number, that he played a part in the important artistic movement of his country. He contributed to some extent by his preferences to the new fashions which were gradually introduced, and his example inspired great lords and financiers to imitate him. His influence was a factor in the development of the Renaissance in France.

This influence was least important in the domain of letters. The literature of the first half of the sixteenth century was too personal in character to submit to any action from without. It is unnecessary to discuss Francis I's literary talents. He composed verses and exchanged rhymed letters with his mother, his sister, Madame de Chateaubriant, and Anne d'Heilly ; and rondeaux, madrigals, songs, and epigrams from his pen are still in existence. They are, however, all specimens of mediocre versification rather than poetry.

But he was quite capable of appreciating good verse. It was he who recognized, protected, and encouraged the most **Marot.** famous poet of his reign, Clément Marot, whose independent humour, essentially French in spirit, and easy graceful verse, with its pretty pictures of rural life, are very typical of the age. Queen Margaret, who took a great delight in him, gave him a pension of 155 pounds and Francis I conferred upon him the title of Groom of the Chamber, which carried with it a pension of 240 pounds. He displayed a great interest in his compositions and urged him to make a verse translation of the Psalms, a task which he actually carried out. But Clément Marot had Lutheran proclivities, and his translation of the Psalms, which had considerable success in Protestant circles and was sung by all the Huguenots of the sixteenth century, provided a pretext for virulent attacks upon him, which finally drove him into exile. He left France and died at Turin in 1544. Francis I, however, remained faithful to him, and the lists of the royal household contained the entry of Marot's name as Groom of the Chamber to the King, together with the pension attached to that office, two years after the death of the poet.

Bonaventure des Périers was also an independent and original character, who was likewise a pensioner of Margaret of Navarre. He was admitted to the Court, and like his royal patroness was a poet and a prose-writer who, in his *Cymbalum mundi* revealed a mocking spirit of scepticism akin to that of Voltaire. He turned Protestant, or perhaps merely atheist, was persecuted by everybody—even Calvin—and ended, it is said, by committing suicide in 1544.

But, save in the case of Clément Marot, it was not so much poetry as the tale and the novel that flourished under Francis I. **Margaret of** This style of writing, copied from Italy, had a **Navarre and** great success among the King's courtiers, as well **Rabelais.** as with the monarch himself. Margaret of Navarre cultivated it sedulously, and in her *Heptameron* left to posterity her best title to literary fame, certainly a stronger claim than can be made for her somewhat colourless poetry. Margaret's tales are a little wanting in relief, perhaps, but they show a pleasant ingenuity and differ from similar productions

102

of the time by the choice of stories of a more actual and "modern" kind. Francis I, who is the subject of at least one of these tales, took a delight in them; he certainly also read the first book, which appeared in 1535, and the third, which came out in 1545, of *Pantagruel,* a work truly representative of the many-sided sixteenth century, so jealously free in spirit, and bold and prompt in accepting new ideas. Rabelais, with his wide learning and his independence of character, his audacities of thought, his open and cynical mind, and his critical and well-informed judgment, charmed an epoch which saw itself reflected in him. The force of a unique creative imagination and an almost unequalled richness of vocabulary, combining to pour out a mingled torrent of inimitable beauty and unblushing grossness, the whole possessing an undisputed philosophical and social value, make his work an incomparable monument of his times. But how individual and isolated he remains, notwithstanding; understood probably by himself alone, and doubtless careful not to be too lucid, on account of the boldness of his ideas, and the vivacity of his criticism. Living a simpler life than has been supposed, and probably a worthy fellow without pretensions of any sort, Rabelais was not cast in the heroic mould of the man who risks his life to maintain his principles.

But one of his contemporaries dared to do so, and duly paid the penalty for his courage. This was Étienne Dolet, a **Dolet.** learned printer of Lyons, who was a sceptic and an atheist. He printed and hawked heretical books which led to his being arrested and tried. According to Calvin "he openly showed his contempt for the Gospel" and declared "that the life of the soul was in no respect different from that of dogs and swine." The Parliament sent him to the stake; the sentence seems very severe nowadays. In the absence of a penal code at this period, Parliament decided the punishments to be inflicted for "crimes" brought within its jurisdiction, and these punishments were, as a rule, extremely harsh. In the case of Dolet, independence of thought was carried to its utmost limits, and natures such as his could be affected by the King of France only in so far as the monarch might interfere with the execution of parliamentary justice, or let it take its course. Thus by reason of its character the literature of his time escaped the influence of Francis I.

With a little more learning the King would have obtained a firmer hold over letters; not that he discovered or directed **Francis I's** men of talent, but his patronage contributed **encouragement** notably to the support of philological studies. **of learned** Thanks to the invention of printing, fresh editions **men.** of Greek and Latin authors came into existence every day, and interest in the works of the ancients, which had hitherto been practically inaccessible, increased considerably. Publications such as Budé's *Commentaires sur la Langue Grecque* and Robert Estienne's *Thesaurus Linguæ Latinæ* facilitated acquaintance with the wisdom of antiquity, and a large number of people developed a taste for the careful study of Greek and Latin forms. Interested in everything connected with the exercise of the intellect, Francis I was greatly attracted by this movement. He was eager to follow it, to know the men who were its most skilled workers, and keep himself informed through them of all that was being done or remained to be done. Thus the most famous scholars of his reign were gradually introduced into his circle; he invited them to his board, conversed with them on terms of familiarity, and listened to their counsels.

The most illustrious of these was Guillaume Budé, the omniscient Budé, who was jurist, theologian, mathematician, **Budé and** philologist, historian, critic, archæologist, and **other Savants.** above all Hellenist, "one of the wise men of Christendom," as he was called, "the French prodigy," according to Erasmus, a typical sixteenth-century *savant* and one of the first scholars to apply himself to the study of antiquity. Louis XII had already noticed him, and with complete confidence in his powers, had sent him as his ambassador to the court of Julius II. Francis I conferred upon him the title of Groom of the Chamber, together with the pension attached to this office, and paid great attention to his opinion. The advice of the learned Hellenist was, above all, invoked for two or three schemes which were set on foot and carried out by the King.

Next in importance to Budé came Lefèvre of Étaples, *Faber Stapulensis*, as he signed himself in his books, thus earning for

himself the surname of *Stapoul*. He was a philosopher, mathematician, moralist, and exegetist, though but little of a philologist. The King, who had a very high opinion of him, made
him tutor to his third son. There were also the Hellenist,
Jacques Toussaint, *Tussanus*, Robert Estiennes' master ;
Robert Estienne himself ; Vatable, whose real name was
Watebled, a Hebrew scholar and also something of a Hellenist,
destined to become a professor in the Collège de France ; and
above all, Guillaume Postel, the Orientalist, one of the first to
unravel the tangled skein of Oriental languages. He was a
strange creature, full of visions, who only escaped the Inquisition later on by passing as slightly mad. Francis I took a
delight in discussing scholarship and philological science with
all these men.

During the course of these conversations certain projects
were discussed, the realization of which will always remain to
The library of the credit of Francis I. In the first place, his
Fontainebleau. attention was drawn to the fact that to help these
learned men in their studies, it would be extremely useful to
find and buy precious manuscripts from all quarters, chiefly
from abroad, and to house them all in one building where they
could be consulted by scholars. This twofold idea was the
origin of the Royal Library, which was destined throughout the
centuries to carry out this policy of buying and preserving texts
most useful to the pursuit of learning. Francis threw himself
heart and soul into the scheme. Venice was at this time the
great market for manuscripts from Greece and Italy. Guillaume
Pellicier, the French ambassador to Venice, was accordingly
charged with the task of collecting as many of these manuscripts
as possible, and money was sent him for this purpose. In 1541
Pellicier dispatched four boxes of Greek manuscripts to Fontainebleau. Guillaume Postel was sent on a mission to the
East to find manuscripts. He went to Constantinople, Syria,
and Egypt, and reaped a rich harvest. Others played their
part in making similar acquisitions. And thus the foundations
of a library were laid which, in spite of various vicissitudes,
continued to grow and finally developed into the Bibliothèque
Nationale of the present day. Francis I placed his manuscripts,
to which he added a collection of books, at Fontainebleau, in a

room above the little gallery painted by Il Rosso, on the second floor, just under the roof. Guillaume Budé was at one time the librarian of this collection, but was succeeded in the post by Pierre Gille.

Francis I also founded the Collège de France. As a matter of fact, as was the case to some extent even with the Biblio-**The Collège** thèque Nationale, he is to be credited with the **de France.** realization of an idea, rather than with any great development of it. It was at the instigation of Budé that the King undertook this work, which aimed at forming outside the ancient and rigid framework of the Universities, a series of free courses on a wider scope of subjects and sciences than those taught by the Universities. It was started on an extremely modest scale. The King allocated 400 pounds for the salaries of the professors who were appointed; Vatable for Hebrew, Postel for Oriental languages, Oronce Finé for mathematics, and Galland for Latin. Budé did no teaching, but supervised the organization. In the absence of a special building the courses were held in the class-rooms of the Collège de Cambray. Each professor took the text of some work, read it aloud, and commented upon it. Such was the system of instruction, and hence we have the title *lecteur* (reader) which is given to professors to this day. Francis I would fain have engaged Erasmus and actually wrote to him, but the Dutch *savant* did not care to come. The institution was founded in 1530, and in that year the *lecteurs royaux* began their courses, under very humble and precarious auspices! In the eyes of its contemporaries the Collège never possessed that distinction it afterwards attained, but was regarded with indifference or jealousy. Francis I, with his usual instability and frivolity, failed to maintain his interest in the institution, and more than once the salaries of the neglected professors fell into arrears. But the establishment was made, and was destined to survive and develop; and the King's reputation had the good fortune to benefit by its happy survival and ultimate celebrity.

Perhaps Francis I has not been given due credit for the incomparable brilliance of the arts in his reign!

There has been much discussion as to whether the Renaissance, *i.e.* that transformation, chiefly in the realm of the arts, by which the realistic, varied, picturesque, fantastic Gothic style, with its undisciplined freedom and disorderly appearance, gave way to an art that was idealized, regulated, subjected to geometrical canons and a well-balanced discipline, was the immediate product of Italian influence alone, or the result of a spontaneous modification of the French genius. The advocates of the first theory attribute the great castles of the Loire to Italy, whilst their opponents refuse to acknowledge Italian influence anywhere. It is probable that the truth lies somewhere between these two extremes. Is the very word Renaissance, which implies a resurrection—that is to say, the resurrection of the artistic principles of the ancient world to new life and honour—itself correct ? This indeed is open to doubt, but it is impossible to modify a term which expresses something that everybody understands.

As a matter of fact, there was first an evolution of French taste ; love of the vital ruggedness of fifteenth-century art with its restless architecture, gave place to an admiration for order, harmony, and grace. This evolution was no sudden transformation, and was not entirely due to the sudden discovery of Italy by the conquering armies of the French Kings. France had for a long time enjoyed an intimate connexion with Italy. Traders and bankers, more especially in Lyons, which was a great centre for international business transactions, were well acquainted with the various Italian towns. Prelates and other dignitaries of the Church were constantly crossing the Alps and visiting Rome in connexion with their work, and they had not failed to observe and appreciate specimens of Italian art, which had reached a high degree of perfection at that date. The proof of this is to be found in the fact that a man like Thomas James, Bishop of Dol in Brittany, had a seal made for himself in Italy in 1478 which might pass for work of the best Renaissance period, whilst in 1507 the Abbot of Fécamp gave a commission in Genoa for a Shrine of the Holy Blood which is still in the church of the old abbey and is one of the most exquisite art productions of the sixteenth century. The great art patrons of the fifteenth century had employed Italian

Evolution of French art.

107

workmen. The good King René, who had stayed a long while in Italy, had taken Piero of Milan and Francesco Laurana into his service and was responsible for the tomb of Charles du Maine in the cathedral of Mans, a piece of Italian work carried out entirely in the new style. Others had studied the ancient monuments and there were signs of a reaction in favour of their severity of style. Jean, Duke of Berry, had had antique cameos and medals in his collection. Thus, at the beginning of the sixteenth century the French were not absolutely unacquainted with Italy or entirely ignorant even of classical art. But artists and works of art gradually made their appearance, bearing witness to a modification in the idea of the beautiful in France, and almost insensibly preparing the public mind for the ideal which was to prevail in the sixteenth century.

There were painters, for instance, like Jean Fouquet, who was born in 1415, died in 1480, and worked for Charles VII, **Jean Fouquet,** Louis XI, and Étienne Chevalier. His incom-
Bourdichon, parably conscientious and talented work was in
Perréal. many respects still realistic, though his realism, it is true, was less harsh than that of the Flemish painters of the same period. But how eloquently his backgrounds of classical architecture, the loftiness of his conceptions, and the arrangement of his subjects, emphasize the change which the data of his predecessors had undergone ! The transition is revealed, and shows itself in a more pronounced fashion in the miniatures of Jean Bourdichon of Tours (1457–1521) who worked for four kings and painted the picture representing the great moments in the life of Anne of Brittany—a masterpiece in which the purity of the figures of the Queen and the saints surrounding her, the lightness and noble delicacy of the detail, and of the values, are much more closely allied to the charming productions of the sixteenth century than to the Gothic ideal, which was beautiful in its way, but extremely rigid and inflexible. We might quote yet another artist of the late fifteenth century, who, like Bourdichon, was attached to the court of Charles VII, Jean Perréal, surnamed Jean de Paris, were it not that there is still some doubt as to the works attributed to his brush.

108

Sculpture was represented by Michel Colombe (1430–1512), one of the best of French artists. He was a native of Brittany, **Michel Colombe.** who took up his abode on the banks of the Loire and seems never to have visited Italy. Like Bourdichon, he represents a very high degree of the evolution of French taste in the direction of more refined forms. His Saint George and the Dragon, made for the Château de Gaillon, is a product of French genius in every respect, both in form and feeling, and owes nothing whatever to Italian influence. And his tomb of Francis II of Brittany, in the cathedral at Nantes, which was ordered by Queen Anne in 1501, is one of the most striking examples of the modifications which were taking place. The figures of the Virtues, standing at the four corners of the tomb, admirable in their harmony, suppleness, intelligence, sobriety, and simplicity, prove the extent to which pre-Renaissance French artists had learnt to apply the best qualities of taste and elegance, before the repeated French expeditions to the valley of the Po had enabled them to take lessons from the Italians. In addition to Colombe, we must mention the anonymous artist responsible for the beautiful sculptures of Solesmes, the tombs of Charles VIII's children at Tours, and various other isolated works of art which critics attribute to Colombe or his school. French sculpture of the sixteenth century was no spontaneous growth; it had its own antecedents.

The same may be said of architecture. The buildings of the late fifteenth and the early sixteenth century, such as **Architecture.** Amboise, the Blois of Louis XII and the Château de Gaillon are French Gothic. The accounts of the Château de Gaillon published by M. Deville contain the names of over one hundred artists, of whom only three are Italians ; two of these had been established in France for a long time and, moreover, played no important part in the building or decoration of the castle. But the elements which were to be characteristic of the new art of the Renaissance : semicircular arches, engaged columns with Corinthian capitals, niches between windows, and carved friezes, gradually made their appearance. These details were not unknown to the painters of the fifteenth century, who frequently made use of them in the backgrounds of their pictures. Obviously, they did not invent them, and Italy alone could have provided them with their models. It was probably due to them that as early as the building of Amboise, the masons introduced those semicircular arches and niches for statues, which are to be found in the plans of Amboise reproduced by Du Cerceau in his work *Les Plus excellens bastimens de France*. The first building to which these principles were largely applied is the portion of Blois built during the reign of Francis I.

Many attempts have been made to discover the names of the architects responsible for the châteaux of Francis I's time, and the fact that none have been found, and that only the names of master-masons have been brought to light, has caused a good deal of surprise. But, as a matter of fact, the architect in the modern sense had not yet come into existence at that period. As in country districts at the present day, there were only builders and workmen, many of them men of taste and skill, with whom contracts for buildings were made. And thus the edifices of that time were the product of a collaboration of the master's idiosyncrasies with the ideas of the craftsmen. Queen Claude, who inherited Blois from her father Louis XII, was anxious to have something better to look out upon than the cold, sombre walls of the feudal castle which enclosed the court to the right of the elegant structure for which Louis XII had been responsible. As soon as Francis I ascended the throne in 1515, she had the work set on foot. An architect, in the modern sense of the word, would have pulled down the existing edifice and raised a grand building on a definite plan. Jacques Sourdeau, however, the master-mason with whom Claude had to deal, preserved the old castle from motives of economy, and rebuilt the façade. Hence the irregularity of this façade, which, in our opinion, gives it additional character. The windows are placed at unequal intervals, and the chimney-stacks defy the laws of symmetry. It was found necessary to construct a staircase, and, as it was impossible to introduce it in the interior, Sourdeau put it outside on the façade, and not even in the middle of this. But his design for the framework is so rich and elegant that it compels our admiration. The windows were still the casement windows of Louis XII's time, but they were enframed by little pilasters with capitals. The whole still preserved the irregular and asymmetric composition of the Gothic style, whilst the new taste was revealed in a greater geometric simplicity and the kind of elegance produced by purity of line. The outer façade on the north side was an even better example of the empirical nature of an art resulting, not from the theoretical conceptions of an architect, working on an *à priori* plan, but from the clever manipulations of masons who built from day to day to meet unexpected demands. In front of the mediæval façade, which was left intact, a terrace was built, and upon this loggias were raised, forming another terrace for the next storey, and so on up to the roof. And as the roof could not be brought into the arrangement, a little gallery of pilasters different from the rest of the façade had to be added to mask the defect.

Queen Claude's buildings at Blois were apparently completed in 1519. Francis I followed the work with great interest and in his turn made up his mind to build.

Francis I was one of the greatest, if not the greatest builder of any of the Kings of France, and was responsible for eight or nine châteaux and palaces. By providing artists with generous supplies for their work, by setting an example which was followed by others, by collaborating as a man of taste with the builders and by his ideas and his preferences, he contributed towards the invention and development of new forms. And thus he set the fashion and inspired the taste of his period.

The first work, upon which he embarked in 1519, was the building of Chambord. Few châteaux afford a better example of the manner in which edifices were raised at this period. They were not built all in one style, previously conceived as a whole, but piece by piece, in accordance with a succession of ideas. Francis I's reason for choosing the site is not known. The hypothesis of some amorous intrigue is a myth. He may have wanted a hunting-box, and it is possible that a feudal castle had already stood on the spot. The central portion of Chambord is, as a matter of fact, nothing but a fifteenth-century feudal castle in plan, very similar to Vincennes : a square structure with four large towers at the corners, and the walls only pierced by high windows. The façade was afterwards continued to the right and the left as far as some towers, in the form of dovecots, which stood a short distance away ; and to complete the general silhouette, a further addition was made still later, in 1544, of a central lantern-tower, built under a special contract with the mason Jacques Coqueau, who furnished the design. The result of this method of construction is a façade which is most magnificent and regal in appearance. But if the edifice be examined minutely it will be discovered that nothing is regular. This is not said in any spirit of criticism, for the fine effect of the whole may be due to this very irregularity in detail. There are more windows on one side than on the other, the chimney-stacks are placed haphazard, the windows in the roof do not correspond, and a turret in the right wing is not balanced by its counterpart in the left. The masons who built Chambord, Denis Sourdeau, Pierre Neveu surnamed Trinqueau, Jacques Coqueau and Jean Grossier, took a tremendous time about their task, over thirty years, if we include prolonged intervals of idleness. In 1530, after his return from Madrid, Francis I employed as many as 1800 workmen. The timbers of the roof were put up in 1534, but the castle was only completed about 1550. As a matter of fact, it is little more than a splendid façade erected in front of a magnificent staircase, a monumental and imposing piece of work. The castle is uninhabitable ; it was the artistic whim of a rich and extravagant monarch. It is, nevertheless, remarkable in every way as an illustration of the genesis of Renaissance architecture and the conditions under which this art developed.

It was above all on his return from captivity in Madrid that Francis I indulged his passion for building. He opened building-yards almost everywhere ; in Paris he conceived the idea of altering the old castle of the Louvre and making it suitable for habitation. At his command the great tower which occupied the court of the fortress was pulled down in 1528. The public regretted this step for, as the *Journal d'un Bourgeois de Paris* says, " it was fair, lofty, and strong." The interior was rebuilt, and large reception-rooms, kitchens, and stables were added on the side of the Rue Froidmantel on the west. In 1534 the Court was able to take up its abode in the Louvre. At the same time, according to the *Bourgeois de Paris*, the King set on foot at the very gates of Paris " near the Bois de Boulogne and the convent of the nuns of Longchamp, the building and erection of a mansion and pleasure-grounds he called Madrid, because it resembled the Spanish building in which he had for so long been a prisoner "—a very doubtful statement. The master-mason who was given the contract was a certain Pierre Gadier. If the façade of Madrid illustrated by Androuet du Cerceau in his *Plus excellens bastimens de France* be compared with that of Blois—the north façade built by Francis I—it is evident that the builder found his inspiration in the loggias which had been an accidental feature of the latter edifice. In 1532 the Château of Villers-Cotterets was begun by the master-masons Jacques and Guillaume le Breton, whilst in 1533 the King conceived the plan of having the Hôtel de Ville in Paris reconstructed, according to one account, by Pierre Chambiges "foreman of masonry for the city of Paris" and according to another by the Italian Domenico of Cortona surnamed Boccador. The building, however, is quite French and shows no traces of Italian influence. At Saint-Germain-en-Laye, a favourite spot of the King's, it was decided to raze to the ground the old pentagonal feudal castle which stood there, and build in its place a new edifice which would be well lighted, airy, lofty, and spacious. This new castle, which had the same ground plan as the former structure, was built in 1539 by the master-masons Pierre Chambiges, Guillaume Guillain, and Jean Langeois, who borrowed their ideas from the Château de Madrid. But Francis I's favourite spot, where he preferred to live towards the end of his life, the home he really loved, was Fontainebleau.

"A harmony of age and season," says Michelet, "Fontainebleau is essentially an autumn landscape, most original, **Fontainebleau.** most wild, and yet most gentle and most serene. With its sun-baked rocks, giving shade to the invalid, its fantastic shadows, empurpled by October tints, which set one dreaming ere winter comes ; and with the little Seine a stone's throw away flowing between golden vineyards, it forms a delicious retreat in which to rest and drink what remains of life's cup ! " According to Benvenuto Cellini, Fontainebleau was " the spot in his kingdom which Francis I loved best." The King began building operations there in 1528. In this case also an old pentagonal castle dating from the time of

H
113

Louis VII and Saint Louis stood upon the site. Without more ado the builders razed the old edifice to the ground, and on its foundations built the new palace. This accounts for the curious shape of the oval court. The keep, at the back, and the chapel of Saint Saturnin were alone preserved. From a distance the general effect is not imposing. It is difficult to say why Francis I conceived the idea of building the great court, afterwards called the Cour du Cheval Blanc, farther on, and joining the two buildings by a gallery, the Galerie de François I, thus turning the castle of Fontainebleau into a strange series of isolated structures without any logical connexion, forming an incomprehensible and inconvenient whole. The only explanation that can be given is that it sprang from the Gothic disregard of order and symmetry, which was not yet extinct, and the successive whims of an owner who had any ideas which came into his mind carried out, careless whether they were compatible with what already existed. The master-masons responsible for the building were Gilles le Breton and Pierre Chambiges. The name of Serlio has been mentioned and is still mentioned in this connexion. But Serlio did not come to France until 1541, when the castle had been furnished for eight or nine years. After his long wanderings Francis I was glad to go to Fontainebleau " for recreation, inasmuch as the place and the country were fair and pleasant and fit for the pursuit of the chase." He had his own suite of rooms there, in the decoration of which he took great interest, superintending it in person.

To carry out this decoration, which was begun about 1532, he had recourse to Italian workmen. Here indeed the influence of Italy in France is an ascertained fact. The employment of transalpine craftsmen in this case was due to several reasons. In the first place, France was somewhat poor in artists. In fact there were practically none of any note, with the exception of the Clouets, who were portrait-painters about whom little is known. They were true to the realistic French traditions in art, though they displayed consummate tact and restraint in their adherence to it, more especially in those chalk drawings, with their clear strong technique, which were so fashionable in the sixteenth century. When Charles V paid his visit to France the King wanted to make him a present of a

114

Hercules in chased silver. A pitiable piece of work was submitted to him which the Parisian craftsmen assured him was the best that could be produced. Moreover, Francis I, a man of taste and culture, loved to surround himself with works of art, and in the top story of the Pavillon Saint Louis at Fontainebleau he had a cabinet where he kept vases, medals, statuettes, and drawings, which he used frequently to visit. Merchants made purchases for him almost everywhere abroad, of tapestries, gold- and silversmith's work, and engraved gems. Pictures also figured in his collections. He had a number of canvases brought from Italy, including Salviati's *Portrait of Aretino*, Bronzino's *Venus and Cupid*, Titian's *Magdalen*, Leonardo da Vinci's *Gioconda*, and Michelangelo's *Leda*, as well as bronzes and statues. He was fully alive to the splendour of Italian art at the beginning of the sixteenth century, the heyday of the Italian Renaissance. Francis was not the first French king who had thought of summoning artists to France to carry out under his own eyes the works he wished to possess. Louis XII made unsuccessful attempts to secure the services of Leonardo da Vinci, and the family of Amboise had employed Andrea Solario. The first artist of any importance whom Francis I asked to enter his service and who consented to do so was Il Rosso.

Il Rosso, who was summoned to Fontainebleau in 1531, undertook the decoration of the gallery called the Galerie de François I, and worked on it until 1541. The work as we now see it was very much restored under Louis Philippe. It was a product of purely Italian decorative art and possessed all its qualities and defects. French taste in no way modified the transalpine conceptions of the artist, which it must have done with singular success in the domain of architecture, if Italian architects were really responsible for the French Renaissance châteaux. After Il Rosso, Francis I summoned Francesco Primaticcio, *Le Primatice*, (1504– 1570) to his Court. This artist remained in France until his death. He helped Il Rosso, continued his decorations at Fontainebleau, and enjoyed a position of great authority under Henry II. The generous and liberal Francis I paid these men handsomely.

Italian artists at Fontainebleau.

CENTURY OF THE RENAISSANCE

Hearing how lucrative a position under Francis I was, other artists flocked to offer their services—among them, Benvenuto Cellini, sculptor, graver, goldsmith, chaser, and a man of great talent, though of somewhat difficult temper. The King welcomed him to his Court, gave him a commission to make a bronze nymph for Fontainebleau, and employed him more particularly on articles in gold and silver, such as a gold salt-cellar, a silver figure of Jupiter, ewers, and dishes. But he kept him barely five years in his service. Around Il Rosso and Primaticcio there was a little constellation of Italian artists and collaborators, none of whom attained any very great pre-eminence. In addition to their decorative work, these men and their pupils produced pictures painted in a particular style of their own. They were somewhat colourless productions, devoid of any very great vigour or merit, though not lacking in elegance and facility. These artists are known as the painters of the Fontainebleau School.

The chief contribution which this group of Italian decorators and Italian influence in general made to French art was the **The Fontaine-** detail of ornament. As a matter of fact, in this **bleau School.** sphere their influence made itself felt very soon. The egg ornament, spirals, candelabra, naked cherubs gambolling and innumerable " grotesque " details appeared very early in the work of French artists, and continued to increase until the sixteenth century. If the statuary, of which there are but few examples under Francis I, bears witness in such works as the statues of the Amboise family, of Louis de Brézé at Rouen, and of Admiral de Chabot and Genouillac, to the maintenance of the best qualities of Colombe: simplicity, firmness, and taste, the intricate and fantastic sculptural ornament of the period reveal the principles of Italian decoration. It is in this domain that Italy chiefly made her influence felt in the artistic movement which took place in France during the sixteenth century.

SOURCES. Same as for preceding chapter with the addition on the subject of the Royal Household, of the French manuscript 7853 in the Bibliothèque Nationale. Also *Poésies du roi François Ier, de Louise de Savoie*, ed. Champollion-Figeac, 1847 ; *Lettres de Catherine de Médicis*, ed. La Ferrière, 1880 ; Th. Hubert, *De vita et rebus gestis Frederici II*, 1624 ; Benvenuto Cellini, *Mémoires*, ed. Leclanché, 1843 ; Deville, *Comptes* *de dépenses de la construction du château de Gaillon*, 1850 ; *Compte des bâtimens du roi, de* 1528 *à* 1571, 1877 ; A. du Cerceau, *Les plus excellens bastimens de France*, 1576.

WORKS. Same as for preceding chapter and Rouard, *François Ier chez Mme de Boisy*, 1863 ; Louis de Brézé, *Les chasses sous François Ier*, 1869 ; De Boislisle, *Semblançay et la surintendance des finances* (*Annuaire-Bulletin de la Soc. de l'hist. de France*, 1881) ; Jacqueton, *Semblançay*, 1895 ; Petit de Julleville, *Histoire de la langue et de la littérature françaises*, vol. iii, 1897 ; Darmesteter and Hatzfeld, *Le XVIe siècle en France*, 1883 ; Faguet, *XVIe siècle, études litteraires*, 1893 ; L. Delisle, *Le cabinet des manuscrits de la Bibliothèque imperiale*, 1868 ; A. Lefranc, *Histoire du Collège de France*, 1893 ; E. Müntz, *La Renaissance en Italie et en France à l'époque de Charles VIII*, 1885 ; L. Palustre, *La Renaissance en France*, 1885 ; E. Müntz, *Histoire de l'art pendant la Renaissance*, 1889 ; L. Courajod *Leçons professés a l'école du Louvre*, 1901 ; P. Vitry, *Michel Colombe et la sculpture française de son temps*, 1901 ; J. de Croy, *Nouveaux documents pour l'histoire de la création des résidences royales des bords de la Loire*, 1894 ; Geymüller, *Geschichte der Baukunst der Renaissance in Frankreich*, 1896 ; Le Père Dan, *Trésor des merveilles de Fontainebleau*, 1642 ; Dimier, *Le Primatice*, 1900 ; F. Bournon, *Blois et les châteaux de la Loire*, 1908.

CHAPTER IV

EXTERNAL PEACE. HENRY II

Henry II, 1547–1559. Queen Catherine de' Medici and her Court;
the King's children; Mary Stuart; Diane de Poitiers; his counsellors—Constable Montmorency, Duke Francis of Guise and the
Guise family. Clearness and precision of French policy under
Henry II; determination to renounce Italy, to conquer in the north,
and to secure peace. Hatred of Henry II for Charles V. Short war
with England and the capture of Boulogne, 1550. The German
princes solicit his intervention : conquest of the three bishoprics—
Metz, Toul, and Verdun, 1552. Charles V makes peace with the
German princes and lays siege to Metz; his defeat, 1552–1553. The
hostilities of 1554, the Duke of Guise at Renty. Abdication of
Charles V : Truce of Vaucelles, 1556. Renewal of the war and the
disaster of Saint-Quentin, 1557. Guise seizes Calais, 1558. Treaty
of Cateau-Cambrésis, 1559. The marriage festivities after the war,
Henry II slain at a joust, 1559.

O F the three sons born to Francis I, the second, who
succeeded him as Henry II, in 1547, at the age of
twenty-nine, was certainly the one least loved by his
father. There had always been a strong contrast between their
characters. Whereas Francis I was lively and outspoken,
Character of Henry, as the Venetian Dandolo writes, was
Henry II. "sombre and taciturn by nature. He rarely
laughs, so rarely, indeed, that many persons about the Court
assert that they have never seen him do so." He was a great
hunter, "all muscles," and had the reputation of having
developed his physical qualities at the expense of everything
else. "He has more bodily than spiritual virtue," said
Tavannes. His melancholy was supposed to be the result of
the indelible impression made upon him by his imprisonment
in Spain. Francis I had other reasons for not being particularly
proud of him, such as the little zeal he showed for learning,
118

and above all his intrigue with Diane de Poitiers, a woman twenty years older than himself. Henry II was to reign for twelve years and three months, and to die in the prime of life at the age of forty-one, as the result of an accident.

The coolness felt by Francis I for his son was not shared by those who came into intimate contact with the new King. Tall and strongly built, extremely elegant in appearance, and with every sign of race about him, Henry II was one of the finest gentlemen among French monarchs. On his well-proportioned body was set a rather small, refined head, which was, however, devoid of much expression owing to the vague melancholy which overshadowed his features. His complexion was very dark; according to Brantôme " he looked slightly Moorish." His hair and beard were black, but he turned grey very young. He had the appearance of a man who enjoyed good health; he was sound in body, solidly built, and robust, and would have had a tendency to grow stout had not a sober life and plenty of exercise preserved his royal dignity of bearing. The only complaint from which he suffered was headache.

He lived a regular and methodical life. Rising early, he began the day by holding a Council of State with the three or four high officials on whose experience and judgment he relied during his reign. This council was called " the select council." Then, every morning, he went to mass, which he attended devoutly, for he was a religious man. After this, having but a small appetite, he partook of a frugal dinner; he would then read a little, go for a ride, and, two or three times a week, hunt, or else grant audiences. His manner on such occasions was easy, courteous, and amiable. Like a true man of the world, he took care to give offence to no one. Nobody left his presence dissatisfied, wrote Giovanni Soranzo, whom he frequently received. He gladly granted anything he was asked and did so right royally, showing himself " extremely affable and kind " to all. Endowed with a very good memory, he never forgot persons whom he had once seen, which flattered their vanity. He spoke Italian and Spanish. At the end of the day he used to spend an hour with Diane de Poitiers, after which he supped in public, when he enjoyed talking to the people about him. His evenings he reserved for receptions given by the Queen,

Catherine de' Medici, who every night had a gathering of the lords and ladies of the Court in her apartments. He would then converse with everybody in a friendly fashion, and retire early to bed.

But Henry II was above all a " sportsman." He was a very good rider and had a passion for horses, of which he had numbers in his possession. He exercised a personal supervision over his studs at Mehun, Saint-Léger and Oiron, and took a delight in showing off the most beautiful animals in his stables. He was particularly fond of hunting, chiefly stag-hunting, and rode to the chase with his packs of grey hounds and white hounds. On a journey he would hunt all along the route to pass the time. But he also indulged in every other form of physical exercise. He played tennis, ball, football, and mall, and also shot, although he had a painful recollection of having when he was Dauphin shot out the eye of one of his equerries, M. de Boucard. He was an admirable skater, and it was one of the joys of his Court to watch him cutting elegant and difficult figures on the ice when the pond at Fontainebleau was frozen. But above all he loved to take part in the great games of the period: jousts on horseback, when two riders, armed from head to foot, charged from either end of an enclosure and tried to unseat each other by a violent thrust of the lance, running the risk of shivering the weapon against the mailed breastplate of the adversary; and the tournament, a violent *mêlée* of mounted knights in heavy armour who endeavoured to unhorse each other by lance thrusts; this was a real battle in miniature. It was this love of sport which led him at the beginning of his reign to give his consent somewhat carelessly to a certain duel in order to provide a spectacle for the Court. The combatants were two young noblemen, Jarnac and La Chataigneraie, who were exasperated because the former had cast some aspersion upon the latter's honour. Francis I had forbidden them to fight as the point at issue was both uncertain and futile. But Henry II ordered the duel to take place, and it was fought with great solemnity. Jarnac, with two thrusts of his sword cut through his adversary's leg, and so brought him to the ground, but there was some difficulty in persuading Henry II to stop the fight and allow La Chataigneraie to escape with his life.

EXTERNAL PEACE. HENRY II

A man of sport, Henry II had but little love of art and letters. He was fairly fond of music and willingly attended the concerts held in the Queen's apartments, but he did not know much about it. He regarded everything of an artistic nature as superfluous, though he confessed that he too would have started the building of some great mansion had the termination of the war given him the leisure to do so. But, unfortunately, the war only ended at his death. As he held the profession of letters in low esteem he naturally had no very high opinion of writers. He preferred soldiers, and kept all his honours and pensions for them.

To sum up, he was, on the whole, a gentle and gracious monarch. His letters, published by J. B. Gail, are those of a man of much fine feeling and great staunchness in his friendships, which were constant, deep, unchangeable and free from all stiffness and hauteur. He was an excellent father who adored his children and took great care of their health, insisting upon their having a change of air as soon as any danger threatened them. On his return from a journey he would gallop ahead of all his suite in order to clasp them in his arms the sooner. His tenderness was touching to behold. Those whom he loved, he loved with all his heart ; but whether his wife, Catherine de' Medici, was included in the number is open to question.

Queen Catherine de' Medici could hardly be called an attractive woman. She was the same age as her husband, her **Catherine de'** birthday falling barely a fortnight later than his. **Medici and** She was afflicted with a fat, coarse face, crowned **her Court.** by black hair, large goggle eyes, heavy eyebrows, a big nose, loose, pouting lips, surmounting a body which lost its shape very early in life. The *bourgeoise* granddaughter of Florentine bankers and merchants, she was distinctly ugly. But to counterbalance this, she became a great lady of high importance when she was very young. She was intelligent, possessed considerable discrimination and prudence, and, moreover, displayed the impenetrable reserve of an Italian woman who has suffered and thought much. From the first, during the reign of Francis I, when she felt that she was unwelcome on account of her origin, she had studied to achieve an attitude

121

of modest retirement and to please every one by her agreeable manners. And she had succeeded. Francis I, with whom she used to ride out to the hunt, appreciated her intelligent firmness, and was fond of her ; whilst she won the sympathy of the Duchesse d'Étampes, as well as of Montmorency, Brion, d'Annebaut, and all who had influence at Court. But she kept a very strict watch over her own conduct.

As soon as she became Queen, however, she was transformed into an accomplished hostess, who received a great deal. Her amiability was unstinted, and she made herself charming and attractive to everybody. People were enchanted with her, and the whole Court considered her perfection itself. She dressed as a rule simply and in a severe style ; but on reception days she wore extremely rich and elegant clothes, covered with numberless chased ornaments, for the designs of which she herself gave instructions to her goldsmiths. She conferred incomparable order and brilliancy upon Court gatherings, and as she inherited vast wealth from her family, she spared no outlay in order to increase the success of her receptions. Her table was abundantly supplied. She attached to her person a host of ladies-in-waiting and maids-of-honour in order to make sure that the composition of her gatherings should be in accordance with her wishes. She was generous in her distribution of costly gifts to those about her, and showed herself very kind-hearted in finding husbands and providing dowries for young girls, spending a great deal on clothes for her dependents and giving generous help to one and all. This conduct was not calculated on her part. For her husband was young and strong, and she had nothing to expect or to fear. But she was a woman of the world who loved to receive, and as she was in a position to do so, she indulged lavishly in her favourite pastime.

The Court became the centre of a society which was one of the most brilliant that has ever existed. Fair ladies and young lords full of life formed the magnetic nucleus attracting the best people in the kingdom, who flocked from all quarters. An uninterrupted succession of balls, musical evenings, and banquets took place. " The Court of Catherine de' Medici," wrote Brantôme, " was a veritable earthly paradise and a

122

school for all the chivalry and flower of France. Ladies shone there like stars in the sky on a fine night." The Queen presided over everything with grace and dignity. " You alone are Queen," Pietro Aretino told her, " you are both woman and goddess ! " Much more intelligent than her husband, she extended her patronage to artists and men of letters. She employed Della Robbia and Léonard Limosin, the enamellist, chose Amyot as a tutor for her children, and arranged performances of the works of Mellin de Saint-Gelais. Later on in the seventeenth century she was credited—as a matter of fact erroneously—with the introduction of refinement into the French Court by the inculcation of Italian manners. Surrounded by charming princesses—her sister-in-law Margaret, a dainty and distinguished personality who presented Ronsard to her, and encouraged du Bellay—her son's little wife, Mary Stuart, and her own daughters, she directed this life of luxury and pleasure with tact and discrimination.

For her husband, that distinguished, somewhat cold, but extremely fascinating prince, she had a real passion. She worshipped him and was terrified of displeasing him, though she was fully aware that Henry II felt nothing but respect for her. In 1560 she wrote to her daughter, the Queen of Spain, " You have seen me as contented as yourself, never imagining the possibility of any other trouble than that of not being loved as well as I could wish by the King your father, who honoured me more than I deserved. But I loved him so much that, as you know, I was always afraid." The knowledge that she did not possess the whole of his affection was a cause of unhappiness to her ; and she stood in dread of alienating him even further. When he went out to war, she put on mourning and begged the Court to pray for the success of their absent King. She brought up her children to respect their father, and after his death she revered his memory.

Henry II thoroughly appreciated his wife. He felt her superiority and had great faith in her judgment. But she never inspired him with love. In the course of time he drew nearer to her and would tell her political secrets, ask her advice, and give proofs of a sympathy which, as a matter of fact, he had always felt. In public, he never failed to show her every

123

possible mark of respect, honour, and deference. But his heart and his affections were in the keeping of another.

The royal couple were long without children. They had none for ten years, and Catherine began to despair. There was **Henry II's** some talk of annulling the marriage. Catherine **children.** threw herself in tears at the feet of Francis I, offering to sacrifice herself, and consenting to retire into a convent. Francis I, with his usual gallantry, raised her up, and kissing her, told her that she was his daughter-in-law and was to remain so. Subsequently she had ten children in thirteen years, thus giving rise to some little consternation. "As their Majesties are yet young," wrote one of the ambassadors, "they are afraid of having more children than they ought, for the King is desirous of leaving to each one of them a heritage in keeping with the greatness of his name." Catherine was a very good mother. She was sedulous in her attention to the smallest details in the lives of the young princes, and, when she was separated from them, wrote every day to their governess, Madame d'Humières. Her two daughters, Elisabeth and Claude, she decided to bring up herself.

Three out of the ten children, a boy and twins, died in infancy. The seven others consisted of four sons and three daughters. Elisabeth, the eldest girl, eventually became Queen of Spain ; the second, Claude, was given to the Duke of Lorraine, whilst the third, Margaret, was the vivacious, intelligent and sparkling Margaret of Valois, the wife of Henry IV, "Queen Margot," as she was called, whose life was so gay and so brilliant. Of the four sons, the youngest, Francis, Duke of Alençon, died young, and the three others were the last three Kings of the House of Valois—Francis II, Charles IX, and Henry III, the feeble scions of an exhausted race, dying out amidst the pleasures, the festivities and the bloodstained dramas of an involved policy.

The eldest of the whole family, the Dauphin Francis, was, at the age of fourteen, a fairly pleasing youth. He was well-proportioned and his figure was made yet more attractive by the becoming Henri II costume of about 1555. He favoured his mother, rather than his father. Of a melancholy temperament, and subject to fits of anger and obstinacy,

124

he was also lazy, a characteristic which was extremely irritating
to his father. Henry II adopted in his case the opposite
system to that which Francis I had followed, and made his
son attend council meetings when he was quite young, in order
to initiate him into his duties. In 1558, when he was fourteen,
Mary Stuart. his father married him to the only daughter
of the King of Scotland, Mary Stuart, who came to live
at the French Court. This exquisite, dainty child, destined
to a tragic end, was very fair, with delicate features. She
was the joy of the Court, " that little Scottish queenlet, who
had only to smile to turn every Frenchman's head," wrote
Catherine de' Medici. She sang well, played the lute, and
was an excellent musician. She was also learned ; she knew
several languages, could write in Latin, took lessons in poetry
from Ronsard, and was loved by all with whom she came in
contact. Henry II delighted in her. " The King has taken
such a fancy to the queen, your daughter," wrote the Cardinal
of Lorraine, to the Queen of Scotland, Mary Stuart's mother,
" that he is content to spend a whole hour in talking to her,
and she is quite as capable of entertaining him with good and
wise conversation as a woman of five and twenty."

But in addition to Catherine de' Medici and Mary Stuart,
there was another woman who filled the Court of Henry II
with the brilliance of her name and the splendour of her reputation : Diane de Poitiers. Hers is a singular history—the
strange romance of the heroine whose fame was sung by poets,
whom artists depicted in so many admirable forms, and who
throughout the centuries has preserved such an extraordinary
halo of love and beauty ! The truth is more modest, and
perhaps more enigmatic.

Born in 1499, Diane was the eldest daughter of Jean de
Poitiers, Sieur de Saint-Vallier, a gentleman of Dauphiny, who
Diane de   had been compromised in the plot of Constable
Poitiers.   Bourbon by the fact that he had not revealed
what he knew about the conspiracy. Diane has been credited
with having saved her father's head by sacrificing her honour,
an episode upon which Victor Hugo founded his play *Le Roi
s'amuse.* It has been proved, however, that this act on her
part was neither probable nor even possible. She was married

at the age of fifteen to a humpbacked old nobleman, Louis de Brézé, Count of Maulevrier, Lord High Seneschal of Normandy, to whom she was faithful. She bore him two daughters and was left a widow at the age of thirty-three. She raised a superb mausoleum to her husband, still to be seen in Rouen cathedral, and made a vow to dress always in black and white She was a tall, beautiful woman, of majestic bearing, proud ·and imposing. She bore a certain resemblance to the Countess of Chateaubriant, though, to judge by the drawings of the period, her features were less refined. But she possessed greater distinction of mind and character. Extremely cold and calm, she had a resolute spirit and a well-balanced judgment. Her letters, which have been published, reveal no sign of a romantic imagination, but rather a precise and definite common sense, combined with a certain dryness, and a lack of enthusiasm and spontaneity.

Henry II, while he was still Dauphin, saw her at Court and fell deeply in love with her. He was seventeen at the time and she was thirty-six. His family was very angry and Francis I reprimanded his son severely, but without effect; for in later years, Henry II was able to remind Diane that he had not been afraid to risk losing his father's favour on her account. Catherine de' Medici was greatly distressed, but Henry II was immovable, and as soon as he became King he made no further attempt to hide his infatuation. He created Diane Duchess of Valentinois, overwhelmed her with gifts of money, and loaded her with crown jewels, which she kept until his death. He took her with him on his journeys, and at each place where he was given a reception the authorities in their speeches made allusions to the favourite, whilst on the triumphal arches, crescents, or figures of Diana the Huntress accentuated their flattery. Henry II adopted her colours— black and white—as his own. He chose as an emblem a crescent moon, and when he wrote to her he signed his letters with the familiar monogram of an H and two interlaced crescents which might also stand for two D's (Diane). His letters, which have been published, bear witness to the extreme tenderness he felt for her. "I cannot live without you," he would say; "He who loves you more than himself"; "I beg

126

you to remember him who has known but one God and one love." Henry II preserved this passion in all its intensity to the day of his death. In 1558 he worte to Diane, " I beseech you ever to remember one who has never loved and never will love any woman but you. I pray you, my beloved, wear this ring for the love of me." Yet he was forty-two at the time, and she was nearly sixty, old enough to be a grandmother, with grey hair and wrinkled cheeks !

This passion lasted until old age, faithful as a friendship. Henry and Diane were both religious, and used to pray for one another. " Do not forget my paternosters," the King used frequently to write to his mistress when he was on a campaign. Moreover, although Catherine de' Medici was violently jealous of her, Diane played the unexpected part of an attentive and sympathetic friend to the royal family. Owing to her influence Henry was an affectionate and considerate husband. Diane greeted the birth of each of the ten royal children with great joy, and if one of them, or the Queen, fell ill, she displayed a touching devotion, nursing them herself, sitting up with them at night, and showing them every attention. Every one noticed that Henry II never treated her with anything but the greatest respect. The King led a very regular life, and as Contarini points out, he never gave the least occasion for scandal on the subject of his relation to Diane. Marino Cavalli, also, mentioning the matter to the Venetian senate in a letter written in 1546, compared the connexion of Diane with Henry II to that of mother and son. Diane had a medal struck of herself upon which she was represented with the attributes of the beautiful goddess whose name she bore, spurning love beneath her feet ; it was surrounded by the symbolic device *Omnium victorem vici,* " I have conquered the conqueror of all " ; and Catherine de' Medici in after years wrote to her son-in-law, Henry of Navarre, the future Henry IV, these words, the meaning of which is perfectly clear : " As for Madame de Valentinois, her position was altogether honourable ; but those women who were foolish enough to make a scandal about her, he (the King) would have been sore displeased for me to keep in my service." And, finally, Henry II, in a piece of poetry, laboured and clumsy enough, which he composed in honour of his friend and the original draft of which corrected by his own hand is still in existence, declares the chivalrous nature of his passion :

> Et si n'estime rien que sa bonne grâce,
> Car autre chose ne veux ni ne pourchasse.*

insists on Diane's calmness :

> Et si ne crains tromperie qu'on me fasse
> Etant tant sûr de sa grande fermeté ;
> Impossible est qu'un autre ait donc ma place
> M'ayant donné si grande sûreté.†

and emphasizes the respect in which he holds her :

> Quand j'aperçois mon partement soudain,
> Et que je laisse ce que tant estimai,
> Je la supplie de vouloir donner
> Pour grand faveur de lui baiser la main.‡

In the light of all these facts it is open to question whether Brantôme and posterity have not been deceived by appearances, which certainly seem to justify all their suspicions, and whether we are not here confronted by the exceptional case of an intelligent and ambitious woman, who, flattered at having inspired so ardent a passion, encouraged it, but intentionally kept it within the limits of a respectful friendship, and turned it to account in order to exercise a power that found expression in useful and salutary counsels. May she not thus have inspired a devotion for which the King had never to blush either in the sight of God, his family, or his kingdom ? At all events, the point is doubtful.

An intelligent woman, gifted with moderation and a sound judgment, Diane possessed conversational powers which were

* Nothing I value but her kindly grace . . .
Nor seek nor follow after aught beside . . .

† No fear afflicts me that she may deceive
Who am so certain of her steadfastness ;
That any rival should usurp my seat
Can never be, while such safeguards are mine !

‡ When I perforce must face the sudden hour
Wherein I part from all I dearly prize,
I pray that she may deign to offer me
The supreme favour—leave to kiss her hand.

a source of infinite delight to Henry II, who confided all his secrets to her, and consulted her on all affairs of State. Her firmness and independence made her a source of happy inspiration to the King. " She was an extremely clever and generous lady," writes Brantôme, " with a great and noble heart, and as such she could not advise, exhort, or persuade the King to anything save to grand, lofty, and generous actions. And this, indeed, she did, as I know on reliable authority." " She was good, charitable and extremely generous to the poor," continues Brantôme. She was a woman of taste, and made great improvements at Chenonceaux, which Henry II had presented to her. In the place of the old manor of Anet, the seat of the de Brézé family, she entrusted Philibert Delorme with the building of the magnificent castle so well known to fame, for the decoration of which she employed the greatest artists of the day. The King used frequently to visit her at this sumptuous abode, and would stay for some time with all his Court, and even receive ambassadors there. As the King's gifts had made her extremely rich, she was able to meet the expenses involved without embarrassment.

The sufferings and tortures of jealousy endured by Catherine de' Medici were unspeakable ! But she bore them in silence, though her hatred for the favourite, in spite of the correct appearances she maintained, was violent in the extreme. As soon as Henry II died, the Duchess of Valentinois was obliged to leave Court, and the crown jewels were taken from her as well as Chenonceaux. " The Queen disliked her so much," says Reguier de la Planche, " that she would have liked to go much further, ruin her completely, and despoil her of all her wealth." Saulx Tavannes seriously offered to cut off Diane's nose, but the Queen refused. She was obliged to tread warily. But in the meanwhile during the King's lifetime, Diane was all-powerful in the State. High and low addressed themselves to her. " It is impossible to exaggerate the pitch to which the omnipotence of the Duchess of Valentinois has attained," said the Florentine Ricasoli. She was one of the most important members of the King's Council. The others either owed their influence to her, or were chosen for qualities of mind that resembled her own.

The chief of these counsellors was the Constable Anne de Montmorency. On the day following his accession to the **Henry II's** throne, Henry II, whom his father had kept **Advisers :** aloof from affairs of State, and who was, conse- **Constable** quently, quite inexperienced, summoned the man **Montmorency.** who had so long held the reins of government under Francis I : Constable Montmorency. As Dauphin, Henry II had had no very great fondness for him, but as King he placed the interests of the State above his own personal predilections. He proved his wisdom in so doing. Anne de Montmorency, a man of fifty-six, sound, sturdy, intelligent, and with the details of administration at his finger-tips, was endowed with practical common sense and prudence, and was above all lucky, for almost everything he had done up to that moment had been attended with success. The only accusa- tion brought against him was that of harshness and arro- gance. He was not much of a favourite at the Court, and at times he gave way to inexorable brutality. For instance, on the occasion of the revolt of Bordeaux in 1548, against the levy of the salt-tax, when the Governor Monneins was killed by the people, the Constable hastened to the scene of insurrection with some troops and twenty cannon. He razed the town-hall to the ground, abolished the privileges of the city, and forced the inhabitants to make honourable amends by digging up the body of Monneins with their fingers in order to give him a proper burial. He then, according to Vieilleville, had over a hundred persons hanged, broken on the wheel, and beheaded. But, on the other hand, he was also reproached with having moments of extreme caution, which were attributed to cowardice. Henry II had great confidence in him ; he consulted him in everything and evinced the liveliest friendship for him. Some of his letters to the Constable are still in existence, in which the King calls him " my friend " and styles himself "his good friend." This affection was both intimate and touching, and sprang from a close sympathy in their ideas and views on the questions which formed the subject of their common deliberations. Although Lorenzo Contarini de- clares that Diane and Montmorency were but rarely in agree- ment, if we are to judge by the letters that passed between them, they seem, on the contrary to have been united by a similar sympathy, the King forming the bond of union. The King and the favourite used to write joint letters to the Constable, signing them : " Your oldest and best friends, Henri, Diane." Montmorency, who had twelve children, five sons and seven daughters, took great pains to push them and find positions for them. He was also solicitous for the advancement of the children of his sister, Louise de Montmorency, wife of Gaspard de Châtillon, Sire de Coligny, who had been made a Marshal under Francis I. On this side he had three nephews, who were destined to become famous and to be converted, all three of them, to the Protestant faith : Odet de Châtillon, Archbishop of Toulouse, and afterwards Cardinal de Châtillon ; Gaspard de Coligny, the Admiral ; and Francis, Seigneur d'Andelot, the Colonel-General.

In addition to Montmorency, Henry summoned to his council board, Jacques d'Albon de Saint-André, his old tutor, whom he held in high esteem, and made a Marshal of France, and also Duke Francis of Guise, a strange and attractive figure, destined to win great popularity by his victories and to perish by assassination during the religious wars, a man whose family played a very prominent part in French history !

At the beginning of the century a younger son of the House of Lorraine, the third son of Duke René II, who could find no **The Guises.**   opening at home, had come to France to seek his fortune. This was Claude of Lorraine, Count of Aumale. He fought bravely at Marignano, and as a reward Francis I created him Duke of Guise in 1527. His brother, the Cardinal of Lorraine, was a very influential member of the King's council. The power of the family increased by leaps and bounds. Claude married Antoinette of Bourbon, the great-aunt of Henry IV, and by her had eight sons and four daughters, a brilliant family which was destined to fill the latter half of the sixteenth century with the splendour of its achievements. The eldest of these was the Francis of Guise mentioned above. He was about the same age as Henry II. They had been brought up together as boys, and had a lively sympathy with each other, born of ideas and tastes in common. Francis

131

was a man of sterling worth ; he possessed good sense, judgment, an extremely lucid mind, and a tenacity that was proof against every assault. He was one of the most remarkable generals that France has ever had. Full of energy and with a keen eye for the right course of action, which he carried out with elegant mastery, he inspired the greatest confidence in his soldiers, and trained them admirably. Monluc has done him justice. "There was nobody," he says, "who did not hold him one of the most alert and diligent lieutenants that could be found in our day, and, moreover, one so full of wisdom in choosing a course of action that after he had given his opinion it was impossible to find a better." In the council he was always in favour of vigorous decisions. Until the death of his father (1550) he bore the title of Duke of Aumale, but when in succession to the aged Claude, he became Duke of Guise, he passed on the title of Aumale to his third brother, who was also called Claude. Another of his brothers, Charles, the next in age to himself, who was born in 1524, was made Bishop of Rheims at the age of fourteen, and became Cardinal de Lorraine after his uncle of the same name. He was twenty-three when Henry II ascended the throne and summoned him to the council. He afterwards managed the exchequer with great ability, but was unpopular on account of his avarice and want of frankness. Louis, the third brother, also went into the Church, and became Archbishop of Sens and cardinal in 1553—he was known as the Cardinal de Guise. The fifth, who was named Francis, like his eldest brother, became General of the Galleys and Grand Prior of France, whilst the youngest, René, was the Marquis of Elbeuf. As for the eldest sister, Mary, a marriage was contrived for her with James V of Scotland, by whom she became the mother of Mary Stuart, who in her turn was given to Henry II's son, the Dauphin.

All the members of this family made brilliant matches. Duke Francis married an Italian, Anna d'Este, a granddaughter of Louis XII, through her mother Renée, Duchess of Ferrara. The Duke of Aumale found a wife in one of Diane de Poitiers' two daughters, an expedient union which, through the agency of the favourite, contributed with various other causes towards securing the unique position at Court enjoyed by persons who

132

became more and more powerful every day. Their prestige was indeed extraordinary! The younger branch of a foreign ruling house — the House of Lorraine; connected with the royal family through Renée of France; brothers of a Queen — the Queen Regent of Scotland; uncles of Mary Stuart, the future Queen of France; supported by two cardinals, one of whom, it was said, even aspired to the Triple Crown, the Guises were superior to all the best families in France and enjoyed a political position that had no parallel!

Montmorency, Francis of Guise, and Marshal de Saint-André formed the nucleus of the council which Henry II summoned to his side to help him in the task of government. They were the three chief personages in it. " Through the hands of this trio," says Monluc, " everything passed," and they guided the policy of the nation. Montmorency was the chief. " The counsellor of whom the King makes most account," wrote Capello, " is the Constable; for he is the senior in age and the man whose advice and exploits have best proved his zeal and devotion." At the beginning, he tried to monopolize the King's favour, more particularly by inviting him to his castles at Chantilly, Écouen, and l'Isle-Adam, and endeavoured to establish himself as the sole master. But in this he did not succeed.

Henry II has been accused of being a pale shadow, devoid of initiative and intelligence, and guided entirely by his coun-

Precision of Henry II's policy. sellors, who did exactly as they pleased. But to prove the error of this view it would only be necessary to call to mind the events which took place after the disaster of Saint-Quentin, when the King, deprived of his three advisers, showed great resolution in the conduct of affairs. As a matter of fact, though he had formed this council at the beginning of his reign, by reason of his inexperience, he derived so much benefit from its deliberations, that he thought there was no need to make any change. Very different in character—Montmorency's love of temporizing contrasting with the vigour and activity of Guise —these counsellors were of one mind with the King in matters of practical common sense. Now Henry II was a man of a

133

very lucid mind. "He is very definite," wrote Marino Cavalli, "and very firm in his opinions. When he has once said a thing he abides by it." From the very first hour of his reign he showed his love of regular and sober living, by changing the over-dissipated tone his father had given to the Court. He reduced the balls and receptions, cut down the expenses of festivals, and exacted less boisterous and more decorous manners. In politics, with the help of his counsellors, he adopted a line of conduct which made his reign one of the most remarkable in French history, for no other was marked by the pursuit of so wise and healthy a policy—a policy absolutely French, and exclusively concerned with useful and tangible realities. This policy may be summed up under three heads:

Renunciation of Italian Wars. the ending of the interminable wars which for fifty years had been ruining the country; the definite renunciation of the absurd Italian will-o'-the-wisp, which had beguiled France out of her natural channels; and, finally, the re-opening or creation of these natural channels by turning all martial endeavour in the direction in which there was a real necessity for expansion, that is to say, to the north and the east, to regions French in language and race, where the close proximity of the frontier to Paris made hostile attacks extremely dangerous, and the smallest defeat fraught with the gravest menace. He waged three wars one after the other. During the first he took Boulogne; during the second Metz, Toul, and Verdun; and during the third Calais—all lasting conquests. The coping-stone of his reign was the Peace of Cateau-Cambrésis, which once and for all put an end to the disappointing expeditions for the conquest of Milan and Naples, and secured him in the acquisitions he had made. "His Majesty in the course of conversation with me," wrote one of the ambassadors, "seemed to covet peace rather than to desire the greatest victories." But if it was necessary to wage war, in order to force the enemy to make peace, the King was of opinion that the French nation "would find it more profitable to turn in this direction (the east and the north) than to Italy." The problem thus clearly defined was firmly and resolutely solved. And the credit for this is due to Henry II.

Of all the passions that stirred the breast of Henry II on his accession to the throne in 1547, none was so profound and **Henry II's** vital as his hatred of Charles V. The memory of **hatred of** the painful hours spent in Spanish dungeons had **Charles V.** been ineffaceably branded on his heart. " As for the Emperor," wrote the Venetian ambassador, " the King hates him and boldly declares his hatred. He wishes him all the evil that it is possible to wish one's most mortal foe, and this complaint is so virulent that the death or the complete undoing of his adversary alone can heal it ! " Henry II's first act was one of defiance and anger against his enemy. Forgetful of the formal treaties by which France had renounced all suzerainty over Flanders, he summoned the Emperor, as a French vassal, to his coronation. The Emperor replied that he would come, but at the head of 50,000 men, and it was clear that the truce between the Empire and France could not last. Henry II realized this and made his preparations. He raised troops, made sure of his usual allies, Turkey and Pope Paul III, and in the spring of 1548 carefully visited his frontiers in Champagne and Burgundy, the provinces which were in the occupation of France, and also Savoy and Piedmont. Before coming to blows in this quarter an episode took place with England. Mary, the sister of the Guises, Queen Regent of Scotland, was having great difficulties with her Protestant subjects, who were supported by Edward VI, King of England. At the urgent instigation of the Guises, Henry II consented to help her, and sent her 6000 men. Amongst other things, there was a question of preventing Edward VI from marrying Mary Stuart, and thus uniting the Crowns of England and Scotland, and of arranging a marriage between the young princess and the Dauphin, Henry II's eldest son. A rupture naturally followed with England. Hostilities broke out here and there, and finally Henry II and Montmorency marched upon Boulogne, which was **Capture of** at that time an English possession, and laid siege to **Boulogne, 1550.** it. The English Government was paralyzed for the moment by conspiracies. It opened negotiations, and con- sented to surrender Boulogne for the sum of 400,000 crowns on March 24, 1550. This was the young King's first victory.

The state of affairs in Germany was propitious for an

attack. After having conquered the rebellious Lutheran princes, and crushed the Elector of Saxony at Mühlberg in 1546, Charles V considered himself the undisputed master of the Empire. Drafts for changes in the constitution were accordingly submitted to him by which the elective principle was to be abolished, and the Imperial Crown made hereditary in his family, thus establishing his uncontested omnipotence. Charles V proved hard and dictatorial. In order to shelve the irritating religious question, he had conceived the extraordinary plan of appointing two Catholic theologians to collaborate with one Lutheran in the drawing up of a sort of declaration, a compromise, which, pending the decision of a general council on these matters, he authorized his subjects of the reformed faith to believe and to practise—Communion in both kinds, the marriage of priests, &c. This basis for beliefs that were to be tolerated was called the Interim of Augsburg. It raised a regular tumult in the Empire. What business had the Emperor to interfere in matters that did not concern him ? Why did he presume to settle points of doctrine which did not fall within his sphere ? The towns refused to recognize the Interim. Fearing that Charles V might succeed in becoming omnipotent in Germany, and in view of his despotic proceedings, the German princes sought a fresh opportunity for rebellion. Alone and unaided they could not do much ; they were perforce driven to ask the support of the monarch whom they knew to be the irreconcilable enemy of Charles V, the only ruler in Europe, moreover, strong enough to help them at that moment —Henry II. From Augsburg, where the Diet of the Holy

Negotiations with the German princes. Roman Empire was sitting, an embassy was dispatched to Fontainebleau, consisting of over a hundred horsemen headed by William, Count of Nassau, the father of William the Silent. The deputation was very well received. The French treated the envoys with great courtesy, and a ball was given in their honour at Fontainebleau, after which discussions were held. The Germans explained that they had been sent by the States of the Holy Roman Empire, to solicit the alliance of the King of France. They had been outraged by the behaviour of the Emperor, who was threatening all the rights, privileges, and statutes of Germany. The Free Towns of the Empire more especially found

136

themselves menaced. They were too weak to resist, and incapable of offering any opposition to the designs of Charles V, who merely laid hands on their territories and added them to his own domains. Three towns, Metz, Toul, and Verdun, which were in close proximity to the French frontier, were at that very moment the objects of the Emperor's designs. If Henry II would consent to give his support to the German princes, the latter saw no reason why the King of France should not temporarily occupy the three towns in question, in order to protect them from the Emperor's ambition.

Henry II admitted to his council that he was very much tempted by the offer of the three French towns ; that he did not intend to occupy them merely temporarily, but "to turn them into a pretext for the extension of the boundaries of his kingdom." This, however, would mean immediate war. Francis of Guise supported the proposal hotly. An excellent soldier, skilful and vigorous, he was all eagerness for the campaign. Anne de Montmorency would have preferred waiting a little longer. But in either case a favourable reply was the only answer that could be given to the Germans, and a treaty drawn up in due form and order was at all events necessary. The German princes gave their consent to the treaty, and, after some discussions, Maurice of Saxony signed in their name the secret convention of Friedwald with Henry II in October, 1551. By the terms of this convention the King of France was to receive the title of " Vicar of the Empire " in the four imperial towns of Metz, Toul, Verdun, and Cambray. The Germans thus obviated the difficulty of abandoning certain of their towns to a foreigner, by making that foreigner enter the imperial system. In return for this the King, in addition to giving them armed support, promised the princes an immediate subsidy of 240,000 gold crowns and, prospectively, regular monthly payments of 60,000 crowns.

It only remained to begin operations. In February, 1552, Henry II made up his mind. In a public manifesto he declared

Conquest of the three Bishoprics, 1552.

war against the Emperor, and confiding the Regency to Catherine de' Medici, he set out for Châlons, where an army of 40,000 men had been collected under the command of Francis of Guise and Montmorency's nephew, Gaspard de Coligny. The nobility of France hastened to join the standards, and the troops were full of enthusiasm, for it seemed clear that in marching eastwards to the conquest of French territory in the direction of the Rhine, a route had once more been discovered which would lead to really useful achievements. As a matter of fact Henry II and Francis of Guise were nursing rather more extensive plans than those proper to a mere Imperial Vicar in three or four towns. Pont-à-Mousson was occupied without striking a blow ; Toul delivered up its keys, and Nancy threw open its gates. At Metz an escort managed to make an entry under some pretext and seizing the drawbridges, let in the rest of the troops. The behaviour of the King of France gave rise to some anxiety. Until that moment the French army had pushed forward boasting, in the words of Tavannes, that " it was marching for the liberty of Germany," and the towns, held in awe by fear of the Emperor, had hailed the deliverers with joy. But now, instead of halting or returning in the direction of Verdun, Henry II was continuing his onward march and penetrating into German-speaking territories, and it was asserted that he meant to let his horses drink the waters of the Rhine. His reception became colder. He succeeded in making an entry into Hagenau and Weissenburg, but Strasburg closed its gates in his face and swore that not a single French pikeman should be allowed to enter. At Spires, the citizens informed Henry that they were quite willing to receive him, but that he must come into the town alone without the shadow of an escort. Public opinion was alarmed, and foresaw the possibility of the King of France over-running the country as far as the Rhine. Disquieting intentions were attributed to him, as, for instance, that he would maintain that these regions had once formed part of France, including the whole of Alsace ; Austrasia was a name given to a fairly wide dominion which extended a long way north. Everywhere the town walls bristled with arms, and it was becoming difficult to advance without turning a hitherto peaceful progress into a bloody march. The German princes were grumbling. Henry II became anxious, and judged it wiser, for the moment, at all events, not to proceed any farther, lest he should compromise the results he had already obtained. He turned back—a course

138

prompted by the profoundest wisdom. One of his regiments occupied Verdun, and excited by the ease of the conquest and occupation of territories which it seemed so natural should return to the possession of France, the troops began to murmur at what they called the King's weakness.

Meanwhile in Germany matters had come to a head. Suddenly attacked by the princes, Charles V, taken by surprise, **Treaty of Passau, 1552.** was hustled and hunted down by Maurice of Saxony, who followed him in hot pursuit. He fled to Innsbruck, with Maurice close on his heels, and was obliged to escape on a mule in great haste, almost alone, across the Tyrol, and seek refuge in Carinthia. His brother Ferdinand, who was forced to sign the Treaty of Passau in his name, on August 2, 1552, granted all the demands of the German princes—the confirmation of the German constitution, that is to say of the Golden Bull, and permission for the Protestants to practise their religion without let or hindrance. The German princes, who were now satisfied, felt that they had no further need of the alliance with Henry II, whose conduct irritated them ; and Charles V, consequently, found himself at liberty to turn with all the forces at his command against the King of France, with the object of recapturing the towns which the " Imperial Vicar " had thought fit to appropriate. Moreover, the princes now joined him, and in September, 1552, 80,000 Germans marched against Metz to drive out the French troops.

Francis of Guise had been the heart and soul of the French conquests, and it was Francis of Guise whom the King appointed **Charles V besieges Metz.** to march to the defence of Metz against the blow that was about to fall. He was given the title of the King's Lieutenant-General in the three bishoprics. The affray looked as though it would reach important dimensions. Crowds of the nobility and of the best families in France flocked, full of zeal and ardour, to join the army : the Prince of Condé, the Duc d'Enghien, the Duke of Aumale, the Prince of Roche-sur-Yon, Monsieur de Nemours, the Marquis of Elbeuf, and the Vidame de Chartres. And indeed the defence of Metz proved one of the great feats of arms of the century. But, above all, it rooted firmly in the popular imagination the warlike renown

139

of the skilful and energetic general in command of the place, and brought into marvellous relief his active qualities of vigour and intelligence.

With the help of his engineers, Piero Strozzi and Marini, Guise immediately repaired the tottering walls of the town. He made entrenchments, put up supports, and pulled down houses and whole suburbs in order to clear the outskirts. From morning to night he was in the work-yards encouraging the soldiers by word and deed. It is even said that he himself and his officers used to help carry the hods. Owing to his forethought, provisions in large quantities were stored. There was plenty of ammunition, and he had powder magazines installed, and organized in advance the hospitals in which the illustrious Ambroise Paré, who has left us a stirring account of the siege, was to win such great distinction. He laid cannon, even placing them on the church steeples by means of platforms. Not content with the forces he had brought with him, he enrolled the able-bodied men of the district, divided them into twelve ensigns or companies of infantry, and had them instructed and trained under severe discipline. He divided the defence of the town up into sections, at the head of each of which he placed a responsible officer, and distributed his troops skilfully, declaring that he could hold out for ten months.

On September 15, Charles V set forth in person at the head of his army, which was under the command of the Marquis of Marignano and the Duke of Alba. He crossed the Rhine, and on October 19 laid siege to Metz. The Imperial troops, amply supplied with provisions of every kind, placed 114 cannon in line. Guise made a few sorties in order to get a change of air, and in one of these his brother d'Aumale was taken prisoner. The Emperor had divided his army into three camps, and had encompassed the town completely. On November 26 the bombardment was begun ; the trenches had already been opened. The besieged defended themselves vigorously. The Duke of Guise, who never left the ramparts, gave orders to all with perfect clearness and self-possession, having the breaches filled as soon as they were made, the walls rebuilt and the platforms repaired. For a whole month the

140

bombardment was kept up. The imperial army used over 15,000 cannon balls, but thanks to the tenacity of the defenders the shots proved futile. The approach by way of the trenches had been no more successful. Meanwhile the winter was making itself felt with cold bleak weather ; there were falls of snow and sharp frosts made the ground as hard as iron. The besieging army, insufficiently provided with shelter, was exposed to terrible sufferings. Some of the soldiers fell in the trenches never to rise again ; the rest dragged themselves along numbed with cold, shivering, with their feet in the frozen mud. Epidemics broke out ; the losses of the imperial army became a hecatomb. It was said that 20,000 or 30,000 men had died and the rest wished to take to flight. Charles V realized that
Retreat of Charles V. his cause was hopeless, and on December 26, after a bombardment of thirty days, forty-five days entrenchment, and sixty-eight days siege, he gave the signal for departure. Bertrand de Salignac, who has left us an account of the siege, describes the terrible shock the defenders of Metz received on visiting the deserted camp. In the midst of miserable accumulations of rubbish of all kinds they found the dead and the dying, half-frozen soldiers and others lying ill in the mud and the filth. Guise had all who could be moved carried into the hospitals, where Paré amputated the limbs of a good many. And the fame of the Duke of Guise rang through the length and breadth of France.

Three months later (in April, 1553) Charles V, determined as ever, in spite of a painful attack of gout which racked him from head to foot, dispatched to the northern frontier a fresh army, which invaded Picardy and captured Hesdin and Thérouanne. On hearing the news that the latter town had fallen into his hands, the Emperor gave orders for it to be razed to the ground. Its destruction caused universal mourning. The French armies did not march until July, and Montmorency was bitterly reproached for the delay. He was always in favour of peace and hoped that it would be secured, with the result that he was never ready at the right time. And owing to his excess of caution the army of 40,000 under his command did not accomplish much, but merely kept watch and ward over the country.

Hostilities were renewed in 1554. The imperial army, attacked in the direction of Hainault by Antoine de Bourbon **Battle of** and Marshal de Saint-André, at first fell back, **Renty, 1554.** but it took the offensive once more under the command of the young and distinguished Duke of Savoy, Emmanuel Philibert, who pushed the French towards the Boulogne district, and forced them to fight at Renty near Saint-Omer. Charles V was present at the battle, carried about in a litter on account of his gout. Duke Francis of Guise, who was in the front ranks, had to meet the shock. With a vigorous onslaught he charged the enemy, and breaking their lines, succeeded in capturing seventeen ensigns, five standards, and four cannon. Unfortunately, Montmorency, who was in command of the main body, considered it more prudent not to support him, and, as the Imperialists held their ground, the engagement seemed indecisive ; finally the French beat a retreat. But the brilliant conduct of Guise added to his popularity. The following month, everything dragged, as the opposing armies found it impossible to accomplish anything. Charles V had retired to Brussels.

All at once the unexpected news was noised abroad that he was going to abdicate ! Endless conjectures have been made **Abdication of** as to the reasons which drove the powerful **Charles V.** Emperor to descend from the throne, he, the master of Europe and the ruler of dominions so vast that since the days of Charlemagne no monarch had been so formidable, he, the despotic, cold, and determined character that history depicts ! Discouragement at his want of success has been urged as a cause. " Fortune is a woman," he said, " she does not love old men ! " It has been asserted that he was weary of the terrible complications of a government which had to fight in Germany, fight on the frontiers, and enter into discussions and conflicts everywhere. His religious feelings have also been held responsible, and the need he felt for retiring into a cloister to end his days in silence and repentance. There is some truth in all these explanations, although the self-reliant and self-possessed character of Charles V must make us accept his alleged discouragement with some reserve. As a matter of fact, his body was crippled by suffering, and it was impossible for him to attend to affairs of state. Gout had cramped all his limbs and shaken him by constant severe pain. " I suffer so terribly," he confessed to the Venetian ambassador, " that I am sometimes forced to bite my hand and pray for death ! " One day when Coligny brought him a letter from Henry II he could scarcely open it, owing to the stiffness of his fingers. "Am I not a brave knight," he remarked sadly to his visitor, " to rush out and break a lance when I can only open a letter with the very greatest difficulty ! " The disease had aged him terribly. Although he was only fifty-three, he was worn out, white-haired, pale, and wrinkled. He sat huddled up in a chair covered with black cloth in a room which some morbid whim had made him have draped entirely with black. He could bear no more. The idea of abdicating had been in his mind for some time before he carried it into execution ; he had long considered the advisability of such a course. He would have liked to hand over to his son, the future Philip II of Spain, who was twenty-eight at the time, the whole of his power, including the Empire. But the German princes refused to be ruled any longer by a Spaniard who had other things besides their welfare to consider. The Protestants, moreover, had no liking for a Catholic prince whom they had every reason to consider dangerous. At the very first overtures that were made they refused to accept Philip as Emperor. After cruel deliberations with himself Charles V decided to leave the Crown of the Holy Roman Empire to his brother, Ferdinand, and keep the rest of his possessions for his son. He handed them over to him one by one, as though he did so tentatively with regret, reserving to himself the position of a supreme master, who could come to a decision at the last moment and go back upon his deeds. He passed on to him one after the other the government of Milan, Naples, the Netherlands, and last of all of Spain. The final scene of the abdication took place on October 23, 1555, at Brussels in the presence of a vast concourse of nobles, courtiers, and the representatives of the various states of the Netherlands. It presented a spectacle that was impressive in its grandiose solemnity—the shrunken old man, looking ghastly white in his black dress, with features distorted by suffering, pronouncing from an armchair raised aloft under a canopy, the few short words which were to transform him from Emperor of the Holy Roman Empire, King of the Spanish dominions, obeyed and held in awe by the whole of Europe, with a name known and respected throughout the world, into an ordinary private citizen, shortly to become a sort of monk. He spoke very slowly, declaring that the state of his health made it impossible for him to continue in the exercise of power, and that he transmitted this power to his son, whom he commended to them all. Philip of Spain was kneeling before him. He laid his hand on his head, and in a voice that shook said: "My beloved son, I give you absolute possession of all my heritage and commend to you the service of God and justice." He then gave him his blessing. His emotion was so great that, according to François de Rabutin great tears " coursed down his pale and withered cheeks and dropped upon his white beard." He then rose, and begging Philip to take the seat he had left, he descended two steps and listened to the new sovereign, who returned a few words of thanks in accents as broken as his own. The proceedings were brought to a conclusion by the administration of the oath of allegiance to the nobles who were present. Charles V went into retirement in Spain, in the monastery of San Yuste in Estramadura, where he died two years later.

When Charles V disappeared from the political stage it became easier for France, which had hailed his abdication with **Truce of** unconcealed joy, to accept a cessation of hos- **Vaucelles, 1556.** tilities. Henry II had always expressed his esteem for Ferdinand, " speaking with respect of his rare virtues and the goodness of his character," and he had no feeling of animosity for Philip II. In default of peace, the details of which it was too difficult to arrange in haste, a truce for five years was signed on February 5, 1556, at Vaucelles, near Cambray, on the basis of the *statu quo* for both sides. This provided a respite. The nation was tired out, and the precarious condition of the exchequer made a period of rest imperative. But, as the word implied, it was nothing more than a truce. From the moment when, during the first discussions, it had been realized that it was impossible to come to an understanding with regard to a definite peace, the vista of fresh campaigns to be undertaken at some future date remained

144

open. By striking the enemy in his weakest spots France would certainly succeed in finally forcing him to the desired end. But for the time being it was necessary to wait.

Francis of Guise, however, whether urged by impatience to fight, or spurred by ambition, or for some other obscure reason, **Guise's** unearthed the rights which he inherited from his **expedition** ancestress Renée of Anjou over the kingdom of **to Italy.** Naples, and asked leave to go and conquer his Italian possessions. Were the chimerical expeditions of former years once more to be repeated ? Montmorency offered a lively opposition to the project, and urged the necessity of reserving the strength of the nation for the approaching conflict with Spain, and of consolidating the frontiers of France whilst scrupulously observing the truce. But backed by Diane de Poitiers, who already saw her son-in-law, d'Aumale, the brother of a King, and also by all the young nobility who were consumed by the desire of following the lucky Duke Francis to fresh victories, the Guises ended by having their way. They were, however, only given 13,000 men. As early as 1554, the King had already lent a gracious ear to the overtures of Monsieur de Termes and some cardinals in Tuscany, who wished to bring about the revolt of certain towns against the imperial sway. Amongst others, Siena had taken up arms, driven out the Spanish garrison, and prevailed upon the King of France to send a force to defend her in case of attack. Strozzi had been dispatched with Monluc and some troops. The town had been besieged, and Monluc had defended it valiantly during a memorable siege made famous by his descriptions of it, which are not free from a certain Gascon exaggeration. But in the end Siena capitulated. Guise accordingly set forth. He manœuvred cleverly, anxious, above all, not to allow any encroachment to be made upon his slender forces, when suddenly a messenger arrived bringing him the news that the King of France had suffered a terrible disaster at Saint-Quentin, and recalled him immediately. What was the disaster that had occurred ?

The expedition against the Kingdom of Naples had made a conflict with Spain inevitable, and war had been declared on January 1, 1557. The government of Philip II, determined to see the matter through vigorously, had collected an army of

K

145

50,000, to which Queen Mary of England, as an ally of Spain, had added a contingent of 6000 men, the whole under the command of the clever and active Duke of Savoy, Emmanuel Philibert. This army crossed the frontier and came and laid siege to Givet. Montmorency was bitterly reproached for his weakness and indecision. Perpetually clinging to the hope that hostilities would not be pushed to extremes, and that he could go on temporizing whilst seeming to keep the peace, he had not collected a sufficient body of troops—barely 26,000 men—and he continued to maintain an attitude of prudent circumspection. Public opinion grew impatient; he was accused of being a "pusillanimous creature and a coward devoid of spirit," and satiric sonnets were circulated at his expense. The imperial army, gaining courage, then made a **Disaster of** vigorous advance and laid siege to Saint-Quentin. **Saint-Quentin,** This time the position of affairs was extremely **1557.** grave, for if Saint-Quentin fell, the road to Paris would lie open. The Parisians were in a state of utter dismay. Coligny threw himself into Saint-Quentin with 700 men, an absolutely insufficient force; he had neither the provisions nor the ammunition he needed. Montmorency made a rapid advance in order to try, if there were yet time, to introduce into the town the reinforcements and provisions which d'Andelot, Coligny's brother, was bringing. With an imprudence incomprehensible in a man like Montmorency, who was generally so timorous, the Constable had the temerity to advance almost on to the enemy's lines, and swerved from his course towards the marshes which bordered one side of the town, in order to allow his troops to advance by night in boats. The boats stuck in the mud and the whole manœuvre was a failure. Thereupon Emmanuel Philibert, profiting by the false position in which the Constable found himself, thus isolated and with an inferior force, opened an attack. A clever general would have endeavoured to fall back in good order, covering his retreat by a series of squadrons on the defensive to protect it, arranged in echelons in favourable positions. But Montmorency gave hurried orders to retreat in columns, as though he had no enemy at his heels. Count Egmont collected all the Spanish cavalry, and charging the French rearguard vigorously, broke its lines.

146

The Constable tried to form the main body of his army into squares, but the imperial forces, galloping headlong upon him supported by all their artillery, charged him *en masse*, and in four or five hours he was overwhelmed.   In the end the French army was utterly destroyed.   The Comte d'Enghien, brother of Antoine de Bourbon, King of Navarre, had fallen, together with a whole host of nobles and soldiers.   Montmorency had been wounded and taken prisoner as well as Marshal de Saint-André, Longueville and Montpensier, whilst the whole of the artillery, baggage, and supplies, and eighty standards had been captured. Monsieur de Nevers, who gathered together the fugitives some distance away, was able to collect barely a thousand men-at-arms and a thousand cavalry.   No such disaster had occurred since the battle of Pavia.

In France there was universal consternation.   As the King no longer had an army to defend his country, the enemy had only to march straight on Paris, for they could meet with no opposition on the way.   And indeed Emmanuel Philibert advised Philip II, who had hastened to the spot, to turn the triumph of his arms to immediate account by marching forward. But upon reflection Philip II deemed it a necessary preliminary to seize the places on the route " in order to have the road behind him more open and secure for further advances and encroachments," says François de Rabutin.   The siege of Saint-Quentin was accordingly pushed on vigorously.   On August 27 the assault was made under the command of the Duke of Savoy. The town was captured, pillaged, burnt, and sacked ; Coligny was taken prisoner and sent to the Netherlands. Philip II then advanced towards Noyon.

When at last the news was received in France that Francis of Guise, summoned back from Italy and returning in hot haste, **Return of** had just landed at Marseilles, a sigh of relief **Guise.** spread through the whole country.   " Joy was everywhere aroused at the sound of his name," says Brantôme, " and in all places the people with one voice exclaimed : ' Now will this man with one touch set everything right and restore all that has been twisted and turned awry.' "

Henry II did not wait for Guise to return in order to take the steps demanded by the state of affairs.   He acted with

great manliness. Deprived though he was of his usual counsellors, he proved that he was a person of will and initiative.
Owing to his efforts, troops were collected from every quarter
and directed towards the places that were threatened. The
towns of Picardy were fortified with men and ammunition. At
his earnest request Catherine de' Medici attended the council of
the City of Paris and asked for 300,000 pounds, which were granted.
On all sides the nobility took up arms at the call of their
King. The towns, vying with each other in zeal, put themselves
in a state of defence and also sent help. There was a sort of
universal outburst of popular enthusiasm, so that when at last
Henry II was advised to leave Paris and seek refuge beyond the
Loire, he refused. " It only remains to be of good courage and to
be surprised at nothing," he wrote bravely to Francis of Guise.

And indeed the Duke of Guise was the only man upon
whom the King and country could rely to repair such a disaster.
In order to confer full authority upon him he was made
" Lieutenant-General-in-Chief in the interior and beyond the
borders of the realm," an exceptional rank which conferred
upon him the same authority as that enjoyed by the Constable,
who was then a prisoner in the hands of the enemy. He took
over the command of the small army which Henry II had just
collected at Compiègne.

This one movement immediately produced an unexpected
result. After the capture of Saint-Quentin and the march
against Noyon, Philip II's army had begun to melt away. The
English, who were tired of the business, had fallen off, and
mutinies had broken out. On receiving the news of the arrival
of a general of the Duke of Guise's determination, Philip II, who
had only an uncertain quantity at his back, came to the conclusion that a march upon Paris was out of the question. It would
be better to end the campaign before the favourable impression
produced by his recent successes had passed away. In October
he accordingly beat a sudden retreat and returned to Brussels.

What was Francis of Guise to do with his impatient army
all eager for the fray ? Public opinion demanded that some
Guise seizes effort should be made after the general impetus
Calais, 1558. given by the whole nation. The popularity of
the young hero was at stake, and he then conceived the bold

148

design of swooping down upon Calais. This port was an English town which had been captured by Edward III two hundred and ten years previously, in 1347, and was now so English that it seemed incredible that it could ever be French again. Guise, however, determined to take it by surprise as it lay unarmed for the winter behind the surrounding marshes, and capture it. No one ever dreamed of such a possibility, least of all the English, who were fully persuaded that Calais was impregnable behind its belt of wide marshland, its deep moats through which ran a river, and its lofty walls. Lord Wentworth, its Governor, had sent home part of his garrison. He had indeed heard rumours that M. de Sénarpont, the Governor of Boulogne, was nursing some vague scheme for taking the town by surprise, but the idea was so absurd that he had given it no further thought.

The engineer Strozzi was sent in disguise to make an examination of the ramparts, whilst Guise had boats collected with the profoundest secrecy all along the coast. Thereupon, when everything was ready, after a feint in another direction, on December 31, in bitterly cold weather, he made a rush for Calais. Fortified outposts guarded the road across the marsh. He bombarded them vigorously, took them by surprise, and then turning towards the sea, he attacked the fortress which commanded the port. The garrison was stunned with astonishment, and a fierce fusillade soon got the better of it. After this Guise directed his efforts against the castle. He placed his batteries on the beach and bombarded the citadel at low tide, covering up his guns when the water rose. As soon as a breach was made, d'Aumale made a vigorous assault. The castle was taken and the town capitulated. The English garrison consisted of 500 men only, but there was ammunition in quantities, huge magazines and 300 cannon.

The news was received with stupefaction! The capture with such marvellous speed of one of the most impregnable strongholds of Europe was " one of the miracles and most astounding feats of the century " ! François de Rabutin wrote that it was the work, not of men but of God : " The deeds of the Almighty," he said, " surpass all the powers and proposals of men however great they may be ! " Bonfires were lighted all over the country, and Henry II hastened to visit his new township. He ordered the English who had taken up their abode in Calais to be driven out, forcing them to sell their houses, and completed the seizure of what was known as the " reconquered territory " by taking Guines and Ham. When he returned to Paris with Guise at his side, the welcome he was given by the people was enthusiastic in the extreme. He was greeted with delirious acclamations of joy. His lucky general enjoyed unparalleled popularity, and the monarchy was still strong enough to bear this with equanimity. For the English, the blow was one of the most terrible they had ever received, and Queen Mary declared that if her heart were opened the name of Calais would be found graven upon it, so inconsolable was she at the loss of this stronghold.

In the following year, 1558, owing to hesitation on the part of Philip II and a desire to make peace on that of Henry II, hostilities dragged on. Guise had managed to raise an army of 50,000 to 60,000 men. In order to make use of them he marched against Thionville, which he captured with his usual luck and rapidity ; but to counterbalance this success M. de Termes, Governor of Calais, was worsted at Gravelines.

In 1559 it seemed that the time had come to consider whether circumstances were not more favourable for negotiat-**Treaty of Cateau-Cambrésis, 1559.** ing a definite peace. The French and Spanish plenipotentiaries met at the Abbey of Cercamps. Philip II was represented by Cardinal de Granvelle, the Duke of Alba and the Prince of Orange, and Henry II by Montmorency and Marshal de Saint-André, who were set free for the proceedings, and the Cardinal de Lorraine. The discussions were stormy. Both sides demanded that all the conquests the other had made should be restored— an agreement by which France would have been the loser. The English insisted above all that Calais should be given back to them. Mary Tudor meanwhile had died and had been succeeded by Elizabeth, the daughter of Henry VIII and Anne Boleyn. At this juncture Elizabeth, partly from conviction and partly from expediency, was inclining to the reformed faith, and Philip II, disgusted at her attitude, decided not to give his support to the demands of England. Finally it was decided

150

that Henry II should keep Calais for eight years, at the end of which period he was to pay 100,000 gold crowns if he did not restore it. Calais, as is well known, has remained French to this day. On the east, Henry II insisted upon keeping the Three Bishoprics. This was a question for the Emperor Ferdinand, who had his hands full for the moment with the Turks and the Protestants ; he made only a formal resistance before yielding. With Spain a rough-and-ready agreement was made. Philip II gave back Saint-Quentin and the neighbouring fortresses, whilst Henry II restored Thionville and Marienburg. As for Italy, the French Government determined to go to the root of the matter, and resolutely renounced all connexion with that country, solemnly renewing its definite abandonment of rights in Naples and Milan. Savoy and Piedmont were kept, but they were restored to their Duke, Emmanuel Philibert, who had put in a vigorous claim for them, as Henry II did not consider he had a right to despoil a third party unjustly. In order to save appearances it was decided that Emmanuel Philibert should marry Henry II's sister, Princess Margaret, who had waited so long for a husband. She was over thirty-six and possessed neither health nor beauty ; but she was gracious and amiable, beloved by all the Court, and Piedmont and Savoy was to be her dowry. But as a precaution Henry II kept, for the time being, a few places such as Turin, Pinerolo, Chivasso, and Villanova. Lastly, to cement the reconciliation with Spain it was arranged that Philip II should marry Henry II's daughter Elizabeth. Everything was at length settled, and on April 3, 1559, the Treaty of Cateau-Cambrésis was signed.

This treaty was one of the most important in French history. After the hard and arduous labours of the first Capets who had to establish their authority in their own possessions ; after the painful efforts of their successors, who had to consolidate the whole of France under their sway, the French Kings had undertaken the task of extending their power beyond the borders of their own country. The campaigns in Italy had been a mistake ; an obstinate determination to make distant conquests in foreign regions, which it was impossible to keep and ruinous to regain, whilst neglecting territory which was really French and whose proximity to Paris made its annexation doubly indispensable, was irrational. The Peace of Cateau-Cambrésis put an end once for all to the Italian wars which had lasted for sixty-five years, and turned the attention of France to the north and the east, that is to say, into its proper channels. The populace was fully aware of the significance of this, and hailed the peace with unfeigned joy.

But on the other hand the "military party" were loud in their recriminations and protests. To abandon Italy, Discontent of which for half a century had provided an un-"Military rivalled school for those who wished to learn the Party." art of war! To sacrifice Savoy and Piedmont, a number of towns and fortresses and quantities of supplies, by a mere signature without striking a blow! Nothing more outrageous could be imagined! "Those who loved France," moaned Brantôme, "wept at the thought!" "In a single hour and by a single stroke of the pen," exclaimed Vieilleville, "to give up everything, and with three or four drops of ink to sully and besmirch all our glorious victories in the past, was indeed depressing and degrading to our souls!" Brissac and Monluc joined the chorus. Monluc declared that 180 fortresses were being surrendered, and calculated that something like a third of the kingdom would be lost, while in the opinion of Brissac, Piedmont alone was worth as much as Burgundy and Champagne together. "And thus France evacuated so many provinces, towns, and castles and such a wondrous tract of country, the conquest of which had cost the late King over forty millions in gold and a hundred thousand human souls!" Monsieur de Vigne, however, the French ambassador at Constantinople, wrote with greater judgment and political discrimination: "A second Salic Law should be passed to have the first man who advises the renewal of the Italian wars or the surrender or exchange of the towns of Metz and Calais, burnt alive as a heretic!" He was perfectly right.

In order to allow the people to join more heartily in the rejoicings at the consummation of peace, Henry II decided that The marriage the marriages of his sister and his daughter should festivities. be solemnly celebrated in Paris, and signalized by a long series of brilliant festivities in June, 1559. The Duke of Alba, accompanied by a magnificent escort of 500 horsemen, was sent from Madrid to represent the King of Spain. Emmanuel Philibert of Savoy came in person. The Parliament was moved to the Augustinian monastery on the quay in order that the whole of the Palace, which was decorated with tapestries, might be free. At the Tournelles, where Henry II was staying—the Louvre having been reserved for the Duke of Alba—a vast temporary hall was erected for the occasion. In the Rue Saint-Antoine, lists, enclosures for tournaments and jousts, were arranged with barriers and stands hung with tapestries.

The festivities began ; there was a succession of feasts and banquets. The Provost of the Merchants and Aldermen of Paris received the royal guests at the Hôtel de Ville. Tournaments and jousts followed one after the other and were attended by vast crowds of people who had collected from every corner of France, and who were delighted by what they considered the superiority of their own countrymen over the Spaniards. Henry II did not hesitate to take part in the games. Mounted on a trained charger and protected by heavy armour, he was anxious to break a lance. On June 30, jousts on horseback were held in the Rue Saint-Antoine. The King announced his intention of riding in them. According to custom he had to break three lances on his adversaries without being unseated. The first two he broke very neatly on the Duke of Savoy and the Duke of Guise. For the third his opponent was Montgommery, the son of M. de Lorges, his captain of the guard, " a tall stiff young man," says Vieilleville. The two riders charged each other and Montgommery gave the King such a fierce thrust with his lance that he almost unhorsed him. Henry II was provoked, and insisted upon having his revenge. His opponent hesitated and declined, but the King persisted and the contest had to be renewed. This time both lances were broken, but Montgommery, in raising the stump of his weapon, caught and opened Henry II's visor, and, as he was carried along by his horse's impetus, his broken spike went into the King's eye and pierced his brain. The King fell forward on to his horse's neck, clasping it with his arms. The animal was stopped and the prince was taken down, laid flat and undressed, after which he was carried to his room, where five or six surgeons tried to extract the splinters. But their efforts were futile, and for nine days Henry II lay **Death of** unconscious. On the tenth he died, at the age of **Henry II, 1559.** forty-two. On the eve of his death the religious ceremonies of the marriages were quickly performed at midnight. "The proceedings were more like a funeral procession and obsequies than anything else." The consternation among the people was universal. Catherine de' Medici was beside herself, and remained for a whole day prostrated by grief without being able to utter a syllable. "I am afraid she will have a terrible illness," Mary Stuart wrote to her mother. And for the rest of her life Catherine de' Medici wore mourning for the man she had loved so well and who was torn from her in such a tragic manner !

SOURCES. *Lettres de Catherine de Médicis*, ed. La Ferrière and Baguenault de Puchesse ; Brantôme, *Œuvres complètes*, ed. Lalanne ; Tommaseo, *Relations des ambassadeurs venitiens*, 1838 ; Alberi, *Relazioni degli ambasciatori veneti al senato*, 1839 ; Maréchal de Vieilleville, *Mémoires*, ed. Michaud and Poujoulat (on this work *see* C. Marchand, *Le maréchal de Vieilleville et ses mémoires*, 1893) ; Gaspard de Saulx-Tavannes, *Mémoires*, ed. Michaud and Poujoulat ; Monluc, *Commentaires et lettres*, ed. de Ruble, 1864 ; François de Rabutin, *Commentaires sur le fait des derniers guerres*, ed. Buchon, 1836 ; Pierre de la Place, *Commentaires de l'état de la religion et république*, 1565 ; *Lettres inédites de Henri II*, 1818 ; J. B. Gail, *Lettres inédites de Henri II, Diane de Poitiers, Marie Stuart*, 1828 ; G. Guiffrey, *Lettres inédites de Diane de Poitiers*, 1866 ; Amb. Paré, *Relation du siège de Metz en 1552*, 1847 ; Bertrand de Salignac, *Le siège de Metz en l'an 1552*, ed. Michaud and Poujoulat.

WORKS. Leopold Ranke, *Histoire de France pendant le XVIᵉ et le XVIIᵉ siècle*, translated into French by Porchat, 1854 ; E. de la Barre-Duparcq, *Histoire de Henri II*, 1887 ; H. Bouchot, *Catherine de Médicis*, 1899 ; M. Hay, *Madame Diane de Poytiers*, 1900 ; F. Decrue, *Anne de Montmorency*, 1889 ; H. Forneron, *Les ducs de Guise et leur époque*, 1877 ; J. Delaborde, *Gaspart de Coligny, amiral de France*, 1879 ; Chabert, *Le siège de Metz en 1552*, 1856 ; Mignet, *Charles-Quint, son abdication*, 1857 ; Gachard, *Retraite et mort de Charles-Quint*, 1852 ; *La guerre de 1557 en Picardie, bataille de Saint-Laurent, siège de Saint-Quentin*, 1896 ; A. de Ruble, *Le traité de Cateau-Cambrésis*, 1889 ; P. Courteault, *Blaise de Monluc*, 1909.

CHAPTER V

THE DRAMA OF PROTESTANTISM. FRANCIS II

The rise of Protestantism in France; its favourable reception at Court at first; subsequent hostility of Francis I; statuette of the Virgin smashed in Paris, 1528; the posting of placards by the Protestants, 1534; several executions, 1535. Case of Merindol and Cabrières, 1545. Repressive policy of Henry II; the Edict of Châteaubriant of 1551; the trial of Anne du Bourg, 1547. The organization of Calvinism, its doctrine and discipline; Jean Calvin, 1509–1564. The first reformed church in Paris, 1555; the first synod in Paris, 1559. Francis II, 1559–1560. The Guises seize the reins of power. Growth and progress of Protestantism; increasingly repressive policy of the Guises, 1560. Press campaign on the part of the Protestants; discontent of the Catholics at the autocratic and miserly government of the Guises; the Conspiracy of Amboise, 1560. The executions following upon it; attempt to compromise the Bourbons in the conspiracy. Signs of the approach of civil war; the moderates succeed in securing the convocation of the States-General at Orleans; arrest of the Prince of Condé. Sudden death of Francis II, 1560.

" IN the year 1520," says the *Bourgeois de Paris,* "there arose in the Duchy of Saxony, in Germany, a heretical doctor of theology of the Order of St. Augustine, named Martin Luther, who said many things against the authority of the Pope and compiled whole books in his

Rise of Protestantism in France. desire to diminish it, writing also against the ordinances and ceremonies of the Church." These books penetrated into France, and Pope Leo X warned Francis I about them with a view to having them condemned. It was thus that the Protestant Reformation was first heard of in Paris. Following the instructions given, the Parliament had the trumpets sounded in the public places and proclaimed that all books by Martin Luther were to be delivered up on pain of imprisonment, with the result

155

that a certain Louis Berquin was convicted of having translated some of these works and was cast into gaol, whilst his books were burnt in front of Notre Dame de Paris. He himself would have been put to death had not Francis I intervened and begged that he should be let alone. Meanwhile the rumour was spreading that the new heresy was making converts in various places, and as a precaution mendicant friars were sent in 1523 all over the country to preach against the false doctrines. In 1525, a Cordelier was arrested at Grenoble, on the charge of having given utterance to Lutheran ideas, and one of the Lords Justices of the place, the Grand Commander of Viennois, sentenced him to the stake. This man was one of the first adherents of the Reformation to pay for his ideas with his life. The measure was hotly criticized, but people in the end came to the conclusion that it was justified on the ground that it was the duty of the magistrates to avenge the honour of the Almighty, which was outraged by heresy, and also to protect society ; for heresy upset society "and tended altogether to the subversion of human monarchy." The first step had been taken. In 1526, on February 17, "*veille des brandons,*" a young licentiate of law named Guillaume Joubert, aged twenty-eight, was sentenced by the Parliament of Paris to be conveyed in a cart to the Place Maubert and there to have his tongue pierced and afterwards to be strangled and burnt " for having held the doctrines of Luther." On August 28 a Picardy scholar was sent to the stake for the same reason in the Place de Grève. What were the doctrines professed by the new heretics ? The people were extremely vague on the subject. They maintained that the Lutherans wished to do away with the images of the Saints, refused the use of holy water, and objected to prayers for the dead ; and they accordingly held them in detestation. The magistrates, for their part, as the vigilant guardians of public order, would not allow any heresy to destroy that order, and consequently thought it their duty to punish the delinquents, who, by attacking the divine majesty and by blasphemy were guilty of an inexpiable crime that deserved capital punishment. As a matter of fact, owing to the comparative rarity of this criminal offence, sentence of death was passed readily enough for the sake of making examples, and Lutherans were either burnt or hanged—sentences which at the time were not regarded as excessive.

These first repressive measures did not stop the spread of the new doctrines. A strong current of criticism was beginning to make itself felt, and suspicion began to fall upon preachers, because even from the pulpit they declared that regrettable abuses certainly existed in the Church. Gradually the idea gained ground that there was obviously something to be said against practices which had needlessly been introduced into the Catholic religion, and at Court this point of view presented itself under a peculiar aspect.

Guillaume Briçonnet, Bishop of Meaux, was a man endowed with an open and inquiring mind. He loved learning and had gathered around him a band of erudite philologists, among whom were Guillaume Farel, a native of Dauphiny, and three men from Picardy, Gérard Roussel, Arnaud, and Jacques Lefèvre. These four philologists studied the Bible together in the Hebrew or Greek texts and hazarded some criticisms which seemed inspired by the Lutheran spirit. The Parliament of Paris was informed of the matter and appointed a commission to inquire into it. The four learned men took fright and crossed the frontier into Germany, whilst Briçonnet, who was reprimanded, made his excuses. But Farel and his friends had left behind them a small nucleus of followers.

It was this element of erudition that had first attracted the attention of Princess Margaret of Valois. Deeply interested as she was in anything that was new, Francis I's sister could not fail to be enticed by what appeared to her the results of research, and the irrefutable truths of philology. In 1527, she married Henri d'Albret, King of Navarre, who was on bad terms with the Papacy; for Julius II had excommunicated his father, Jean d'Albret, in 1512, and had given Spanish Navarre to Ferdinand of Aragon—an illegal manner of disposing of kingdoms that were not fiefs of the Church, against which the Kings of Navarre, supported by the King of France, had lodged violent protests. The Albrets were consequently perfectly ready to listen with favour to anything that was said against the Pope. As soon as she was installed at Béarn, Margaret of Valois welcomed

Margaret of Valois favours the Protestants.

157

Jacques Lefèvre to her house, as well as Gérard Roussel, who passed for a saint and whom she made her spiritual director. These men were not actually "Lutherans," but in the name of history they criticized the Catholic institutions of their day, demanding the Communion in both kinds, refusing to admit the strict doctrine of the Real Presence in the Eucharist as the Church did, and proclaiming that the Church had corrupted the purity of the religion of Christ by superstitious inventions. When Margaret returned to Francis I in Paris, she tried to make him share these new opinions with her.

As a matter of fact, the new teaching had already found a sympathetic echo in the frivolous society at Court. After all, **Attitude of** it was argued, why should it not be possible to **the Court to** take and keep hold of the substance of the Christian **Protestantism.** faith " just as Jesus Christ had founded it, and the Apostles had published it abroad and drawn it up in writing," and to reject " the superstitions and accretions " which had been added by time, recognizing only the pure Word of God and the life of the primitive Church ; to worship God in spirit and in truth ; to exercise that " Christian liberty that shakes off the yoke of superstition and man's traditions and clings to God alone," in short " to reform morals and do away with certain abuses that had crept into the Church." This did not mean separation from the Church. With their minds set at rest by such arguments as these " everybody," says Florimond de Raymond, " wished to sample the novelty." When the " sweet and soothing " fashion of singing Marot's French translation of the Psalms was introduced it was thought very beautiful. Everybody joined in the singing, and it became a regular furore at Court. " The metrical version of the Psalms attracted the souls of men by their harmony."

At first Francis I, in his easy way, paid no particular attention to the new ideas. Though he did not share them he did not regard them with antipathy. He had had Berquin released, and at one moment he even consented, at Margaret's request, to send to Germany for the Lutheran, Philip Melancthon, upon whose influence the princess counted to touch her brother's heart. But he gradually changed his mind on the subject. Francis I was after all a ruler, and in conjunction with his
158

counsellors, the Cardinal de Tournon and the Cardinal de Lorraine, he came to the conclusion that to favour the spread of heresy meant to compromise the unity of the State, to shake the foundations of the kingdom, and to lay himself open to all manner of trouble, as the populace would remain firmly attached to the Catholic religion. He made up his mind, and certain incidents shortly afterwards occurred which greatly incensed him.

On the morning of Whit Monday, 1528, the statuette of the Virgin which stood at the angle of Monsieur Harlai's house in front of the door of Petit Saint-Antoine's Church in the parish of Saint-Germain in Paris, was found mutilated. The heretics had smashed the heads of the Virgin and Child. Public opinion, which had already been roused against the Lutherans, was extremely excited, and there was a considerable uproar. The King and the government thought it incumbent on them to share the general resentment. Francis I promised a reward of a thousand crowns to anyone who would denounce the culprits, and replaced the mutilated statuette by a new one in silver. He brought it solemnly in person accompanied by an impressive procession in which all the parishes of the city were represented, as well as Parliament, officials, prelates, nobility, and gentry, surrounded by a vast concourse of people.

Parliament began to take severe measures. Louis Berquin, who was imprudent enough to draw attention to himself again, was once more arrested and tried. He frankly confessed his ideas, did not conceal the fact that he had written Lutheran books, and showed copies of them. He was condemned to death. The King was at Blois, and in order to prevent the royal intervention from saving the culprit as on the previous occasion, he was executed at once before the news could reach Francis I.

The Provost of Paris, the head of the criminal department, and all the judges tried cases and condemned the accused. When the Provost gave a lenient sentence, and the prisoner nevertheless appealed to the Parliament, the latter made the penalty more severe. But, as is always the case when persecution intervenes, the zeal of the adherents of "the new teaching," far from being cowed, merely grew stronger, and the Lutherans retorted by various reprisals.

The mutilation of the Virgin on Monsieur Harlai's house had been an isolated incident. But it was now repeated. In

Protestant outrages and Catholic reprisals. May, 1530, the statuettes of Our Lady, of the Infant Christ, of Saint Roch and Saint Fiacre, which stood at the angles of houses, were broken during the night, and each outrage necessitated an expiatory procession on the part of all the parishes. The Parliament, in scarlet robes, accompanied these processions and promised a reward of twenty gold crowns to any person giving information against a Lutheran culprit. The populace was furiously excited, and a further outrage, which was even graver and more audacious, brought their rage to boiling-point. On October 18, 1534, heretical placards were discovered posted up everywhere, attacking " the Holy Sacrament of the Altar and the honour of the Saints." There were even some in the Louvre, on the door of the apartments of the King, who happened to be away at Amboise ; and some were also taken to Amboise itself. There was a universal outburst of indignation. The King was furious, and commanded the magistrates of Paris to do " rigorous justice." They forthwith proceeded to make numerous arrests, followed by executions. The year 1535 was the first blood-stained year in the annals of Protestantism All kinds of people were arrested. It was quite enough for a man to have a Lutheran book in his house for him to be suspect. Shoemakers, woollen-drapers, printers, booksellers, clerics, rich merchants, scholars, and attorneys were seized, and the Parliament and the head of the criminal department vied with each other in condemning the culprits, who were burnt at the Halles, at the Croix du Trahoir, at the end of the Pont Saint-Michel, at the Place Maubert, at the Carrefour du Puits Sainte-Geneviève, and in the cemetery of Saint Jean ; at the pig-market they hanged in iron chains those who had been condemned to death, after dragging them on hurdles to the front of Notre Dame. Those who were most leniently treated were banished after doing penance by standing in their shirts with bare feet, holding a candle in their hands, in front of a church or during the celebration of High Mass ; they had previously been birched on a cart, and had had their goods confiscated. When the accused persisted in their blasphemies and refused to

160

recant, their tongues were cut out. Numbers of people fled in fear. The Parliament summoned seventy-three persons who had disappeared to stand their trial—among them Clément Marot. Men, women, and children of all ages and all ranks fell victims ; and public opinion signified its approval. Matters reached such a pitch that Francis I began to think the authorities were going too far. At his request Parliament stopped the persecutions. A lull followed, and the seventy-three Lutherans who had been banished by proclamation were authorized to return. Prisoners were released with a warning that if they were arrested again they would be sent to the stake. The King explained to the ambassador Giustiniano that he had some difficulty in getting heretics burnt, especially as it was not done in Flanders.

But the impetus had been given, and Francis I was obliged once more to see his magistrates, with the sanction of public opinion, exceed the limits he himself would have set. In the villages of Provence there were a certain number of people who were said to have held somewhat heretical ideas for a long time, ever since the thirteenth century. They drew their inspiration from the Holy Scriptures and maintained that as the words Mass, Pope, and Purgatory could not be found in the Gospel, they were not bound to accept them. These people hated Catholicism. They were known as the Vaudois. Attracted by a certain community of feeling, the Protestants studied their doctrines sympathetically, as those of precursors. The Vaudois, on their side, adopted the ideas of Luther ; and out of this certain incidents arose. The Vice-Legate of Avignon intended to lodge information against some of them ; they thereupon took up arms, and committed some acts of pillage and murder. The Parliament of Aix opened an inquiry into the matter, and having convicted the inhabitants of two **Case of** particular towns—Mérindol and Cabrières—of **Mérindol and** heresy, passed sentence on November 18, 1540, **Cabrières.** to the effect that these two places should be destroyed and their inhabitants banished. Francis I, who was annoyed by these proceedings, ordered the execution of the sentence to be postponed. But after the lapse of four years, the Parliament of Aix determined to put an end to the matter and, at the instigation of d'Oppède, the First President, and Guillaume Guérin, the Advocate-General, they appointed a commission of five members to proceed to the execution of the sentence. The commissioners made an agreement with Captain Paulin, Baron de la Garde, who let loose his soldiers and allowed them to commit all kinds of excesses. They massacred the people and burned twenty-four villages. It was said that the victims numbered 3000, whilst 900 houses were burnt down. The matter made a great stir in France and the King, in hot indignation, resolved not to allow such excesses to pass unpunished ; he ordered the magistrates of Aix to stand their trial before the Parliament of Paris. The proceedings dragged on interminably. Francis I did not live to see the end of them, and under Henry II, when ideas had undergone a change, after a final trial, which lasted for fifty sittings, d'Oppède and three of the commissioners, together with Paulin, were acquitted. Guillaume Guérin alone was found guilty of having forged certain documents, and for this offence was beheaded in the Place de Grève. On the whole, Francis I, although his ruler's instinct told him that it was impossible to countenance heresy without compromising the unity of the State, would have inclined to toleration had he not been irritated by various provocations. But his magistrates, who were whole-heartedly Catholic and anxious to preserve public order with a firm hand, over-ruled him.

Under Henry II, however, the aspect of affairs changed. Protestantism had continued to spread. Pierre de la Place, **Repressive policy of Henry II.** in his *État de la Religion et de la République*, says : " Men talked of nothing but the increase in the numbers of the Lutherans, in spite of the severe measures and punishments inflicted on them, and of the secret meetings which were held both by day and by night in many places, more particularly in the City of Paris." And, indeed, the Lutherans, formerly isolated individuals, had now formed themselves into groups, meeting secretly for common prayer and mutual exhortation. Like everything mysterious, these meetings excited the suspicions of the multitude, and one night the wrath of the populace broke out. In the Rue Saint-Jacques, in front of the Collège du Plessis, an assembly of about 100 or

120 people was discovered. Crowds flocked to the spot, and when the congregation tried to escape they were attacked and overwhelmed. The women were beaten, had their hair pulled down, and were rolled in the mud, whilst a few people were killed. Among those present were some ladies of rank— Madame de Rentigny, Madame de Champagne, and Madame de Graveron ; a Parliamentary lawyer, Monsieur de Gravelles, and an aged University Professor, Monsieur Clinet. Arrests were made, and the Parliament had the culprits burnt in the Place Maubert after their tongues had been cut out.

These meetings provoked a fresh outburst of persecution. Henry II, less broad-minded than his father, had not the sort of scepticism which predisposes to toleration. He was a stricter Catholic and was scandalized at seeing what he held to be divine truth a matter of dispute. Moreover, the progress of the Reformation, which daily became more threatening, constituted a growing menace to the State, and the Council was even more alarmed than the King. The first measure taken by Henry II in 1549 was to open a special court in the Parliament of Paris for the prosecution of heretics. It was called the " burning chamber " (*Chambre ardente*). In 1551 he published an edict known as the Edict of Château-briant, which classified in forty-six articles all the measures passed against the Lutherans and codified the laws dealing with them. It was high time, asserted the preamble to this document, that precautions should be taken. " The error grows from day to day and from hour to hour, and has become a common plague " . . . " this is the cause of God, in which every man is bound to lend a hand and use all his strength." The printing, sale, or possession of heretical books was accordingly forbidden, informers against heretics were to be given a third of their goods, and any individual convicted of holding Lutheran ideas was to be condemned to death. In order to free the Parliaments from the burden of prosecuting these crimes, inferior tribunals, called presidial courts, were allowed to take cognizance of them. But, in curious contrast to the state of affairs under Francis I, when the magistrates had been the most ardent instigators of persecution, the rumour now became rife that heresy, which was gaining

The Edict of Châteaubriant, 1551.

ground rapidly, had even invaded their ranks, and that they could no longer be trusted. The Edict specified that in future information might be lodged against judges who were suspected of negligence towards the Lutherans ; that every three months sessions, called mercurial sessions, would be held in the Law Courts, when religion would be discussed, in order to keep the magistrates true to right doctrine, and to discover whether any of them were tainted with heresy ; finally, that no man would be made a judge in future without producing a certificate to prove that he was a good Roman Catholic.

But it was not only in the ranks of the magistrates that the new ideas found converts. Every class in society was in turn corrupted. Under Francis I the nobility had for a time been drawn towards the new doctrines, but their convictions had not been very profound. Now, however, great personages **Heresy gains** at Court, nobles of high standing, and even princes **ground.** betrayed an intelligent sympathy with the heretical creed. In 1558, the Cardinal of Lorraine, who had been sent to the frontier of the Netherlands to arrange a peace with the Spanish Minister, Granvelle, Bishop of Arras, was informed by the latter that he possessed proofs showing that the kingdom of France was infested by Lutherans, of whom one of the most distinguished was d'Andelot, the nephew of Constable Montmorency himself. D'Andelot, he said, had just sent to his brother Coligny, who was a prisoner, a book which contained abominable language on the subject of the Mass. On his return to Paris, the Cardinal of Lorraine warned the King, who was irritated by the news and also, by reason of his affection for the Constable, somewhat embarrassed. However, he charged d'Andelot's brother, the Cardinal de Châtillon, to try to obtain from the culprit some satisfactory explanation on the subject of his beliefs. D'Andelot confined himself to declaring that no man should force him to say anything of which his conscience did not approve. At this juncture it chanced that he had occasion to visit the Château de Monceaux, where Henry II was staying. The King was unable to restrain himself, and questioning him sharply, asked him whether it were true, as people declared, that he regarded the Mass as an abomination. D'Andelot replied very firmly, that f the Mass were regarded as a propitiatory sacrifice for the sins of the living and of the dead, he certainly did regard it as " a detestable and abominable thing," in no wise instituted by God, seeing that the death of Christ constituted once and for all a sufficient sacrifice and oblation. Henry II indignantly ordered d'Andelot to leave his presence on the spot, and then had him arrested by his Master of the Robes, Babou de la Bourdaisière, and conducted by a strong escort under the command of Monluc to the Château de Melun, where he was shut up. D'Andelot's assurance proved the confidence he felt in the general progress of the new doctrine. His brother Coligny was a convert, as well as the King of Navarre, Antoine le Bourbon, his wife Jeanne d'Albret—daughter of Margaret of Navarre and Henri d'Albret—and Antoine's brother, the Prince of Condé, these three composing an important group of princes of the blood royal. The Bourbons, together with the Châtillons—d'Andelot and Coligny—were to form a kind of impressive and formidable general staff.

This spirit of confidence increased. It was certainly true that the magistracy was becoming more seriously infected every day. The criminal court of the Parliament of Paris showed itself singularly indulgent towards heretics, whom they no longer condemned, but merely sent before the Bishop. If the number of Lutherans was rapidly increasing, declared the Cardinal of Lorraine in anger, it was because the public knew the judges were conniving at heresy. The Government was extremely irritated. On one occasion, when Séguier, President of La Tournelle, came to the King for the magistrates' salaries, which had not been paid for twenty-two months, the Cardinal of Lorraine answered sharply, " Your salaries would not be kept back if you performed your duties faithfully ! " When Séguier answered that he did not think they had failed in this, the Cardinal exclaimed, " But you have ! For you are not punishing the heretics." The President protested. " You send them up to their Bishops," continued Lorraine, " a fine expedition indeed ! " Séguier replied that they could not pronounce against their consciences. " Then you are the cause," cried the minister, " that France is filled to overflowing with this vermin, which, trusting in you, brings forth and multiplies."

Shortly after this the mercurial session prescribed by the law was held. The King commanded the Bar to speak with great firmness. On the appointed day—the last Wednesday in April, 1559—the session was opened in the Augustinian monastery on the quay, as the Palace was engaged for the marriage festivities. The Parliament assembled in large numbers, some 100 or 120 magistrates being present. Bourdin, the Attorney-General, made a speech in which he vehemently arraigned the magistrates " for disaffection to the faith and adhesion to the false doctrines of Luther " ; which meant that La Tournelle did not condemn heretics to death, but let them go free contrary to the ordinances. There was a disparity between the sentences of the Grand Chamber, which carried out the edicts and those of La Tournelle, which merely banished Lutherans. This disparity was a " scandal " ! After the speeches were finished, the opinions of the members were asked in the usual way, and all the magistrates, one after the other, expressed their views. Those who had leanings towards the new doctrines bravely declared that abuses and errors had undeniably crept into the practices of the Catholic Church ; that numbers of good men were demanding the summoning of a general council to decide the matter, and to extirpate these abuses ; and that in the meantime it was only reasonable not to inflict capital punishment upon people who adopted a critical attitude, inasmuch as their objections might be proved by the council to have some foundation. Amongst those who were of this opinion were Du Ferrier, the President of the Court of Inquiry, and Antoine Fumée. The session was terminated before all opinions had been taken, and the further discussion of the question was adjourned till the next meeting. In the meanwhile the Presidents, Le Maître and Minard, went to the King to give him an account of the views that had been expressed at the mercurial. There was no longer any room for doubt ! the heretics had the effrontery to advertise their beliefs before the whole Parliament, and from the magisterial benches, under peculiarly irritating circumstances ! Henry II decided that he would be present at the next mercurial and listen to the speeches. At this session, over which the King presided, the Catholic magistrates demanded the application of the existing

166

edicts without any alteration whatever. But the counsellors, Claude Viole, Louis Dufaur, and Anne du Bourg, pronounced for the suspension of capital punishment until the council had met. Dufaur was highly intelligent, and Anne du Bourg, a young magistrate of thirty-seven, extremely eloquent. He made a passionate and vivacious speech in which he displayed more courage than prudence. When all was over, Henry II curtly ordered Saint-Germain, the Registrar, to read the minutes of all the opinions that had been expressed, and then declared that there were certain magistrates in the Parliament who had " strayed from the faith," and that he had decided to punish them. Thereupon, turning towards the Constable, who was also present, he ordered him immediately to arrest Louis Dufaur, Anne du Bourg, Claude Viole, Antoine Fumée, du Ferrier, and three others, whom a captain of the guard was to conduct to the Bastille forthwith. On his return to the palace the King, beside himself with rage, exclaimed " that he would go and see Du Bourg burnt with his own eyes." A judicial commission, consisting of a President of the Parliament, a Master of Requests, two counsellors, the Bishop of Paris and an Inquisitor of the Faith was appointed to judge the prisoners. Henry II, however, was not destined to be present at the end of the trial or " to see du Bourg burnt "—for Montgommery's lance laid him low a few days afterwards.

Far from arresting the spread of the Reformation, Henry II's repressive policy merely increased it. But in addition to these temporary conditions, a circumstance of considerable importance had for some time been conducing to the growth and spread of heresy : Calvin had just provided it with a creed, a discipline, and an organization.

Martin Luther, a vigorous and fiery spirit, had contributed not so much to the founding of a new " religion " as to the overthrow throughout Christendom of the ancient compact faith of the Middle Ages. He had begun by criticizing the abuse of putting up spiritual indulgences for sale by auction. Rome would not tolerate criticism of any kind, but Luther, sure of his ground, persisted, and supported by public opinion, extended the scope of his invective. In the face of coercive measures of the ecclesiastical authorities, who declined to enter into any discussions, but merely condemned him, he had opened an attack, arousing the enthusiasm of the multitude by his fiery eloquence in support of a cause which [was becoming popular. Little by little, carried away by his own feelings, and the favour of public opinion, he had succeeded in undermining the very foundations of Catholicism. And he thus destroyed the prestige of absolutism in the eyes of the people, who had hitherto regarded the teaching of the Church as the expression of eternal truth. Everybody now thought himself capable of dissecting the ark of the covenant, and of discriminating in accordance with his own private tastes, knowledge, and tendencies between doctrines he regarded as acceptable and those he rejected as false. Lutheranism to the subjects of Francis I was merely the right to criticize Catholicism. It was in this sense that scholars like Farel and his friends at Meaux were Lutherans, and, as a matter of fact, though they may have agreed upon the points to be rejected, they were not unanimous as to those that were to be accepted. It was reserved for Jean Calvin to formulate the creed of Protestantism.

Jean Calvin was born at Noyon in 1509. His father was a certain Gérard Cauvin (Calvin is the Latinized form of Cauvin), **Jean Calvin,** who was attorney, registrar to the diocesan courts, **1509–1564.** notary to the Chapter, and procurator fiscal to the episcopal county—in short, a sort of ecclesiastical lawyer. Thus, Jean Calvin's earliest recollections were connected with his father's quarrels with dignitaries of the Church. When on one occasion he was summoned to show his accounts, Gérard Cauvin refused. He was abused, threatened, and excommunicated, and in 1531 the unfortunate attorney died in disgrace and was denied religious rites at his burial. Charles, the eldest of his four sons, succeeded to his father's business, was in his turn excommunicated, and died three years later in similar circumstances. Jean Calvin, who was the second child, could hardly have been expected to feel sympathetically inclined towards Church officials. He was placed at the college of Noyon to begin his education, and was afterwards sent to Paris to live with his uncle, a locksmith, who made him attend classes at the Collège de la Marche and, later on, at the Collège de Montaigu. At the age of nineteen he went to study for a

168

law degree at Orleans, where the University was famous for its courses in jurisprudence. He was a diligent, hard-working student who ate little, was delicate in health, and suffered from a bad digestion. He was recognized as a scholar of a supple intellect with a great gift for dialectics. When he had taken his law degree he devoted himself to the study of Greek literature and developed a strong taste for literary subjects. He even abandoned the law, and gave himself up entirely to the humanities, returning to Paris at the age of twenty-two. In the following year (1532), twelve months after the death of his father, he brought out his first book, a commentary on Seneca's *De Clementia*. This reduced him to poverty, for he was not rich and the printing of his work was expensive. The feelings aroused in his heart by his family's misfortunes and his own studies had already prepared the ground, and he began to show a sympathetic curiosity about Lutheran ideas. He became a constant visitor at the house of one of his fellow-townsmen, a rich merchant of the Rue Saint-Martin, named Étienne de la Forge, who habitually entertained a whole band of heretical friends, among them Gérard Roussel. The development of Calvin's faith was slow and gradual and he passed through periods of great difficulty. The blood-stained year of 1535 proved fatal to the band of the Rue Saint-Martin. Étienne de la Forge was denounced and arrested, and on February 16 was sent to the stake. His friends were hounded down, and Calvin was obliged to flee in haste. He wandered about, going to Nérac, to Poitiers, and to Noyon, where he was recognized, arrested, and thrown into prison. Upon his release he crossed the frontier and reached Bâle, where he finished a book on religion which was destined to enjoy considerable success— his *Christianæ Religionis Institutio*, printed in 1536. Finally, in this same year, at the age of twenty-seven, he arrived at Geneva, as yet a modest and obscure young man.

An ancient town contemporary with the Romans, Geneva had had a turbulent history during the Middle Ages, owing to Calvin in perpetual disputes between its Bishop and the Geneva. Count, afterwards the Duke of Savoy, as to the lordship of its territory. In opposition to both competitors, the inhabitants had ended by declaring that they belonged to

169

neither, but were citizens of a free imperial town that ought to be independent. The partisans of this theory were called "the Libertines." This party endeavoured to gain support from outside. They succeeded, and formed a confederation with the cantons of Freiburg and Berne, whence arose the appellation *Eidgenossen*, the German word for confederates, and the origin of the term *Huguenots;* eventually, having driven out the supporters of the Duke of Savoy—the Bishop's adherents had long since disappeared—they remained masters of the situation. Geneva became a kind of free republic governed by a grand council under the vague suzerainty of the Emperor of Germany. Lutheran ideas were favourably received there and developed without much difficulty. At one moment they met with some opposition, but the grand council decided to allow the citizens absolute freedom of belief. Whereupon heresy grew so rapidly that it ended by establishing a majority in the city. At this juncture, a phenomenon occurred which, as we shall see later, was repeated in France. The Protestants, having acquired the ascendency, decided that it was impossible to tolerate "error, idolatry, and superstition in their midst," and that it behoved them to "shake off the yoke of the Roman Antichrist." Accordingly, on August 27, 1535, the grand council forbade the exercise of the Catholic religion in Geneva. The images and crucifixes in the churches were thrown down, the altars overturned, and the priests banished. From this time forth Geneva became the sanctuary of the new creed and a refuge for the fugitives from persecution in France, who speedily flocked to its gates. One of the first of these was Guillaume Farel, whose gift of eloquence quickly won him a position of considerable influence in Geneva ; and in the following year, 1536, Calvin reached the city.

As he was obliged to work for his living, Calvin asked and obtained permission to give lessons in theology. He was favourably received on account of his remarkable precision, conciseness, and lucidity, and was admired for his learning, the thoroughness of his methods, and a certain inflexibility of character. It was not long before he was given leave to exercise the functions of a pastor. His success was rapid, and he speedily won a position of incontestable authority. Shortly after this

170

the pastors had a meeting to consider the question of compiling a catechism, and Calvin was entrusted with this duty. Thanks to the neophyte zeal of the Protestants in the city, the pastors' assembly possessed an extraordinary moral influence, capable even of checkmating the political powers of the grand council. In their religious enthusiasm, the pastors decided that with the view of making the morals of Geneva compatible with the Christian faith, disciplinary regulations should be drawn up to compel the inhabitants to practise virtue and eschew vice under threat of severe penalties. This amounted to the institution of ecclesiastical government. Calvin drafted the regulations, which were extremely severe. A number of citizens at once lodged a vehement protest against this invasion of matters of conscience in the domain of politics. A party was organized which claimed to defend the old families of Geneva, who were anxious to protect the liberties of the city, as well as the independence of the body politic against the " strangers," as they called them. The pastoral body retaliated by dubbing their adversaries " Libertines," and a fierce conflict was inaugurated. The Libertines gained the upper hand and drove out the pastors. Calvin, who thus became an exile once more, sought refuge in Strasburg, where he opened a fresh theological class in order to earn his livelihood, for he was in great distress and was obliged to sell his library and take in boarders. But in the meanwhile a revolution was changing the aspect of affairs in Geneva. Aggravated by the excesses of the Libertines, the people rebelled and returned a majority in favour of the pastoral party, now called the " Evangelicals." Calvin was recalled and returned on September 13, 1541. This time the pastors **Organization** had definitively gained the upper hand ; they **of Calvinism.** proceeded to enforce their disciplinary regulations and, at the instigation of Calvin, reorganized the city in conformity with his ideas. The functions of teaching the doctrines of the new faith and of administering the sacraments were assigned to the ministers. Twelve elected elders and the ministers together formed a consistory which kept watch and ward over the morals of the community, punished the guilty by reprimands, censures, and excommunications, and in cases requiring corporeal chastisement, summoned

171

the delinquents before the grand council. All luxury was prohibited ; festivals were forbidden, rejoicings were restricted, every man's opinions were scrutinized, and life was made sad and austere. Under the guidance of Calvin, whose authority daily increased, and who gradually succeeded in imposing his ideas upon the rest of his colleagues, religion assumed a severe and forbidding aspect. All ceremonies were abolished ; sermons, prayers, the reading of the Gospel, and the singing of the Psalms were considered sufficient. Baptism and the Lord's Supper being the only sacraments mentioned in the New Testament, Calvin preserved them, but the bread and wine of the Lord's Supper were regarded merely as signs or symbols and not, as in the Catholic Church, as the actual body and blood of Christ. By his sermons, and by his continual courses of theology, which soon became so famous that people from far and wide came to hear him, Calvin defined and circumscribed the faith. His fame spread through the length and breadth of France, and letters asking for instructions reached him from every quarter. With indefatigable zeal and prodigious activity, he carried on a world-wide correspondence, encouraging and fortifying his followers, recommending the foundation of churches on the model of the Church of Geneva, and upholding the persecuted, all in the language which made the success of his *Institutio Christianæ*—a style supple, concise, firm, and lucid, which places him in the ranks of the best French writers. Crowds flocked to his side. The population of Geneva, which in 1543 had numbered 13,000, rose in 1550 to 20,000. Calvin instructed the ministers and then sent them forth to preach the Gospel ; Geneva became the seminary and the " Rome " of Protestantism.

But whilst he defined the doctrines of Protestantism, Calvin was also determined to fix them categorically. With an extraordinary lack of consistency, the reformer, who had taken such liberties in connexion with Catholic doctrines, would not allow anyone to discuss his creed. He used to terminate the prayer with which he ended his sermons by asking God to preserve His Church from " all false doctrine, heresy, and schism, which are the seeds of trouble and divisions among His people." Rigid and merciless, he persecuted all who differed from him with inexorable severity. Sebastian Castellio, who had ventured

172

to dispute the inspiration of the Song of Solomon, was driven from Geneva, and certain pastors whose opinions did not seem above suspicion, or who were over-bold, were deposed, imprisoned, or banished. A certain Spanish doctor of medicine, named Miguel Serveto, attacked some of Calvin's ideas, to the extreme irritation of the latter ; and in his book *Christianismi Restitutio* Serveto dared to make certain assertions which Calvin regarded as inadmissible. Some time after this the Spanish doctor rashly supposed that it would be safe for him to pass through Geneva ; he was arrested, tried, and burnt there on October 27, 1553. Calvin was bitterly reproached with the death of this man, and in order to defend himself he wrote in 1554 his *Déclaration où il est montré qu'il est licite de punir les hérétiques.* And, indeed, the Protestants, true children of their age, after having repudiated the authority of the Catholic Church, continued to profess the intolerant opinions prevalent in their time. Melancthon agreed with Calvin ; and Theodore Beza published in 1554 his *De hæreticis a civili magistratu puniendis libellus,* in which he maintained that liberty should be allowed to truth, but denied to error, the devotees of which should be punished—a statement which was the very theory of the Inquisition itself. Castellio was the first to proclaim the necessity of liberty of conscience, and to maintain that ideas should be defended by ideas and not by the sword ; but it was some time before this opinion was accepted by the reformers.

His implacable spirit, supported by prodigious activity, indefatigable energy, and lofty unbending faith, is sufficient to account for the immense authority wielded by the founder of Calvinism. He wore himself into his grave. Exhausted by headaches and indigestion, gout, gravel, and asthma, his emaciated body and hollow cheeks revealing the weakness of his constitution, Calvin's life flickered out on May 27, 1564. He was fifty-five years old, and he died in poverty.

Thus it was at the instigation of Geneva and following in her footsteps that the Lutheran bodies who had met together **First Reformed** here and there secretly in France, organized them-
Church in selves into churches. In September, 1555, there
Paris, 1555. arrived in Paris a minister from Geneva, named La Rivière, who gathered together a certain number of converts

173

to the new faith in a house in the Pré-aux-Clercs. He was elected pastor, and had a consistory of elders nominated, thus founding the first reformed Church in Paris. Churches of a similar kind were afterwards created at Meaux, Angers, Poitiers, Agen, Bourges, Blois, and Tours, and at the end of two or three years, some twenty of them were in existence. Ministers from Geneva arrived in the towns all over the country, but if they did not find enough followers, or if, on account of the hostility of the people, secret meetings were impracticable, they went away. They preached and prepared the ground, and, as in Geneva, they read aloud from the Scriptures, prayed, exhorted their congregations, and sang psalms. When once it had been organized, the Church in Paris in its turn sent out ministers in all directions. These men, in concert with the assemblies, nominated the elders of the consistories, and these latter collected the money for the pastor's salary and for almsgiving. Advice and directions were asked from Geneva. Calvin had issued orders that the pastors should be well versed in theology, that scandals should be energetically suppressed, and that the lives of the faithful should be narrowly scrutinized. And thus, little by little, the organization of Geneva spread throughout the whole of France. Soranzo wrote in 1558 that the Protestants numbered 400,000. They were now called "the Calvinists," and their numbers became so large that it was thought necessary to complete their organization by securing the unity of all the churches among themselves. Variations existed in the doctrines that were taught, and, in conformity with Calvin's ideas, it was thought necessary to discipline the teaching and come to some agreement as to a general formulary. This led **The first** to the meeting in Paris in May, 1559, of the first **Synod in Paris,** national Synod, an imitation of the Councils of **1559.** the Catholic Church. This Synod, at which each church was represented by its pastor and its elders, sat in the Faubourg Saint-Germain and lasted for four days in the midst of perils and dangers without number. It adopted a formulary, the text of which was inspired by Calvin, and then proceeded to the regulation of discipline. All the churches were to be equal among themselves, and no one of them was to claim primacy; in every church the pastors were to be equal; the

174

representatives of several churches in the same neighbourhood were to meet together in assemblies called colloquies ; the representatives of churches in the same province were to meet once a year in provincial synods, and at the head of all was to stand the national synod. The Synod of 1559, which completed the foundation of the Protestant churches in France, formed the starting-point for the triumphant rise of Calvinism, which spread so rapidly that in 1561 there were over 2000 reformed churches in the country. It was this swift and unexpected growth which so alarmed the government of Henry II and caused that monarch such profound anxiety. And when he died, the future looked dark and disquieting indeed to the ministers of his successor.

This successor, Francis II, was a delicate and unhealthy boy of fifteen and a half. According to Régnier de la Planche, **Francis II,** he had " a pale, puffy face " covered with pimples **1559–1560.** and blotches ; he suffered from some affection of the nose—probably adenoids—and was, moreover, morose, taciturn, and obstinate. He was destined to reign only a few months, and his personality is a negligible quantity in history. He had been married to the charming Mary Stuart, and showed a tender affection for his " little wife." He passed his time by her side ; they were delightful to see, as they fondled each other and went apart from their companions to whisper unimportant secrets.

The Guises, taking advantage of their position as the Queen's uncles, at once seized the reins of power. Duke Francis had in his favour his brilliant military exploits and the prestige of his popularity and glory. His brother, the Cardinal of Lorraine, was already in the government ; both were powerful, fiery, and autocratic spirits. The Cardinal had everything connected with the finances and internal administration of the country in his hands. He was extremely clever, and a good speaker, and brought great application to bear upon all he did Grave in demeanour and dignified in person, he possessed much knowledge, more especially in the domain of theology. But he was treacherous, miserly, and violent in temper, He directed everything, his brother, the Duke, confining himself to military matters. It was impossible to resist them ! Their niece, the Queen, Mary Stuart, was on their side, and consequently the King himself. They were in possession of practical power, and they made their authority felt harshly, with the result that everybody stood in awe of them. Catherine de' Medici, the King's mother, finding that she was altogether powerless, adopted a cautious attitude of circumspection and reserve. She was now forty; she felt herself to be a woman of capacity, who could rule if she had the chance, and over her son, the new King, she maintained an ascendency which made him fear and respect her. But political events were for the moment too strong for her, and matters had so fallen out that she had no alternative but to wait in silence. Constable Montmorency held aloof. The Bourbons and the Châtillons remained. For the Guises, who were half foreigners, to be everything, whilst the Bourbons, who were princes of the blood, were ciphers, was intolerable. But at first the notorious sympathy of the King of Navarre and his family for the Reformation placed them, as well as the Châtillons, in a particularly false position. The Guises profited by the state of affairs to make the situation of their rivals even worse. They resolutely isolated the Châtillon-Bourbon group from Court, and on pretence of religious expediency, excluded them from the councils of state. Thus the stage was left free for themselves. The Bourbons and the Châtillons gathered together at Vendôme in order to see what could be done. Condé, who was hot-tempered and impatient, supported by the Vidame de Chartres, proposed having recourse to arms. Coligny, calmer and more cautious, and naturally straightforward and honest, was in favour of more conciliatory methods and suggested that they should appeal to Catherine de' Medici against the unauthorized usurpation of power by the Guises. The meeting voted in favour of this resolution, and Antoine, King of Navarre, was chosen to represent the case to the Queen Mother. Antoine was a quiet, irresponsible person, whose thin face, darkened by a short, sparse beard, and poorly illuminated by a pair of shifty eyes, masked a mediocre character, deficient in courage. He came to Court, where he had a very bad reception. Francis II kept him waiting two days for an audience, and when he finally granted it, treated him, in obedience to his uncles' instructions,

176

with marked coldness. When, disconcerted by this treatment, Antoine addressed himself to Catherine de' Medici, she gave him evasive replies, telling him that he must be patient, that in time things would arrange themselves, and that later on the Bourbons would return to their legitimate position of power about the King's person. The King of Navarre, who by this time was thoroughly disgusted with his mission, came to the conclusion that he must be contented with these fair words. Moreover, there was no one else to whom he could turn, as the Guises had secured the King's immediate circle by keeping him under the constant surveillance of their own friends and supporters, notably, the Chancellor Olivier, Marshal de Saint-André, and Marshal Brissac. By thus isolating the Bourbon-Châtillon faction on account of their Calvinistic proclivities, as well as with the object of keeping the rivals of their power out of the way, the Guises threw them into the arms of the Protestants, and ended by providing the latter with leaders.

Meanwhile, from all quarters news came to Paris of the daily increasing audacity of the Reformers. Thus in one small Growth and southern town, where hitherto the ministers who progress of came from Geneva had only been able to preach Protestantism. by night hidden away in private houses, they now dared to hold public meetings in broad daylight in the schools. If the magistrates hastened to the spot, with the object of reporting them, altercations ensued, and the ministers gave explanations, which, in the end, left the King's officials undecided what course to pursue. In other places, too, meetings were held with perfect freedom, and the number of Calvinists grew from day to day with astonishing rapidity. "The conflagration is spreading everywhere," wrote Soriano, and he was perfectly right. The Guises, ardent Catholics—especially the Cardinal of Lorraine, a man of uncompromising ideas—were also, as heads of the Government, devotees like Francis I of the principle of authority, which was compromised by the very existence of heresy. Naturally combative, energetic, and resolute, they revived and exaggerated the repressive policy of Henry II.

A series of merciless measures was the result. Edicts were published throughout the country commanding the immediate imprisonment of anyone known to be a Calvinist. Orders were sent to the judifical commission charged with the trial of Anne du Bourg to terminate the matter. Du Bourg had tried dilatory methods of procedure, appealing from one jurisdiction to another, maintaining that as a cleric he was entitled to appear before the episcopal judge in the Bishop's court, and raising an agitation through his friends. The trial was hastily concluded, but passions had been roused to such a pitch of excitement that one of the judges, the President Minard, was assasinated by a Calvinist. In the end du Bourg was condemned to death and executed. The Protestants called his death " a triumph," and the murder of Minard " the judgment of God."

The King's procurators, magistrates of all ranks and callings, bailiffs and sergeants bestirred themselves in the provinces with feverish activity. Everywhere there was a constant succession of citations, arrests, and imprisonments. The year 1560 was particularly calamitous. " It is impossible," wrote Hubert Languet, " for this to go on any longer. The prisons are full ! "

The Protestants, however, who now possessed a regular organization, with colloquies and synods, were in a position to combine and offer resistance, or at least to demand some abatement of the draconian measures with which they were being overwhelmed. It was useless for them to approach the King or the Guises, and, like the Bourbons and the Châtillons, they determined to address themselves to Catherine de' Medici. The Queen Mother made no sign. Possibly, she was not so rigid in her opinions as those who held the reins of government ; she represented a latent influence, and at least exercised some moral authority. Unfortunately, however, she was powerless, and once again, as in the case of the King of Navarre, she maintained an attitude of reserve. In her reply she confined herself to advising the Protestants to remain calm and to say nothing, adding a few vague words of toleration and peace.

Thereupon the Calvinists, the most fiery among whom, realizing the strength of their movement, had come to the **The Calvinists** conclusion that they had at least the right to **appeal to** demand liberty to meet and to preach, turned **the Bourbons.** to the Bourbon-Châtillon faction. After all, were they not princes and the highest nobility in the kingdom ?

178

How could they allow foreigners like the Lorraines to seize the government, drive them from Court, and use the power thus usurped to inflict intolerable persecution upon them, their friends, and their creed ? The Bourbons must be induced to return to Court, to drive out the Guises, and take their place. Once masters of the Government, they would put an end to persecution, and grant the Calvinists the liberty they demanded.

But they were once more unfortunate in having to deal with a man like the King of Navarre, who was not great enough for the part they wished him to play. The nobility liked him because he was cordial, good-natured, and, though he was not rich, generous, open and simple " in the true French style," says Giovanni Michiel, also gallant enough in battle though a mediocre general. But his was a soft nature, devoid of daring. He recoiled in terror. In vain did they try to act upon him by means of his wife, the intelligent Jeanne d'Albret, who, unlike her husband, was fiery and determined. Nothing came of it, and he refused his help. No other champion was to be found. His brother, the Prince of Condé, would have been more ambitious and active, but he lacked the solid qualities necessary for a leader, and, moreover, as he was a younger brother, it would have been difficult for him to undertake a task refused by his senior. As for the Châtillons, they had not the requisite authority.

The Protestant ministers, finding they could get nothing from the persons they had relied on, then decided to fight their
Protestant Press campaign. own battles with the only weapon they possessed —the Press. They multiplied their pamphlets and entered upon a campaign of eloquent and inflammatory polemics. " The blood of the just crieth aloud," wrote La Planche, " and God useth persecution as bellows to fan the flame of His Word ! " They made a passionate attack upon the Guises, denouncing their tyranny and their unjust usurpation of the royal power, and anathematizing their ambitions. What was their goal, they asked, but the appropriation of the Crown, the deposition of the King, and the usurpation of the throne by one of themselves ? After having driven away the princes of the blood, they aimed at nothing less than their destruction in order that every

179

obstacle might be removed from their path. And in the meanwhile they were ruining the finances, corrupting the Court, and sowing the seeds of hatred on every side. Now in connexion with the various points just enumerated the complaints of the Protestants found an echo in the breasts of others besides heretics.

The harsh and autocratic rule of the Guises had not been established without arousing a certain amount of discontent even among Catholics. After the Peace of Cateau-Cambrésis, in view of the financial difficulties of the situation—past debts and heavy liabilities to be met—the Guises had decided to make substantial economies. They had reduced the expenses of the Court, cut down the army considerably, and restricted pensions. These measures had called forth loud protestations from their victims. A large number of the nobility who had but slender fortunes and had hitherto made a livelihood by war, were deprived of their means of subsistence. Arrears of pay were due to them, and they laid claim to them. The straitened condition of the Exchequer made it impossible to satisfy them, but they insisted and agitated. The Cardinal of Lorraine was not the man to tolerate such methods of intimidation and showed himself hard and overbearing. Even under ordinary circumstances, says Brantôme, " he was extremely insolent and short-sighted, having no respect for persons, and showing them no consideration ! " A fierce animosity was kindled against him and his brother. The refusals were attributed not to the penury of the Exchequer, but to the avarice of the Cardinal, and loud murmurs were heard on all sides. Lorraine imagined that he could close people's mouths by holding out the threat of the gibbet for all grumblers, which did not tend to smooth matters. Thus there was a strong party among the nobles extremely hostile to the government of the Guises. The arguments of the Protestants went home, and a large heterogeneous political opposition was formed. From this opposition the elements of that strange enterprise called the Conspiracy of Amboise were recruited.

A certain gentleman of obscure origin, a native of Périgord, named François de Barry, Sieur de la Renaudie, was at this time roaming about the world. He had come into conflict

180

THE DRAMA OF PROTESTANTISM

with the judicial authorities in the past, had been compromised in a case against du Tillet, condemned for forgery and for uttering a forgery, and had been compelled to cross the frontier. He took refuge in Switzerland and became a Calvinist. His family had been unfortunate, and one of his brothers-in-law had been sent to prison by the Guises. He wandered about from town to town until the idea of attempting to wrest the power by force from the House of Lorraine and give it to the Bourbons germinated in his brain. On the part of this insignificant exile the notion was little short of madness. However, he confided his scheme to some Calvinist pastors, and even to Calvin himself. The pastors replied vaguely that even if it were wrong to make any attempt against the King himself, no doubt it might be allowable to overthrow a tyranny of usurpers. They did not attach much importance to La Renaudie's proposals, and Calvin, upon being pressed, avowed his disapproval of the idea. However, it became more and more firmly rooted in the mind of its originator, who returned to France secretly in the month of February, 1560. He went to Nantes, where the assizes of the Parliament of Brittany were being held at the moment of his arrival. These assizes had attracted a large number of people, amongst whom La Renaudie found some old friends, Calvinist gentlemen like himself. He talked to them, and entirely engrossed by his scheme, communicated it to them, but in the following cautious terms. He proposed that they should go in a body to the Court and present a petition to the King asking him to allow members of the reformed faith liberty to practise their religion. If they went in large numbers—several hundreds—the demonstration would make some impression. La Renaudie's secret hope, at which he merely hinted, was that if the manifestation were only large enough, a rising might perhaps be organized, which, if it succeeded, might lead to the arrest of the Guises. In the shape, however, in which he represented his plan—as a sort of petition—it seemed to his friends capable of realization. It amounted, in short, to a respectful and orderly proceeding which the King could not regard as abnormal, organized with the object of modifying the persecutions from which all members of the reformed faith suffered. The date and place of the

181

rendezvous was fixed for March 10 at Blois, where the Court
was to be staying. The main point was to ensure that the
members of the deputation should come in imposing numbers.
La Renaudie's friends told those they knew about the plan, and
asked them to pass the secret on in confidence. The news
spread from mouth to mouth and gradually assumed the aspect
of remonstrances to be made to the King on the subject of the
Guise government. From that moment the opposition joined
the movement. Among the crowd which was making for Blois
at the beginning of March were not only Calvinists, but also
officers and discontented soldiers demanding arrears of pay.
Meanwhile La Renaudie, still engrossed with his cherished
project—an attempt at a *coup de main*—confided his secret to
some of his most trusty supporters, and in order to secure
larger numbers, and more resolute auxiliaries, he recruited
bands of unemployed soldiers, though without informing them
of his intentions. He exhorted his adherents to keep the
secret and to come to the rendezvous one by one, or in very
small groups. In short, out of all the people who were on their
way to Blois in March, some, the hired soldiers, did not know
why they were going; others, the majority, believed they
were about to attend a mere respectful demonstration; whilst
an exceedingly small group were aware of the fact that it was
a question of provoking an insurrection at the last moment.
It is open to question whether the Bourbons and Châtillons
were in the secret. They probably knew something about the
proceedings, but were ignorant of the proposed attack. The
whole affair was very badly organized. It was ambiguous and
uncertain, at once too much and not enough of a secret, shared
by too many and too few, foolishly short-sighted and naïvely
cautious. The conspirators might have foreseen that the Government would never allow such a body of armed men, arriving
suddenly in so menacing a fashion, to approach the King, who
was always surrounded by his guards and well defended.

The Guises were informed of the enterprise in all its minutest
details by one of La Renaudie's friends, a Protestant lawyer
named des Avenelles, who lived in Paris. The instigator of
the plot had confided it to this man, who was alarmed at being
made the depository of a secret which might land him in a
182

criminal suit if he did not betray it. With men of the Lorraine temperament, the news naturally provoked an outburst of fury, the results of which were to become cruelly manifest.

As Blois was too open and not sufficiently isolated to be securely protected, the Guises decided to transfer the Court at a moment's notice to Amboise, which was more inaccessible, surrounded by high walls, and easy to guard. This sudden change upset the plans of the conspirators, and La Renaudie postponed the date of the rendezvous from the 10th to the 16th, substituting Amboise for Blois. The Government then took speedy and vigorous action. Bands of cavalry were immediately ordered to beat the woods in the neighbourhood of Amboise as far as possible, and to collect all the people they found in them. The conspirators arrived singly, one after the other, or else in small groups, and they were accordingly seized without any idea of what was going on. Some, who had clear consciences, offered no resistance. Others, seizing their pistols, were attacked and cut down, whilst a few succeeded in making good their escape. A certain number, who were warned in time, took to flight ; but most of the unfortunate victims walked straight into the trap. On the morning of March 20, La Renaudie, feeling somewhat anxious, was making his way through the forest of Château Renaud, when he found himself confronted by a troop of horsemen, commanded by Monsieur de Pardaillan. "Who goes there?" demanded Pardaillan. "Liberty!" replied La Renaudie. "Long live the King!" was Pardaillan's retort, as he bore down upon La Renaudie and fired his pistol at him. The shot missed La Renaudie, who, drawing his sword, plunged the blade into Pardaillan's body with deadly effect. But at this moment one of the latter's companions rode up, shot La Renaudie through the head at close range with his pistol, and killed him on the spot. Thus the chief of the conspiracy disappeared before it had so much as taken shape. "Never," said Calvin, "was an enterprise so badly conceived or so stupidly put into execution!"

The news of the conspiracy aroused a tremendous commotion. The Guises represented it in the light of a plot against the King's person, got up by the heretics, an infamous crime and an

183

unutterable outrage ! Their indignation was sincere, not so much on account of the alleged plot against Francis II as by reason **The Execu-** of the danger they themselves had run. They **tions following** ended by believing that this danger had been more **upon it.** real and menacing than they had at first supposed, and the reaction resulted in a series of merciless measures. Francis of Guise began by having himself appointed Lieutenant-General of the kingdom, which gave him an unrivalled position of authority and put the whole army under his command. He then set about repression of the revolt. The cells of Amboise were filled with people who had been surprised in the woods. They were summarily sentenced and executed *en masse*—hanged, beheaded, or drowned. It was a pitiless slaughter in which no quarter was given. The Protestants were all the more indignant as the guilt of the victims in general was by no means established, and in many cases was certainly venial ; they accused the Guises of taking vengeance for the terror they had felt. To crown all, the Lorraines had the audacity to hang the bodies of La Renaudie and the chief conspirators from the balconies of the royal residence itself, facing the river at Amboise. The corpses of all these gentlemen swinging in the wind, dried and withered, in full view of the great bridge over the Loire, was a horrible spectacle. Jean d'Aubigné, who chanced to pass by the spot with his son Agrippa, the future writer, then a boy of eight and a half, remarked to him as he pointed out the sinister string of human heads : " My child, look well at them ! Your head, when my own has fallen, must not be spared in avenging these honourable leaders. If you spare yourself, my curse will be upon you ! " And Agrippa d'Aubigné never forgot the indelible impression made upon him by the terrible sight of those dangling corpses and his father's deep emotion as he made him swear to avenge the blood of the " martyrs ! "

But the matter did not end here. At Court and through the country generally a rumour spread abroad that there were **Attempt to** yet other leaders responsible for the attempt. **compromise** A conspiracy of such importance could not have **the Bourbons.** been organized by so insignificant an individual as La Renaudie ; and it was permissible to seek the real instiga-
184

tors among those who would have profited by the success of the enterprise, that is to say, among the Bourbons. They were accordingly accused of having inspired the plot, and as Antoine, King of Navarre, was not the sort of man to have conceived such a project, the Prince of Condé was marked out as the leader of the enterprise. In the King's immediate circle, the imputation was promptly accepted. It coincided only too well with the interest the Guises had in isolating and ruining the Bourbons.

Condé was summoned before the King and his council to offer an explanation. He was cross-questioned and returned indignant answers, humiliated at having suspicion cast upon him and being made to appear as a culprit before his enemies. He protested, and defied anybody to produce the smallest shadow of evidence that he had had anything whatever to do with the matter. He even offered to fight anyone who maintained that he had. The whole family joined in his protestations with such warmth that the Calvinists, to whom the severity of the repressive measures had endeared the victims of Amboise, considered this method of denying all connexion with the vanquished somewhat excessive, and accused the princes of "cowardice." The incident went no farther, but it left in the breasts of all concerned a fermentation of hatred and anger which was destined to bear fruit at no very distant date. The Conspiracy of Amboise was the first tentative effort, the fore-runner of civil war. The experiment of gathering together a crowd of armed men had been made. The sword-thrusts and pistol-shots exchanged in the woods round the royal residence had been a rehearsal, and the Guises' mistaken policy of forcing the Bourbons against their will into the ranks of the rebels provided the latter with leaders who, as princes of the blood, satisfied the scruples of loyalists. Finally, the political question which had been grafted upon the religious problem—the tyrannical usurpation of power by strangers, who deserved to be driven out—added infuriated partisans to the opposition. The two parties, facing each other in a state of great excitement, were ready to come to blows.

But at this juncture there began to appear between the two camps a certain number of honest men who deprecated the passions that had been aroused and would have liked to arrange an understanding upon a basis of mutual toleration. They were advocates of the tradition outlined by Francis I—the tradition of conciliation and intelligent good-will. And as it happened, just after the Conspiracy of Amboise, Olivier was succeeded as Chancellor of France by a magistrate of a little over fifty, a learned and dignified man of great experience and high character, whose " grey beard, pale face, and grave manner " were very impressive—the famous Michel de l'Hôpital. His name in history stands for a whole policy. He kept repeating " Patience ! patience ! " In his eyes this was the guarantee and condition of improvement. " Everything will come right," was his assurance. But for the time being this party was too small to have any influence.

In view of the general state of fermentation the Guises raised troops everywhere. The Bourbons, exiled from Court, kept a disquieting silence. The Protestants, exalted by martyrdom, had revived their services in all the towns, whilst the magistrates still carried out the severe decrees against them. " In a year's time," wrote the King's secretary, Robertet, " the fire will be even more surely kindled than it is now." Indeed, it was felt that far from dying down, passions were becoming excited to boiling-point, and that before very long a conflict would break out. The peace party made an attempt at conciliation. They approached Catherine de' Medici, and induced her **The Assembly** to demand an Assembly of Notables to consider **of Notables,** means of pacification. The Guises gave their **1560.** consent, and the assembly met at Fontainebleau in August, 1560. It was composed of great personages in the State and of distinguished members of the reformed church. The Châtillons came, but the Bourbons refused to appear, and their absence did not pass unheeded by the Court. At the meetings, over which the King presided, Michel de l'Hôpital spoke eloquently in favour of peace. Coligny, who possessed great influence, owing to the respect his character inspired— " for he was," says Brantôme, " a noble knight, a good man, wise, mature, prudent, diplomatic, brave, critical, judicious, and a lover of honour and virtue "—presented a petition from the Calvinists of Normandy, who begged to be allowed freedom

186

of belief and liberty to practise their religion without let or hindrance. Coligny added that he was in a position to collect over 50,000 signatures to the petition. The Duke of Guise answered him by an irritable speech, declaring that if Coligny could collect 50,000 signatures from people who claimed liberty for Calvinism, he could find millions against it. A discussion ensued. Monluc, Bishop of Valence, was of opinion that the States-General should be summoned, as this assembly would carry more weight than a mere gathering of Notables, and that a National Council should be convoked to settle the disputed points in the Catholic doctrines, and, if possible, to reform abuses. The idea of summoning these two assemblies seemed to meet with a favourable reception. The Cardinal of Lorraine gave his consent to the States-General, but opposed the Council. In the end, however, the proposed resolution was passed to the effect that the States should meet in December 1560, and the Council in January 1561, unless the Pope took the initiative and summoned a General Council. Nothing was decided on the subject of Coligny's demands, the consideration of which was postponed till the next meeting. The moderate party had gained the upper hand.

But everywhere the signs of impending conflict became more menacing. News kept arriving of sporadic rebellions on the part of the Protestants. In Dauphiny, Montbrun tried to make his co-religionists take up arms. Normandy was in a state of ferment. Villars, Lieutenant-General of Languedoc, said that he could no longer answer for his province ; and bands of armed men were reported to be scouring the country. The King and the Guises suspected the Bourbons, and above all the Prince of Condé, of instigating these movements, in preparation for a general rebellion. Military precautions were increased ; recruits were raised, even in Germany ; and reinforcements were sent to the garrisons in the towns. It was arranged that a clear explanation should be demanded from the Bourbons at the States-General, and that if it were necessary they should be treated with the utmost rigour. The question was whether they would attend the States-General.

The place for the meeting of the assembly, which had at first been fixed at Meaux, was changed to Orleans as being more

187

secure. The King arrived there surrounded by an imposing body of troops. He had summoned the ban and rear-ban of

Meeting of the States-General at Orleans. the nobility. A whole army surrounded the town, the inhabitants of which had been disarmed. All the garrisons along the route by which the Bourbons would have to travel had been reinforced. In the face of such precautions the Bourbons were undecided what course to pursue. Their immediate followers begged them to remain at Béarn and not to run any risk. Catherine de' Medici, on the other hand, advised them to come, and offered them safe-conducts, provided only that they did not come in force, as the Government had determined at once to attack any concourse of people that seemed the least suspicious. After numberless hesitations they at last made up their minds to attend. A general feeling of anxiety had prevailed at Orleans, which was relieved on hearing this news. "The majority of the madmen," wrote Francis II to the Constable, "perceiving the path I am taking, are drawing in their horns a little." It was supposed that methods of intimidation had been successful.

The Bourbons arrived at Orleans a few days before the meeting of the States-General. They were frigidly received, and were immediately called upon to give a categorical explanation of the events that were taking place in the provinces and of their own attitude. The Prince of Condé retorted angrily, and exclaimed in great irritation that he was the victim of infamous calumnies on the part of the Guises. If he had had a guilty conscience he would not have come! On other points his answers were vague and dilatory. Antoine de Bourbon maintained an attitude of reserve and indecision. The Government promptly decided upon the course to be pursued. At

Arrest of Condé. the command of Francis II, the Prince of Condé was arrested, and his officers and secretaries were thrown into prison. The King of Navarre, in deference to his rank, was merely placed under close supervision. A judicial commission composed of magistrates belonging to the Parliament of Paris and presided over by de Thou, the father of the historian, was instructed to prepare the indictment of Condé on a charge of high treason. Condé, in his exasperation, kept

188

repeating that he would settle the whole matter personally with the Guises, his enemies, " at the point of the lance." At first he consented to answer his judges, but suddenly he refused to do so any more, and demanded to be tried by his peers before the Parliament of Paris. In order to give him some sort of satisfaction the number of the commissioners was increased by the addition of the Knights of Saint Michael, an order to which the Prince belonged, and on November 26 the tribunal returned the verdict that the prisoner was guilty of treason, heresy, and conspiracy. Michel de l'Hôpital refused to sign the decree, on the pretext that the case had not been proved, as the judges had only had presumptive evidence to act upon. The whole proceeding had a disastrous effect. The Protestants were indignant at the fact that a political manœuvre had been falsely hidden beneath legal forms. The party in favour of toleration deplored an incident calculated to aggravate matters rather than to improve them ; whilst the Catholics could find no answer to these protests except the fact that an adversary had been warned and that it was a fair fight.

It was in the midst of the painful impression produced by this trial that the members of the States-General met. They **Sudden death** were extremely troubled in their minds. Em- **of Francis II,** boldened by the success of their enterprise, the **1560.** Guises had decided to guide the deliberations of the Assembly towards the most rigorous repression of Calvinism. Their plans were already laid. They proposed to have a formulary of the Catholic faith signed by all the judges and Crown officials of every rank in the State, and even by all the King's subjects, one by one, parish by parish, under pain of summary arrest. By this means heresy would be stamped out, and the complete annihilation of the Bourbons would leave the uncontested supremacy in their own hands. Through the States-General, which they had in their grip, they would at last get the better of the Reformation. The Guises might well have thought they had reached the pinnacle of their power and greatness, when an event, upon which they had not counted, suddenly cast them down. Francis II died after an illness of only a few days.

Always puny and ailing, after having suffered for some time

from a suppurating ear, the unfortunate young King was seized with sudden weakness accompanied by high fever. Every effort was made to save him. The Cardinal of Lorraine multiplied prayers, vows, and processions on his behalf. The Duke of Guise flew into a passion with the doctors, threatening to hang them, and accusing them of stealing the King's money. Francis II rapidly lost consciousness, and on December 4 at eleven o'clock he died, according to one theory, from the effects of an abscess on the brain caused by the suppurating inflammation of the ear from which he suffered, and, according to another, from the rupture of the temple bone, followed by a cerebral effusion. Politically his death meant a revolution.

SOURCES. *Journal d'un bourgeois de Paris sous le règne de François I,"* ed. Lalanne, 1854; Jean Barrillon, *Journal*, ed. De Vaissière, 1897; Tommaseo, *Relations des ambassadeurs vénitiens*, 1838; Catherine de Médicis, *Lettres*, ed. La Ferrière and Baguenault de Puchesse; Brantôme, *Œuvres complètes*, ed. Lalanne; Pierre de la Place, *Commentaires de l'état de la religion et de la République*, 1565; Régnier de la Planche, *Histoire de l'état de France sous François II*, ed. Mennechet, 1836; Florimond de Raymond, *Histoire de la naissance, progrès et décadence de l'hérésie de ce siècle*, 1610; Hubert Languet, *Epistolæ politicæ*, 1646; J. Calvin, *Lettres françaises*, ed. Bonnet, 1854; and, *Opera omnia* in the *Corpus reformatorum*, vol. x to xx; d'Aubigné, *Histoire universelle*, ed. de Ruble, 1887.

WORKS. Th. de Bèze, *Histoire ecclésiastique des Eglises reformées au royaume de France*, ed. Baum and Cunitz, 1883; Lutteroth, *De la réformation en France*, 1859; P. Imbart de la Tour, *Les origines de la Réforme, la France moderne*, 1905; Weiss, *La Chambre ardente, étude sur la liberté de conscience en France sous François Ier et Henri II*, 1889; Haag, *La France protestante*, 10 vols. ; Doumergue, *Jean Calvin, les hommes et les choses de son temps*, 1899; Kampschulte, *Johann Calvin, seine Kirche*, 1869; Roget, *L'Église et l'État à Genève depuis la Réforme*, 1870; F. Buisson, *Sébastien Castellion*, 1891; C. Bouvier, *La question Michel Servet*, 1908; Le P. Maimbourg, *Histoire du calvinisme*, 1682; J. Crespin, *Les actes des martyrs*, 1565; A. de Reumont, *La jeunesse de Catherine de Médicis*, translated by A. Baschet, 1866; Capefigue, *Catherine de Médicis*, 1856; de Ruble, *Antoine de Bourbon et Jeanne d'Albret*, 1882; René de Bouillé, *Histoire des ducs de Guise*, 1849; H. Forneron, *Les Guise et leur époque*, 1877; Guillemin, *Le Cardinal de Lorraine*, 1847; J. Delaborde, *Gaspard de Coligny*, 1879; Dupré-Lasale, *Michel de l'Hôpital*, 1875; C. Paillard, *Additions critiques à l'histoire de la conspiration d'Amboise*, 1880; Potiquet *La maladie et la mort de François II*, 1893.

CHAPTER VI

BLOODSTAINED ANARCHY. CHARLES IX

Charles IX, 1560–1574 : Regency of Catherine de' Medici with Michel de l'Hôpital as her Chancellor. Change of policy with regard to the Protestants ; the results of this new policy ; the *Diary* of Faurin of Castres. The Triumvirate of Montmorency, Saint-André, and Guise ; resistance of the Catholics. Attempts to come to an understanding, the Colloquy of Poissy, 1561 ; its failure. Violence of men's passions ; the Massacre of Vassy, 1562. First Civil War : terrible disorders of the year 1562. Battle of Dreux ; the Protestants beaten, they fall back on Orleans ; assassination of the Duke of Guise, 1563. The Peace and Edict of Amboise, 1563. Travels of the Court through France ; the Conference of Bayonne, 1565. Attempt on the part of the Protestants to kidnap the Court, 1567. Second Civil War ; Battle of Saint-Denis, 1567 ; Peace of Longjumeau, 1568. Fall of l'Hôpital. Third Civil War ; Battle of Jarnac won by the Duke of Anjou, 1569 ; death of Condé ; Coligny becomes the leader of the Protestants ; his defeat at Moncontour, 1569, is followed, owing to the distress of the Government, by the disastrous Peace of Saint-Germain, 1570. Marriage of Henry of Béarn to Margaret of Valois : the Massacre of Saint Bartholomew, August 24, 1572. Death of Charles IX, 1574.

FRANCIS II, who passed away at the age of seventeen after a reign of one year and five months, was succeeded by his brother Charles IX, a child of between nine and ten. He was at the time and continued to be throughout his life an amiable prince, lively, extremely alert, graceful, as were Charles IX, all the members of the elegant House of Valois, 1560–1574. and with much ease of manner. He was also a sportsman, and loved riding, hunting, shooting, and tennis ; he had artistic tastes and tendencies, and took an interest in painting and sculpture, though, on the other hand, he hated study and business. His health, which had been delicate from the beginning, betrayed the degeneracy of his race. He was

191

tall and slight, with thin legs, and was short of breath. He ate and drank very little, and was easily overcome by fatigue, whilst his pale face and bowed head suggested a feeble constitution. Giovanni Michiel, the Venetian ambassador, who recognized his generosity, ardour, and intelligence, considered him handsome. He had fine eyes, and an expression that was by no means unpleasing, but the exaggerated angularity of his face gave his protruding mouth a disagreeable, sulky expression. The personality of this monarch, who died in his twenty-fifth year, had the qualities and the defects of youth. An evil fate destined his reign to be one of the most sinister in French history, and this has sufficed to make him almost a detestable figure.

By the laws and traditions of France which fixed the majority of kings at the age of fourteen, Francis II had been accounted **Regency of** a major when he ascended the throne, a circum-**Catherine de'** stance which allowed the Guises to seize the **Medici.** reins of power on the pretext that the King was free to confer authority. But with Charles IX the case was different. He was a minor, and it was necessary to have a regency. Now, by these same traditions the Queen-Mother usually became Regent. Catherine de' Medici, with characteristic promptitude and intelligence, did not wait for the death of Francis II before securing the government. The Guises had no legal rights to maintain ; they accordingly held their peace. Princes of the blood alone—in this case the Bourbons—had any claims to urge. But Catherine came to an understanding with them and promised them all they asked : Condé's release, and the admittance of the King of Navarre to the council and to a share in the government with the title of Lieutenant-General of the Kingdom, provided he made some profession of the Catholic faith. She obtained their support, and they for their part were well pleased at such a significant change in their position. In order to prevent them from wreaking vengeance on the Guises, she insisted on a reconciliation. She welcomed Montmorency, made herself extremely agreeable to the Châtillons, and spoke of toleration for the Huguenots. In fact she tried to be conciliatory to everybody. It is essential that her policy should be clearly understood.

192

BLOODSTAINED ANARCHY

As a woman and a foreigner, springing from a family of newly enriched merchants, she felt that she had no authority. " God has left me with three young children," she wrote to her daughter, the Queen of Spain, " and a kingdom divided against itself, without a soul in whom I can place the slightest confidence." Prudence—a quality of which she possessed no small share—counselled her to act warily, and to use soothing and conciliatory measures. In the midst of conflicting passions she had to try to be friendly to all. She has been condemned for dissimulation. But the position in which she was placed, her Italian blood, her education, and her former habits combined to make this almost inevitable. She had but a single object in view—the preservation of the King's authority and her own. Rightly or wrongly, she thought that but one method could secure this object—the method of conciliation. She failed, and has been accused of weakness and treachery. Greater ability, greater luck, or better conditions enabled Henry IV to succeed. He is called a great man ; and yet fundamentally their two policies were identical.

Moreover, her own character predisposed her to this conciliatory attitude. A healthy, robust woman, who had a **Character of** large appetite, took plenty of exercise, and was **Catherine de'** extremely brisk and lively, though she was so **Medici.** enormously stout that Brantôme calls her " a lady of masculine proportions," she was now more kind and amiable than ever. Every one agreed in thinking her " an extremely agreeable and gentle princess." The smile never left her poor plain face with its sallow olive complexion, baggy cheeks, and large goggle eyes, and she was affable and modest, without ever losing the dignity of a great lady. Generous to the point of prodigality and disorder, loving comfort, receptions, and all the splendour of a sumptuous Court life, she was honoured and loved by the courtiers who thronged about her. Her greatest joy was to see the nobility at peace enjoying themselves at her festivities. But she was far too intelligent to be deceived. " It is difficult to keep up this farce [the government of the kingdom] before so large an audience without displeasing some one ! " she wrote disconsolately to the Bishop of Limoges, her ambassador in Spain. In public she assumed a demeanour of calm self-possession. But Correro declares that more than once he found her weeping hot tears in her own room over what she called the troubles and misfortunes of France. What course was open to her but that of conciliation ? Did not reason agree with necessity ? Speaking of Protestantism and her system of toleration towards it, she wrote : " For twenty or thirty years we have tried cauterization to stamp out the contagion of this evil in our midst, and we have found by experience that violent measures do but increase it. . . ." " In this respect," she added, " I have acted as a woman, the mother of a royal ward, who thought that mildness was more suited to this disease than any other remedy." She realized her own powerlessness and the necessities of the political situation.

Even if she herself had not felt as she did, the man who was destined to be her most trusted counsellor, the Chancellor, Michel de l'Hôpital, would have imbued her with this spirit. A cold, dry man, with a firm, precise mind, l'Hôpital hid behind a thin bony face, rendered venerable by a long white beard and illuminated by a pair of clear eyes with a straightforward, penetrating glance, a vigorous intellect and decided ideas. He was a resolute and determined partisan of liberty of conscience for the Protestants, and a policy of conciliation towards the nobility. He supported, inspired, and encouraged Catherine de' Medici.

When once Francis II was dead and Charles IX proclaimed King, Catherine de' Medici, in her capacity as Regent, began by bringing the meeting of the States-General to a speedy conclusion. L'Hôpital attended it and made an eloquent speech during which, exhorting to toleration, he pronounced the famous words, " Let us do away with these diabolical terms, Lutherans, Huguenots, and Papists, the names of parties, factions, and seditions ; let us cling to the title of Christians ! " The States drew up their list of grievances, which showed a wide diversity in the desires of the three orders. On January 31, 1561, they were declared closed, and as the corollary demanded by custom, the Chancellor prevailed upon the Regent to publish a grand ordinance, containing 150 articles, in which he inserted several of his own ideas about reform. Amongst them were

194

the re-establishment of canonical elections in the Church, which had been suppressed by the Concordat, abolition of the sale of judicial offices, limitation of the jurisdiction of the ecclesiastical courts, injunctions to the sheriffs of the North and South to leave trials to the care of lieutenants of various ranks, etc.—reforms which were only partially or imperfectly carried out.

The Government then made public its resolution with regard to the Protestants. Catherine explained that after so many years of repression, now recognized as inefficacious, the experiment of a policy of gentleness and liberalism was to be tried. On February 24, 1561, an edict was published, by the terms of which all Protestants who were in prison were to be released, and judicial suits brought against them were to be stopped. Huguenots who had been banished were authorized to return, and those who had been sent to the galleys were recalled. The Act added, it is true, " on condition that they become Catholics " ; but no notice was taken of this proviso. As a matter of fact, this edict of toleration gave Protestantism the most decided impetus that it had ever received. Hitherto as a restricted, threatened, and dangerous faith, the Protestant religion had succeeded in collecting but a small number of converts. But from this moment it assumed a prominent position. People began to attend the services out of curiosity, and the simple piety of the new religion attracted and converted many. Gradually a movement was inaugurated which became a force and a fashion, accelerating the development of Protestantism before the very eyes of the astonished Catholics, who were held in check by the idea that the King approved of it, or that it was an irresistible power. At the end of six months in one of the southern towns the Huguenots were in the majority. To prove this we need only refer to the curious *Diary* of Jean Faurin, a Protestant hosier of Castres, in which he relates the events which took place from day to day in that little town :

The end of the year 1560 was marked in Castres by a terrible persecution. Magistrates arrived from Toulouse and Carcassonne and multiplied the number of summonses, arrests, and imprisonments. The services were celebrated secretly by

195

night, but enormous difficulty was experienced in holding them without provoking outbursts of fury on the part of the popu **Faurin's** lace, which was ready to stone the hated Hugue **"Diary."** nots. In February, 1561, the edict arrived. All the Protestants in the prisons were at once set free. Monsieur de Lostau, the Huguenot minister, began to preach in the houses. Nothing was said to him. On April 18 he preached publicly in the school to an audience of 500 or 600 people. The magistrates were angry and ordered him out of the town. He refused to go, and they did not dare to force him " for fear of a popular outbreak." On April 26 and 28 ministers arrived from Geneva. On June 5 the procession of the Holy Sacrament of Corpus Christi took place in the town, and, for the first time, the Protestants did not decorate their houses with hangings. "But no one took any notice of it." On July 6 the Lord's Supper was celebrated at the school, and 600 people received the Sacrament. One Tuesday in August the Protestants all shut their shops at midday and went to prayers with their servants. They repeated this every Tuesday, and nobody said anything. On Sunday, August 31, the first Huguenot funeral took place, and "there was not the slightest commotion." On September 1 the election of borough consuls and of the procurator royal was held. Protestants were returned for all the posts. The consuls and the members of the consistory went to the clergy of the second most important parish in the town, Notre Dame de la Platé, and demanded the keys of the church in order that they might hold a Calvinistic service in it. The priest in charge refused to admit them, and they thereupon broke open the doors of the church and held the service in spite of him—"nobody raised any commotion." On October 5, the Lord's Supper was celebrated in the same church. At the end of October "by order of their honours the magistrates, all the idols—the statues—and all the altars " of this church were pulled down "without any opposition." And thus, before the end of the year 1561, Protestantism, which at the beginning of it had been restricted, repressed, and punished, was installed at Castres with the enjoyment of full liberty of conscience and freedom of worship, and was in possession of the municipality and the churches. Much the same thing

196

took place almost everywhere. From one end of France to the other, the Catholics, unable to understand what was happening, looked on in stupefaction.

Meanwhile at Court complications were arising. Catherine de' Medici, true to her promise, had released Condé. But he wished to be legally rehabilitated and not merely pardoned, and had demanded and obtained a verdict from the Parliament attesting his innocence. The Guises, already enraged by all that was taking place, protested loudly, and declared that this verdict amounted to the repeal of an act of the late King. The Cardinal of Lorraine left the Court, and Condé informed Catherine that he would only return to her on condition that his mortal enemy, Francis of Guise, was driven from her presence. By dint of manœuvring, Catherine succeeded in calming this first storm. She summoned Condé to Fontainebleau and received him in the most charming manner. Condé himself, according to Brantôme, was " extremely agreeable, amenable, and amiable " ; and allowed himself to be won over. The cloud passed by. The King of Navarre had been made Lieutenant-General of the Kingdom.

But it was impossible for the Catholics to remain indefinitely silent in face of the changes which were being introduced to Montmorency, the detriment of their religion. The Duke of Saint-André, Guise consulted with the Constable Montmorency Guise. and Marshal de Saint-André on the situation, and agreed with them that they must combine to resist a movement which threatened to ruin the State. The three men made a compact and formed themselves into a sort of triumvirate. As soon as their agreement became known adherents flocked to them from all quarters. Like Chantonnay, the ambassador of Philip of Spain, they all considered that whether deliberately or not, Catherine de' Medici by her policy of toleration was paving the way for the triumph of Protestantism. Was not Condé already freely inviting Huguenot ministers to preach at Court ? Were not the Protestants influential enough to bring about the disgrace of Catholic officials, like Montmorency's brother-in-law Villars, in Languedoc, who had been over zealous against the Calvinists ? The triumvirate was welcomed with acclamations, and the Cardinal de Tournon and the Dukes of Montpensier and Brissac lent it their support. The Catholic sovereigns, the Pope, the King of Spain, and the Duke of Savoy, displayed their deep sympathy, for Europe was watching the events that were taking place in France with the closest attention. Philip II more especially was concerned to know whether Protestantism was going to win yet another great kingdom—an anxious question for the King of Spain, seeing that the Netherlands had already gone over to the new religion. Catherine, who was greatly harassed, tried to calm them and reassure them as to her intentions. She wrote to her daughter, Elizabeth of Spain, " I am obliged to have the King of Navarre at my side. The laws of France insist upon it." She explained to her ambassador in Spain that, as a matter of fact, with Protestants on one side and Catholics on the other, the Bourbons and the triumvirs, she was trying " to find a *via media* between the two parties." She informed foreign Courts and the Pope that nothing had been changed in France with respect to the Protestants, and that there was no need for them to be concerned. But causes for further alarm were not slow to arise.

Like a plague spot, Protestantism gradually spread farther and farther with astonishing rapidity. But as the inevitable **Protestant** consequence of this, in those places where the **outrages.** Protestants were in a majority, they declared, as they had done at Geneva, that they could not tolerate what they called " idolatry " in their midst, and the scandal of " Romish superstition." They had demanded toleration, and it had been granted them. They had taken freedom of worship, and the officials had been obliged to let them have their way. And now, intolerant in their turn, they wished to destroy Catholicism. Irritated chiefly by the worship of images, the Protestants began to smash the statues in the churches all over the country.

The Catholics resisted, and conflicts took place, resulting in a certain number of deaths. The Huguenots attacked religious processions and tried to disorganize them, whilst the Catholics invaded the Protestant services. Disorders occurred throughout the kingdom, and from all quarters there reached the Government in general, and l'Hôpital in particular, unani-

198

mous complaints on the part of the Catholics against his policy
of weakness and concession. The Chancellor was regarded as
a Huguenot. What had he done with the ancient laws ? Had
he or had he not repealed them ? The Government, in some
anxiety, published a new edict in July, 1561, recommending
people to keep the peace and to practise toleration, prohibiting
the bearing of arms, and whilst renewing the retrospective
armistice with regard to the Protestants, forbidding them, in
accordance with the old edicts of the past, to hold public or
private meetings on pain of being summoned before the civil
tribunals and being punished with imprisonment or the confisca-
tion of their goods, the extreme penalty of death being prohibited. This timorous expedient contented nobody, and the
universal seething of discontent continued unchecked whilst
l'Hôpital was declared to be absolutely powerless.

The Chancellor thereupon conceived an unexpected plan—
that of reuniting the Protestant and the Catholic communions
by endeavouring to reconcile their doctrines. The Catholics
were to make concessions on questions of discipline and ceremony, whilst the Protestants on their side were to give way
on points of dogma. A conference was to be convoked between
the bishops and the Protestant ministers at which the conditions
of the agreement were to be discussed. Catherine approved
of the plan, and the Protestants gave their consent to it. The
bishops, humiliated by the thought of a discussion of this kind,
would never have agreed to take part in it, had not the Cardinal
of Lorraine, who hoped to win a great oratorical victory by
his eloquence, prevailed upon them to do so. The Colloquy,
The Colloquy as the meeting was called, was summoned to
of Poissy, meet at Poissy in August 1561. Twelve Protestant
1561. ministers arrived headed by the illustrious Theodore Beza, Calvin's favourite disciple, a supple-minded, elegant,
and fiery-tempered divine ; and Peter Martyr from Zurich.
On their way they passed through Saint-Germain where the
Court was staying and were granted a gracious reception, "far
more friendly a one than the Pope would have received if
he had come," as Claude Haton petulantly observes in his
Diary. The assembly was opened on September 9 at Poissy
in the old refectory of the Dominican monastery dating from

199

the time of Saint Louis, and was attended by enormous numbers. The little King, Charles IX, presided over it with his mother, Catherine de' Medici, at his side. Theodore Beza spoke temperately. He had, according to Haton, " an eloquent tongue combined with a beautiful and apt use of the French language, whilst his face and gestures attracted the hearts and minds of his hearers." He held the attention of the audience. But, unfortunately, he made some unhappy comparison on the subject of the Eucharist. Exclamations burst forth from the assembly, and the Cardinal de Tournon sternly called the speaker to order. " I was on the point," Catherine afterwards wrote, " of bidding him be silent ! " At the next sitting, the Cardinal of Lorraine replied, and speech succeeded speech without any result. At length it was decided that it would be wiser to appoint a commission of ten members—five Catholics and five Protestants—to find some formula of agreement. But they too failed. The proceedings had been altogether barren, and it was realized that reunion was out of the question.

The Colloquy of Poissy served only to increase the general disorder. The Protestants considered themselves the victors. " The Protestants," wrote d'Aubigné, " exalted by their rights, proclaimed the victory of their ministers." And it was indeed a triumph and a distinction to have been allowed to enter upon a discussion on equal terms with prelates who had hitherto regarded the Huguenots as criminals and infamous heretics ! Protestantism was now becoming a recognized religion, worthy of attention and respect ! The courage of the Calvinists rose high, and all over the country the result immediately made itself felt. Let us return to Faurin's Diary.

On December 14, 1561, in the Cathedral church of Saint Benoît at Castres, a certain friar, Claude d'Oraison, preached **Further** a sermon in which he vehemently denounced the **Protestant** Reformation. A Protestant scholar interrupted **outrages.** him, and at the top of his voice shouted out that " he was a liar." The congregation kicked the scholar out of the church, with the result that there was a great commotion among all the Huguenots in the town. In the evening they all gathered together carrying arms, went to the cloisters of Saint Benoît, where the friar lived, seized him, and cast him into prison. The Catholics were terrified and made no protest. The next day Father d'Oraison was conducted to the gate of the town and told to depart. On December 31 the borough magistrates, still all Protestants, ordered the statues and images in the churches to be demolished. On January 1, 1562, they formally forbade the Roman Catholic clergy to say Mass inside the town—thus abolishing the Catholic religion in Castres. On January 4 the magistrates went in a body to the Convent of Sainte-Claire and drove out the twenty nuns they found there. On February 2 a Trinitarian monk was discovered celebrating the Mass in secret in the presence of a small congregation of the faithful. He was seized, put on a donkey with his face to the tail, to which he clung with both hands, and, dressed in his sacerdotal vestments, was marched through all the streets of the town. After this exhibition he was taken to the square, set upon a chair and shaved, and was then shown the consecrated wafer, and asked whether he were ready to die for it. The poor man was terrified and replied in the negative whereupon his sacerdotal garments were burnt, and he himself was driven away after having been made to promise that he would never again celebrate the Mass.

Similar occurrences took place on every side. In all quarters the Protestants invaded the churches, drove out the priests, and usurped their places. The church bells were suppressed, and were replaced by drums. The altars were overthrown and the images of the saints were destroyed. Here and there the Catholics were either less patient or stronger than their co-religionists in Castres, and attacked their adversaries. In December, 1561, a scuffle took place in Paris in the Faubourg Saint-Marcel, during which the Huguenots invaded the church of Saint-Médard and pillaged it. The Catholics retaliated by rushing to the Protestant meeting-house and burning the contents.

In face of the advancing tide, Michel de l'Hôpital came to the conclusion that he must swim with the current if he hoped **Concessions** ever to stem it, and in January, 1562, he published **to the** an edict authorizing the Protestants to hold **Protestants.** meetings—which was merely the legal recognition of an accomplished fact—but only on condition that they took

201

place outside the towns, in the suburbs, for instance, and that no places of worship should be built; there was a further proviso that the Calvinists should give back to the Catholics all the churches they had seized. The Protestants were satisfied with this concession. And, indeed, it was considerable. For the first time they had received official recognition. Their meetings were authorized, and the practice of their religion was no longer an offence, but the regular exercise of a right. They accepted the conditions. At Castres the Huguenots gave up the churches of La Platé and Saint-Benoît, and held their meetings on the boulevard of the Porte de l'Albinique under tents put up for the occasion. No priest, however, had the courage to enter the town to celebrate Mass.

The edict was greeted by a violent outburst of indignation on the part of the Catholics. The Government was accused **Discontent of** of definitively giving way to the heretics. The **the Catholics.** latter, it was argued, were only a minority, and " in the wrong," yet they were gradually gaining privileges equal to those enjoyed by the majority, who had remained faithful to the true religion. The Catholics were no longer in a position to insist that the Calvinists should not be allowed to practise their religion ; they were now called upon to defend themselves against adversaries who, after having demanded and obtained freedom of worship, were arrogating to themselves the right of interfering with the religious liberty of others, and from being persecuted had themselves become persecutors. There was no longer any room for doubt—the Regent and her Chancellor were giving the country over into the hands of the Protestants ! Urgent complaints were addressed to the Government from abroad on the subject of its weakness. Philip II wrote angrily that if the Regent were not in a position to cope with the heretics, she might have the use of his troops. When Catherine in high dudgeon replied that it was out of the question for the affairs of France to be managed " by any other than her own forces," the King of Spain retorted that if this were so, he would offer his soldiers to the Catholics, a reply which only enraged the Queen-Mother the more. However, as Philip II, in his anxiety at the thought of the effect which events in France might have in his own provinces of the Netherlands,

202

remarked : " It was better to go and put out the fire in a neighbour's house than to wait for it to spread to one's own." The Regent wrote letter after letter to explain and justify her attitude, and gave him every assurance that she was firmly resolved to suppress heresy. She was merely accused of double dealing, and Maisonfleur gave her the nickname of *Madame la Serpente*. The Duke of Alba, the Governor of the Netherlands, was of opinion that in the end it would be necessary to interfere in France. Owing to the absence of forces sufficient to maintain public order in the country, the smallest incident was sufficient to produce civil war, which was already imminent. An incident of this nature occurred on March 1, 1562, at Vassy.

Duke Francis of Guise chanced to be returning from Saverne to Paris with an escort of over two hundred horsemen, when, **The Massacre** as he was going through Vassy, on the frontier **of Vassy, 1562.** of Champagne, one Sunday morning he passed a barn where a Protestant service was being held at which about 400 or 500 people were present. The members of his train and some of the congregation exchanged taunts. This led to blows, and the Duke of Guise's nobles backed their own men, with the result that the whole body attacked the Protestant assembly. The Huguenots tried to defend themselves by throwing stones, one of which wounded the Duke, whose followers thereupon drew their swords in fury, and struck out right and left. The Protestants fled helter-skelter, but twenty-three were killed and over a hundred were wounded. It was the first really serious incident in the struggle that was about to begin, and the first in which there had been much bloodshed.

The incident was turned to account by the Protestants, among whom it aroused a considerable commotion. The Catholics tried to make light of an affair which they termed " an accident," " a mere scuffle." The Huguenots could talk of nothing but " the Massacre of Vassy," and indignantly declared that the plot on the part of their enemies to destroy them had now been unmasked. Catherine, much alarmed, forbade Francis of Guise to enter Paris, where the populace, who were fervent Catholics, might, in their ardour, provoke fresh complications, and ordered him to join her at Montceaux.

The passions which had been unloosed were, however, too strong to be curbed. Guise disobeyed her orders and went to Paris, where he was received by the two other triumvirs and greeted by the frenzied acclamations of the mob. The Provost of the Merchants welcomed him at the Porte Saint-Denis and hailed him as the " Defender of the Faith." Catherine de' Medici, growing more and more anxious, left Montceaux, with all the Court, and shut herself up in the Château de Melun, a safer and stronger position. From thence she reached Fontainebleau. There was no knowing what might happen next. The Prince of Condé was in Paris, surrounded on all sides by resolute partisans, and never going out without arms and an escort. A hostile encounter between the two foes was inevitable. By dint of entreaties the Cardinal of Bourbon succeeded in inducing Condé to leave the city. But he merely went to Meaux, whither he summoned all his friends, servants, and supporters. The Châtillons joined him, though Coligny did so unwillingly—recognizing that this concentration of forces at Meaux was neither more nor less than the nucleus of an army of revolt, and unable to reconcile his conscience to the idea of becoming a rebel. In a very short space of time 100 gentlemen and 1500 horsemen were collected. In order to allay Coligny's scruples, Condé explained that the King was a prisoner in the hands of counsellors, of whom they themselves were the victims, that there was no question of taking up arms against his Majesty, but that they purposed to release him, and inaugurate a wiser plan of government in his name. In this way the semblance of legality was preserved.

In point of fact the Court, hemmed in between the two opposing parties, the Catholic triumvirs on the one side and the Protestant Bourbons on the other, was faced with the problem of deciding which of the two it should support. Paris was in a state of acute agitation, and Catherine de' Medici made up her mind to advance at all costs, and use her authority. She left Fontainebleau and together with the King came and shut herself up in Vincennes. The triumvirs, however, interpreted this as a public avowal that the Government was on their side. A council was held at the Louvre at which the Regent was present. The triumvirs proposed that they should march out resolutely against Condé. Catherine and l'Hôpital refused to sanction this step.

The Court, however, was practically in the power of the Catholics, and Condé made up his mind that the die had been cast. He left Meaux, which was too near Paris—as he had not sufficient forces at his command—and reached Orleans, where he published a manifesto, declaring that the King was no longer free, and must be set at liberty, and calling upon all the Calvinist churches in the kingdom to raise troops and send them to him. He declined all responsibility for the conflict, which he laid to the charge of the Guises and their provocative behaviour, and ended by repeating that he wished to liberate the King, his brother, and the Queen-Mother, and secure the carrying out of the edicts. According to him, right was entirely on his side.

Meanwhile, civil war was breaking out all over the country. Catholics and Protestants were attacking each other on every **First** hand. The Parisians refused to acknowledge the **Civil War.** edict of January, and would not tolerate the presence of any known Huguenot in their city. In the provinces anarchy reigned unchecked. The Protestants went about in bodies attacking the churches, smashing the statues with their muskets, breaking open the doors, collecting in a heap in the choir all the ornaments, reliquaries, pyxes, and chalices they could find, and making a bonfire of them. They then turned to the tombs, broke them open, and scattered the bones. The tomb of Louis XI at Cléry was violated in this way, and the remains of the Bourbons at Vendôme were disinterred. Claude de Sainctes, who recounts these deeds, was scandalized by them. They carried country towns by assault and drove out the Catholic priests. "The walls of Puylaurens," writes Jean Faurin, "were scaled and the town was captured by members of the reformed faith. When once they had made an entry they put down idolatry and the Mass, and established the ministry of the Word of God according to the Holy Scriptures. And in so doing they acted after the manner of the good Josiah." Catholic services were abolished in every place where the Protestants had the upper hand—in the south and in Normandy, at Caen, Rouen, and Bayeux. They sent help to each other from town to town, exchanging men, ammunition, etc., from enormous distances. The open country, traversed by companies marching to their destinations, was no longer secure, and men with fire-arms lurked in every hedge and ditch. The royal officials were powerless, and some of the Governors were murdered by the rioters. In Dauphiny the terrible Huguenot Baron des Adrets scoured the country, killing, burning, and pillaging. Bands of Catholics and Protestants, driven out of the towns, wandered about until they fell in with armed troops who massacred them. Ardent Catholics carried out the repressive measures pitilessly. Monluc, for instance, on the banks of the Garonne, hanged every Huguenot he met. " One man hanged," he said, " is a better example than a hundred killed." He carried out his decrees swiftly without either verdict or writing, " for," he added, " in these matters I have heard tell that it is best to begin with the execution. If all who had charge of the provinces had acted as I do, the conflagration which has burnt up everything would have been stamped out." The year 1562 was one of the most lamentable in French history. Never had the country presented such a terrible spectacle, not even during the Hundred Years War, when the misery was not nearly so widespread. " There is not a corner of land that has escaped devastation," wrote Hubert Languet. " All business in the kingdom is suspended," Chantonnay, the Spanish Ambassador, informed Margaret of Parma, " which is a great pity " ; whilst Castelnau declared " the civil war is like a raging fire burning and consuming the whole of France."

Meanwhile Catherine de' Medici in despair was leaving no stone unturned to postpone the conflict with the Prince of Condé. She kept writing to him, trying to calm him and bring him back, bidding him come to see her, and asking him to name his conditions. Condé replied that he demanded the expulsion of the triumvirs, and the punishment of those responsible for the massacre of Vassy. The triumvirs consented to absent themselves from Court, but on condition that the Government should ensure the exclusive exercise of the Catholic religion in France. The dilemma was insoluble. From the provinces news kept arriving day by day which added fuel to the fire. At Toulouse fighting in the streets had lasted for four days, one quarter of the town had been set on fire, and 400 people had been killed. The taxes were no longer paid, and the whole country was in a state of terror. Under the stress of public opinion, which had become exasperated, and at the instigation of the Papal Nuncio and the Spanish ambassador, Catherine de' Medici decided to allow the army mustered against Condé to march. It consisted of 6000 infantry and 4000 cavalry, under the command of Antoine de Bourbon, King of Navarre, Lieutenant-General of France. This frivolous, inconsistent, and apathetic individual who, reviewing his position, preferred to keep the honours and dignities which the State had conferred on him, had abandoned the Protestants, and made profession of the Catholic faith, with the result that he was constrained to lead a body of troops against his own brother.

Before the hostile forces met Catherine made one last attempt to come to terms. Conferences were held at Toury, but both sides persisted in making irreconcilable demands. The Protestants declared that these negotiations were mere feints, and Condé's gentlemen insisted upon war. Gradually the Court became convinced that the Government would soon be in the same position as the towns ; that if once the Huguenots secured toleration, they would claim equality ; when they had equality, they would want to be masters, and if they were masters they would destroy Catholicism in France.

On July 3 Condé attempted a *coup de main* and tried at night to take the Catholic army by surprise. He failed, and **The Protestants negotiate with England.** retreated towards Blois and Tours. The army of the triumvirs pursued him, and Poitiers was occupied without much difficulty by Marshal de Saint-André. The Protestant forces, which were badly disciplined, began to disband and offered no resistance. The Government thereupon decided to march upon Rouen, and a rumour spread abroad that Condé had entered into negotiations with Elizabeth, Queen of England, with a view to obtain her support. Condé had, as a matter of fact, sent La Haye and Jean de Ferrières to Hampton Court to discuss matters with Elizabeth. Moved purely by self-interest, she had replied that she would consent to furnish 6000 men and pay a sum of 100,000 crowns on condition of being allowed to occupy Havre, adding that, by the terms of the Treaty of Cateau-Cambrésis, Calais was to be returned to her at the end of eight years, and that she would keep Havre as a security for that town and evacuate it if Calais were given back to her at once. La Haye and Jean de Ferrières thought that the occupation of Havre would terrify the French Court, and they accordingly signed an agreement with Elizabeth. As soon as the clauses of this convention were made known they aroused violent indignation. Condé and Coligny protested, and informed the Queen of England through her ambassador, Throckmorton, that they regarded the occupation of Havre as purely temporary, that anything else would be an everlasting blot upon their memory, and that if, when peace was made between the Huguenots and the King of France, the English did not evacuate the place unconditionally, all the forces of the country would be sent against them. Jean de Ferrières, heart-broken at his own error, wrote to Elizabeth's minister Cecil : " I cannot tell you the grief I feel ! Do your best to prevent my being tempted to despair at seeing *jacturam honoris esse sine fructu.*" He realized that he had disgraced himself.

At the head of 18,000 men, Charles IX marched in person upon Rouen, where the garrison had been reinforced, as soon **The Catholics capture Rouen.** as Havre had been occupied, by 500 English under the command of Montgommery—the slayer of Henry II. The King of Navarre accompanied the King of France. The attack was made on October 26. It was successful ; the town was captured, and Montgommery fled. The victory, however, cost the life of the unfortunate King of Navarre, who was shot by an arquebusier. He was forty-four at the time of his death, which he met in the service of the Catholics after having been the hope and mainstay of the Huguenot cause. He died unregretted.

Meanwhile, however, Condé had reorganized his army, reinforcing it with a body of 2600 German *reiters* and 3000 lansquenets, had marched boldly upon Paris and pitched camps at Gentilly, Arcueil, and Montrouge. The city, which was well defended, held out against him, whereupon he decided to fall back upon Chartres, proposing to reach Normandy

208

and co-operate with the English. But the army of the Royalists and Catholics, consisting of 14,000 infantry and 3000 cavalry under the command of the three triumvirs in person, was tracking him down, and fell in with him at Dreux. This time an **Battle of** encounter was inevitable, and it took place on **Dreux, 1562.** November 19, 1562—the first battle of the civil wars. Every one was deeply moved. " Each man," says La Noue, " thought within himself that the soldiers he saw advancing were French, that some of them were his own relatives and friends, and that in an hour's time, they would have to kill each other ; which filled him with horror at the thought of battle." In order to recognize each other the Huguenots had adopted the " uniform " which they wore throughout the civil wars—a white cloth doublet ; whilst the Catholics carried crucifixes and images in their hats. Under the skilful and vigorous generalship of Francis of Guise the battle was decisive. By five o'clock in the evening all was over, and the Protestants had been defeated and routed. But the victory had been dearly bought. Marshal de Saint-André had been killed, and the old Constable, Montmorency, unhorsed and wounded, had been made prisoner by the Huguenots, who carried him off with them in their flight. On the other hand, Condé had been surrounded and was in the hands of the Catholics. Six thousand men lay dead upon the blood-stained field of battle.

The news of the victory gave rise to unparalleled rejoicings throughout France. Processions were formed and *Te Deums* sung. As the death of Antoine de Bourbon left the post of Lieutenant-General of the Kingdom vacant it was offered to Guise, who thereupon took over the command of the troops.

After Condé, the leadership of the Protestant forces devolved upon Coligny, who prudently beat a retreat and fell back upon **Murder of** Orleans, where he shut himself up. With his **Guise, 1563.** habitual determination Guise followed in pursuit, resolved, in his own words, to catch the foxes in their holes. He pitched his camp beneath the walls of the town, whilst he himself together with his family found lodging at Valins, some distance away. He stayed in the camp all day and went home at night. On February 9 the fort of Les Tourelles was taken, and everything was progressing favourably. On the 18th, as

Guise was returning to his lodging between six and seven o'clock in the evening, a horseman was observed riding up and down the road, asking the passers-by whether the Duke would really return that way. Guise had sent one of his gentlemen on ahead at a gallop to inform the Duchess that he would be late, but was coming. He rode his horse at a walk and was preceded by a page mounted on a mule, and accompanied by Tristan de Rostaing. As soon as he saw the group, the horseman, who was on the watch, plunged into a thicket and allowed Guise to pass him; but the moment he was five or six feet ahead he covered him with his pistol and fired. The weapon was loaded with three balls, and Guise was wounded in the right arm-pit. He fell back exclaiming: "I am killed!" but pulling himself together with a violent effort, he tried to unsheathe his sword. He had not the strength to do so, however. Rostaing sprang in the direction from which the shot had come, but the murderer succeeded in keeping him off for some time at the point of the sword, and then setting spurs to his horse, disappeared into the darkness of the wood. He wandered about the whole night and lost his way; in the morning, worn out with fatigue he went into a barn belonging to a farm to rest, and there fell asleep. He was under the impression that he had been riding away from the camp, but, as a matter of fact, he had come back to it in a circle, and was on the Pont d'Olivet, near the spot where the Swiss were encamped. Monsieur de Seurre, one of Guise's lieutenants, discovered him in the barn and arrested him. He offered no resistance. He was a young man of six-and-twenty, a Protestant from the Angoumois, whose name was Poltrot de Méré.

For six days Guise hovered between life and death. He bore his sufferings courageously, and died on February 24, between ten and eleven o'clock in the morning. **Coligny accused of the murder.** The news of his death caused a profound sensation. The chief of the nation had passed away, the skilful and lucky general, the glorious victor in many a battle. Smith, the English ambassador, wrote to Queen Elizabeth: "He was the greatest warrior that France or even Christendom has ever seen, hardened to fatigue, courteous and eloquent, loved alike by the common soldier and by men of rank." Public opinion with one accord accused Coligny of having armed the hand of the assassin; but this has never been proved, nor is it likely to have been the case. Poltrot, when he was cross-examined, confessed that he had received 100 crowns from the Admiral to do the deed; and the Government published this avowal all over the country. Coligny was obliged to answer the accusation, and did so very clumsily. He acknowledged that on two different occasions he had given Poltrot £50 and £300. The Duke of Guise, he added, was an enemy of God, of the King, and of the country, who had planned, so he had been informed, to have him, Coligny, killed. But though he never actually instigated anyone to murder the Duke, he certainly never tried to stop those who talked of doing so from carrying their threats into execution; and he ended this reply, which was addressed to Catherine, by saying, " Do not imagine, Madam, that what I have said means that I regret the death of Monsieur de Guise; for I think it was the greatest blessing that could be conferred upon the Church of God and this kingdom in general, and more particularly upon myself and all my house." This letter produced a deplorable effect. " Though he does not frankly confess to having consented to this murder," wrote Pasquier, " he nevertheless defends himself so coldly that those who wish him well would fain he had either held his tongue or made a better apology! " And Brantôme added, " Many people were astonished that a man who was so cold and modest in speech should have given utterance to such words, which served no purpose and with which he might well have dispensed! " With all his great qualities Coligny was guilty of certain errors of judgment. The Guise family, convinced that he was the murderer, were for the future imbued with the one idea of avenging the death of Duke Francis by the blood of the Admiral. Poltrot de Méré was hanged and quartered on the Place de Grève on March 18.

With Condé a prisoner, Guise dead, and Coligny discredited, Catherine de' Medici's task was simplified. An agreement was **The Peace and** reached and a peace concluded, the terms of which **the Edict of** were proclaimed by a royal edict—the Edict of **Amboise, 1563.** Amboise of March 19, 1563. The prisoners on both sides, Montmorency and Condé, were set free. The exercise of the Protestant religion was definitely authorized in any town on permission being obtained from the sheriff, as well as in all towns where the Calvinists were the undisputed masters, but it was forbidden in Paris. Huguenot nobles were empowered to have services held in their own houses. In return, the Protestants were to evacuate the churches, which were to be given back to the Catholics, and they were still to be excluded from public office. Condé was extremely dissatisfied. He wanted better terms, but his eagerness to be set free made him agree to the peace. The Catholics, who would hear of nothing but repressive measures, were even more discontented. But Catherine de' Medici was determined to re-establish order at all costs; which, indeed, was extremely necessary; for the misery throughout the country was terrible, the cultivation of the fields having been abandoned, and the life of the people interrupted. She laboured under no illusion, however. "We have only recoiled to spring the further," she remarked sadly in one of her letters. But it was above all necessary to gain time. In the meanwhile troops were sent against Havre to drive out the English, a task which was accomplished without difficulty, and on the return of the expedition, Charles IX was proclaimed of age at Rouen. He was now fourteen, but he begged his mother to continue the direction of the government.

The leaders of the Catholics and the Protestants once more returned to Court, but with what implacable feelings of mutual hatred may well be imagined! The Guises—more especially the mother and the widow of Duke Francis—demanded the trial of Coligny. The son of the murdered man, Henry, who was now Duke of Guise, and his uncle, the Duke of Aumale, were constantly uttering threats against the Admiral, who only dared to put in an appearance surrounded by a number of gentlemen. But Condé, delighted at having regained his liberty, threw himself with careless frivolity into all the joys of Court life, and the Protestant ministers were scandalized at seeing this lively little man assiduous in his attentions now to the widow of Marshal de Saint-André and now to Mademoiselle de Limeuil. Everybody felt that the Peace of Amboise was nothing more than a truce.

At this juncture, Catherine de' Medici decided to keep all

this company of people occupied by taking them a journey across France. She resolved to hold festivals and to amuse the

Travels of the Court through France. nobility in order to prevent them from hatching conspiracies, and more particularly she wished to show the new monarch his kingdom, and prove to the provinces, which had been plunged in anarchy, that they really had a sovereign whom it was their duty to obey.

On January 24, 1564, the expedition set forth, and the lengthy caravan passed through Troyes, the Lorraine districts, Dijon, Lyons, and Dauphiny. The Catholics flocked to welcome the procession, assuring the King of their devotion and urging him to pursue an energetic policy. " This belongs to you," Tavannes informed his sovereign at Dijon, placing his hand upon his heart, " and here is a weapon you can use," he added, striking the handle of his sword. Solemn entries, receptions, banquets and balls followed each other in close succession. " And they all dance together," Catherine informed the Duchess of Guise, " Huguenots and Papists alike ; and so happily indeed, that I do not think they would have gone so far as they have, if God had disposed others elsewhere to act as wisely." The royal procession crossed Provence and Languedoc slowly, paying long visits to the various towns, and only reached Toulouse in February, 1565. From thence it passed on to Bordeaux, and arrived at Mont-de-Marsan in the month of May ; on June 3 it reached Bayonne, where Elizabeth, Queen of Spain, the daughter of Catherine de' Medici, came to see her mother, accompanied by the Duke of Alba. This meeting at Bayonne excited general interest.

For a long time Catherine de' Medici had been dreaming of some sort of " international understanding " between the **Conference of** Catholic Powers, in order that they might agree **Bayonne, 1565.** as to the policy they intended to adopt towards Protestantism. A " Holy Alliance " of this nature would have strengthened her own position in France. To gain this end, she was anxious to have interviews with the Emperor of Germany, the King of the Romans, and, above all, the King of Spain. " My aim," she wrote on November 9, 1563, to the Bishop of Limoges, one of her ambassadors, " is none other

213

than to see whether we, who are the greatest and most powerful of Christian Princes, cannot, if we meet together, come to some agreement, and unite in order to secure the peace and tranquillity of Christendom by some better method than that of taking up arms." But the Catholic sovereigns did not respond to her overtures. The King of Spain and his lieutenant the Duke of Alba, who were combating a revolt of the Protestants in the Netherlands, cared only for one thing : that the King of France should strengthen them by stifling heresy in his own kingdom. " I can see quite clearly," Catherine replied, " that the Duke of Alba would like everybody to be joining in the dance with his master. But, for our part, as God by His good grace has allowed us to escape from it, I am content never to return to it again if I can help it." Philip II was not anxious to have an interview, and wanted to know beforehand what would be the outcome of it. But owing to the persistence of Catherine and his wife, Elizabeth, he at length unwillingly consented. " This interview has been postponed for various reasons," he wrote to Granvelle, " but I have given in at last to the importunity of the two Queens. It will, however, have no political object, and it is important that this should be made perfectly clear and the interview be represented in its true light." Then at the last moment he decided not to go himself, but to send his wife Elizabeth alone to Bayonne under the escort of the Duke of Alba. The Duke was given precise instructions. He was to insist most emphatically that the King of France should take energetic measures to suppress heresy in his kingdom ; the Protestant ministers were to be driven out ; Protestant worship, whether public or private, was to be formally forbidden ; all Calvinist judges and officials were to be dismissed ; and the decrees of the Council of Trent, which had just come to a conclusion, and the validity of which French jurists refused to acknowledge, on the plea that they were contrary to the law of the land, were to be promulgated. A tall, straight, thin man, with hollow cheeks and a long sallow face lit by two keen black eyes, the Duke of Alba, who was fifty-seven at this time, was ready to play his part with brutal severity.

The meeting took place in June. From the beginning the

214

Duke of Alba conjured Charles IX " to chastise the offences which were every day committed in his kingdom." But Charles IX, who was beginning to think for himself, answered evasively, " I do not wish to take up arms—that would mean the ruin of my country." With Catherine de' Medici the discussion was very strenuous. The Spaniard attacked the question resolutely, and demanded rigorous measures against the heretics. " You must banish this sect from France," he exclaimed, " the King, your son, has no alternative." Catherine answered by suggesting a League with the Emperor Maximilian. " That is impracticable," the Duke replied, and the debate grew hot. Alba declared that l'Hôpital was a Huguenot. " Indeed he is not ! " the Queen retorted. " You are the only person in France, Madam, who is of that opinion," answered the Duke. On the question of the Council of Trent the discussion was equally futile. Catherine evaded the issue by consenting to appoint a Commission to decide whether "the decrees that had been passed by it were in any wise hostile to the liberties of the Gallican Church." On the whole the interview was fruitless. A last solemn conference was held on June 30. In order to give more weight to her declarations, which were those of the Government, Catherine summoned the chief leaders of the Catholic party, the Constable Montmorency, the Duke of Montpensier, and the Cardinals of Guise and Bourbon, to the meeting, at which Charles IX was present. Montmorency made a speech, and summing up the feelings of his whole party, declared that whilst they were all good Catholics they regarded civil war as dangerous and uncertain ; the King would nevertheless be capable of suppressing heresy. These last words were vague, and were only uttered to save appearances. In a letter to Philip II dated July 6, Catherine repeated this declaration : " You may rest assured," she wrote, " of our good-will and zeal in the cause of our religion and of our desire to see all things conducing to the service of God—a matter which we shall never forget but will endeavour so to carry out as to do His will." But at the same moment she wrote to the King's ambassadors abroad : " Their Majesties in no way either desired or arranged to alter any of the promises made (to the Protestants) by the edicts of pacification and the declarations which have since been published!" Thus both sides failed in attaining their object, Catherine in her project of a League, and the Duke of Alba in his attempt to drag the French Government into a policy of violence.

This interview, however, the details of which were not made public, produced great anxiety among the Huguenots, who were convinced that their extermination had been demanded— in which they were perfectly right—and that it had been determined, which was not the case. After the massacre of Saint Bartholomew, ten years later, however, the Conference of Bayonne appeared in a somewhat sinister light. But in reality, when the Duke of Alba consulted some French Catholics upon the best means of stamping out heresy in France, the Duke of Montpensier's confessor replied, " The shortest way would be to behead Condé, the Admiral, d'Andelot, La Rochefoucauld, and Grammont." This was all that was said on the subject, and it was merely the private opinion of an irresponsible person.

From Bayonne, the Court returned to Paris through Nérac, Angoulême, Tours, and Blois. At Moulins Michel de l'Hôpital **Return of** made the authorities sign one of the grand ordin- **the Court.** ances supplementing the Ordinance of Orleans and continuing the reforms required to simplify the administration of justice. In Paris they found religious hatreds and passions in a more excited condition than ever. The Guises and the Châtillons hurled threats and defiance at each other daily. The Duke of Aumale was talking of challenging Coligny ; and d'Andelot, it was said, wanted to have d'Aumale assassinated. In the provinces the mutual hatred between the Catholics and the Protestants was at its height. The Edict of Amboise, which had been carried out with brutal rigour, had in some places given rise to a fierce reaction. At Castres, royalist troops invaded the town and reinstated the priests and nuns, forcing the Protestants to hold their services secretly in garrets, and removing all the arms and pieces of artillery with which the Huguenots had previously furnished the place. In Provence the Protestants were banished after being forced to sell their goods, and the sheriff of Troyes forbade any Protestant meetings to be held. But in other cases the heretics remained masters of the situation, and refused to acknowledge the edicts. " We have no power," wrote Bourneuf and Masparault from Saintonge, " to enforce the observation of the edict. Not a single cleric has the courage to risk returning to the villages and unfortified towns, and no officer of the law dares to do his duty ! " From Thouars, Monsieur de Sanzay wrote : " There are a hundred parishes in which divine service has not been held for two years." Here and there the clergy were murdered, and the gentlemen, it was said, were selling their goods to buy arms, whilst quarrels resulting in bloodshed were too numerous to be counted.

The truth had at length to be faced. If the repressive policy of Henry II and Francis II had failed to arrest the development

Change in Catherine's policy. of Protestantism, the conciliatory method inaugurated by Catherine de' Medici had produced effects very much more disastrous. Disorder, anarchy, civil war, and all the worst conditions of a State that was falling to pieces were the lamentable results. The country was going to ruin. A gradual change then began to take place in the mind of Catherine de' Medici, who was thoroughly discouraged. So nothing, it seemed, could be done with the Protestants, who were clearly aiming—and this conviction little by little gained ground in her mind—at nothing less than a usurpation of power with the object of destroying Catholicism and forcing the French people to become Huguenots, whether they liked it or not ! Her travels through France had given the old Queen the opportunity of realizing that they were, as a matter of fact, in the minority, and that the Catholics were the more numerous and the stronger party. Surely then it was unnecessary to submit to the tyranny of the heretics ! Charles IX, who was young and ardent, began to feel more exasperated than anyone, and in a discussion with Coligny he lost his temper and exclaimed angrily, " Not so very long ago you were content with being tolerated by the Catholics, but now you demand equality ! Soon you will want the power for yourselves alone, and will wish to drive us out of the country ! " He understood the state of affairs. Anger against the rebels rose high, and the imprudent and provocative conduct of the Protestants aggravated the exasperation of the Government.

217

The Reformers, regardless of the fact that in a number of places their co-religionists were violating the edicts and making themselves absolute masters, made loud complaints that in many districts the Edict of Amboise was not carried out, to the detriment of the members of their faith, as indeed was true. For even murders of Huguenots were allowed to pass unpunished. To these complaints, Catherine's Government returned curt and dilatory answers. " I can do nothing more here," exclaimed Condé, beside himself with rage, and he thereupon left the Court. Conferences between the Protestant leaders were held under his roof in the Château de Valery and in Coligny's home at Châtillon, at which they came to the definite conclusion that they were being deceived, and that the Edict of Amboise was not being carried out, owing more to the powerlessness than to the ill-will of the Government ; they were not allowed to practise their religion in a town even after they had got permission from the sheriff. The question was raised as to the objective of the foreign troops which the King was summoning from Switzerland and Germany. A rumour was current that the Government intended to arrest the Protestant leaders. Clearly they were menaced, and under these circumstances it would be wiser to steal a march upon the Government than to wait for it to open the attack. D'Andelot made the daring proposal that they should attempt the manœuvre which had succeeded in Scotland against Mary Stuart, and kidnap the King and the royal family at Monceaux ! Coligny objected strongly to the idea, but the majority were in favour of the scheme, and it was decided that troops should be secretly collected with the object of surrounding Montceaux.

Catherine de' Medici was warned in time, and she barely managed to beat a hurried retreat from Montceaux on September **Protestant** 25, 1567, and take shelter behind the walls of **attempt to** Meaux. But the sense of shame, anger, and **kidnap the** humiliation with which this attempt and the **Court, 1567.** flight it necessitated filled a Queen who was extremely sensitive on the score of her dignity, already sorely wounded, and its even deeper effect upon an impetuous young man like Charles IX, cannot well be imagined. " Never should I have believed," wrote Catherine to the Duke of Savoy,

" that such great and grievous designs against their King could have occurred to the minds of subjects." " ' They shall not give me any further alarms of the kind,' exclaimed Charles IX, with oaths of unseemly vigour," wrote Bouchefort, in a letter to Renée of Ferrara. " ' I will go into their houses and even into their beds to fetch out those who furnish them!' " Tavannes was right—the Protestants had gone too far in conceiving such a plan, and in failing to carry it out, not far enough. The attempt was destined to weigh heavily on the future, inasmuch as it definitively alienated Catherine from the Huguenots, and more especially because it filled her mind with a perpetual terror of abduction and, perhaps, of a general massacre.

Closely guarded by 6000 Swiss, the King and the Court returned to Paris. Condé, feeling that a fresh civil war—the **Second Civil War.** second—was upon the point of breaking out, rallied his followers, and collecting a force of 4000 men, began to send out scouts round Paris. With 16,000 men Constable Montmorency, Marshal de Damville, and the Duke of Aumale, left the city in order to surround him. They reached him at Saint-Denis on November 10, 1567. The aged Montmorency, notwithstanding his weight of seventy-four years, charged like a young man. He was mortally wounded and fell from his horse. Three days afterwards he died! The Huguenots did not hold their ground ; at the end of an hour they took to flight, and their troops disbanded themselves. Hostilities dragged on for some time. But eventually Michel de l'Hôpital proposed to make peace. " The good pilot never insists upon fighting the storm," he remarked sadly; " he lowers his sails and waits." The Protestants gave way and a peace was signed at Longjumeau on February 23, 1568, by the terms of which the Edict of Amboise was ratified, and its execution promised. But the Catholics raised endless objections ; was it seemly that the King should treat with rebels, his subjects, on terms of equality, and give way to them out of weakness ? This peace was destined to be the Chancellor's last success. The years that had passed had brought a change in men's ideas, and, as his policy had failed, the time for conciliation and liberalism, which had clearly proved disastrous, was over. " It is you," exclaimed Catherine, who was now disillusioned, " it is you, who with your fine words about moderation and justice have landed us where we are ! " At the end of the month l'Hôpital gave up the seals and left the Court in disgrace.

Everybody felt that the Peace of Longjumeau was nothing more than a truce. And as far as the provinces were concerned, it mattered little whether the country were at peace or at war, for the state of anarchy remained unchanged, with mutual intolerance, surprises, and massacres. After the incident at Montceaux, Condé and the Protestant leaders felt that it was out of the question for them to return to Court ; their position there would have been too insecure. In all their discussions the Catholics kept reiterating that the evil sprang from five or six leaders, and that if these were suppressed there would be a change for the better. This opinion gained ground, and was far from reassuring for the Protestants. Condé accordingly retired to La Rochelle with the Châtillons. They were joined by their followers, and almost imperceptibly a Protestant army was formed. The fiery Jeanne d'Albret brought her son, Henry of Béarn, the future Henry IV, who was then fifteen years old. The third war was on the point of breaking out.

The Government thereupon threw off the mask, and casting away all show of forbearance, published an edict on September **Third** 28, 1568, unconditionally forbidding the exercise **Civil War.** of the reformed faith in France in any form whatsoever, ordering the Protestant ministers to leave the country within a fortnight, and excluding all Calvinists from public office. This was a return to the repressive policy of Henry II. Condé's only reply was to set out on the march with his army of 21,000 men, including 3000 cavalry, representing the largest force the Protestants had yet been able to raise. The Government with difficulty collected 20,000 men whom they dispatched to meet Condé under the command of the Duke of Anjou, the King's younger brother, the future Henry III, with Tavannes as his lieutenant. For a long time the two armies watched each other's movements, manœuvring and countermanœuvring, and not daring to open battle. The conflict eventually took place at Jarnac on March 13, 1569, and was

220

in the nature of a surprise. Condé led a charge at the head of 250 men against 2500, and was surrounded. A kick from a horse broke his leg. His charger fell and he was brought to the ground ; he was just giving up his sword when a gentleman named Montesquiou, came up behind him and shattered his skull with a pistol shot. Thus, at the age of nine-and-thirty

Death of Condé. fell this prince, a brilliant and inspiring general, a supple and gracious man, self-willed and obstinate, but frivolous and unstable. In the Bibliothèque Nationale a letter has been preserved which was found in his pocket on the field of battle, and which Jeanne d'Albret had written to him on the very morning of the fight on the subject of her son Henry. This letter is stained with Condé's blood !

The disaster of Jarnac and the loss of their leader discouraged the Protestants. They could no longer pretend, if they rebelled again, that they proposed to deliver the King from tyranny, for they had fought against the monarch's own brother. The fact that they had had a prince of the blood to lead them had saved appearances hitherto ; but for the moment they were deprived of this advantage. Jeanne d'Albret hastened to present her son, the young Henry of Béarn, and her nephew, Henry of Condé, to the Calvinists. The two cousins were about the same age—fifteen and sixteen years old respectively. Jeanne harangued her co-religionists at Saintes and tried to raise their spirits. Condé was succeeded as active leader by Coligny, a man of a calmer temperament, more deliberate and more mature, but lacking his predecessor's vigorous qualities. As his brother d'Andelot had died two months after the battle of Jarnac, Coligny had become the virtual head of the Protestant party in France.

He marched against Poitiers with the intention of making for Paris, but lost seven weeks and 3000 men in besieging the

Battle of Moncontour, 1569. former place which he failed to take in the end. The Duke of Anjou, still accompanied by Tavannes, was marching against him with an army. The two forces met at Moncontour on October 3, 1569. After a moment of indecision, the Protestant lines wavered, then broke and fled. A veritable massacre took place, and some 5000 or 6000 men were left lying upon the field. Coligny fled to

Niort and from thence went south, where he raised fresh recruits with the intention of making his way back towards Paris from the east. He was endowed with the patience, the constancy under disaster, and the calm decision which inspire troops with confidence. Simple in his manners and easy of approach, although his face, while extremely sweet in expression, had a touch of melancholy, he gained influence by his dignity and his absence of personal ambition. Men followed him readily.

In July, 1570, he reached Charité-sur-Loire. The Protestants, though beaten, were ever ready to raise their heads again. But at this juncture the Government was in a most pitiable plight. They had no money, for, after several years of universal disorder, the taxes had ceased to come in, and they did not know how to subsist; it was impossible to raise troops or to pay them. Were they destined to find themselves at the mercy of the Huguenot leader, they asked themselves anxiously. It is possible that they may have exaggerated the critical nature of their situation, but in the dilemma in which they found themselves, Catherine and Charles IX came to the conclusion that it was necessary to treat for peace at all costs and accept any terms that were demanded, however exorbitant—and **Peace of** they were indeed disastrous. By the Peace of **Saint-Germain, 1570.** Saint-Germain of August 8, 1570, it was stipulated that liberty of conscience and freedom of worship should be definitely accorded to the Protestants throughout the country with the exception of Paris and in the immediate neighbourhood of the Court. A general amnesty was pronounced in favour of the rebels; the Huguenots were to be eligible for all public offices, and for a space of two years, as guarantees for the execution of the treaty, they were to receive four cities as guarantees—La Rochelle, Montauban, Cognac, and La Charité. In return for these concessions Catholicism was to be re-established in all the districts where it had been suppressed by the Protestants. Thus at one fell swoop the King granted full liberty to the heretics. It was the first time such a thing had been known in France! The King had actually made a treaty with rebels whom he had conquered, and had submitted to their terms; and he had given them towns as a guarantee—a monstrous proceeding, indeed! The Catholics

222

were dumbfounded and called the peace " a humiliating capitulation." Monluc wrote : " We had beaten our enemies over and over again ; we were winning by force of arms, but they triumphed by means of their diabolical writings ! " The Catholic Powers protested, but Charles IX replied that he had learnt " by experience that it was impossible to end the trouble by force of arms," and that he had acted under the pressure of necessity. To the Pope Catherine wrote that the King had made peace with the Huguenots " the better to arrange everything in accordance with his wishes." The moderates remarked philosophically in the words of Pasquier that the Government had " ended where they ought to have begun."

But this time the Protestants were satisfied, and peace was established. Catherine seized the moment of respite to arrange **Marriage of** a match for Charles IX, and married him to **Charles IX.** Elizabeth of Austria, daughter of the Emperor Maximilian II. The Protestants talked vaguely of a marriage between their prince, Henry of Béarn, and Elizabeth of England, but the Queen decided to give him her own daughter, Margaret of Valois, and proposed her second son, the Duke of Anjou, as a husband for the Queen of England. On the latter point, however, she did not succeed. She was extremely fond of the Duke of Anjou, who was her favourite son and the apple of her eye, a gentle boy, whom she had well in hand. As early as the Conference of Bayonne, she had tried to arrange a match for him with a Spanish Infanta, but without success. England kept the question in suspense for some time as a matter of policy. But the union was impracticable ; Elizabeth, an ardent Protestant, was thirty-seven, whilst the Duke of Anjou, a no less ardent Catholic, who had every intention of remaining true to his faith in England, and even of endeavouring to restore it in that country, was only nineteen. The negotiations had no result.

But the suggested marriage between Henry of Béarn and Margaret of Valois was a very different affair. Catherine saw various advantages in this alliance ; she would be giving her daughter to a King, the King of Navarre ; she would be laying hands upon the nominal chief of the Huguenots, a prince of the blood, with the vague hope of one day converting him ;

and she would be realizing a project which Henry II had nursed for many a long year. Difficulties arose in the first place in connexion with Jeanne d'Albret on the score of religion. Jeanne hoped that Margaret of Valois would become a Protestant, but Margaret refused. Catherine had then insisted upon the marriage being celebrated in church, to which Jeanne would not consent. But in the end the Queen of Navarre, who in her heart was rather proud of the fact that her son was to marry the sister of the King of France, gave way. It was from Rome that protests were next raised, and the Pope demanded that Henry of Béarn should make profession of the Catholic faith. Catherine de' Medici paid no attention to this and persuaded the Cardinal of Bourbon to perform the ceremony without waiting for the dispensation. This marriage determined the reconciliation between the Court and the Protestant party. Jeanne d'Albret and her son came to Blois, as did also Coligny (September 18, 1571) with over 500 Protestant nobles. They were received as cordially as possible. Owing to a certain lack of decision in their ideas, Catherine and Charles IX gave themselves up entirely to the peaceful sentiments of the moment.

Charles IX and Coligny. The young King was touched by Coligny's character. The fine melancholy features and gentle, deep-set eyes of the Admiral attracted him, and he felt himself moved by a sudden sympathy for his upright, honest character. During the long conversations they had together, the young King of twenty gained confidence in the veteran of fifty, who had seen so many wars and had lived under four reigns. Their intimacy increased rapidly, and Coligny took advantage of it to impart to Charles IX a project which he had deeply at heart. The Netherlands had rebelled against Philip II, and Coligny suggested that France should support them, with the object of laying hands on the French provinces, which might be induced to return to their allegiance. By this means the martial ardour of the nobility would be engrossed by a foreign war, whereas otherwise they might seek satisfaction in civil conflicts. "If we do not give them amusement abroad," said Coligny, "they will begin their quarrels at home again." Moreover, he added, he felt that the King must be extremely irritated by Philip II's proceedings, his constant remonstrances,

224

and the protective attitude he had assumed. Had not the Duke of Alba offered to come and command the Catholic forces in France? Did not Philip II negotiate with the Guises without consulting the Court, and did he not act as though he were master of France? An attack upon him would be perfectly legitimate. Charles IX lent a ready ear to these suggestions.

But the Catholics protested vehemently. Not only, it seemed, had the Treaty of Saint-Germain given everything to the Protestants, but now the King himself was ready to go over to them. The Guises left Blois. Already the new Duke, Henry of Guise, the son of Duke Francis, a brilliant, ambitious young man, of great courage and strength of will, and his brother, Mayenne, were becoming conspicuous among them. The hatred this family felt for Coligny, the reputed murderer of Duke Francis, was aggravated by the menacing popularity of the Admiral at Court.

The marriage contract between Margaret of Valois and Henry of Béarn was signed at Blois on April 11, 1572, and the date of the wedding itself was fixed for August. Jeanne d'Albret was not destined to witness the ceremony, for she died somewhat suddenly in June. " She was a great Queen," says d'Aubigné, " who had nothing feminine about her except her sex. Her whole soul was absorbed by virile interests, and she had a heart that was undaunted by adversity."

Coligny turned Charles IX's favourable attitude to account, and in his capacity as Admiral began to make military prepara-

Coligny the head of the Government.

tions, and raise troops for the proposed war in the Netherlands. His influence at this juncture was preponderant at Court, and he was regarded as the head of the Government. But a strong opposition began to be formed against him. It was natural that Catherine de' Medici and her counsellors should regard his power with apprehension. As the Chancellor de Birague subsequently explained to the Venetian ambassador, Giovanni Michiel, Coligny was actually the undisputed leader of the Protestant cause ; the Protestants never carried a royal edict into execution without securing a favourable opinion on the matter from their leader, and they were in a position to raise for him a force of 7000 or 8000 cavalry and 25,000 or 30,000 infantry within one month—

numbers which the King could only collect in four. Thus the country had another master besides the King—an intolerable state of affairs. As far as the Netherlands were concerned, moreover, Coligny's plan of war was absolutely unreasonable. The kingdom was in debt and its own internal troubles had barely calmed down. Surely to engage in a foreign war against Spain with the provinces rising up in rebellion in the rear was sheer madness? And were the Catholics, forsooth, to march under the command of the very men they had conquered at Jarnac and Moncontour, in order to help the Huguenot cause abroad and thus add such additional strength to Coligny's position in France that on his return he would be able to Protestantize the whole country? Tavannes, in high dudgeon, threatened to leave the Court. By what right, he demanded, was Coligny now raising troops without the King's command? His preparations were giving people cause for alarm.

Impatient at the opposition which he felt rising against him, Coligny asked that the question of the Netherlands might be settled at a grand council. This council was held, and the majority was against intervention. Coligny was annoyed and confessed that he had promised the Prince of Orange, the leader of the rebels in the Netherlands, the support of France, and that if the King backed out of the war he would be under the necessity of going himself together with his followers and friends, in order to fulfil his engagement as a private individual. Then, turning towards Catherine de' Medici, he ended his speech by saying, " The King, Madam, refuses to enter upon this war. God grant that another may not break out, from which it will not be so easy for him to escape perhaps ! " Was this meant as a threat? Catherine was startled, and began to feel seriously anxious.

August, and the date fixed for the marriage of Henry of Béarn, was fast approaching. From all quarters the news came **Marriage of** that the Protestant nobility intended to present **Henry of** themselves *en masse* for the festivities. Haunted **Béarn.** by the dread of some plan of kidnapping similar to the Montceaux incident, or even worse, Catherine de' Medici had refused to allow the ceremony to take place in any small provincial town where the Court would be at the mercy of the

226

Huguenots, and had insisted upon Paris, a thickly populated Catholic city. At the time arranged Henry of Béarn and Condé entered Paris followed by an escort of 800 cavalry, and by all the roads the Protestant gentry made their way to the city, hastening to take part in the festivities which were to consecrate the triumph of their church, and curious to behold the splendid pageant about to be unfolded. The influx of all these heretics put the Government and the Catholics into a state of extreme excitement. Charles IX, alone, who was still on the best of terms with Coligny, remained unmoved. The marriage, which had been fixed for August 10, was not celebrated until the 18th, and in accordance with custom it took place in the open air outside Notre Dame, whilst Mass was said inside the church in the presence of the bride alone. The festivities then followed. But the conversations which took place betrayed the irritable condition of men's minds. The Protestants were filled with indignation at the Government's refusal to interfere in the Netherlands; they kept insisting on the dilemma pointed out by Coligny: " either civil war or a foreign war "; and they were extremely outspoken in their criticisms of the King, Catherine de' Medici, the Catholic leaders, and the Guises. Among the Catholics, too, the flood of discontent rose daily higher. They declared that the Court was being carried away headlong in the tide of Protestantism, and hinted covertly at a fresh stroke of violence on the part of the Huguenots, like the attempt at Montceaux, which would aim at placing the royal family entirely in the hands of the Protestants. Coligny's position, above all, aroused their ire, and the Guises uttered furious threats against him. Anger was seething on all sides. A continual muttering of discontent was heard, and the air was heavy with two opposing electric currents, the first spark from which would fire the mine. This spark was kindled on Friday, August 22.

On the morning of that day Coligny was making his way to the Louvre from his house at the corner of the Rue de l'Arbre **Attempt to** Sec and the Rue de Bétizy (the present Rue de **murder** Rivoli). As he was going down a narrow street **Coligny.** which skirted the Hôtel du Petit Bourbon between the Rue des Fossés Saint-Germain and the quay, he bent down to arrange his shoe which was slipping off his foot, when he was shot from behind a small curtained window. The bullet cut off the first finger of his left hand, ripped up his arm, and entered his elbow. " This is how honest men are treated in France ! " he exclaimed. His companions rushed towards the house, and burst open the door, but found only a smoking arquebuse. The assassin had made his escape in the rear on horseback. They discovered that the house belonged to the Guises, that the murderer, whose name was Maurevert, was a member of their suite, and that the horse had come out of their stables. A unanimous outcry was raised that the Guises were responsible for the attempt. Coligny was carried back to his house, where he was placed under the charge of Ambroise Paré. The bullet was extracted with great difficulty, and the arm was badly mangled in the operation. The surgeon, however, answered for the life of his patient.

Charles IX was playing tennis when the news of the crime was brought to him. " Am I never to have any peace ! " he exclaimed, throwing down his racket in a violent fit of anger. He returned to the Louvre where considerable excitement prevailed. It was useless to blink matters—the event which had just occurred was very probably the signal for a catastrophe. The royal palace was immediately cleared, and the guards at the gates doubled.

Coligny's house was besieged by all the Protestants in a state of feverish commotion—the Prince of Condé, the King **Agitation in** of Navarre, the leaders of the party, and a constant **Paris.** influx of Huguenots who went to and fro asking for news amidst a babel of violent language, curses, and furious oaths. Vengeance must be wreaked upon the Guises at once, they kept repeating. They must be killed if necessary in the presence of the King himself, in the heart of the Louvre. " They used extremely insolent language," writes Brantôme, " declaring that they were prepared to strike and to kill ! " Coligny expressed a desire to see the King, and the Government, knowing how matters stood, thought it would be best for the whole of the royal family to go to the Rue de Bétizy, as this courtesy might perhaps calm the Protestants. The visit was accordingly paid in the afternoon, and Catherine de' Medici together with

228

her two other sons accompanied Charles IX. " You feel the pain," the King said, as he greeted the Admiral, " but it is I who feel the grief." And he assured him that he would have strict and exemplary justice done him. He even proposed to have him conveyed to the Louvre, but Coligny refused. They discussed matters, and Coligny kept reverting to the idea of an expedition to the Netherlands as the sole solution for the difficulties of the existing situation. In the evening Charles IX informed all the ambassadors of the crime. " This evil act proceeded," he declared, " from the hostility between the House of Châtillon and that of Guise, and I shall take good care to ensure that they do not mix up any of my subjects in their quarrel." He was doing his best to limit the sphere of danger. " I am determined," he continued, " to have justice done on such a scale that it shall be a warning to every man in my kingdom."

On the morning of the following day, Saturday, August 23, the Duke of Guise and the Duke of Aumale presented themselves to the King and asked permission to leave Paris. " Go wherever you like," Charles IX answered curtly, and as soon as their backs were turned, he added, " I shall always be able to find them again ! " Instead of taking their departure, however, the Guises went back to their house, the Hôtel de Lorraine, where they barricaded themselves. Huguenots kept passing to and fro beneath their windows shouting threats of death. As a precaution the Court sent fifty arquebusiers to guard Coligny ; an inquiry into the crime was instituted and opened by de Thou, the First President.

Meanwhile, however, the excitement among the Protestants was increasing every moment. The house in the Rue de Bétizy, its court and its staircase were crowded with people uttering vehement threats. " That arm shall cost 30,000 other arms ! " they cried. They wished to kill the Guises, if necessary, they repeated, in the Louvre itself, and they threatened even to burst open its gates and massacre the guards. Other names were mentioned, and among them that of the Duke of Anjou, who was accused of having connived at the crime of the Guises. But in the tumult what would happen to the King, the Queen-Mother, and the princes ? In vain did Briquemaut try to put a stop to these declarations. The agitation was beginning to spread to the streets, and the people, irritated by the attitude of the Huguenots, were leaving their houses and forming menacing groups in open spaces ; some of them even carried arms.

In the evening a council was held in the apartments of Catherine de' Medici, at which the Duke of Anjou, the Chancellor **Agitation of** de Birague, Nevers, Tavannes, and Gondi were **the Government.** present. They had to face the facts of the situation. The position was most critical ; they were within an ace of civil war in Paris, and in the midst of such a fiery populace this would mean nothing short of butchery. The lives of the King and of the royal family were in danger. Echoes of the threats pronounced round Coligny's sick bed reached them from without, and in any case, civil war, whether in Paris or in the provinces, was once more a foregone conclusion. The council was in a great state of agitation, when suddenly Bouchavannes arrived from the house in the Rue de Bétizy, announcing as a fact that the Protestants had decided to attack the Louvre, and to massacre the King, his brother, and the Queen-Mother " on the following day at supper-time." What truth was there in the allegation of this terrible conspiracy? It is possible, nay probable, that Bouchavannes mistook for a general decision the mere approval expressed by a few minor personalities of a suggested plan of action. However this may have been, the effect produced was terrible. At the thought of the impending catastrophe consternation filled the breasts of Catherine de' Medici and her counsellors, who were already in a state of alarm, and brought the nervous terror which had possessed them for some hours to a climax. They thought they were lost. To order the arrest of the conspirators was impossible ; their friends would defend them or rescue them. And after all, as Catherine de' Medici afterwards explained to her ambassador, du Ferrier, Charles IX was " sovereign King and prince " and supreme judge of the realm— for the magistrates only passed sentence as delegates of his unique power. He had the right, *motu proprio*, summarily to punish all criminals known to be such. For ten years everybody had been repeating *ad nauseam* that if the heads of five

230

or six of the leaders were forfeited, the diabolical conspiracy of the heretics, which was bringing the country to ruin, would be stopped once and for all. The hour had come. They must either strike or perish! It would be better to prevent the war that was on the verge of breaking out by one bold move than to drag on for months in all manner of perils and miseries. The Duke of Anjou was particularly emphatic on this head.

It only remained to win over the King. A terrible scene took place. According to Pibrac, who was given a minute description of it afterwards, Charles IX, utterly disconcerted, began by offering a fierce resistance. He proposed having the instigators of the plot of which he was informed arrested, and an inquiry opened. But he was told that time pressed, and that if the business were not stopped within a few hours, the royal family was lost. " But since the conspiracy has been discovered," exclaimed the King, " surely we can ward it off without having recourse to murder ! " "There are too many of them," was the retort. " You might capture one or two, and even so you would be obliged to kill them, and you would not escape a fourth civil war." For two hours the discussion continued, passionate and breathless, Charles IX holding out, in feverish agitation, with Catherine, the Duke of Anjou, and the rest arguing and imploring, beside themselves with terror. At last the King gave way, but with a cry of rage and fury, exclaiming: " Well then, kill them all, that not a single man may be left to reproach me ! "

The die was cast ! In the mind of Catherine and of her counsellors it was merely a question of the death of five or six men—Coligny, the Count de la Rochefoucauld, Téligny, Caumont la Force, Montgommery, and the Marquis of Resnel. Preparations for the deed were made. The Provost of the Merchants was summoned to the Louvre. He was informed of the conspiracy that was threatening the King, and ordered to have all the gates of Paris closed immediately, to call out and arm all the city militia, to concentrate them in the squares and on the quays, to mass the artillery in front of the Hôtel de Ville so that it might be used whenever it was found necessary, and to await further orders. For the execution of the sentence passed upon Coligny, none were better fitted than the Guises.

Duke Henry and the Duke of Aumale were summoned, and the mission, which they accepted, was confided to them. The parties entrusted with the other executions were also appointed. Unfortunately the instructions issued were not sufficiently precise. It was arranged that the signal should be given on the following day, August 24, the Feast of Saint Bartholomew, at three o'clock in the morning by the bell of the Palais de Justice.

That night no one in the Louvre closed his eyes. The King, his mother, and his brothers kept vigil, the prey of

Massacre of Saint Bartholomew, 1572. indescribable emotion. In their deadly anxiety they were even on the point at one moment of giving up the whole project and countermanding their orders. But about one o'clock in the morning news was brought that fighting was going on all over Paris. Had the conspirators been warned? They decided to give the signal earlier, and sent to have the bell of Saint-Germain-l'Auxerrois rung. At half-past one the fatal peal rang through the silence of the night. Guise, who was ready, sprang on his horse, accompanied by the Bastard of Angoulême, and at the head of 300 soldiers rode rapidly to the house in the Rue de Bétizy, which he surrounded. Coligny was in bed, watched by Ambroise Paré, the Protestant minister, Merlin, and his own servant, Nicolas. The tramp of the soldiers arriving in the street together with the clang of the tocsin, awoke him. Violent knocking was heard below, and voices ordering the inmates to open in the name of the King. The gate was unbarred. As soon as Coligny heard the troops marching into the court, he understood. Rising from his bed, he put on his dressing-gown and asked Merlin to read prayers. Cornaton burst hurriedly into the room exclaiming, "They are breaking in the door! We are lost!" Their last hour had come. Coligny replied calmly: "I have long been prepared for death; save yourselves. I commend my soul to the mercy of God!" Up the stairs heavy footsteps were hastening. The soldiers burst in, headed by one Besme, a German by extraction. "Are

Death of Coligny. you the Admiral?" he demanded brutally. "I am!" Besme then drove his sword into Coligny's breast, drew it out, and slashed his face. The Admiral fell to the ground, and the soldiers thrust at him again and again. A voice from the court below cried out, " Is it done ? " It was Guise. " Yes," one of the soldiers replied. " Well, throw him out." The body was pushed through the open window, and Coligny, who was not dead, clung to the ledge. He was forced to let go, and his body fell with a thud on the pavement. Guise approached it, and Angoulême, wiping away a little of the blood from Coligny's face with his handkerchief, said, " Yes, it is he " ; then kicking him he exclaimed, " Now for the others." Whereupon they remounted their horses and rode away to finish their work.

A regular man-hunt took place. The Count of La Roche-foucauld was stabbed, and died in his bed. Téligny ran over the roofs of three or four houses, and was finally laid low by a shot from an arquebuse. Caumont la Force and his son had their throats cut. Resnel was killed by a pistol-shot and thrown into the Seine ; whilst Montgommery had time to mount his horse, and clearing the city moat, made good his escape.

But at the news of what was happening a rumour immediately ran through Paris that the Huguenots were being massacred, with the result that Catholic nobles, soldiers of the guard, archers, members of the populace, and people of every rank rushed out armed into the streets to take part in the execution. A general massacre began to the sound of ferocious yells of " The Huguenots ! The Huguenots ! Death to the Huguenots ! " They were slain, drowned, and hanged. No one who was known to be a heretic escaped, and private revenge completed what religious passion had begun. Terrible incidents occurred ; illustrious victims fell, among them Ramus ; innocent persons were massacred, and then, as was inevitable, pillage ensued. The envoy from Mantua wrote : " I with my own eyes saw soldiers of the royal guard bearing away money and objects of value." " Paris," said Tavannes, " was like a conquered city. As soon as blood ceased to flow, the sack began." At eleven o'clock in the morning the terrified aldermen came to inform the King that " princes and nobles of his Court, lords, archers, soldiers of the royal guard, and all sorts and conditions of men mingled with them, and under their protection,

233

were pillaging, sacking, and killing in the streets." Thus the Government in giving the signal had let loose the beast. Anarchy reigned, bloodthirsty and destructive. Public order was at an end.

Horrified at their handiwork, Charles IX and those about him endeavoured to stem the torrent. Everywhere proclamations were made to the sound of the trumpet, ordering the crowd to go home. Patrols of mounted archers, guards, and city officials were sent to scour the streets, and in the afternoon the uproar seemed to be dying down. It began again, however, on the following night, and was only quelled next day, the 26th. How many victims had fallen ? It is impossible to tell the numbers exactly ; de Thou says 2000.

The Government immediately dispatched letters to all the provincial Governors informing them that a terrible conflict **Paralysis** had broken out in Paris between the House of **of the** Guise and the House of Châtillon, and that the **Government.** King had found it impossible to hold it within bounds. In the evening Charles IX wrote to the French ambassadors abroad to tell them that " a conspiracy had just been brought to light which the members of the so-called reformed religion had formed against himself, his mother, and his brother," and that a " commotion " had resulted, of which nothing could be said until the full details were known. It was clear that the Government was paralysed and did not know what attitude to take. On the 25th, the day following the massacre, as the Guises refused to accept responsibility for the events that had occurred, the Government was forced to confess, more especially as the triumphant Catholics were acclaiming the King as the avenger of their religion. Charles IX went to the Parliament, and at a *lit de justice* * declared that the Guises had acted by his orders " for the punishment of those who so frequently before and now once again had conspired against his person, desiring to annihilate religion, overturn the monarchy, and by means of heresy establish a new form of

* This ceremony, which consisted in the meeting of the King and the Parliament with the object either of conferring upon some matter of law or policy, or merely of honouring the Parliament, was one of the most solemn and important functions of the monarch. (Tr.)

government in France." All Protestant services and meetings were forbidden throughout the country, and further communications were addressed to the provincial Governors, imperatively commanding them to maintain order. The Government, embarrassed and confused, babbled contradictions and incoherencies.

The effect of the events that had taken place in Paris made itself felt in the provinces, and massacres took place in many of the towns—Orleans, Troyes, Meaux, Bourges, La Charité, Rouen, Lyons, and Toulouse. The strife was fiercest at Lyons and Orleans, where the inmates of the prisons were put to death. According to de Thou 800 victims fell at Lyons and 1000 at Orleans. The Governors set to work energetically to hold the populace in hand, and there were no outbreaks in Burgundy, Provence, and Dauphiny. The Massacre of Saint Bartholomew stirred the provinces less than Paris.

But, as Tavannes wrote: "When once the blow had fallen and the danger was past, the bloodshed weighed heavily on men's consciences!" And, indeed, the Massacre of Saint Bartholomew had been a terrible surprise. "The suddenness of the danger," de la Mothe Fénelon, the French Ambassador to England, informed Queen Elizabeth on behalf of his Government, "had not even left the King time for reflection, and he had been constrained to allow that to be done to the Admiral and his followers which they had planned against his own person." "As the conspiracy was on the eve of realization," the first President of Bordeaux informed his Parliament, "matters were so pressing that it had been impossible to wait for justice to take its ordinary course: it had been thought better to surprise the conspirators than to be surprised by them, and this the King had declared in his court of Parliament to have been his sole reason for taking action." "The event," said Tavannes, "had been the result of necessity and wise counsel, owing to the errors and recklessness of the Huguenots." Catherine de' Medici, whom the envoy of the Duke of Savoy described as looking "like a person who had just escaped from a great peril," kept repeating to every one "that it was better for the blow to have fallen on them than on us!" The Catholics certainly approved the course the

Catholic
exultation.

Government had taken, maintaining that they had escaped from an intolerable situation by a measure of public safety, and that the revolutionary schemes directed against the royal family necessitated the employment of exceptional, though legitimate measures. Philip II in a transport of joy had a *Te Deum* sung, and wrote to his ambassador in France : " This has given me one of the greatest joys of my life, and will be the greatest title to glory of the King, my brother, with posterity." In Rome Pope Gregory XIII, radiant with triumph, attended a thanksgiving celebration of the Mass in the Chapel of Saint Louis. He also had a medal struck representing an avenging angel, with the inscription *Ugonotorum strages*, and prescribed an annual *Te Deum*, which was destined to be celebrated longer than is generally known. But the full consequences of the act had also to be faced.

In Vienna the impression produced was lamentable, and the Emperor Maximilian did not hesitate to make this felt. **Horror of Europe.** In England Elizabeth received the French Ambassador arrayed in deep mourning and addressed him with grave melancholy, whilst her minister, standing by her side, openly told the envoy in severe accents that the deed had been too bloody. In Switzerland, the Netherlands, and Germany, the effect was deplorable. The event was described and exaggerated, and it was even said that the marriage of Henry of Béarn and Margaret of Valois had been nothing but a monstrous snare. Schomberg, the French Ambassador, wrote in despair : " These calumnies turn everything upside down. I shall die of vexation." At Geneva pamphlets were printed stigmatizing the monarch who murdered his subjects, and François Hotman, in his *De Furoribus Gallicis*, attacked the very principle of royalty. The *Réveille-Matin des François* took a delight in publishing gruesome details, and a legend was current that Charles IX had shot at the Huguenots with an arquebuse from his window in the Louvre. This rumour, indeed, was persistent—but, as a matter of fact, there was not a single witness of the act, which was highly improbable, if only for material reasons. In Italy, under the pretext of exalting the deed, the massacre was compared to the action of a Cæsar Borgia or a Catherine Sforza, and was represented as having been consciously prepared with Machiavellian craft for many years, led up to with incredible coolness and audacity, and executed with incomparable skill at a marvellously opportune moment. The Cardinal of Lorraine, who was at Rome at the time, and was flattered by these insinuations, allowed people to believe in their truth. But this only increased the horror felt by the rest of Europe. " King Charles IX," William of Orange wrote to his brother Ludovic of Nassau, "is condemned not only here but throughout the world " ; and he even went so far as to tell Mondoucet, the French envoy, that his master would never be able to wash the blood of the massacre of Saint Bartholomew off his hands.

The French Government, through the medium of its ambassadors all over Europe, thus learnt the truth as to the impression that had been made. Catherine de' Medici held her ground, at all events in public, and put a bold face on the matter, declaring that they had only intended to execute five or six men, and that all the rest was due " to the excesses of the populace, which she deeply deplored." But Charles IX, **Remorse of** utterly prostrated, was stricken to death. In **Charles IX.** the eyes of the world, he told himself, he was merely a criminal, a dastardly assassin, a miserable wretch, covered with the blood of his own people. Under the weight of grief and remorse he changed visibly. He did not long survive the Massacre of Saint Bartholomew, for tuberculosis, to which he had always had a tendency, began to make swift ravages in a body rendered anæmic by sorrow.

The French Protestants, utterly cast down and disconcerted, were for the moment terror-stricken, and many of them abjured their faith. Henry of Béarn and the Prince of Condé, who as a precautionary measure had been kept in the Louvre, upon being invited to change their religion, consented to do so. In order to impress upon men's minds that a conspiracy had really existed and was the true cause of the event, though the public had lost sight of it in their horror of the consequences, the Government made the Parliament pass a resolution confirming their action, so to speak, in which Coligny was declared guilty of conspiracy and rebellion, and condemned to be hanged in effigy at Montfaucon, to have his goods confiscated and his children degraded from their rank. Two " accomplices " were unearthed who had escaped the assassins—Briquemaut and Cavagnes—and they were publicly tried and solemnly executed. But all these measures served no purpose. Both contemporaries and posterity quickly forgot the circumstance which had caused a panic in the government of Charles IX and remembered only the atrocity of the deed.

Beneath the lowering clouds created by August 24 and in the humiliating isolation into which the Massacre of Saint **Anjou elected** Bartholomew had plunged the French Govern-**King of** ment, one single gleam of light appeared—a **Poland.** semi-successful stroke of diplomacy. Catherine de' Medici succeeded in placing her favourite son, the Duke of Anjou, upon the vacant throne of Poland. He left France, to the great joy of Charles IX, who was jealous of him and had scenes with him which caused their mother many bitter tears. On behalf of her youngest son, the Duke of Alençon, Catherine revived the negotiations for a marriage with Elizabeth of England. D'Alençon, who was a young man of a frivolous and discontented disposition, and held in very slight esteem, was flattered by this prospect, and had the Queen of England informed that he would not be so irreconcilable on the score of religion as his brother had been. He showed signs of sympathy for Calvinism, and gained the reputation of being favourably disposed towards heresy. But Elizabeth eluded him. Finally, he decided to flee from Court in the company of Henry of Béarn, a species of conspiracy which once more filled the royal family with alarm, and resulted in the arrest, trial, and execution of two nobles, La Môle and Coconas, who were regarded as the instigators of the escapade.

Meanwhile, however, Charles IX gradually sank into a decline. Since the terrible catastrophe he had never been **Death of** himself. Bowed down with melancholy that **Charles IX,** nothing could alleviate, he looked like a mourning, **1574.** terror-stricken shade. The foreign ambassadors, and among them Giovanni Michiel, noticed that he always held his head down, that he no longer dared to look men in the face, but kept his eyes closed. Occasionally when he was addressed he made an effort and raised his eyelids, but after a swift glance

238

he dropped them again. A contemporary portrait, of the school of Clouet, which was till recently in the Château d'Azay le-Rideau, depicts him with pale tired features, haggard eyes, and transparent tremulous hands—an arresting image of a man racked by remorse and the haunting obsession of a fixed idea. He spat blood, and the doctors declared that he was " consumptive." Day by day, consumed by fever, he grew gradually feebler and thinner. In the spring of 1574 he was nothing but a skeleton dragging himself painfully along. In May, reduced to a state of extreme weakness, he took to his bed which he never left again. During the night of the 29th–30th he had an attack, when he was thought to be *in extremis,* and exclaimed in agonized tones : " Oh, what streams of blood ! . . . God forgive me ! . . . I don't know where I am ! . . . I am lost ! " He was in a bath of perspiration and wept bitterly. The nurse who was watching him wiped his face with a handkerchief. On the morning of the 30th he sent for the Duke of Alençon and the King of Navarre, and told them that after his death his mother would be Regent, and that they must obey her. He confided a little child he had to the care of Henry of Béarn. He then received the Sacrament and was given Extreme Unction. On the 31st, Catherine de' Medici, who never left him, tried to say a few words to him on affairs of State, but he gave her to understand that " earthly things were no longer of any account to him." The end was at hand, and at four o'clock in the evening he died. The last word that passed his lips was " Mother ! " . . .

SOURCES. Same as for preceding chapter, and : Monluc, *Commentaires et Lettres,* ed. de Ruble, 1864 (on the subject of this author *see* P. Courteault, *Blaise de Monluc historien,* 1908) ; Michel de Castelnau, *Mémoires,* ed. Le Laboureur, 1731 ; Claude Haton, *Mémoires,* ed. Bourquelot, 1857 ; La Noue, *Discours politiques et militaires,* 1587 ; Jean Faurin, *Journal,* ed. Pradel, 1878 ; Claude de Sainctes, *Discours sur le saccagement des églises en 1562* in Cimber and Danjou, *Archives curieuses,* vol. iv ; *Mémoires-Journaux* of the Duc de Guise, ed. Michaud and Poujoulat ; Marguerite de Valois, *Mémoires,* ed. Guessard, 1842 ; J. Blanchet *Recueil de lettres missives adressées à Antoine de Bourbon* (1553–1562),1905 ; Saulx-Tavannes, *Mémoires,* ed. Michaud and Poujoulat ; Vicomte de Turenne, *Mémoires,* ed. Baguenault de Puchesse, 1901 ; Michel de la Huguerye, *Mémoires,* ed. De Ruble, 1877 ; Bertrand de Salignac-Fénelon, *Correspondence,* ed. Teulet, 1840 ; Cardinal de Granvelle, *Papiers d'Etat,* ed. C. Weiss, 1841 ; *Correspondence de Philippe II sur les affaires des Pays-Bas*, 1851 ; *Correspondence inédite de la maison d'Orange-Nassau*, ed. Groen van Prinsterer, 1836 ; Jeanne d'Albret, *Mémoires et poésies*, ed. de Ruble, 1883 ; Et. Pasquier, *Œuvres*, 1723 ; de Thou, *Histoire universelle*, 1734, vol. iv.

WORKS. H. de la Ferrière, *Le XVIe siècle et les Valois*, 1879 ; Soldan, *Geschichte des Protestantismus in Frankreich bis zum Tode Karl's IX*, 1855 ; Kervyn de Lettenhove, *Les Huguenots et les Gueux*, 1883 ; Amphoux, *Michel de l'Hôpital et la liberté de conscience au XVIe siècle*, 1900 ; H. Klipffel, *Le colloque de Poissy*, 1867 ; A. de Ruble, *Le colloque de Poissy*, 1889 ; J. Calas, *Le massacre de Vassy*, 1887 ; Coynart, *L'année 1562 et la bataille de Dreux*, 1894 ; H. Hauser, *François de la Noue*, 1892 ; de Ruble, *L'assassinat de François de Lorraine, duc de Guise*, 1897 ; F. Combes, *L'entrevue de Bayonne*, 1882 ; Kervyn de Lettenhove, *La conférence de Bayonne*, 1883 ; H. de la Ferrière, *L'Entrevue de Bayonne de 1565*, 1883 ; G. G. Soldan, *La France et la Saint-Barthélemy*, 1855 ; H. Bordier, *La Saint-Barthélemy et la critique moderne*, 1879 ; J. Loiseleur, *Les nouvelles controverses sur la Saint-Barthélemy*, 1881 ; and, *Trois énigmes historiques, la Saint-Barthélemy*, 1883 ; H. de la Ferrière, *La Saint-Barthélemy*, 1892 ; H. Monod, *Un document sur la Saint-Barthélemy (Revue de Paris*, August 1908) ; S. C. Gigon, *La troisieme guerre de religion, Jarnac et Montcontour*, 1911 ; P. de Vaissière, *De quelques assassins*, 1912.

CHAPTER VII

THE CATHOLIC REACTION. HENRY III

Causes of the Catholic reaction against Protestantism. The character of Henry III, 1574–1589; his difficulties with his brother the Duke of Anjou and Henry of Béarn; the Peace of Monsieur and the Edict of Beaulieu, 1576. The League, 1576. The States-General of Blois, 1576. The Peace of Bergerac with the Protestants, 1577. The Duke of Anjou in the Netherlands. The Lover's War and the Peace of Fleix, 1580. Fresh expedition of the Duke of Anjou to the Netherlands, 1581; his defeat; his death, 1584. The Protestant Henry of Béarn heir to the throne of France; violent protestations; the Committee of the Sixteen in Paris. The unpopularity of Henry III; his minions; Henry III obliged to give way to the League, Treaty of Nemours, 1585. War against the Protestants: defeat of Joyeuse at Coutras by the King of Navarre, 1587; Guise's victory at Vimory and Auneau, 1587. Growing hostility of the mob towards Henry III: the day of the barricades, 1588. Defeat of Henry III. The States-General of Blois and the assassination of the Duke of Guise, 1588. Upheaval of France. Henry III reduced to a combination with Henry of Béarn: march on Paris; assassination of Henry III, 1589.

AT the conference of Saint-Bris held in 1586, Catherine de' Medici, discussing matters with the Vicomte de Turenne, Henry of Béarn's envoy, said: "The King will have but one religion in France." The Protestant replied, "We are of the same mind, madam, but it must be

Causes of Catholic reaction.

our religion." This had long been the case in Béarn, where Jeanne d'Albret had succeeded in abolishing Catholicism. The Huguenots would fain have ended by making France a Protestant country against her will. But France was recalcitrant. The reign of Henry III is the history of the definitive Catholic reaction against the exclusive designs or aspirations of the Protestants.

Until about 1564 Protestantism had steadily increased and developed. From that time forth it ceased to grow. The causes of this arrest are numerous, but amongst the reasons which led to the revival of Catholicism, the sight of the destruction for which the Huguenots were responsible was certainly one of the most potent. Lippomano on his journey across France in 1577 noted with horror all the unrepaired ravages with which he met—devastated towns, plundered monasteries, cathedrals in ruins, crumbling churches, violated tombs and disinterred bones. Orleans, Blois, Tours and Poitiers were in a deplorable condition. "The sight of these things is truly lamentable," he said, "and it is difficult to understand how men can let themselves go to such a pitch of ferocity and barbarity as to rage against mere stones." The public conscience awoke in revolt. But the work of destruction did not cease. In spite of the peace that had been proclaimed, Jean Faurin remarks, acts of hostility were continually perpetrated. During the course of twenty-seven years this same Faurin had witnessed 459 sieges, captures of castles, and surprise attacks in the region round Castres. The people were exasperated beyond endurance. The conclusion of the Council of Trent made a favourable impression upon public opinion, for the Catholic Church in the face of hostile criticism, had revised and defined her doctrines, formulated her teaching, and reformed her discipline. The Council had lasted a long while, in the midst of various vicissitudes ; but it had accomplished its task, and had formulated decrees the terms of which seemed to give satisfaction to the troubled minds of the Catholics, and to strengthen their faith. Finally, a new army adapted to the fresh needs of the time was fighting against the Reformation. This was the Jesuit militia, founded by Saint Ignatius Loyola in 1540, with the object of opposing the Protestant principle of free inquiry by the contrary doctrine of passive obedience. This order abjured all ecclesiastical dignities, while adapting itself to every form of priestly function—oratory, teaching, hearing confessions, and the study of theology ; its members preached and founded colleges everywhere. The Jesuits spread with such rapidity and became so powerful that by the end of the century they inspired universal fear and were driven out everywhere. They contributed, however, to the accentuation of the Catholic reaction, which took place under the reign of one of the most extraordinary and complex characters among the Kings of France.

A man above the average height, extremely thin, with a very long face, the half-veiled glance of his father Henry II, **Character of** a broad forehead and mocking mouth, Henry III **Henry III,** was far from being a fool. He was a prince **1574–1589.** endowed with a lively intelligence and much perception ; but he was a sceptic, and a scoffer with a touch of the dilettante, amused by life and at times himself amusing. He once wrote to Villeroy " There was a certain King of Judah who owing to bad counsels was lost. May God preserve the King of France from such a fate ! I know very well, it seems to me, what I ought to do, but I am like a man who feels he is drowning, and from an instinct of obedience is content to do so rather than save himself. And then, nobody else would agree with me and I may possibly be wrong ! " For a King of France who came to the throne when his country was passing through a most critical phase in her internal history, this state of mind was by no means desirable. In other respects Henry III was an amiable man with a gentle, affable disposition. He had eyes that were charming when they looked at his inter-locutors, and, when he spoke, the corners of his mouth had an attractive curve. He held himself extremely well and had a noble and graceful bearing. In short he was every inch a King, and very conscious of his own dignity. It was he who laid down the rules for an augmented ceremonial about his person—a Court etiquette which was destined to be applied more particularly under Louis XIV and resulted in keeping people at a distance from the King, and in multiplying the " idolatrous " obeisances performed, not only in his presence, but even before the common objects he used ; " apish tricks," wrote Claude Dupuy, " imported *ab ultimis Sarmatis* to our country of France : *barbari moris sunt !* "

But if Henry III had the intelligence and wit to understand the course of events without having the energy to direct them ; **Henry III's** and if, conscious of his rank, he aimed at inspiring **tastes.** respect by means of external signs of deference, many other elements contributed to contradict these qualities. " Everything about him is contradictory " said Morosini.

Extremely delicate in health, with a sickly constitution, subject to violent headaches, abscesses in his ear, and a skin disease—which the doctors called a sort of " itch " and for which they ordered him sea baths—and suffering from constant attacks of indigestion, he had the characteristic tastes and habits of a degenerate. All who came into contact with him regarded him as " effeminate." Contrary to the traditions of his family, he hated physical exercise, regarded riding and hunting with horror, and lay late in bed. On the other hand, his attention to his toilet was carried to the point of ridiculous excess. He invented fashions each more extravagant than the last, covering himself with precious stones, wearing ear-rings, bracelets, and numberless rings, and curling his hair. But above all he delighted in perfumes, scattering musk violet powder and bags of rose-leaves everywhere, even in his bed. He also loved amusement. Utterly indifferent to affairs of state—especially at the beginning of his reign, though later on he was obliged to take part in them—and detesting work, he threw himself into a life of gaiety. He was essentially a man of pleasure, and Germain Pilon's medal of him certainly gives this impression. In the company of comrades and friends of his own age who never left his side, he gave himself up to all the follies in which rich and overbearing young men, in a position to venture upon anything, can afford to indulge. He once arranged a dinner-party where the task of waiting upon the guests was performed by ladies of the Court dressed as men, and every one was clad in green silk. And on another occasion, at Chenonceaux, a dinner was given on the terrace at which young ladies of the Court played a similar part, with their hair hanging loose about their shoulders and their dresses cut excessively low. But his most successful entertainments were masquerades. On Shrove Tuesday he would dress himself up as a woman, in a " fish-wife's skirt " of red, black, white, and orange, and wearing a mask over his face, would scour the streets with ten young boon companions, jostling people, entering houses and playing a thousand impudent pranks all through the night until six o'clock in the morning. For balls he disguised himself in a lady's gown " opening his doublet and uncovering his neck, round which he wore a pearl necklace and three linen collars."

244

His weakness for his friends and companions, which amounted to infatuation, and his relative indifference to women have laid him open to certain imputations. But there is not the slightest evidence of a taste which would brand him as a man of perverted instincts. The abnormality of his character, however, was displayed in other strange caprices. He affected an attitude of excessive piety which, in a man of pleasure, presented a somewhat surprising contrast. He went on pilgrimages to Chartres and Cléry from Paris on foot. He used to wander from one church to another with two or three companions " holding large *Paternosters* in his hand, which he kept muttering and repeating through the streets." He marched at night by torchlight in the processions of the Blue Penitents, with his body tied up in a sack which had two holes for the eyes. He founded the Brotherhood of the Penitents of Our Lady, and took part in their processions with a monk's cowl on his head, carrying a candle in his hand. The people derided him, calling him " the churchwarden of Saint Germain-l'Auxerrois, the son-in-law of Colas." * He had a chaplet made for himself the beads of which represented death's heads—the death's head was his chosen emblem, and is seen on the bindings of his books —and he danced at balls wearing this chaplet suspended from his waist. He had no children. This distinguished, witty, effeminate and fantastic prince represents the degenerate end of a royal race.

Henry III was at Cracow, in Poland, when he heard of the death of his brother, Charles IX, whose heir he was. As he detested life in that remote country, he took flight by night, galloping away on a mare, which he killed by riding her hard for seventy-two hours, and leaving his followers to manage as best they could without him. He passed by Venice where he was given a very friendly reception. Catherine de' Medici awaited his arrival in France, carrying on the government

* A reference to an old sixteenth-century term of abuse applied to Huguenots, and in its original form " the cow of Colas " (*la vache à Colas*). It arose out of an incident at Bionne, where a stray cow belonging to one Colas Pannier entered a Protestant place of worship. The Huguenots, thinking the cow was driven in among them on purpose, seized and killed it. The Sheriff, however, made them indemnify its owner. Songs were soon written and sung by the Catholics in memory of the incident. (Tr.)

meanwhile. Henry III, overjoyed at his accession to the throne, was extremely amiable to everybody. He set free his brother, the Duke of Alençon, and the King of Navarre, who had been kept in a state of semi-confinement ever since their last escapade ; he was attentive to the Guises, assured the Huguenots that he was ready to grant them an amnesty for the past, and won the hearts of the Catholics by his reverent piety. In February, 1575, he married, taking to wife a charming young **Henry III's** girl of twenty, Louise de Vaudémont, a niece of **marriage, 1575.** the Duke of Lorraine. It was not a brilliant match, but in spite of Catherine de' Medici's opposition, he insisted upon it, having fallen in love with the girl, whom he had met at the time of his departure for Poland. Queen Louise, with her pale face and pretty, delicate features, her graceful carriage and elegant slender figure, her laughing eyes and extremely sweet, simple, and modest nature, was destined to retire somewhat into the background. She adored her husband and never took her eyes off him, but later on she was rather neglected by him. Henry III bought her an estate at Ollainville, near Paris, where she used to spend the long summer months.

Though the Queen took no part in public affairs, the Duke of Alençon, the King's younger brother, caused him much anxiety. This youth, who was two years younger than Henry III, and consequently twenty-two at the time of his accession, was small, squarely built and fat, extremely dark in complexion, with curly black hair. He was amiable and jovial, however, although wild, turbulent, and unruly; he was jealous of his brother, whom he accused of being their mother's favourite, and had no affection for him. On the pretext that he was being spied upon, he fled from Paris on September 15, 1575, hidden in a carriage, and reached Dreux, where he published a manifesto declaring that the King wished to cast him into prison. The situation became somewhat serious, as he opened negotiations with Condé and made overtures to the Huguenots. Grave complications were feared if the party should adopt him as its leader. Catherine de' Medici set out in pursuit of him with the object of inducing him to come back, and followed him to Chambord. At that moment a body of 2000 *Reiters* was actually crossing the frontier on their way to join Condé. Fortunately, however, the Duke of Guise, who was Governor of Champagne, attacked and dispersed them at Dormans, when he received a volley in his face which left a deep scar. From that day forth he went by the nickname of *Le Balafré* (the scarred man). Catherine succeeded in allaying the storm by paying Condé 160,000 crowns, and giving the Duke of Alençon a bodyguard to make him feel safe.

But at a Court under a King of four-and-twenty who passed his days in revelry surrounded by excitable young men, it was **Difficulties** inevitable that the passions that were surging in the **with Henry of** provinces should have free play; and Protestants **Béarn.** and Catholics alike committed acts of provocation. " We are nearly always ready to cut each other's throats," Henry of Navarre wrote to Monsieur de Miossens. " We carry daggers and wear coats of mail and very often breastplates under our cloaks. I am only waiting for the opportunity to have a little fighting, for I am told that they are plotting to kill me and I want to steal a march on them." The threats against him became so alarming that he in his turn fled from Court on February 3, 1576, during a hunting-party, and hastened to join Alençon, publicly declaring that he was a Calvinist, and announcing that his recantation after the Massacre of Saint Bartholomew was of no account. He then made for Béarn, where he summoned all his gentlemen to him. The Duke of Alençon and Condé showed an inclination to support him, and the position of the Government was embarrassing in the extreme. The King did nothing but amuse himself, and the Exchequer was empty. " The only topic at Court at the moment was that there was nothing for the King's dinner." The Court was living upon loans—and miserable loans—of 500 or 600 pounds, borrowed from parliamentary counsellors, lawyers and procurators. How could they raise the funds to pay an army ? Catherine de' Medici, who continued to be the guiding spirit of the Government, was of opinion that every sacrifice should be made to avoid war. Her fears were exaggerated ; she was growing old. The result of her negotiations was that the Duke of Alençon was allowed to add the title of Anjou to his honours and to become Duke of Anjou ; whilst

247

Condé was made Governor of Languedoc. This treaty, concluded May 6, 1576, was called the Peace of Monsieur. With

Peace of Monsieur, Edict of Beaulieu, 1576. regard to the Protestants, the concessions made them were ratified by the Edict of Beaulieu. The terms of this edict were so unexpected and so extraordinary that the country was filled with stupefaction. The Protestants were granted full liberty of worship everywhere without restrictions of any sort ; eight surety cities, mixed chambers in the parliaments, that is to say, chambers with two Presidents, one Catholic and the other Huguenot, and twelve counsellors, four of whom were to be Huguenots ; Coligny and the other victims of the Massacre of Saint Bartholomew were to be rehabilitated and the verdicts against them rescinded ; Protestants were to be eligible for all posts, and the meeting of the States-General was promised. Never had the Court conceded so much—and this, too, so soon after the Massacre of Saint Bartholomew ! It was inexplicable, and the Catholics were completely at a loss to understand the reasons for such indulgence. In Paris the public refused to light bonfires, and when the government wished to have *Te Deums* sung to celebrate the solemnization of peace, the precentors and canons refused to take part in them. The Edict of Beaulieu was destined to lead to many other dangerous complications for France.

The destitution of the Court was indeed pitiable. In spite of the loans they had raised they had not a penny to go on with, and it became necessary to pawn the crown jewels, to sell offices, and live by all manner of expedients. " In whatever direction we turn our eyes," wrote Monvillier, " nothing but despair stares us in the face." And unfortunately, the public was exasperated because Henry III did not stop his merrymaking, but continued to squander and give away the little money at his disposal to his boon companions. Thus on the one hand the King was indifferent, and on the other the feeble Government was yielding everything to the Protestants. In these circumstances the Catholics came to the conclusion that as the power of the Crown could not or would not defend them, the only alternative was for them to take their own cause in hand. Thus the League—the famous League—was formed ;

a lamentable expedient to which subjects were driven, creating a State within the State, in order to demand from a new **The League, 1576.** organization the protection which the old could no longer afford them. Its results, however, were war, disorder, and anarchy.

The origin of the League was accidental. By the terms of the Peace of Monsieur, the town of Péronne had been given over to the Prince of Condé, as a guarantee-city. But the inhabitants of the place refused to accept a master who would they feared insist upon making Huguenots of them all. They accordingly combined with the clergy, the magistrates, and the nobility of the neighbourhood, none of whom were anxious to see Péronne turned into a Protestant town. The idea of a Catholic league was thus inaugurated; it spread rapidly and other districts followed the example set by Péronne. In Paris it was owing to the initiative of a certain lawyer, Pierre Hennequin, and a citizen named La Bruyère, that the association was formed with the consent of the Guises. A definite programme was formulated : the defence of the Catholic religion and the re-establishment of the royal authority, the weakening of which was bringing ruin upon the Catholics. The populace joined with astonishing rapidity and enthusiasm, so ripe was the moment for such a project. Everywhere leagues were formed and provinces, towns, and boroughs gave in their adhesion, but all were merged in a general association inspired by one spirit and one desire. The question of choosing a leader arose, and public opinion pointed to Henry of Guise. Of the same age as Henry III, taller than the King, with fair curly hair, bright eyes and a sparse beard, his majestic features rendered more manly by his scar, the young hero whose family was so popular attracted the sympathies of every one by his easy grace of bearing. He accepted the post.

From the very first Henry III realized how humiliating and how exceedingly dangerous the formation of the League was for him. He tried to oppose it. " I am greatly displeased," he wrote, " inasmuch as the inhabitants of Péronne have resolved not to obey my commands." When he saw the extent to which the association was developing, however, he had to give way and make the best of a bad business. He then

249

declared that he had encouraged it, and wrote to the Duke of Nevers: "The Huguenots maintain that these associations have been formed without orders from me. This is false. I shall establish them throughout my kingdom and shall not rest till I have done so." On reflection he had come to the conclusion that he might profit by the League, and use it as an instrument.

To the Protestants, already weakened by the feeling that the Reformation was no longer spreading, and still suffering from the effects of the Massacre of Saint Bartholomew, the violent revolt on the part of Catholic public opinion attested by the League, had all the appearance of intimidation. They held special prayer-meetings and fasts everywhere. "The ministers of Geneva offered up special prayers on behalf of the French churches." Formerly, under similar circumstances, they would have raised troops, bought arms, and fortified towns. But times were changing and the new attitude adopted by the Calvinists betrayed their sense of inferiority.

The first result of this dual situation was the composition of the States-General summoned to meet at Blois, in 1576, in **States-General of Blois, 1576.** accordance with the terms of the Peace of Monsieur. The elections proved favourable to the League. The Protestants, certain of being defeated, did not even stand. Three hundred and sixty-two deputies were returned. As a matter of fact, Henry III, who since the formation of the League had become seriously anxious and had begun to direct his Government himself, had consented to the meeting of the States for the sake of getting money from them, and in order to lay hands on the formidable association. The opening meeting at which he presided took place on December 6 in the ancient Salle des Etats at Blois, still in existence. He made an extremely dignified speech in which, after paying tribute to all his mother had done, and saying: "All who love France will be bound for ever to praise her great vigilance," he assured the assembly that he intended to re-establish order and public peace, and to redress abuses. He spoke well. At the proposal of an eloquent lawyer, named Versoris, the house declared that there could be only one religion in France—the Catholic religion—and a formal resolution to that effect was carried. Determined to side with the majority, Henry III replied that he would abide by the Edict of Beaulieu. Did this mean war against the Huguenots? Henry of Béarn protested in those firm, moving, and loyal terms which made all the letters he wrote at this time so beautiful, and said: "Religion is implanted in the hearts of men by force of doctrine and belief and is confirmed by living example and not by the sword. We are all Frenchmen and fellow-citizens of one country and as such it behoves us to come to an agreement founded upon reason and kindness and not upon harshness and cruelty." But as the States wished for war against the Huguenots, Henry III opined that they would forthwith contribute the money for it. On the motion of a deputy from Vermandois, named Jean Bodin, however, the assembly voted for the re-establishment of religious unity "in all gentleness without recourse to war." The question of the finances was then raised, and when the Government confessed that there was a deficit of 100 millions, the States loudly condemned the extravagance of the Exchequer. On being asked for a grant of two millions by means of a hearth-tax or a tax on the alienation of demesnial property, they refused to give it, or only granted insignificant subsidies. Henry III felt that he had been fooled. In vain he had himself supported the League in order to conciliate the deputies and had even declared himself the head of the movement—a strange manœuvre indeed! To insist would have been undignified. He accordingly dissolved the States, informing them that as they refused to make war he had no alternative but to treat with the Huguenots. By way of compensation he confined himself to drawing up, out of the voluminous papers presented to him by the States on February 9, 1577, one of those grand ordinances which were always so full of good intentions, but never operative. It contained 363 articles and formed the Ordinance of Blois of 1579.

After the dissolution of the States, and a few insignificant acts of hostility, Henry III signed a definite peace with the Protestants. This was the Peace of Bergerac of **Peace of Bergerac, 1577.** September 17, 1577, by the terms of which the Calvinists were granted liberty of conscience, though freedom of worship in any place was allowed solely on condition of obtaining the sanction of the authorities. The mixed chambers were re-established, but only in the southern Parliaments. This peace, which was confirmed by the Edict of Poitiers, was destined to secure seven or eight years of tranquillity. The Protestants, with ministers and princes at variance, Henry of Navarre an unwelcome leader to many, and some of their towns, La Rochelle, for instance, taking up the attitude of independent republics, were divided against themselves. They had lost their pristine vigour and were now in a condition of weakness and paralysis.

The Protestant question being at rest for the moment, it remained for Henry III to face the problems presented by the **Anjou in the** League and the Catholic princes. The most **Netherlands.** pressing of these was the conduct of the latter. The turbulence of the ex-Duke of Alençon, who had become the Duke of Anjou, was, in the first place an occasion of perpetual alarms. The master of five duchies and four counties, with an income of 400,000 crowns and an establishment almost as large as the King's, the Duke of Anjou was an extremely dangerous rival. In 1577 an opportunity for getting rid of him occurred which Henry III seized with alacrity. Ever since 1572 the Netherlands—that is to say the northern Dutch provinces—had been in a state of rebellion against Spain, and in 1577 the southern provinces of Flanders joined the movement. The Governor, Don Juan of Austria, found it impossible to hold his own, and anarchy reigned. The French envoy, Mondoucet, conceived the idea of summoning the Duke of Anjou and placing him at the head of the rebellious Catholics, thus making an attempt to win back at least those southern provinces that had once belonged to France. The Duke of Anjou, like the reckless madcap he was, consented to this plan, and Henry III, who was enchanted, allowed him to go, though to avoid offending Spain he refrained from formal recognition of the expedition. The Duke of Anjou entered Flanders at the head of 7000 men, nobles eager for war, disbanded soldiers and volunteers. The States-General, the deliberative assembly of the rebel provinces of the north, made a pretence of accepting this succour, though determined, as was also their military leader, the Prince of Orange, to insist upon the French returning over the frontier the moment they had no further need of them. Anjou took Hainault, Maubeuge, and Binche. But at this point he was obliged to stop short. His troops were plundering, and the inhabitants were protesting, and betraying them on all sides. The affair was hopeless and Anjou, unable to accomplish anything, returned to France at the end of three months. The adventure, however, had only been postponed.

On the side of Henry of Navarre all was peaceful. The prince had loyally accepted the Peace of Bergerac, and had

Henry of Béarn at Nérac.

retired to his gay castle of Nérac, devoting himself entirely to a life of ease and pleasure. Henry III gave his consent for his sister, Margaret—Queen Margot—to join her husband in Gascony ; and Catherine de' Medici decided to go with her. The two set off together and took the journey slowly, giving balls and festivals everywhere and preaching peace and good-will, visiting the towns and sojourning in them ; their travels took them a year. Though they found the provinces fairly tranquil they were nevertheless received with loud complaints on the part of the people, who inveighed against the taxes and the poverty-stricken condition of the State. "They are ready to believe anything against the King," said Estoile, "who daily burdens them with fresh impositions and new officials and pays none of his debts out of the vast sums he raises thereby, but spends them on prodigal luxuries and huge gifts." When he heard of these complaints Henry III replied : "These are the results of the League that are beginning to make themselves felt. But I will put a stop to them if I can." The arrival of Margaret at Nérac served to redouble the gaiety of the little Court, at which there was a perpetual round of dances, hunting-parties, and festivities. The Protestant ministers were scandalized. Henry and his wife, who vied with each other in frivolity and inconstancy, passed the time joyously. A cloud, however, arose and for a moment cast a gloom over the period of tranquillity which had begun to set Henry III's fears at rest. In the north, Condé, irritated by provocations on the part of the League, had suddenly seized La Fère ; whilst in the south, the town of Cahors, which was part of Margaret of Valois' dowry, refused to receive the Governor sent by the King of Navarre. The latter, enraged by this, set out hurriedly for the place, and on May 29, 1580, placing a petard at the entrance, blew up the gate and threw himself into the streets at the head of a troop of cavalry as if he had been a simple carabineer. At the same moment Lesdiguières in Dauphiny showed signs of activity. Full of anxiety at these commotions, Henry III dispatched Matignon to La Fère, Mayenne to Dauphiny, and Biron in the direction of Guyenne, at the head of bodies of troops. La Fère was recaptured and a treaty signed at Fleix, in Périgord,

Peace of Fleix, 1580. reiterating the articles of the Peace of Bergerac, put an end to disturbances which, according to l'Estoile, had been merely " a little straw fire," " a lover's quarrel " ; the brilliant life at Nérac resumed its course. An unexpected event, however, was destined to give it a rude shock, and to change the whole future of the King of Navarre. It was to place both him and the Kingdom of France in a terrible situation, confusing the problems presented by the princes and by the Protestants to Henry III in such a way as to make the reign of Henry III one of the most dramatic and most bloodstained through which a King of France had ever lived.

The Duke of Anjou, who had never abandoned the idea of the expedition to the Netherlands, was making preparations to return to Flanders. He had paid a visit to England with a view to obtaining the good-will of Elizabeth. But she was holding herself in reserve. The success of Alessandro Farnese, Prince of Parma, the new Spanish Governor of Brussels, who proved more fortunate than Don Juan of Austria, had induced the States-General of the United Provinces and the Prince of Orange to make a fresh appeal to the French King's brother. They offered to make him commander-in-chief of the forces. The moral support of the great neighbouring kingdom would, they thought, strengthen them, in spite of the fact that Henry III refused to recognize his brother's activities. Anjou, on his side, hoped to be made king. Every one was buoyed up with false hopes. In June, 1581, the Duke of Anjou assembled his troops, and in July, Holland and Zetland definitely declared themselves independent of Spain. At the head of 14,000 men, of whom 3000 were gentlemen, Anjou set out on the march, raised the siege of Cambray, entered Ghent **Anjou returns** and Antwerp, and was crowned Duke of Brabant **to the** and Count of Flanders. Attracted by success, **Netherlands.** adventurers of all nationalities hurried to join him, and the young victor, finding himself well supported, and impatient at the equivocal attitude assumed by the States-General, determined to make a dash for " his sovereignty," to take it *à la française* and grasp it vigorously, with or against their will. As Busbecq, the imperial ambassador remarked, " his head was turned." He captured places belonging to the States-General by surprise, and tried to lay hands on Antwerp in a similar manner. But the citizens of this town rose up against him. Hunted through the streets, the Duke of Anjou's troops found it impossible to get the upper hand. Two thousand of them were massacred and the rest driven out. This defeat proved Anjou's undoing. Irrevocably compromised in the eyes of the Netherlanders, he had no alternative but to take his departure. He held out for two months longer and then returned to France ; his adventure was at an end. Casting about for some one to blame, he accused Henry III of not supporting him, sulked, and refused to return to Court. Catherine de' Medici succeeded in reconciling the two brothers, who met again in 1584. The Duke of Anjou, however, like all the members of this unfortunate family, was constitutionally delicate ; worn out by excesses, he was suddenly attacked by violent hæmorrhage of the lungs. The end came rapidly. On June 10 he breathed his last at Château Thierry at the age of thirty-one, after a few hours of illness.

But now the King's last brother was dead, he himself had no children, and the question of the succession became pressing. **Henry of** By virtue of the traditional rules of succession **Béarn heir to** in order of primogeniture, the nearest heir was **the throne.** Henry of Béarn, King of Navarre, descendant of a sixth son of Saint Louis and cousin in the 22nd degree of the reigning monarch. The throne of France was the heritage of a Protestant prince ! The country was filled with consternation at the idea. A Protestant King was an impossible eventuality. The eldest son of the Church could not be a heretic; as such, he could not even be crowned. A violent campaign broke out in the press. The year 1584 gave the signal for an outburst of publications which continued throughout the reign of Henry III, forming, with the reign of Louis XIII and the period of the Fronde, one of the three epochs under the old régime when "the political press" was most prolific. The agitation was extremely lively in the immediate circle of the princes. In the opinion of Henry III there was but one solution —that Henry of Béarn should become a convert. He approached him on the matter, and the King of Navarre's friends added their counsels to his. Henry of Béarn, however, loyally replied that he could not present the nation with a spectacle of such fickleness of conscience merely for his personal advantage. Let them call a council together, he suggested, to discuss the two religions with a view to his instruction. He asked for nothing better than enlightenment. Any other course was alien to his straightforward character. The members of the League thereupon declared that under these circumstances, there was no alternative but to summon the States-General and make them alter the order of succession to the throne; the nation should revive its ancient rights. The partisans of Henry of Navarre retorted that there was a legal order of succession, which the States had no power to modify. But already future candidates for the throne were being discussed, and the name of Henry of Guise was in many mouths. Genealogists even proved that the illustrious family of Lorraine was descended from the Carlovingians—a very fantastic theory— and all extolled the steadfast faith of those who had so valiantly defended the Catholic religion. At all events, they declared, the States would do as they pleased. Others brought forward the name of the King's uncle, the aged Cardinal Bourbon; which meant postponing rather than solving the problem. Foreign countries followed the discussion with interest. Philip II, alarmed at the prospect of a Protestant King in France, offered to come to an understanding with the Guises, to which they agreed. They were somewhat surprised at the turn things were taking, but did not dare to stipulate that the throne should revert to them. By the Treaty of Joinville of January, 1585,

which they signed with Spain on behalf of the League, it was
Treaty of decided that Cardinal Bourbon should succeed
Joinville, 1585. to the throne. The King of Spain was to give
subsidies, in return for which Béarn and Navarre were to be
ceded to him later on. Thus, not content with forming
a State within the State, the League was treating with the
foreigner !

But they were emboldened by the fact that the sentiment of
the great majority in the kingdom was on their side. It
was clear that the country would not have the Huguenots
at any price, much less, therefore, would they tolerate a king
who was a heretic. The League increased with amazing rapidity
and everybody hastened to join it. From the pulpits preachers
inflamed their congregations at the mere idea of becoming the
subjects of a Calvinist ; and pamphlets were issued in vast
numbers. During the general effervescence the League formed
a committee in Paris composed at first of five members ; but
after 1587 this number was raised to sixteen, who rapidly
assumed a revolutionary authority, and laid down the law as
masters. They were known as the " Sixteen." The forces
of anarchy began to be organized.

In the midst of all this turmoil Henry III was reaping the
fruits of his life of dissipation ; he was hated by the people.
Unpopularity Far from restraining his fantastic tastes, he had
of Henry III. exaggerated them, and, in spite of the general
poverty, continued to heap honours and money upon his boon
companions, for whom he displayed a ridiculous attachment.
These young men, Caylus, Saint Luc, d'O, d'Arques, Saint
Mesgrin, Mauléon, Maugiron, Livarot, Grammont, and La
Valette had exasperated the public by their absurdities, their
haughty and insolent airs, their pretentious manners and their
excesses. The people called them the King's "minions."
Duels, however, and acts of revenge were thinning their ranks.
Caylus and Maugiron had been killed in duels, and Saint Mesgrin
had been assassinated. Henry III was weak enough to raise
mausoleums of exaggerated magnificence to their memory,
after giving way to excessive grief. He had three special
favourites : d'Arques, whom he had made Duke of Joyeuse
and married to one of the Queen's sisters during the course of

some scandalous festivities, when seventeen banquets were given to a crowd of people bedizened with gold and precious stones; La Valette, who was created Duke of Épernon; and d'O, who afterwards fell into disgrace. The King called them "his three children." Joyeuse and Épernon were extremely powerful "grand viziers" as the people dubbed them. The latter, in the end, became "the most conspicuous of them all," the King's first "minion" "his eldest son." In 1587 he married the Countess of Candale with great pomp; the King gave the bride a necklace of 100 pearls valued at 100,000 crowns, and the bridegroom 400,000 crowns in cash. The public and "the press" thereupon attacked Henry III.

The King at last became seriously anxious. He cross-examined the Guises and demanded an explanation. They replied that public opinion was greatly disturbed by the question of the succession, but that guarantees were all that was required. Even in the King's immediate circle the Court was divided. Many were in favour of the League, whose intentions were, they said, radically just. Among these were the Queen's brother, Philip Emmanuel of Lorraine, whom Henry III had created Duke of Mercœur, and made Governor of Brittany; the Duke of Nevers, and Joyeuse. Épernon, on the other hand, supported the cause of Henry of Béarn. Henry III could not come to a decision. If he had been master of the situation he would have persuaded the King of Navarre to recant, and suppressed the League. As it was, he could do neither the one nor the other.

The League went its way. In March the Duke of Guise, *le Balafré*, occupied Châlons in its name, and his brother, the Cardinal Bourbon's manifesto. Duke of Mayenne, who was thirty-one, a tall, elegant man with a gentle expression, and great courage and vigour, seized Dijon. Cardinal Bourbon had retired to Péronne. On March 31 he published a grand manifesto—or at least it was published with his signature —in which the League declared that it aimed at securing a Catholic successor to the throne, the establishment of one religion only in France, the convocation of the States-General, and their regular assemblage every three years, and all this without prejudice to the privileges of the clergy, the nobility,

258

the Parliaments, and the *bourgeoisie*. The unfortunate King of France found himself in the most precarious predicament. He had neither an army nor money. " About his person," wrote Busbecq, " he has only a few feeble and powerless friends." The provincial Governors followed the example of the public and pronounced themselves in favour of the League. Even the ministers, Cheverny, Bellièvre, and Villeroy hesitated. The entire sympathies of the nation were on the side of the Catholic association. Henry III published a manifesto in reply **Henry III's** to the one issued by Bourbon, in which he en- **reply.** deavoured to defend his policy, by explaining that he had concluded peace with the Huguenots because the States-General had refused to provide him with the funds to make war upon them ; that after all he had secured long years of peace by this means ; and without discussing the principles of the League, he reprobated its methods. The manifesto was a colourless production, devoid of dignity, and its effect was negligible. Only one solution remained : to treat with the League. Catherine de' Medici devoted herself to the task, and went to Épernay, in Champagne, to discuss matters with the Duke and Cardinal Bourbon. But they insisted upon war against the Protestants. The problem was insoluble, for the King no more had money or men at his command for an attack upon the Huguenots than he had for fighting the Guises and their party. Catherine therefore replied that in this case the League must bear the burden and expense of the war. The Guises in return demanded some towns as guarantees. Thus, with territory and authority alike divided, the kingdom was threatened with dismemberment on every side.

These painful negotiations dragged on for three months and finally the Government had to give way. By the Treaty **Treaty of** of Nemours of July 7, 1585, the King consented **Nemours, 1585.** to publish an edict making Catholicism the only religion allowed in France, and commanding the people to conform within six months or else leave the country. The mixed chambers were abolished and the towns given to the Protestants were withdrawn, whilst others were handed over to the League for five years. Its leaders, Cardinal Bourbon, Guise, Mercœur, Aumale and Elbeuf, were granted the right of maintaining a private bodyguard, and, to crown all, it was formally acknowledged that the League had acted in the best interests of the State. It was a pitiful business! After having made every possible concession to the Protestants, the Government was now handing itself over bound hand and foot to the members of the League and making itself their chattel. " The King was on foot," said l'Estoile, " and the League was on horseback."

The person who suffered most was Henry of Béarn. He had always declared that he did not know whether he would ever ascend the throne, but that he was certain that men's consciences should not be forced, and that they should be free to believe what they liked. The Treaty of Nemours overwhelmed him. " My fear of the evils I foresee," he told the Marquis de la Force, " is so great that it has made my moustache turn white." He wrote an eloquent letter of protest to the King of France whilst the Huguenots in despair prescribed prayers and fasts. After twenty years of struggle they had returned to the point from which they had started, and they were now in the presence of a formidable foe indeed, the nameless mob, whose strength was increased tenfold by their confidence in a successful issue, and the knowledge that they were sailing before the wind.

But at this juncture Henry III's cynical and mocking spirit came once more to the surface. He was as indignant as any one Preparations at the extremities to which he had been reduced. for Civil War. He informed the League that it was now obviously necessary for him to make war upon the Calvinists, but that he would require three armies for this object, which it would be their business to raise for him. Secondly, he would need money, and as he himself was ready to ruin himself and give " his last shirt " in the cause, he considered that the Catholics should be prepared to do as much. He therefore informed them that he should cease to pay the salaries of the officers and the interest on the Hôtel de Ville funds, that he intended to tax the citizens, and put ecclesiastical property up to sale. This retort provoked vehement protests. " I am very much afraid," Henry III replied, " that if we try to stop Protestant services we shall greatly endanger the mass! " Of the three armies demanded, one was to protect the King in Paris, the second, under the command of Mayenne, was to march south against Henry of Béarn, and the third—since news had been received that German Protestants were on the way to help their co-religionists in France—was to keep watch over the eastern frontier under the leadership of Guise.   Having made up his mind to act, Henry III wrote to the King of Navarre, asking him to recant, and ordering the Huguenots to stop their services and give up the towns they held.   This amounted to a declaration of war.   Henry of Béarn sent out in all directions letters which he made public with the object of justifying his conduct, and throwing the responsibility for the events that were taking place upon the Guises.   He reiterated his desire for instruction in the matter of religion, on condition that a council were summoned for this purpose, and declined to obey the King's command to stop the Protestant services and give up the towns.   The Protestants increased their manifestos, but took up a defensive instead of an offensive attitude, clumsily accusing the Catholics of undermining the authority of the King, the offence with which they themselves had been so bitterly reproached in the past.

Whereupon, on September 9, 1585, there arrived from Rome a thundering Bull, which the League had demanded from the Pope, Sixtus V, solemnly excommunicating Henry of Béarn and his cousin the Prince of Condé, declaring them both heretics and renegades, cutting them off from the succession, and definitively discrediting them in the eyes of convinced Catholics. It was a rude blow. The King of Navarre appealed to the Court of Peers.   "As it is contrary to the laws of the land," he exclaimed, "for the Pope to arrogate to himself the right of determining the succession to the throne in such a manner, the Bull is null and void in France." Pamphlets appeared, supporting his protestations.   Jurists were also of opinion that this act on the part of the Pope was an infringement of the rights of the Crown.   The clergy, taken by surprise, held their peace, whilst the moderates openly expressed their indignation.

Nevertheless, the League put three armies in the field. Hostilities, however, were merely tentative. Condé had collected troops in Poitou, but they were disbanding. Mayenne

Excommunication of Henry of Béarn and Condé.

261

occupied a few places in Limousin, and Henry of Béarn
Civil War.   manœuvred, holding himself in reserve. Once again
Catherine de' Medici endeavoured to arrange matters, and
conferences were held at Saint-Bris, between Cognac and Jarnac,
on October 18, 1586. The solution of all the difficulties was
still to be found in the conversion of the King of Navarre, but,
Henry of Béarn, ever loyal to his cause, returned the same reply.
And, indeed, such was the condition of men's minds after the
issue of the Papal Bull, that his conversion would have lost him
his friends without winning over his enemies. He demanded
that the League should be severely reprimanded, and even
completely suppressed. The conferences were foredoomed to
failure. Meanwhile in Paris, the public, uneasy at these negotiations, began to agitate. The Sixteen declared that no reliance
could be placed on Henry III, and proposed to seize his person.
This was a serious insurrectionary design, the prologue, possibly,
of a deliberately planned revolution. Terrified by this demagogic spirit, the Guises refused their support, and here the
matter ended for the time being.

The Germans, whose arrival had long been expected, at
last appeared upon the frontier to the number of 35,000, cavalry,
lansquenets, Swiss and Grisons under the command of the
Baron von Dohna. Their intention was to go to the support
of the King of Navarre in the south. The Duke of Guise set
out in pursuit at the head of 15,000 men. The Germans
captured Châtillon-sur-Seine, and marched towards La Charité
in order to cross the Loire. Henry III with some troops took
up a post of observation at Gien. To hold Henry of Béarn in
check he had already dispatched his young favourite, the
beloved minion, Joyeuse, to whom he had confided his best
soldiers. Joyeuse advanced, took Saint-Maixent, and at
Battle of   Coutras fell in with the troops of the King of
Coutras, 1587. Navarre. His own forces were twice as strong,
and he decided to attack (October 20, 1587). To judge by the
appearance of the Catholic army, which was well equipped and
numerous, and that of the Huguenot force, poor, ragged, and
armed with rusty swords, the result seemed a foregone conclusion. But Joyeuse had to reckon with the valour of Henry
of Navarre, who charged with an impetus which carried along
262

his whole army. The Catholics were repulsed. Four hundred nobles of the League remained upon the field, whilst Joyeuse, **Death of** thrown from his horse, was struck by three bullets, **Joyeuse.** and killed. He was only twenty-eight. The battle of Coutras was the first victory won by the Huguenots since the beginning of the civil wars. It produced a profound impression and once more aroused a feeling of exasperation on the part of the League, expecially against Henry III. They reproached the King with having sacrificed his army and the public interest to a foolish wish to give an inexperienced young man, his minion, the opportunity of distinguishing himself in the field. The victory, however, was a barren one for the Calvinists, who were much divided, and had comparatively few supporters under arms. After the battle Henry of Béarn rejoined the Countess of Guiche, whom he adored. He was sharply censured for this proceeding.

The Germans, abandoning the intention of crossing the Loire near La Charité, returned northwards towards La Beauce, **Battles of** with the intention of fetching a compass and **Vimory and** descending upon Vendôme and Saumur, where **Auneau, 1587.** they could cross the Loire more easily. The Duke of Guise followed them. At Vimory, near Montargis, he seized an opportunity to attack part of their columns, burning a camp and seizing the money-chest and horses. This success was vociferously applauded. On another occasion, by means of a forced march accomplished by a body of picked men, he surprised the enemy at Auneau (November 24, 1587) and cut them to pieces ; 2000 Germans were massacred. The rest were discouraged. The winter was setting in cold and raw ; they had no clothes and lacked provisions. They went to Henry III, who had advanced towards Vendôme, and he consented to treat with them and allow them to return to Germany in peace. The Guises, who declared that they could make a speedy end of the remaining invaders, were loud in their disapproval.

On his return to Paris, Guise was greeted with acclamations. **Popularity** The King, it was said, had done nothing except **of Guise.** send his unworthy favourite, Joyeuse, to bring about the defeat of the Catholic army at Coutras, whilst Guise alone, with the modest army at his command, had

achieved some result. " Saul hath slain his thousands, but
David his tens of thousands " was the cry that was repeated
on all sides. The Duke was called " Moses, Gideon, and David,"
and his popularity increased proportionately as Henry III lost
favour and incurred public odium. The King, conscious of
the state of affairs, was irritated to the last degree. He felt
the menacing power of Guise increasing daily before him. The
absence of a direct heir to the throne, the prospect of a Huguenot
successor who was unacceptable to the country, the public discussions on the rights of the States-General to revive the ancient
privilege of the nation to choose its own king, the latent candidature of Guise to the throne, and the danger that if public
feeling became embittered, means would be found to hasten
the moment for the transmission of the crown, provided an
aggregate of elements which made his situation intolerable.
He began to be seriously alarmed. His crown, nay, his very
life, was in danger. He had Polybius and Machiavelli read
aloud to him. He made up his mind to form about his person
a nucleus of firm, reliable and devoted partisans, who would
at least be capable, in case of extremity, of defending his life.
As early as 1578, when his mind had been vaguely preoccupied
with considerations of this nature, he had created a new order
of chivalry, the famous order of the Holy Ghost—in imitation
of that formerly founded by one of the Anjous—to take the place
of the Order of Saint Michael, instituted by Louis XI, which
had been discredited by abuse. The new knights, whose number
was limited to a hundred, wore a blue ribbon, and took most
rigorous oaths of loyalty. " His Majesty," wrote l'Estoile,
" conceived the idea of strengthening himself by means of these
new knights, who would, he believed, be swift and faithful to
defend him should any commotion arise." But he did not stop
here. He created a special body of forty-five nobles, chiefly
men of Gascony, vigorous and courageous fighters in the prime
of life—from twenty-five to forty years of age—lively and
unscrupulous swashbucklers. He paid them a salary of 1200
crowns, which was a large amount for those days, fed them,
provided them with everything and refused them nothing, but
demanded of them absolute devotion. These ruthless individuals
understood his intention : they were to be the " King's trusty

bodyguard," ready for any emergency. Events in Paris seemed to justify these precautions.

Day by day the agitation in that city increased and hatred for the King waxed stronger. People no longer hesitated to speak of him in terms of contempt, as though the ancient cult of royalty were already a thing of the past. He was called a royal drone, a Sardanapalus, and abusive placards about him were posted up. Finally, it was currently agreed that it was absurd to keep upon the throne a monarch so weak, so false, and so maleficent in matters of religion, so scandalous in his life, and so revolting in the manner in which he abandoned himself to unworthy favourites. The Sixteen, who little by little, were forming a sort of revolutionary government, outside the regular authorities, wrote to the magistrates of the large towns in France, such as Lyons, Rouen, Amiens, and Orleans, asking them whether it would not be as well to face the possibility of deposing Henry III. The Duchess of Montpensier said that " she carried in her girdle the scissors which would give a third crown to brother Henry of Valois."

In the presence of provocations such as these, Henry III determined to have done with moderation. The Guises had **Insubordination of Guise.** demanded the vacant Governorship of Picardy for the Duke of Aumale, a member of their family. The King refused it, and nominated the Duke of Nevers instead. Events were coming to a climax with dramatic rapidity. D'Aumale occupied some towns in Picardy, and the Duke of Guise had the impertinence to write and tell him to keep them. Henry III gave due warning that unless d'Aumale immediately ceded the towns in question to the new Governor, he would be regarded as a rebel and his head would be forfeited ; he himself would go and arrest him. " If the King leaves Paris," the Duke of Guise insolently replied, " I will make him think of returning before he has advanced a day's journey towards Picardy." The conflict was on the verge of breaking out. The King of Spain, who was keeping a watchful eye on the course of events, exhorted Guise to break off all relations with the King of France, and offered him 300,000 crowns and a force of 6000 men.

Henry III immediately summoned a body of 4000 Swiss to Paris. The Sixteen invited the Duke of Guise, who was at

Soissons, to come and join them. The King informed the Duke that he forbade him to enter the city. For a moment **Guise enters** Guise hesitated; then he sprang upon his horse, **Paris.** and accompanied only by eight persons hastened to the capital as fast as he could ride. On Monday, May 9, 1588, he entered Paris through serried ranks of people, who greeted him with enthusiastic cheers, and so dense was the crowd that he could scarcely make his way through it. They covered him with flowers, and kissed the corner of his cloak. "France," said Balzac, "was crazy about the man; to say that she was in love with him would be to understate the case." Calm and cold, bare-headed, sitting erect upon his horse, his face, with its fair curling locks, keen eyes, and warlike scar, sternly set, this hero of eight-and-thirty, the most popular personage who lived under the old régime, had the grand manner. As Madame de Retz said: "One had only to look at him to become a Leaguer." He dismounted at his house in the Rue Saint-Antoine.

It was Villeroy who came to announce the news to Henry III. "How do you know?" the King demanded, beside himself with rage. "Has he actually arrived? 'Sdeath, he shall die for it!" and in his fury "he swore, contrary to his habit." Guise went to see Catherine de' Medici in her own house—she did not live in the Louvre, but occupied a mansion built for her, afterwards known as the Hôtel de Soissons, near the Rue Coquillière—and begged her to go to the palace with him. The old Queen got into her litter and accompanied the Duke to the royal abode. As they entered the Louvre, all the King's guards were standing ready, the French and Swiss lined **Interview** up on either side. The King's reception of them **between** was icy, and he curtly asked Guise why he had **Henry III** come in spite of his prohibition. The Duke **and Guise.** replied that he wished to clear himself of the calumnies that were being circulated against him and that, moreover, he had not supposed the King's order to be a formal one. Henry III made an exclamation of annoyance, and an altercation would have taken place had not Catherine de' Medici interfered to prevent it. Whereupon Guise, on the pretext that he was tired, went home, followed by an excited crowd which cheered him without ceasing. In the evening the Sixteen held a consultation at his house together with the captains of the city quarters and over 400 gentlemen. At the Louvre a surprise was feared, or at all events some commotion, and the inmates passed the night in terror. On the following morning, the 10th, Guise returned to the palace escorted by a numerous retinue. He was admitted to the King's presence, when he demanded the dismissal of the most obnoxious of the favourites, the Duke of Épernon. Henry III refused and then spoke himself. He said that he was exasperated at the encroachments made by the League upon his sovereign power, and, consenting to enter into further details, confessed his embarrassment with regard to money, and pointed out the inextricable difficulties of his situation, and the conflicting interests he was called upon to reconcile. Guise replied with a few vague phrases in which the words help and succour were noted.

Meanwhile the troops summoned by the King had reached Paris, and were marching through the streets. They concentrated at the Louvre, where Henry III had shut himself up. Swiss and French guards were then stationed round the palace to hold the approaches, and detachments even advanced as far as the Place de Grève and the Cemetery of the Holy Innocents. The city was full of soldiers and the bridges were barred. What did all these precautions mean? Paris was filled with terror. A rumour was rife that Henry III was meditating the arrest of 120 persons, the leaders of the League, intending to put them to death, and then proceed to a massacre of the Catholics similar to the Massacre of Saint Bartholomew. Ten thousand Huguenots, it was said, were arriving in the Faubourg Saint-Germain! The Swiss drums, beating a muster, gave the alarm. The shops were closed, and everybody rushed out into the streets, filling the squares and public places, The day of the where the crowds held eager discussions. At the barricades. corner of one of the streets some people conceived the idea of stretching chains across the road, planting barrels filled with earth and paving-stones, and piling up beams and furniture—barricading, in fact! This gave the signal. To the cries of " Long live the Union! " burghers, workmen, and magistrates set to work to raise similar barricades everywhere, in order to prevent the royal troops from advancing. Henry III commanded Crillon and d'O to push forward on one side as far as the Place Maubert and on the other to the Rue Saint-Antoine in order to secure an outlet. But it was too late. Neither Crillon nor d'O was able to force a passage. The tocsin was ringing and the roar of the growing tumult filled the streets. In the Marché Saint-Innocent, where a body of 900 Swiss was stationed, the sound of shots was heard. The people had fired on them and twenty men fell. The rest laid down their arms. In the Rue Neuve Notre-Dame, near Saint Denis de la Châtre, in the Cité, when some other Swiss fired one or two shots, a fusillade was immediately opened upon them to shouts of " Kill them ! Kill them ! " From the windows women hurled projectiles and struck down the soldiers, screaming at the tops of their voices, " France, France ! We are Christians ! " Some fifty or sixty victims fell. Many of the French guards laid down their arms. In the Louvre Biron declared that nothing could be done unless they were prepared to besiege every street, which was impracticable. He was accordingly dispatched together with d'Aumont to try to hold a parley, but at the first barricade they were received with a volley and were obliged to retreat. About four o'clock in the evening Guise rode out on horseback, recommending the people everywhere to keep calm, telling them to stand firm, but not to move. He sent back to the Louvre the royal troops who had laid down their arms. According to Nicolas Poullain's Diary, the people replied that the King must be killed or at all events captured, and that his Government must be changed and he himself reduced to impotence.

The demoralization of the Louvre was complete. The terrified princesses were in tears. Catherine de' Medici had **Demoralization** herself taken by night through side streets to **of the** the Hôtel de Guise, and there demanded an **Louvre.** explanation from the Duke, asking him what he wanted and what he demanded. Guise replied that he wished to be appointed Lieutenant-General of the kingdom, and stipulated that the chief provincial Governorships should be reserved for members of the League, that suspicious characters should be dismissed, that Huguenot princes should be excluded

268

from the succession to the throne, and that the States-General should be summoned. Catherine returned without having made any promises. On the following night all remained on the watch and the next day Catherine sent to the Duke of Guise, proposing that he should come to the Louvre and discuss matters with the King. But the Duke refused, on the grounds that he could not thus deliver himself up into the hands of his enemies. Thereupon violent incidents broke out in the streets. Students rushed down in a shouting disorderly throng from the Montagne Sainte-Geneviève and tried to make their way to the Louvre. The tumult was increasing and preparations were on foot indicating that a violent effort was about to be made to attack the royal troops and force the King's residence. The danger was indeed pressing. It is true that the King might have escaped through the Tuileries, which at that time was outside Paris, for the town walls only reached to the middle of the gallery on the river-bank, where there was a gate opening on to the Seine, called the Porte Neuve. This gate was still free. The Provost of the merchants and aldermen of Paris informed Henry III that the situation was becoming more alarming every moment. There was only one remedy : the withdrawal of the troops whose presence had provoked the outbreak. Henry III replied that he would not withdraw his troops unless the barricades were removed. The insurgents retorted that they would only remove the barricades when the troops had departed. An agreement seemed impossible. At this juncture—four o'clock in the evening—a messenger arrived to warn the King that a strong detachment of Parisians was skirting the walls outside the town, coming round the Tuileries, and making for **Flight of** the Porte Neuve with a view to seizing it. Henry **Henry III.** III was about to be blockaded. There was no time to be lost. He went down to the garden as if he were going for a stroll, reached the Tuileries where the stables were situated, changed his clothes quickly, and springing on horseback accompanied by a very small escort—the Parisians had not yet secured all the outlets from the city—galloped away in the direction of Saint-Cloud. The Court nobles and secretaries of State followed shortly afterwards, though they had to make their escape through occasional volleys aimed at them along

269

the banks of the Seine. The Queens remained behind. Once Henry III had made good his escape the troops were ordered to fall back, after which the French guards and the Swiss left Paris in their turn to rejoin the King. Henry III slept that night at Rambouillet and the following day took up his quarters at Chartres. In 1575 his mother had written to him: " You would rather be dead than a fugitive or a vanquished man." He was now both.

Guise remained master of the situation. He secured the Bastille, Vincennes, and the Arsenal, had a new municipality **Guise master** elected as the existing one was not sufficiently **of Paris.** subservient to him, and invited Achille de Harlay, the first President of the Parliament, to carry on the regular administration of justice. Harlay, however, answered haughtily : " It is lamentable, sir, for the servant to drive out the master ! " He deposed the Provost of Paris and nominated a fresh one. The Sixteen, for their part, on their own initiative removed from their benefices clerics suspected of liberalism, and filled their places with other men. " They are playing the King and the Pope," remarked Henry III, shrugging his shoulders. Colonels, captains, and quartermasters of the city militia who were considered lukewarm, were also superseded.

The news of the events which were taking place in Paris was received in the provinces with mixed feelings. Between the rabid Catholics and the Protestants, a moderate party consisting of those who were concerned at seeing the State falling into anarchy—a party of reputable and reasonable people, known as royalist or political Catholics—increased in numbers. The Day of the Barricades, as it was called, caused as much indignation to some as it aroused joy in the breasts of others. Many were utterly perplexed. " This day," wrote d'Aubigné, " clove in two the kingdom, the court, every province, every town, every family, and often the very brain of an individual man." Many protestations of fidelity and loyalty reached the King, even, nay above all, from Paris, either on behalf of individuals or organized bodies. This unexpected movement embarrassed the League. They began, indeed, to wonder what they could do with their victory, now they had achieved it ; to what decision could they come ? Mechanically, they tried to justify themselves to the King at Chartres—a grave concession! Henry III, however, was even more embarrassed than themselves. Deeply wounded by his humiliation, and a prey to excessive uneasiness, he found it impossible to sleep. What was he to do? On whom or on what could he rely? As the moderate Catholics were not yet sufficiently strong to be counted upon, he found himself under the hard necessity of turning to the League, which was his worst foe. This he endeavoured to do in a dignified manner. To the overtures

Henry III treats with the League. made him by the Parisians, he replied, in a few haughty and disdainful words, reproaching them with their ingratitude and their forgetfulness of all he had done for their city, in which he had resided longer than any of his predecessors. It remained to settle the conditions of an agreement. Henry III consented to sacrifice the Duke of Epernon; he deprived him of the Governorship of Normandy, to which he nominated the Duke of Montpensier, and begged the favourite to retire to Provence. He sanctioned some of the changes that had been made in Paris, and promised to convoke the States-General at Blois. With regard to the Huguenots, it was agreed that he would chastise them, that he would not acknowledge the King of Navarre as his heir-presumptive, and that he would support the candidature of Cardinal Bourbon. He gave four more towns as guarantees to the League, and appointed Henry of Guise Generalissimo of the royal forces. The treaty, known as the "Edict of Union" was concluded, and Henry III endorsed his own defeat. Not realizing the absolute impotence of the King, the moderate Catholics, indignant at his weakness, wrote lampoons against him. "Many steps lead up to the throne," they said, "but none lead down. You should not allow persons to receive you, and expect you to go to them; they must come to you, and you must receive them. To be King is your function. The man who has taken upon himself to make you a fugitive to-day, may compass your death to-morrow!" Compass his death to-morrow! That was precisely Henry III's private opinion as to the projects of the Guises. The question between him and his new Generalissimo, who was already King in deed though not yet in name, was which of the two was to get the better of the other. The drama was developing apace.

The results of the elections for the States-General were entirely favourable to the League. The royalist Catholics were **States-General** beaten; the Protestants did not even face the **of Blois, 1588.** conflict. The Assembly was opened at Blois in October, 1588, by a procession of the Order of the Holy Ghost, and the King took his seat on the 16th. The session was held as usual in the great hall of the ancient counts, in the presence of the princes and princesses, the Crown officials, and the nobles of the Court. As Grand Master, the Duke of Guise was seated just below the King, facing an assembly of which he was, in reality, the actual chief. The King's speech was lofty, resolute, and personal. He protested that he intended to defend the Catholic faith loyally, that he was ready to lend a willing ear to any proposals of reform the States might make, but that it was impossible for him to tolerate any League which intrigued against him, and by raising subsidies and troops, made an attack upon his sovereign power. He would consent to grant an amnesty for the past, provided acts of this sort were never repeated. His attitude was courageous enough. He did not mention the question of the succession.

The debate was at once opened, and the hostile feeling of the assembly became evident from the first moment. It began by demanding the exclusion from the succession of the King of Navarre, and intimated that it expected vigorous war to be made upon him. The question of finance was raised, and the budget of the country's receipts and expenditure presented by the Government excited mistrust and was regarded as incorrect. The States insisted upon the suppression of certain offices, the abolition of taxes that had been recently raised, and the reduction of the *taille* to the amount at which it had stood in the time of Francis I. Henry III proposed the raising of a loan for war expenses. The assembly retorted that if they sanctioned this loan it would be on the understanding that they superintended the spending of it. They became aggressive and waxed bolder, dismissing thirty-five financial officers—a most extraordinary innovation. They passed a resolution to the effect that their decisions should immediately have the force of law without further confirmation—which amounted to revolution; and that as soon as the assembly was dissolved, a procurator should represent them and superintend the execution of their wishes. In the face of all these measures, what was to become of the traditional absolute power of the Crown and "its full authority"? Henry III was exasperated. It was an open secret that the States were entirely under the control of a committee, which prepared the motions, and included amongst others Henry of Guise, his brother Cardinal Guise, Cardinal Bourbon, and d'Épinac, Archbishop of Lyons. What were they all—and more especially Guise—aiming at? Clearly they wished to begin by reducing the reigning monarch to a cypher in order to set him aside more easily later on. As Henry III descended, Guise would ascend. The words "Guisards" and "Royalists" became current terms denoting opposite factions. Further extensions of power were demanded for the Duke, and there was even some talk of having him made Constable by a decree of the States and not by the King—yet another revolutionary measure. Guise, **Murder of** surrounded by the States, who were devoted to **Guise pro-** him, and by his own partisans, was practically **jected.** master at Blois. At this juncture, the problem in all its terrifying simplicity presented itself to the agonized mind of the King. One of his own subjects, nay more, a foreigner, rising up against his lawful sovereign, had made himself all-powerful in the State, and spurred on by an inordinate ambition, was endeavouring to overthrow that sovereign, and usurp his throne. As King, Henry III found himself face to face with a rebel guilty of high treason; as a man, he was confronted by the murderer who wished to kill him. Once the problem had been defined, the solution presented itself automatically—it was necessary for the King to forestall him and take action himself. The idea of a trial hardly entered his thoughts. " I might have appointed judges! " he exclaimed later in answer to one of the Presidents of Paris, who made the suggestion. " Where, pray, was I to find them? " And, indeed, almost the whole of France was on the side of the League. Before making up his mind to strike the blow Henry III consulted his faithful friends—d'Aumont, Rambouillet, d'Angennes, d'Ornano and Beauvais-Nangis. With hardly a dissentient voice they declared he must not hesitate. The occasion was unique. Guise was at Blois, in the King's hands. It would be easy to take him by surprise. They recalled his threatening speeches and the provocation he had given. It would be best to put an end to it all. A step taken by the Duke himself precipitated the catastrophe.

On Thursday, December 22, as Henry III was coming away from Mass, he was followed by Guise, who demanded an explanation from him. The Duke declared with animation that he found himself the object of a growing antipathy on the part of his Majesty, that all he said or did had an unfavourable construction put upon it by the King, and that the situation, under these circumstances was " intolerable." He had had enough of it and wished to leave and send in his resignation of the post of Generalissimo. Surprised by this outburst, the King refused to accept the resignation. A stormy discussion ensued ; Guise reiterated the tale of his grievances and renewed his offer to retire. Henry III persisted in refusing it. The interview lasted a long time, causing grave anxiety to those who were following it at a distance without understanding what was going on. But as soon as he got home the King felt convinced that Guise " only wished to resign his office because the States had promised to make him Constable." He was certain that the Duke would flee. There was not a moment to be lost. Henry III sent for Crillon, who was in command of the regiment of guards, and cross-questioned him. Crillon replied that he was quite ready to kill Guise in a duel, if he were called upon to do so, but not otherwise. Whereupon Loignac, the leader of the forty-five gentlemen, assured the King that he might count upon his men and that he would answer for them.

Henry III made his preparations with extraordinary coolness and presence of mind. In the evening, after supper, he **Preparations** ordered his coach for the following day at four **for the** o'clock, as if he meant to make an excursion. **murder.** He commanded the council to attend a meeting at six o'clock in the morning, and sent a special summons to Guise, his brother the Cardinal, and the Archbishop of Lyons. The forty-five were to be at the castle at five o'clock, and

274

Loignac was to choose out ten resolute fellows from among them. At nine o'clock in the evening Monsieur de Larchant, the captain of the guard, was ordered to station himself with his men at seven o'clock in the morning on the grand staircase, and to prevent anyone from ascending or descending the stairs after the Duke of Guise had passed. He was also to send a detachment to guard the stairs which led from the Galerie des Cerfs to the King's old cabinet in the court. At midnight Henry III went to bed in the Queen's room, after having given du Halde, his valet, instructions to call him at four o'clock.

At four o'clock in the morning du Halde accordingly came and knocked at the door. " Who's there ? " demanded Madame de Piolant, the woman of the bedchamber. " It is du Halde ; tell the King that it is four o'clock." " The King and the Queen are both asleep ! "—" Wake him up, then. He told me to call him." Henry III had not closed his eyes. He jumped to the foot of his bed. " Piolant," he called " here ! my boots, my gown, and my candle." And he went out into his cabinet. The grand staircase at Blois leads on the second storey to a guard-room on the left. Crossing this to come to the façade, which now overlooks the town, but formerly faced the garden, we find on the right the Queen's apartments, which extend as far as the great hall where the States-General used to meet ; the first room is the bed-chamber ; on the left, three rooms open into each other—the council-room, the largest of the three, where the King took his meals ; the King's bed-chamber or state room ; and the King's cabinet. Adjacent to the state room, but looking into the court, was the King's old cabinet, *le cabinet vieil*. The King found du Halde and de Termes in his cabinet. The men who had been picked out of the forty-five arrived one by one in the state-room and as they came Henry III, followed by de Termes, who carried the candle, led them by a secret stair to the floor above and shut them up in little rooms which were supposed to have been prepared for some Capuchin monks. At six o'clock the members of the council arrived and took their seats in the council-chamber. The King, thereupon, made the guardsmen he had shut up come down into his state-room, telling them to make no noise, in order not to awaken the Queen, his mother, who was sleeping below. As soon as this was done he entered the council chamber. Guise had not yet arrived. Henry III proceeded to make a speech in which he ennumerated everything the Duke had done for some years past to undermine his authority, the insolence of that " ungrateful and disloyal soul," and his audacity in coming to Paris on the eve of the barricades, in spite of having been commanded not to do so. " And now," he continued, raising his voice, " in his unbridled ambition he is on the eve of making an attempt against my Crown and my life, so that he has reduced me to this extremity, that either I must die or he must die not later than this very morning." He had made up his mind to forestall his enemy, and he asked the members of the council for their consent. Speechless with surprise, they tamely acquiesced. Thereupon Henry III returned to his state-room and collecting those of the forty-five who were there, he reminded them of all he had done for them, how he had honoured them by attaching them to his person, and how he had absolute confidence in them. Never had he refused them anything, but on the contrary, had loaded them with benefits. And now it was his turn to ask them a favour. They must, of course, be aware of the violent conduct of the Duke of Guise towards him—his insolence and the provocation he had given. Matters had reached such a climax that at that very moment his life and his Crown were in danger. And he repeated the phrase: " I am reduced to this extremity, that this very morning either he must die or I must die ! " Would they consent to kill the Duke ? He spoke with great energy, and with one voice the bullies declared that they were ready. "Cap de Diou, Sire," one of them, named Sariac, exclaimed in his Gascon dialect, " I'll kill him for you ! " The band consisted of eight men armed with daggers and their chief, Loignac, who had a sword. They were hidden in the old cabinet. It was arranged that Guise was to be called from the council-chamber to the old cabinet on the pretext that the King wished to speak to him, and that as he crossed the state room he was to be executed. When all was ready Henry III retired into his cabinet, the room next door, and waited, walking up and down in feverish agitation.

276

THE CATHOLIC REACTION

Cardinal Guise and the Archbishop of Lyons had arrived at the council. The Duke of Guise, who had spent the previous evening in agreeable company, had not gone to bed till nearly three o'clock in the morning. Various notes had been delivered to him bidding him beware. He had merely shrugged his shoulders exclaiming: "There would be no end to it if I paid attention to every warning. He would never dare!" At eight o'clock he awoke, and putting on a suit of grey satin came to the council. As soon as he had gone upstairs all the exits were guarded in accordance with the King's instructions. He went in, saluted the council, said he felt cold, and ordered the fire to be heaped up. He thereupon said he would like something to eat, and some Brignoles plums were brought to him. A Master of Requests was making a report on some question of taxation. Monsieur de Révol, the usual gentleman in attendance, came in looking rather pale, and whispered in the Duke's ear that the King wished to see him in his old cabinet. Guise rose, slung his cloak over his left arm, and putting down the plums on the table asked: "Who would like some?" Then picking up his gloves he added, "Farewell, gentlemen!" and passed through the state-room door which Nambu, the usher, locked behind him. The nine men who had been chosen from the forty-five were sitting round the room. They rose as if in deference to the Duke. Guise returned their salute, and went towards the door of the old cabinet. He was stroking his beard with his hand, and was only a couple of paces from the curtain over the doorway, when, as the men were following him, he turned round to see what they wanted. Whereupon one of them, Monsieur de Montféry, seized him by the arm and stabbed him violently in the breast. "Ah!" exclaimed the Duke, as he sprang back hastily. But another man had already flung himself upon him, and laid tight hold of his legs in order to prevent him from moving, whilst all the rest rushed forward striking at him. There was a horrible scuffle. In the room next door, the counsellors, hearing Guise's hoarse cry, had sprung to their feet, pale to the lips, guessing what was taking place. They heard the tramp of feet during the struggle, and the heartrending appeals of the Duke—"Ah! . . . What treachery!

277

. . . Oh ! my God ! . . . Mercy ! " . . . Then followed the dull thud of a heavy fall. Dragging along his assassins, who clung to him, Guise had managed to stagger across the room, and, mortally wounded, panting, and covered with blood, had sunk down beside the King's bed. " They are killing my brother ! " exclaimed Cardinal Guise hoarsely." 'Sdeath, sir, don't move," answered Marshal d'Aumont, roughly, as he drew his sword, " the King will deal with you." Henry III, informed that all was over, raised the curtain of his room and with face convulsed, gazed upon the scene. Guise was in his death agony. They searched him hurriedly ; he died in a few minutes. An Oriental carpet was flung over his body ; two great pools of blood stained the floor.

The King went downstairs to announce the sinister news to his mother, who was ill at the time. " What have you done ? " exclaimed Catherine de' Medici, wringing her hands in terror. Then after a moment's silence she continued : " God grant you may benefit by it ! " Henry III answered firmly : " Now, I alone am King ! " He was wrong, however. He was King no more !

He then gave orders for the arrest of Cardinal Guise, the Archbishop of Lyons, Elbeuf, Nemours, and Joinville, and **Murder of** commanded Cardinal Bourbon to be strictly **Cardinal Guise.** guarded. His first intention had been merely to imprison Cardinal Guise ; the following morning he changed his mind and gave orders for his execution. But this time no one could be found to carry out his commands, and he was obliged to fall back upon three soldiers, who were prevailed upon to kill the Cardinal with their halberds in a gallery whither he was summoned for the purpose.

The news of the tragedy that had been enacted at Blois reached Paris on December 24, Christmas Eve, between three and four o'clock in the evening. It produced an upheaval in the city, and the streets were thronged with people crying : " Murder ! Fire ! Death and vengeance ! " The council of the Union met at once in the Hôtel de Ville, appointed the Duke of Aumale Governor of Paris, put the militia under arms, seized the gates, and deliberated what course to pursue. After a moment's stupor the whole of France was filled with rage and hatred. No! Henry III was no longer King, the people repeated, he was merely "Henry of Valois, sometime King of France." He was nothing but "a murderer, an assassin, a false heretic!" Violent pamphlets appeared, and the name of the King was vilified, insulted, and dragged through the mud. No King of France was ever treated as Henry III was treated at this moment. His authority was virtually extinct. He was "the tyrant." Sermons in the pulpits, couplets at the cross-roads, lampoons and placards poured imprecations on his head in unanimous chorus. Morally speaking, Henry III was already deposed. He received anonymous letters announcing that he himself would very shortly be executed ; he felt as if his kingdom were crumbling to pieces around him.

Throughout the country religious ceremonies were held for the repose of the souls of the victims of Blois, at which funeral sermons were preached denouncing the murderer. The Faculty of Theology in Paris announced at the Sorbonne "that as the tyrant had fallen" no one was called upon to obey him. Parliament was suspected of harbouring among its magistrates certain "politicians," dangerous and sinister people, "the enemies of the Catholic religion," amongst others the First President de Harlay. He was accordingly sent to the Bastille together with the Presidents Potier and de Thou and a number of counsellors. Brisson was nominated First President and Molé Procurator-General. A declaration was published in which the League announced its intention of defending religion, avenging the death of the Guises judicially, and protecting the States-General. And, indeed, a judicial commission appointed by the Parliament opened an inquiry. Some of its depositions have been preserved. A herald who presented himself on behalf of Henry III was soundly thrashed, and public notice was given that the League refused to hold any communication whatsoever with "Henry of Valois." Paris was in a state of insurrection. The Sixteen wrote to all the towns in the kingdom calling on them to judge in the case. Nearly all pronounced in their favour—Rouen, Amiens, Chartres, Rheims, Troyes, Angers, Marseilles, Le Mans and Toulouse. In Bordeaux, Matignon remained loyal, but Périgueux and Agen declared against the King. Lyons issued its manifesto on

February 24. The provincial governors in their turn followed the example of the towns.

Henry III was beside himself, weeping and declaring that "he would think himself lucky if somebody had already killed **Despair of** him." Only Blois, Tours, Saumur, Bordeaux, **Henry III.** and a few isolated spots remained to him. He declared the States-General dissolved, and in order to explain his conduct dispatched a proclamation throughout the country which no one would even receive. In May a finishing stroke in the form of a Bull from Rome arrived, in which Sixtus V declared that if within ten days "Henry of Valois," as he was called in the text, did not release Cardinal Bourbon and the Archbishop of Lyons, he would be excommunicated; it summoned him to Rome to stand his trial for the blood of Cardinal Guise criminally shed by him. This was the *coup-de-grâce*. The whole of France regarded Henry III as excommunicated.

The Duke of Mayenne, who assumed the title of Lieutenant-General, now found himself at the head of the League. He convoked the States-General. In his pitiable state of distress Henry III declared both him and d'Aumale to be felons and called to his aid the ban and rear-ban of the kingdom—that nobility, who in despair at the events which had taken place, and humiliated by the demagogic excesses of Paris, at heart still felt some remnant of loyalty for him, though they remained silent and perplexed. In spite of the fact that he had no money and that the taxes were not being paid, Henry III sent Monsieur de Sancy to Switzerland to raise recruits for him. But, in the midst of the universal hatred against him, whither was he himself to turn? Would it be possible for him to hold out for long at Blois? At this juncture his friend of old days upon whom he had once heaped so many favours, d'Épernon, hastened to him, and reviving the idea which he had always upheld and which had been the cause of his disgrace, begged Henry III to throw in his fortunes with those of his heir, the King of Navarre. At this opportune moment, March 4, Henry of Navarre published a declaration noble and lofty in tone, in which he generously held out his hand to the fallen monarch. "Misery, confusion, and want everywhere," he said, "such

280

are the fruits of war. I ask for peace in the name of us all from my Lord, the King. I ask it for myself and for every Frenchman—for France herself!" He begged the King to pardon and to welcome those who might come and offer him their allegiance. It was impossible to hesitate any longer, and du Plessis-Mornay and Sully secretly came to Tours, where Henry III was staying, to hold a consultation with him.

Henry III. combines with Henry of Béarn. The coalition was decided upon and a treaty signed defining the conditions. But hereupon the whole kingdom exclaimed that "at last the lying features of the arch-hypocrite of France have been unveiled!" The "tyrant" had put the coping-stone to his "treacheries, perfidies, sacrilege, exactions, cruelties, and deeds of shame;" he had cast aside the mask and had openly declared himself the defender of heresy.

The meeting between the two Kings took place on April 30, 1589, in the park of Plessis-les-Tours. Henry of Navarre, that needy hero, arrived clad in a "doublet worn on the shoulders and sides by the rubbing of his cuirass, velvet breeches the colour of dead leaves, a scarlet cloak and a grey hat with a large white plume—the costume of a soldier on campaign." The throng of people was so great that the two sovereigns had some difficulty in coming together. With deep emotion they embraced each other, and Henry of Navarre even wept. He had been warned against taking so dangerous a step, considering the character of the man with whom he had to deal. But he remained true to his purpose. "The ice has been broken," he wrote that evening to du Plessis-Mornay, "I have crossed the water after commending myself to God."

Under a leader so distinguished as Henry of Béarn the conditions of the conflict assumed a very different aspect. A **March on Paris.** man of clear and resolute judgment, the King of Navarre decided that all the troops that were ready to hand should be collected at once to march straight on Paris. The nobility, who, in spite of everything, had a certain sympathy for him on account of his brilliant qualities, and who now saw him at the side of the lawful King, gathered round him. The Protestant forces had rallied; the march was begun and vigorously led by Henry of Navarre. They won a few successes in small skirmishes and met with no serious opposition. On July 24 Pontoise was taken. On the 25th Sancy joined them, bringing a reinforcement of 16,000 men which he had succeeded in raising in Germany and Switzerland. The royal army almost reached the imposing number of 42,000 men. On the 29th the bridge of Saint-Cloud was occupied and the troops extended from this point to Vaugirard. Hope began to revive. Noting the energetic measures of the two Kings, the people of Paris became anxious and hesitated; the moderates held deliberations. On the 30th, Mayenne had 300 persons arrested in the hope of suppressing the threatened reaction. But entrenchments had been begun; the work advanced apace. Henry of Béarn had decided to attempt an assault on August 2, and his success seemed certain. Mayenne, in despair, had already determined to make a sortie from the town, and, rather than allow himself to be surrounded and taken, to hurl himself upon the royal army in the open country, when on the morning of August 1, a piece of news was suddenly spread abroad which put an end to the hopes of some and the fears of others: Henry III had been assassinated!

In the midst of the passions that had been let loose and the seething of an infuriated mob, one individual of distorted

Plan to murder Henry III. intelligence had taken the curses hurled against the tyrant King, the destroyer of religion, literally, and, choosing as his example similar instances described in the Old Testament, had thought he would accomplish a noble deed in ridding " the Church of God " of the " monster " who wished to ruin her. He was a Dominican monk, or, as he was called, a Jacobin, of twenty-eight. The idea had taken firm hold of his mind, and he believed himself to be a Jehu, or a Judith, a weapon designed by Providence for the salvation of his people. Deterred by one last scruple he had consulted doctors of theology with the object of ascertaining—the question, he said, had been put to him theoretically, by a third party—whether one might without sin, assassinate Henry of Valois, and whether if the King's murderer were killed upon the spot, he would go to heaven. The doctors had replied that, theologically speaking, if the murderer had in

282

view any personal interest or the satisfaction of a desire for revenge, he would be guilty of a grave sin, but that if he acted for the public good and the interests of religion, his deed would be a meritorious one, " and that there was no doubt that if he died after having carried it out he would be saved and win eternal bliss." Clément, accordingly, made his preparations ; he fasted, prayed, and received the Sacrament. The announcement that an assault was to be made decided him. After some difficulty he obtained a letter of introduction to the immediate circle of Henry III from a royalist prisoner confined in Paris, the Count of Brienne. The King was staying at Saint-Cloud in the house of Monsieur de Gondi, called " the red house," which was situated on the hill a little above the town, on the left in the direction of Meudon. Clément presented himself at the outposts, and was taken to Monsieur la Guesle, Procurator-General of the Parliament, who was close at hand. He asked La Guesle to present him to the King on the pretext that he wished to tell his Majesty of a certain plot that was being hatched in Paris for delivering one of the gates of the city into his hands. La Guesle cross-questioned the monk, and, thinking that his story might, after all, be true, promised to conduct him to the King on the following morning.

The next day, August 1, Clément went to the " red house." Here he waited an hour ; the King was getting up. Henry's **Murder of** retinue did not wish him to receive an unknown **Henry III, 1589.** man in this way, but he replied that it would produce a very bad impression if he refused an audience to a priest and a monk. At eight o'clock the Dominican was shown into his presence. In his loose white sleeve he carried a little common knife. The King had on only his breeches and a dressing-gown over his shoulders. Clément bowed before him and presented his letter ; as the King perused it, he pretended to be seeking for another paper in his sleeve ; and drawing out the knife with a swift, violent movement he plunged it into the King's belly. Henry III had guessed his intention, and bent forward quickly to parry the blow. But it was too late. " Ah ! the wretch, he has killed me ! " he exclaimed. " Kill him ! " The suite rushed at Clément, and hustled him into a corner of the room where he fell dead, riddled with sword-thrusts. After bleeding copiously Henry III was carried to bed, where his wound was dressed. He did not suffer much. The physicians told him that it would be nothing; but Portail, the head surgeon, in probing the wound had discovered that the intestine was pierced and knew that there was no hope for the King. In the evening the wound became inflamed, and fever accompanied by violent pains set in. Henry III knew that all was over. But he was calm and resigned. He embraced the King of Navarre and said : "I am dying happy in the knowledge that you are by my side. The Crown is yours. I command all the officers to recognize you as King after me." Henry of Navarre kissed the hand of the dying man, his eyes full of tears. The spectators, on their knees, promised to do their sovereign's bidding, and turning to Henry of Béarn the King added : "You will have many troubles unless you make up your mind to change your religion. I exhort you to do this ! " At midnight he became unconscious, and at three o'clock in the morning he was dead.

Catherine de' Medici had preceded him to the grave. Shocked beyond measure by the execution of the Guises at **Death of** Blois, she had afterwards had a scene with **Catherine de'** Cardinal Bourbon. He had reproached her with **Medici, 1589.** the events that had taken place, and had exclaimed : "Ah ! Madam, this is your doing. It is you who are killing us all ! " She had protested vehemently, saying that she had had nothing whatever to do with the matter ; and then she added : "I can bear no more. I must go to bed." She never left it again. She died of pneumonia on January 5, 1589, at the age of seventy. The public, absorbed in other matters, was quite indifferent to her death. "They paid no more heed to it than they would have done to the death of a goat," and the Parisians declared that if her body were brought to Saint-Denis they would throw it out into the gutter. Of the numerous and brilliant family of Henry III no single prince remained, and the Crown reverted to a heretic whom the majority of Frenchmen repudiated.

SOURCES. Same as for two preceding chapters, and : *Mémoires du duc de Nevers*, ed. Gomberville, 1665 ; *Mémoires d'État de Villeroy*, 1665 ; *Mémoires de la Ligue*, 1758 ; Combes, *Lettres inédites de Henri de Guise*,

THE CATHOLIC REACTION

de Catherine de Médicis et de Henri de Navarre, 1879 ; Henri IV, *Lettres missives,* ed. Berger de Xivrey, 1843 ; Sully, *Économies royales,* ed. Michaud and Poujoulat ; du Plessis-Mornay, *Mémoires et correspondence,* 1824 ; Pierre de l'Estoile, *Mémoires-Journaux,* ed. G. Brunet, 1875 ; *Lettres de Busbecq, ambassadeur de l'empereur,* in Cimber and Danjou, *Archives curieuses,* vol. x ; H. Davila, *Histoire des guerres civiles de France,* ed. Mallet, 1757 ; Loutchizky, *Documents inédits sur la Réforme et la Ligue,* 1875 ; Dubois, *La Ligue, documents relatifs à la Picardie,* 1859 ; *Documents historiques sur l'assassinat des duc et cardinal de Guise,* in *Revue retrospective,* vol. iii and iv, 1834 ; Nicolas Poullain, *Journal,* in Cimber and Danjou, *Archives curieuses,* vol. xi ; Diegerick and Müller, *Documents concernant les relations entre le duc d'Anjou et les Pays-Bas,* 1889.

WORKS. Same as for the preceding chapter, and : Marquis de Noailles, *Henri de Valois et la Pologne en 1572,* 1867 ; M. W. Freer, *Henry III, King of France, his Court and Times,* 1858 ; E. Frémy, *Henri III pénitent,* 1885 ; Comte de Baillon, *Histoire de Louise de Lorraine,* 1884 ; E. Charleville, *Les États généraux de 1576,* 1901 ; V. de Chalambert, *Histoire de la Ligue,* 1854 ; H. de l'Épinois, *La Ligue et les papes,* 1886 ; F. Decrue, *Le parti des politiques au lendemain de la Saint-Barthélemy,* 1892 ; Robiquet, *Paris et la Ligue,* 1886 ; B. Zeller, *Le mouvement guisard en 1588,* 1889 ; A. Gérard, *La révolte et le siège de Paris* (in *Mem. de la Soc. de l'hist. de Paris,* 1906) ; Baguenault de Puchesse, *Les négociations de Catherine de Médicis à Paris après la journée des barricades,* 1903 ; Richard, *Pierre d'Épinac, archeveque de Lyon,* 1901.

CHAPTER VIII

INTERNAL PEACE. HENRY IV

Henry IV's difficulties (1589–1610) in obtaining recognition of his title to the throne. The siege of Paris raised. Battle of Arques, 1589 ; fresh march against Paris and failure to capture the city. Battle of Ivry, 1590. Renewed unsuccessful siege of Paris. Henry IV seizes Chartres. Violence of the demagogic faction of the Sixteen in Paris : execution of President Brisson, 1591. Attempts at negotiation with Henry IV : Mayenne convokes the States-General, 1593. Philip II's attempts to have his daughter nominated Queen of France. Conference with Henry IV at Suresnes. Recantation of Henry IV, 1593. His coronation at Chartres, 1594. All parties enter into negotiations with him. Surrender of Paris, 1594. The end of the League. Henry IV drives out the Spaniards : Battle of Fontaine-Française, 1595. Peace of Vervins, 1598. The end of war : Henry IV sets his kingdom in order ; Sully ; the finances ; Assembly of Notables at Rouen, 1596 ; agriculture, commerce, public works, colonization. Religious peace and the Edict of Nantes, 1598. Annulment of Henry IV's first marriage and his alliance with Marie de' Medici, 1600. The case of Marshal de Biron, 1602. Scant popularity of Henry IV during his lifetime. His assassination, 1610.

THERE was a moment of singular confusion in Monsieur de Gondi's " red house " at Saint-Cloud on the morning of August 1, 1589, when the death of Henry III left the nation to face the inevitable fact that France had a new King and **Henry IV.,** that this King was a Protestant. The prevailing **1589–1610.** sentiment in the monarch's immediate circle, which was chiefly composed of Catholics, was that of rage. " With cries and yells," said d'Aubingé, " they pulled down their hats over their eyes or flung them to the ground, clenched their fists, and with the airs of conspirators, shook each other by the hand, and made vows and promises, the conclusion of which was : rather would we die a thousand deaths ! " They hardly knew Henry IV.   D'O, d'Entraigues, and Châteauvieux

286

kept repeating that there was no one they would not have
preferred as master. On the night of the 2nd, the chief
Catholics of the Court met together to consider the situation.
A few of them, such as the Duke of Longueville, Baron de Givry,
and Monsieur de Rambouillet, were of opinion that as the
siege was in progress, it was necessary to recognize the King
of Navarre, and push on the attack upon Paris with the object
of avenging Henry III. The majority, however, were against
this, saying that it was impossible to take as their King a man
who was excommunicated. Henry of Béarn would never be
converted ; his vacillation in the past had conclusively proved
this. Finally, at the instigation of d'Épernon, it was decided
that a deputation should be sent to explain to Henry IV, that
if he would immediately abjure the Protestant faith, he should
be proclaimed without further delay.

The new King of France was a man of five-and-thirty, of
medium height, wiry, vigorous, and nervous, the most in-
Character of telligent of all the French Kings, endowed with
Henry IV. one of those lively and supple intellects which
see all the shades of a question and make prompt decisions.
In addition, he was witty, charming, simple in manners and
bearing, and an excellent soldier. He possessed too lofty a
conception of his own personal dignity and that of his position
to accept the terms offered him, though he was fully conscious
of his precarious situation. The army by which he was surrounded contained barely 2000 Huguenots, encamped apart
at Meudon, the butt of the rest of the troops, who mockingly
dubbed them " the highwaymen." At the very first moment
he had despatched Biron to administer the oath of allegiance
to the Swiss, foreigners, mercenaries, and Protestants, who
would obey him. But outside these groups he had no supporters.
A few Catholics might follow him ; the rest might go ; he would
remain a King without a country, and a general without an
army. He was a proud man, and held his ground firmly
against the deputation which came to bid him be converted.
He answered with vehement emotion that they were holding
a knife at his throat and demanding from him an action that
would dishonour him. He promised to give the Catholics
every possible guarantee and was ready to receive instruction

by means of a national council. Let those who did not wish to stay take their departure. "My supporters among the Catholics," he said nobly at the end of his speech, "will be those who love France and who love honour ! "

This determined attitude disconcerted the Catholic leaders, and they held another meeting. What were they to do ? **Provisional** Whom could they take as King ? The prince's **recognition** scruples were certainly worthy of respect. Some **of Henry IV.** one, thereupon, proposed that Henry IV should be provisionally recognized, and given six months in which to be converted ; a resolution to this effect was carried. Henry IV accepted the terms. An agreement was signed on August 4, by which it was arranged that the King should be instructed, that during the course of the six months he should summon a national council, and that in the meanwhile no alteration should be made in the position of the Catholics and the Huguenots respectively. But was this really a solution ? Unfortunately, a number of stubborn Catholics refused to accept the compromise. They collected their baggage and left the army, one man taking his departure with the whole contingent under his command—a body of 7000 men. And, on the other hand, the Protestants, discouraged by the promises Henry IV had just made, also retired. La Trémoïlle broke up his camp and left with nine battalions. The royal army was thus thoroughly disorganized, and Henry IV, who, to add to his misfortunes, had no money, finding it impossible to carry on the siege, retreated from the banks of the Seine and fell back in the direction of Normandy.

The country received the agreement of Saint-Cloud with mixed feelings. A minority accepted it, but the mass of the people remained undecided, uncertain, and troubled, not willing to go as far as the League, and yet refusing to submit to a heretic King. The League regained confidence. It was no longer a question of defending themselves against the possible accession of a Reformer ; the heretic was actually King. "A second rebellion," said Palma Cayet, "almost took place." Mayenne, realizing that he could not himself lay claim to the Crown, made up his mind to abide by the decision of the States-General at Blois, and to proclaim Cardinal Bourbon King with the title

of Charles X. Cardinal Bourbon was shut up in the Château
Cardinal de Loches. He let Mayenne proceed and wrote
Bourbon pro- to Vergnètes : "I have embarked on the enterprise
claimed King. and nobody knows why. They (the League)
have a grudge against the House of Bourbon. As long as I
side with them they will be obliged to recognize the Bourbons.
Meanwhile, the King of Navarre, my nephew, will make his
own way. What I am doing is merely to preserve my nephew's
rights." The Cardinal was a wise man. Notification of the
accession of Charles X was sent to all the towns in France,
and Mayenne assumed the title of Lieutenant-General of the
kingdom.

Fortified by the knowledge of his rights and penetrated by
a sense of duty, inspired, not by any personal ambition, but by
a strong and admirable conviction of what he owed to France,
Henry IV realized that he would have to conquer his kingdom
step by step. He made up his mind to the task. He had
10,000 men at his disposal, and with them he marched upon
Rouen. The fall of that important town would have had a
considerable effect. Mayenne hastened from Paris with a much
more powerful army to force him to raise the siege. As it
was impossible to await him in such a disadvantageous position
Henry IV retreated towards Dieppe. Wherever he went he
was cordial and affable to all. "I want no ceremony, my
children," he remarked on entering Dieppe, " but your friendship, and good bread, good wine, and kind, hospitable faces."
He entrenched himself strongly at Arques, whither Mayenne
came with 32,000 men to attack him. For twelve days, the
army of the League endeavoured to force the lines of the
Battle of Royalists in spite of the cannon of Arques and
Arques, 1589. Dieppe. At last on September 21, they thought
they had succeeded. A breach had been made in the entrenchments through which they poured in. Henry IV, however, collecting his soldiers, threw them against the enemy so
vigorously that the latter was obliged to give way after suffering
severe losses. Mayenne tried to turn the tables, but failed ;
whereupon he gave up the enterprise in disgust and went
away.

This success at Arques produced an extremely favourable

T

impression. Supporters hastened to Henry IV's side, and Longueville with his troops joined him. He received everybody with smiling cordiality. In a short time, he found, to his surprise, that he had mustered a force of some 23,000 men about him. They were miserably equipped, it is true, and in rags, but they were fairly well in hand and confident of success. Few French generals before Henry IV were more clear-headed and resolute than he. He immediately made up his mind to march to Paris, "the bull's-eye of the target," as he called it. He was fully aware that if he held Paris the rest would follow. On November 1 he attempted an assault on the city at three different points on the left bank, more particularly at the Porte de Nesle. Unfortunately for him, however, the League made a strong defence and repulsed him. The news that Mayenne was advancing swiftly against him made him fall back, and, not wishing to be caught between two fires, he retreated to Tours. Still attracted by the "target," however, he soon set out again, and occupied Le Mans, Alençon, Falaise, and Honfleur, always hovering round Paris. He went about gaily, full of energy, and was popular with his soldiers on account of his brilliant and thoroughly French qualities. He called himself "a King without a country, a soldier without money, a husband without a wife" (owing to incompatibility of temperament and mutual infidelity, Henry IV and Margaret of Valois had long been separated). In that quick incisive style, which makes him one of the great writers of France he ordered : " To horse, Fervagues, I want to see at once of what feather are the geese of Normandy. Come straight to Alençon." People followed readily. Meanwhile the situation of his enemies was becoming more and more complex.

In Paris, Mayenne's cause was far from prosperous. The tyranny of the faction controlled by the Sixteen was increasing. **Mayenne's difficulties.** Exasperated by their humiliating and demagogic conduct, the nobility had adopted the attitude of holding aloof, more especially as they were attracted by secret feelings of sympathy for a gallant soldier like Henry IV. Mayenne, deprived of the swords of the nobility, was obliged to get troops where he could, that is to say, from abroad. Now the foreign country where these were most plentiful was

Spain. The King of Spain was still keeping a watchful eye on events in France. He had conceived the extraordinary idea, not merely of profiting by her troubles in order to lay hands on certain portions of territory, but actually of seizing France and turning it into a province of his vast empire. He had accordingly charged his ambassador, Mendoza, to offer Mayenne all the troops and money he required on condition that he made a treaty recognizing Philip II as " Protector of the State and of the religion of the kingdom of France." This was the first step. Mayenne, who was in sore need of help, hesitated. But Villeroy persuaded him not to accept Philip's offers. One of Henry III's old ministers, who had entered public life at the age of eighteen under Catherine de' Medici, and had quickly risen to the position of Secretary of State, Monsieur de Villeroy had been dismissed by Henry III on the eve of the assassination of the Guises, and had thrown in his lot with the League. He was a man of vast experience, extremely calm and deliberate, with a clear mind, and endowed with skill and plenty of good sense and judgment. He was destined to be minister under Henry IV and Louis XIII, and to die at the age of seventy-four, having served for fifty-six years under five Kings in succession. It was his secret aim to arrange a definite understanding between Henry IV and the League— an understanding of which he would be the author. He offered a vigorous opposition to the Spanish pretensions. " It would be absolutely disgraceful," he said, " even to lend an ear to such proposals, which are only directed towards a usurpation of the State and its destruction." Public opinion would never tolerate them and they would be the undoing of Mayenne. Mayenne, thereupon, declined the offers. But he was now holding out without any forces to support him. News was arriving that, encouraged by the impotence of France, foreigners were preparing to invade her territories—that the Duke of Lorraine proposed to occupy the Three Bishoprics, and the Duke of Savoy, Provence and Dauphiny. Everything was going wrong. But in his distress Mayenne at length found an ally in the Pope. Sixtus V had sent Caietano to Paris as Legate Extraordinary to study the situation, and Caietano had pronounced in favour of the League, declaring that the idea of recognizing Henry IV, who was a heretic and excommunicated, could not be discussed for a moment. In the name of the Pope he forbade a national council to be summoned for the conversion of the King of Navarre, on the ground that it was quite unnecessary for the King of Navarre to have the assistance of a national council in order to be converted. He also provided Mayenne with money. Strengthened by this moral support and assisted by this subsidy, Mayenne left Paris and marched against Henry IV, hoping to reduce him by force of arms.

Henry IV had retreated towards Dreux, to which he laid siege. He had at this moment an army of 11,000 men including 3000 cavalry. The army of the League amounted to 16,000. At the approach of this force, which outnumbered his own, the King decamped from Dreux and descended the valley of the Eure. Mayenne followed cautiously. Then, suddenly, Henry IV made up his mind to attack his adversary. On **Battle of Ivry, 1590.** March 14, 1590, he arranged his army on the plain of Ivry with six cannon in the centre surrounded by cavalry and flanked by companies of infantry. His own battered helmet adorned, according to du Bartas, "with a horrible plume" he galloped along the front of his troops, who were miserably clad and poorly armed, repeating the famous words : "Rally round my white plume; you will always find it on the road to honour and victory ! " Mayenne would have preferred not to fight, but he was obliged to accept the encounter. After a few cannon shots his cavalry broke up. Their retreat was badly managed, however, for the horsemen, fleeing in haste, hustled each other, and confusion prevailed. The King of Navarre seized the opportunity to charge right through them, and carried along by his vigorous onslaught, his cavalry wrought havoc in the enemy's lines. Henry IV fought like an ordinary carabineer, bravely and heroically. Galvanized by his example his men followed him shouting, "Long live the King ! " As soon as the cavalry was beaten they hurled themselves upon the infantry. The Swiss contingents belonging to the League laid down their arms, and Mayenne, seeing that the battle was lost, took to flight, leaving 6000 men and eighty standards on the field. "God has shown," Henry

IV wrote that evening, "that he loves right better than might." He invited all the chiefs of the victorious army to dinner at the Château de Rosny.

Having beaten the enemy, Henry IV, ever faithful to his goal, turned towards Paris. Unfortunately, the impracticable **Siege of Paris** condition of the roads made the march of his **renewed.** army slow, and want of money obliged him to remain a fortnight at Mantes in order to reorganize his forces. It was only in April that he was able to begin the investiture of Paris by occupying Charenton, the Buttes-Chaumont, and Montmartre. Mayenne had left for Picardy in order to raise an army, leaving Paris under the charge of his brother, the Duke of Nemours, a young man of two-and-twenty, an extremely active and intelligent youth. He took advantage of the fortnight's respite which Henry IV's delay at Mantes gave him to prepare for the siege. The city was very badly equipped. It had neither provisions nor ammunition, the ramparts were in ruins, and there was but one mounted cannon, the rest having been removed for use on campaign. He had provisions brought in, strengthened the walls, obliging everybody, workmen and citizens alike, to lend a hand ; and made ready to receive the attack. The organized militia, it was said, gave him 50,000 men. Henry IV had only 13,000, and not daring to attempt a capture by assault, he tried to starve out the garrison. All the exits of the city were guarded and the roads occupied. Not a single waggon was allowed to pass the roads, nor a boat to navigate the Seine. In time, it was hoped, success would crown his efforts. On May 9, the news arrived that Cardinal Bourbon was dead. Mayenne sent word to say that this event made no difference, that he was still Lieutenant-General of the kingdom, and that the States-General would decide the question of a successor. The beleaguered capital continued to hold out. In order to keep up the spirits of the inmates grand processions were organized. A solemn one was held on May 14, in which the Papal Legate, three bishops and all the clergy and authorities joined. A yet more extraordinary exhibition took place later, when some 1300 priests, monks, friars, and students, wearing breastplates and helmets, with muskets on their shoulders, marched through the streets.

The upper middle classes who were favourable to Henry IV afterwards derided these demonstrations.

But the days were slipping by. Provisions began to run short and prices were raised. Well-to-do people sold their plate. Finally, to avoid reproach, the Papal Legate gave a sum of 50,000 crowns and all his own plate for the benefit of the poor. He also allowed Church vessels to be pawned. The ambassador, Mendoza, talked of advancing 120 crowns a day ; and princes, communities, and people of importance subscribed to aid the sufferers. In the streets " huge caldrons of soup " were to be seen from which the destitute were fed. What was Mayenne doing all this time ? Why did he not come to the help of the city ? Mayenne in despair was trying to collect troops in Picardy, where he only succeeded in raising 3000 or 4000 men. He begged Spain to help him. But Spain, now assuming a haughty attitude, insisted upon his first delivering up some towns in Picardy. This Mayenne refused to do. He appealed to Alessandro Farnese, the Governor of the Netherlands, a less harsh and grasping man than Philip. The Duke at first objected that he had not yet completed the conquest of the Netherlands, but he nevertheless consented to send a contingent of troops. As a precaution Mayenne hastened to garrison the towns of Picardy, the gates of which were kept carefully closed. Farnese, indeed, talked of coming to France himself.

Mayenne advanced towards Paris with the Spanish contingent, and Henry IV, accompanied by a few detachments, marched to meet him. Somewhat alarmed, Mayenne took refuge behind the walls of Laon. The King of France left him there and returned to the beleaguered city. He felt more confident than ever. From all sides recruits, both numerous and important, were flocking to his standard, saluting him as the King of to-morrow on the eve of victory. They included Châtillon, La Trémoïlle, Conti, the Duke of Nevers, and their followers. He now had 23,000 men at his disposal. On July 7, 1590, he took Saint-Denis ; on the 24th he attempted a general assault on Paris by night at about two o'clock in the morning. It was unsuccessful, but it had the effect of drawing the blockade closer. In the city provisions became gradually

294

scarcer and scarcer. Famine was staring people in the face, and they were eating dogs, cats, and rats, after having lived on **Horrors of** a wash of oatmeal and water. Butter was sold at **the siege.** three crowns a pound instead of twopence-half-penny ; eggs, if there were any at all to be had, were sixpence a piece. In three months 1300 people died of want. Miserable wretches were to be seen devouring raw remains and the entrails of animals out of the gutters ; it was even said that there were cases of cannibalism. Moved by pity at the description of these horrors, Henry IV is said to have allowed provisions to be sold to a few people of rank, and permitted many poor persons to leave the city. Meanwhile public opinion in Paris began to be exasperated by all this misery. Crowds collected demanding " bread or peace." Violent manifestations took place, and so lively a pressure was brought to bear upon the Duke of Nemours that he was obliged in terror to ask the Bishop of Paris to see Henry IV and discover what conditions he would accept. The King of France demanded the submission of Paris, pure and simple ; but, allowing his feelings of pity to get the better of him, he granted a week's respite during which the women and children were allowed to leave Paris. This concession proved his undoing, for during this interval, the Duke of Parma kept his word, and joined Mayenne at Meaux on August 23, with a force of 13,000 men. The Duke of Nemours, informed of this, took measures to hold out, whilst the army of the League, now 23,000 strong, one-third French and the rest foreigners, a well disciplined, well armed and well equipped force, followed by 1500 waggons stocked with provisions, was hurrying towards the place it was to relieve. The struggle became impossible for Henry IV, who was caught between two fires ; his soldiers were worn out and the nobles were anxious to return home. He himself, as usual, was short of money and was living on **Siege of Paris** loans. He raised the siege, dismissed his volun-**raised.** teers, and contented himself with distributing his companies of infantry and cavalry in the various garrisons round about Paris behind the shelter of solid walls, so that the League's sphere of power might at least be kept within bounds.

This was a serious check. The Papal Legate had a solemn *Te Deum* of thanksgiving sung. Mayenne congratulated himself. His joy, however, was destined to be but short-lived. Once the siege had been raised, the Duke of Parma, declaring that he had come for that purpose alone, took his departure and began to make his way back to the Netherlands. Meanwhile, the indefatigable Henry IV, far from losing heart, was returning to his campaign with more energy than ever. His plan of action was to harass the capital, with the support of the garrisons belonging to him, and thus prepare the way for a fresh investment, and starve out the city once more. He consequently kept hovering about "like a bird of prey," blockading roads and stopping the entry of provisions. He reinforced his garrisons, raised loans in Italy, and begging all his partisans to join him, laid siege to Chartres, which he took **Capture of** at the end of a month. Mayenne, in great anxiety, **Chartres.** begged for and obtained a reinforcement of 4000 soldiers from Spain.

More clearly than ever did Henry IV realize that he would only win his kingdom by forcibly laying hold of it. *Dieu et mon droit*, he kept repeating. This was his motto, and he believed in it. In vain did Rome hurl her thunderbolts against him. Pope Sixtus V had been succeeded by Gregory XIV, who, in a brief, dated February 1591, had commanded his Legate, Philip Sega, Caietano's successor, to forbid the French bishops to recognize Henry IV, and summoned the King's Catholic partisans to withdraw their allegiance on pain of excommunication. This was a heavy blow. His Catholic supporters had begged the King of France to make up his mind to recant, and his whole family had supported this request. Vendôme and Soissons had pointed out that he would lose the crown for the House of Bourbon and the moderates added their voices to the general chorus, in the name of reason, common sense, and prudence. Henry IV, greatly irritated, had resisted their demands, telling his relatives to hold their peace, and protesting hotly against the interference of the Pope in political questions that did not concern him. At his instigation protests were made by the Royalist Parliaments, who remained true to the old Gallican traditions, and even by a small assembly of nine archbishops and bishops. The French clergy were extremely anxious, divided, and uncertain.

Landriano, a fresh legate, who was sent to Paris, advised Mayenne to settle the matter by summoning the States-General and having a King elected. But the time was not ripe for this. The King of Spain and his ambitious designs excited suspicion ; elections, in a country so divided in opinion, were no easy matter ; nor was it feasible to get the deputies to Paris. All Mayenne's counsellors, including Villeroy and Jeannin, advised him to give an evasive reply. He accordingly declined to act, utterly at a loss what course to pursue.

The Sixteen thereupon attributed this irresolute attitude to the growing influence of the moderate party ; and there was **Violence of** an outburst of anger against the "politicians." The **the Sixteen.** more ardent imperatively demanded that measures should be taken against the moderates in order to secure the safety of the cause. They insisted upon expulsions, arrests, and even the use of the harshest measures. Lists were issued, called red papers, containing the names of suspects, with letters against them—P. D. or C. (*pendu, dagué*, or *chassé*, hanged, stabbed, or exiled). Amongst those most seriously menaced were members of the Parliament, calm and sedate adminis-trators of justice, who were indignant at the demagogic transports of excited persons, for the most part of low birth, vulgar, brutal people who set themselves up to be masters of Paris, and tried to lay down the law for everybody. An in-cident occurred which made the bolt fall. The procurator royal at the Hôtel de Ville, a certain Brigard, was caught in the act of sending a letter to Saint-Denis, to the enemy's camp. It was couched in enigmatical terms, but was thought to contain the proofs of his treachery. He was arrested. The extremists demanded his trial ; but the Parliament, regarding the charge as non-proven, acquitted him. The indignation of the violent **Execution of** spirits was unbounded, and they vented it chiefly **Brisson, 1591.** on the President, Brisson, a somewhat feeble and complaisant individual, the victim of his own vacillation. "I feel I am drowning," he said. "I should like to save myself and reach some landing-place, but I am unable to do so and am carried away by the strength of the current." On November 15, 1591, as he was on his way to the Parliament, he, together with the counsellors Tardif and Larcher, was stopped by a band of zealots and conducted to the prisons of the Petit Châtelet. Here he was brought before a sort of judicial board, over which one of the Sixteen presided ; and after a farce of a trial was hanged with the two counsellors from the beam of one of the rooms in the Châtelet. These summary executions produced a profound impression. Parliament declared that the administration of justice had been taken out of its hands, and begged Mayenne, who was away from Paris at the time, to come back and put a stop to the bloodthirsty fury of an intolerable oligarchy. Mayenne hastened to the city with 3000 cavalry, and seized fourteen of the ring-leaders, among them those who had been responsible for the execution of the magistrates. He had four of them hanged from the rafters of the great guard-room at the Louvre, and the rest cast into prison. Their accomplices fled. With one energetic blow he had punished the outrage they had committed ; but the situation remained as gloomy as before. He still stood irresolute between the extremists and the moderate party, unable, unwilling, or afraid to express his wishes clearly.

Henry IV was constantly in the saddle, galloping and laying about him. "I am making good progress," he wrote, "I go **A fruitless** wherever God leads me, for I know not where I **campaign, 1591.** shall end." He conceived the idea of capturing Rouen, which was defended by Villars Brancas, a member of the League. On November 11, 1591, his lieutenant, Biron, began the siege. Mayenne again appealed to the Duke of Parma, who consented to come to his aid with 25,000 men. The season was bad. It rained and snowed, and the country was broken up. The two armies skirmished continuously, the Royalist forces taking shelter behind entrenchments. Nothing decisive occurred. After some time the two adversaries each went his way. Farnese returned home, and Henry IV, whose army, composed half of Huguenots and half of Catholics, always quarrelling with each other, was worn out and famished, dismissed the main body of his troops, and set himself to harassing the retreating Spaniards with the help of a few intrepid and faithful followers. The campaign had been fruitless, and matters had not advanced a single step.

In this state of general uncertainty, Villeroy thought it

might be possible to come to a solution by negotiation with
Henry IV on the one hand, and by summoning the States-
Attempts at General on the other. If only the King of
negotiation. Navarre could be brought to understand that his
conversion was the one possible way of escape from the conflict! Mayenne let him have his way, and Villeroy had an
interview with du Plessis Mornay and Henry IV. He was
insistent, and pressed his case home. The League, he said,
was about to find itself involved in very unacceptable pretensions on the part of Spain. A choice had to be made. Every
day Henry IV was besieged by similar arguments from his
Catholic supporters, whilst even a few Protestants, like his
faithful friend Rosny, afterwards Duke of Sully, ended by
acknowledging that the only way out of the difficulties seemed
to be a recantation. Henry IV accordingly decided to send
the Marquis of Pisani and Cardinal Gondi to Rome to negotiate
with the Pope. Was he wavering?

In Paris the news of Villeroy's mission produced a considerable agitation, resulting in the strengthening of moderate
ideas. Public opinion was gradually veering towards the
solution it felt to be inevitable. Moreover, the arrival of the
Spanish troops, the foreigners, had upset the people. The
moderate party, headed by a certain d'Aubray, an ex-Provost
of the Merchants, grew bolder. They won over the Parisian
militia, thirteen out of sixteen of whose colonels were already
on their side, as well as the commandants and a number of
captains. They proposed that an exhortation (*semonce*) should
be presented to King Henry asking him to be converted. The
party was accordingly dubbed the "exhorters" (*semonneux*).
After having been overwhelmed by the extremists, Mayenne
was now overwhelmed by the moderates, so little did he command the situation. The truth was that he wanted the crown
himself; but caught in the toils between the dangerous ambitions of Spain, the extremists, the moderates, and the supporters
of Henry IV, and feeling that his own candidature was not
even admissible, he was uncertain as to the course which would
best further his own interests. In this state of indecision he
convoked the States-General. They might perhaps be able
to hold the "exhorters" and the extremists in check, and give

time for deliberation. From Rome the news came that the Pope had refused to receive the King of Navarre's envoys.

The States-General, summoned to meet in Paris, assembled on January 26, 1593. They could hardly be called "General." **The States-General of 1593.** A large number of provinces had refused to send deputies, and many had found it impossible to reach Paris owing to the dangers of the journey. There were barely 128 representatives : forty-nine ecclesiastics, twenty-four nobles and fifty-five members of the Third Estate ; whereas the States which had met at Blois had consisted of 505 deputies. It was the ghost of a parliament. The *Satyre Menippée* covered it with ridicule, but it deserves a better reputation than it possesses ; for it showed judgment, moderation, dignity and patriotism in peculiarly difficult circumstances.

Mayenne presided over the opening session in the Louvre, sitting under a royal canopy of cloth of gold, as if to prepare the minds of the assembly for his election. He explained that the States had been summoned in order to nominate a Catholic King of France. But unfortunately for Mayenne nobody took his candidature seriously, a fact which embarrassed him, and made his address vague and devoid of character. The envoy of the King of Spain was seated in one of the tribunes, and the Papal Legate was also present. In the first place it was proposed to open negotiations with Henry IV, with a view to examining the situation. The Legate then spoke and opposed the suggested conferences. The States, irritated by this interference, voted in favour of the conferences. In the end they even refused to hold their debates in the presence of the Pope's envoy. The feeling that obsessed all minds was the fear of Spain. They stood in need of her help—her money and her soldiers. She was sending yet another contingent of 5000 men under the command of the Count of Mansfeld. But her pretensions were disconcerting. It had been known **Philip II's pretensions.** ever since the battle of Ivry, that Philip II's dream was to be elected King of France. France would thus become a province of his Empire. The privileges to be accorded her would certainly be appreciable : municipal freedom, the regular convocation of the States-General, which would have passed laws and voted taxes, the

300

exclusive nomination of Frenchmen to official posts—in short a broad and intelligent autonomy. Many men in France had admitted the possibility of this combination, and committees had been formed to defend the idea, adding the stipulation that France should be allowed free trade with the Spanish colonies. But on reflection Philip II had renounced this plan and turned to another scheme. As he himself had married a sister of the last three Valois, he considered that his daughter, Isabella Clara Eugenia, as a descendant of Henry II, might claim the vacant throne of France. The Salic law, it was true, precluded this, that famous Salic law which everybody talked about, though no one could quote the text bearing on the succession to the throne—a text, as a matter of fact, which was non-existent. The Salic Law could be set aside. This was the candidature which the States expected to have presented to them under the most embarrassing political conditions. The Duke of Feria was sent from Spain as ambassador extraordinary to follow the proceedings. Mayenne had an interview with him at Soissons, when he renewed his demand for troops. Feria was somewhat curt with him; he offered, if Mayenne would accept the King of Spain's proposals, to make him Lieutenant-General of the kingdom and Governor of Burgundy and Picardy. Mayenne answered evasively, saying that he would refer the matter to the States. The ambassador retorted with considerable vivacity and the discussion became heated, Mayenne even going so far as to tell Feria that the French would not be treated like the Indians.

Feria came to Paris and attended the assembly of the States, where he was given an official reception on April 2, 1593. He made a long speech, in which he dwelt on all the King of Spain had done and was doing for the Catholic cause, but confined himself to concluding that it was high time that the States elected a king. Their attention, however, at this moment was occupied by the conferences with Henry IV, the principle of The Con- which had been adopted. These conferences were ferences of being held at Suresnes. The League was re-Suresnes. presented by Villeroy, Jeannin and d'Epinac, Archbishop of Lyons ; the Royalists by de Thou, Schomberg, and Regnault de Beaune, Archbishop of Bourges. They were

301

inaugurated under excellent conditions, for on the eve of their first meeting, Henry IV, in conversation with the Superintendent d'O and the Archbishop of Bourges, had confessed that he certainly saw no solution of the dilemma with which they were grappling save to turn Catholic. The vital word had been spoken. If the League, argued Henry IV, appointed a King, an interminable struggle would begin against the new monarch. It was obvious that France would not acknowledge a Protestant sovereign at any price, and under these circumstances it would perhaps be best for him to yield. These confidential remarks, which were repeated at Suresnes, greatly facilitated the task of the negotiators. They began by deciding upon an armistice of ten days, the news of which was received with great joy in Paris as foreshadowing a possible speedy conclusion of peace. The extremists had the ground cut from beneath them. When they were asked what they would do if the King of Navarre were converted, they replied that they would await a decision from Rome. But the possibility of his recantation disconcerted them.

No one was more embarrassed than Mayenne, whose personal interests were inextricably involved! He maintained an enigmatic attitude. "Nobody," wrote Estoile, "can discover what part the Duke of Mayenne is playing. He is a mystery to all." He confined himself to saying that he would always defend the interests of Catholicism—a vague declaration! The Spaniards, partly from insolence and partly from ignorance, kept demanding the election of a king of France; and finally officially proposed the candidature of the Infanta Isabella Clara Eugenia. "The abscess of the King of Spain's ambition has burst at last!" people exclaimed. The Salic Law was invoked, and the Parliament protested vigorously in the name of the fundamental laws of the land. The ambassadors wrote memoranda answering these objections, and one of their theologians came to the States and explained to them that there was nothing to prevent the proposed election. The States listened in silence. The Spanish ambassador, thereupon, boldly called upon them to proceed to the election of the Infanta Isabella as Queen of France in her own right, and even went so far as to add that the princess would probably marry an Austrian Archduke, the Archduke Ernest, who did not know French perhaps, but who would certainly learn it. To this proposal the States refused to give their consent: the plan presented to them was contrary to the "laws and ordinances of France." Mayenne then suggested that the States should elect a king who should marry the Infanta. This proposal seemed to meet with a certain amount of favour, and the Spanish envoys said they would accept it, on condition that Isabella was recognized as Queen in her own right, and that Philip II chose his daughter's husband. The States retorted that they must first know the name of the husband in question. It was clear that they were merely trying to gain time whilst awaiting the result of the conferences at Suresnes.

Public opinion was slowly turning in the direction of Henry IV and demanding peace. Petitions were signed, and Villeroy **Opposition to Spanish demands.** deliberately abandoned the League and went over to the King of France. Many others followed his example, and all were graciously received by Henry IV. The Parliament issued decree after decree against the Spanish demands, declaring them contrary to public law, and Le Maistre, the President, maintained that as the States were not represented in their full numbers, they were not qualified to make any fundamental change in the laws of the land. The States thereupon decided to tell the Spaniards that after due reflection they had come to the conclusion that the moment was unfavourable, and that they could not proceed to the election of a King whom the League was not in a position to defend. Philip II's ambassadors then retreated step by step, saying that they would accept the candidature of the Duke of Guise, and proposing a marriage between that prince and the Infanta. But the Duke of Guise was unwilling to accept a position which he could not maintain ; he refused. To the demands for money and soldiers which they received from all quarters, the Spaniards returned evasive replies, with the result that they were reproached with trying to back out of their agreements, and taunted with being unable to give anything. "There is not a single person," Mendoza wrote to Spain, "who does not cast it in our teeth that we lack everything." Mayenne seized the opportunity to propose a truce with Henry IV.

The forthcoming conversion of the King of France was awaited and counted upon by everybody; it went forward **Recantation** apace. In July, 1593, Henry IV had a con-**of Henry IV,** ference with the bishops at Saint-Denis, to discuss **1593.** certain religious questions that occupied his mind. The conference lasted five hours and was extremely lively. The theologians were obliged to pass over certain points to which they could not get the King to agree—the doctrine of Purgatory, for example, the worship of the Saints, which Henry IV regarded as "an absurdity," and the authority of the Pope. He gave way, apparently without much faith in the things he was told. "You do not fully persuade me," he kept repeating. "I am not as satisfied as I could wish to be. But to-day I put my soul in your hands. I pray you take care of it; for wherever you make me enter I shall leave only by the gate of death—that I promise and vow to you." And so saying he wept. He was sincere though he was not firmly convinced. The Protestants of France, who still doubted his conversion, were fasting and praying "that it might please God to grant their King constancy of purpose." He was made to sign a formal act of recantation. On July 23, he wrote to his mistress Gabrielle d'Estrées, half jestingly, half anxiously, "On Sunday I shall make the perilous plunge." He was taking this step not from any personal ambition but for the good of the State. The solemn recantation took place on July 25 at Saint-Denis, under the great porch of the Abbey Church, in the midst of a vast concourse of spectators. Henry IV was dressed entirely in white, and was surrounded by princes, nobles, Crown officials and guards with drums beating. Sitting on a chair covered with white damask the Archbishop of Bourges awaited him, supported by about ten bishops and the monks from the monastery. "Who are you?" asked the prelate. "I am the King." "What is it you ask?" "I ask to be received into the bosom of the Church." "Do you really desire this?" "Yes, I wish and desire it." Henry IV then knelt down and read his profession of faith. "I promise and vow before the face of Almighty God to live and die in the Catholic religion."

He was thereupon conducted to the choir, whilst the swarming crowd shouted, "Long live the King!" He made his confession, heard High Mass, and was present at a *Te Deum*. His recantation was consummated.

In Paris furious preachers declared that it was null and void, and the Papal Legate announced that the prelates at Saint-Denis had no power to withdraw the pontifical excommunication. Throughout the kingdom, however, *Te Deums* of joy were sung, and public opinion became more and more favourable to the new King. Mayenne signed a truce of three months and also adjourned the States-General for that period, asserting, however, that until the Pope had pronounced his verdict, nothing was decided. The Spaniards, somewhat taken aback, held themselves in reserve and waited. Rome had yet to be persuaded to give her consent, and Henry IV sent the Duke of Nevers, together with some prelates, to discuss matters with Pope Clement VIII. The Holy Father received them coldly in a private audience, and not as ambassadors. He raised numerous difficulties, saying that Henry IV had offered no guarantees, that the Papacy did not wish to abandon Spain, and that the Catholics of the League were superior to the others. In vain did the envoys insist that the King had two-thirds of the country on his side, together with the various Parliaments, and that he was the lawful King of France ; Clement VIII vouchsafed no reply.

When the three months truce had expired, Mayenne was at a loss what course to pursue. He had neither money nor Gradual men, and the growing impotence of the League recognition was now patent to all. Its leaders, well aware of Henry IV. of the fact, and seeing that their cause was lost, dropped off one by one, recognizing Henry IV independently of each other, and endeavouring to make the best of a hopeless position. On all sides negotiations were opened with the King. The least the Governors of provinces and towns demanded was to be allowed to retain their offices ; and to this request Henry IV, ever smiling and sceptical, gave a ready consent. "All I want is to get back the kingdom that belongs to me," he said, "and any who help me to do so I shall recognize as my servants." Vitry, the Governor of Meaux, made an agreement with him on December 24 ; La Châtre, Governor of Orleans and Bourges, followed suit ; those Parliaments which still adhered to the League imitated them and pronounced for Henry, whilst even the towns were unwilling to be left behind. The inhabitants of Lyons revolted against their Governor, the Duke of Nemours, a member of the League, and putting up barricades, drove him out and summoned Monsieur d'Ornano, Henry IV's lieutenant in Dauphiny, to take his place, on condition that the privileges of their town were recognized—a condition which was granted.

Thus the League gradually drifted towards dissolution. The press attacked it with an ardour all the more efficacious inasmuch as it was now a question of completing the downfall of the vanquished. It was at this juncture that the *Satyre Menippée* made its appearance, an eloquent, vigorous journal, full of freshness, good sense, and natural wit, in the pages of which a few moderate men succeeded in covering with ridicule a turbulent and violent party which had exposed itself only too freely to criticism. Far from giving way as everybody else was doing, but feeling, nevertheless, that the end was near, Mayenne would not wait for it in Paris. He left the city on March 6, 1594, on the pretext that he was going to arrange with Mansfeld about collecting troops, and left Monsieur de Brissac in charge—an extremely injudicious choice.

Meanwhile, to the various elements of success which secured his right to the throne, Henry IV now added yet another, **Coronation of Henry IV, 1594.** a decisive and sovereign element ; he had himself crowned King, and prevailed upon the Church to bestow that sacred unction which transformed him into a semi-religious personage with quasi-pontifical powers, and constrained Christian consciences to bow to his authority. As it was impossible for him to have the ceremony performed at Rheims, which was still in the hands of his enemies, he had it celebrated on February 27, 1594, in the ancient cathedral of Chartres, a church beloved of his Vendôme ancestors. The choir was hung with tapestries ; the bishop was enthroned beneath a silken canopy ; the royal chair placed against the rood-screen was surmounted by a canopy of purple velvet studded with gold *fleurs de lis*, and stands set up in the choir provided seats for the princesses and ladies of the Court. A new sceptre, crown, and *main de justice* * of chased gold had been made for the occasion. The coronation produced a profound sensation throughout the country, and it was felt that it must succeed in forcing the hand of the Pope. Brissac, Mayenne's lieutenant in Paris, thought the time had now come for him to escape from the conflict and safeguard his own interests. He accordingly negotiated with Lhuillier, the Provost of the Merchants, Langlois, the Sheriff, Molé, the Procurator-General, and the various captains, and notified his conditions to Henry IV, who at once accepted them. On the date agreed upon, the night of March 21–22, at four o'clock in the morning, three **Surrender of** of the gates were opened to the troops of the **Paris, 1594.** King of France, which, to the number of 2500 infantry and 1500 cavalry, were waiting a short distance away. Vitry entered by the Porte Saint-Denis, d'O by the Porte Neuve, on the banks of the Seine, alongside the Louvre ; and some detachments disembarked in the Quartier Saint-Paul. The bridges and squares were occupied, and the Parisians, taken by surprise, made no resistance. As soon as it was light Henry IV rode on horseback to the Porte Neuve where Brissac received him, accompanied by the Provost of the Merchants, and handed him the keys of the city. He entered Paris wearing his helmet and breastplate, the former adorned by his great white plume, and with an escort of 500 or 600 men-at-arms with pikes in their hands and muskets over their shoulders. He went to Notre-Dame where he heard Mass, and then returned to the Louvre. Astonished and inquisitive crowds rushed into the streets trying to get a glimpse of him, but with no hostile intention. " Let them alone," the monarch commanded his soldiers, who wanted to drive them off, " they are eager to see a King." Heralds went through the streets announcing a complete amnesty, and the church bells rang out in full peal. There was a festive air about the whole proceeding, and the crowd, completely won over, shouted " Long live the King ! ' The Duke of Feria had ordered the foreign contingent of 4000 Spaniards, Walloons, and Neapolitans lent to the League by

* A sort of sceptre with a hand at the top, forming part of the regalia of the French Kings. (Tr.)

Philip II to take up their arms and keep in their quarters. The King, however, sent Matignon to tell him to send them quietly away ; and on the same day, these troops marched out by the Porte Saint-Denis with drums beating and flags flying. Henry IV went to see them pass from the top of the gate, and called out, as he saluted them, " Gentlemen, commend me to your master, but do not come back again." By the evening all **The end of** was quiet ; the Papal Legate had taken his **the League.** departure, and life had resumed its peaceful course. Without striking a blow, the League had melted away.

The amnesty was observed, except in the case of some 120 monks, preachers and others, who had compromised themselves too deeply, and were obliged to leave the city. The religious orders said that they were awaiting the decision of Rome. The Parliament was reinstalled ; the Sorbonne acknowledged Henry IV, and everybody breathed again. " All good citizens," said Estoile, " of the middle and lower classes were extremely glad to find themselves delivered from slavery, and out of the power of the party and government of the Sixteen ; restored to liberty, with the honours and goods that belonged to them ; and freed from the tyranny of the Spaniards and foreigners, which was regarded by Frenchmen as harsh and intolerable." When once Paris had been won the rest of France followed without delay.

The various governors were won over by bribes of money and honours. " Do not bargain," Henry IV told Rosny, who was discussing terms with them, " the things they are delivering up to us would cost us ten times as much if we had to take them by force." Paris had exacted 482,000 crowns. At Rouen, Villars Brancas was given 715,000 crowns, together with the title of admiral and the governorship of seven fortresses. On March 27, 1594, he gathered together the merchants of Rouen and the garrison captains at a great dinner, and at the end of the feast rose and told them bluntly : " Gentlemen, the League has gone to the devil. Let us shout with one accord ' Long live the King ! ' " And he thereupon put on the white scarf. The House of Lorraine gave way one by one ; its head, the Duke, on November 16. Altogether they cost 9,000,000 pounds, which they extracted as an indemnity for their losses during the civil wars. Mayenne was the last to yield, together with the Duke of Mercœur in Brittany.

Henry IV now settled down. Difficulties, however, soon confronted him on every side. He was besieged by people **Henry IV's** demanding reprisals, and objecting to seeing **difficulties.** those who had stood loyally by him placed on the same footing as those who had gravely compromised themselves. " If you said the Lord's Prayer every day with real sincerity," Henry IV replied, " you would not talk as you do. As God has pardoned me, so too will I pardon others. If there are some who forgot themselves, it is enough for me that they should return to their senses. I wish to hear no more about it." All his appointments aroused recriminations : the reinstallation of Villeroy, who was hated by Catholics and Protestants alike, as minister ; and the elevation of the Duke of Bouillon, who was a Huguenot, to the rank of Marshal of France. Not only did the rivalry between Catholics and heretics continue, but amongst the Catholics themselves a conflict now began between the Royalist Catholics, who became advanced Gallicans, and the Catholics who had been members of the League and remained Ultramontanes. The Order of the Jesuits formed one of the chief points at issue. They were accused of having given too much support to Spain and the League, and of not having acknowledged Henry IV ; they were still awaiting the decision of Rome. The Parliament and the University attacked the Order vigorously upon various pretexts of minor importance ; but it was really a war upon principles. On December 27, 1594, a certain pupil of the Jesuits, a youth of eighteen named Jean Chatel, stealing up to Henry IV, dealt him a blow with a knife, which cut his lip and broke two of his teeth. The wound was a slight one, and the would-be assassin merely a fanatic. He was hanged and quartered, and the hot-heads tried to place the responsibility for the deed upon the Jesuits. They were accordingly banished by acts of Parliament from the confines of Paris, Rouen, and Grenoble. " The end of the year 1594," wrote Estoile, " was as grievous for the Parisians as the spring had been full of rejoicings ; for Chatel's attempt filled them

309

with fear of future misfortunes, and tightened their purse-strings, cooled the enterprise of the merchants, and plunged them, together with the people, into fresh poverty." Moreover further troubles were threatening. In default of a direct heir—for Henry IV had no children by Margaret of Valois—the throne reverted to his nephew, the Prince of Condé, another Protestant, a fact which irritated the Catholics. The Protestants were displeased at the King's recantation, and altogether the horizon was dark and lowering.

In order to clear it Henry IV decided to make war upon Spain, and drive out the Spaniards from French territory. By this means he would win victories which would consolidate his position, he would give occupation to the martial lust of the nobility, and deprive the Leaguers of their last vestige of support. Philip II accepted the conflict, and dispatched the Count of Fuentes at the head of an army. Henry IV, marching against the troops commanded by Mayenne and Velasco, fell

Battle of Fontaine-Française, 1595. in with them near Saint-Seine, at Fontaine-Française, and had the boldness to attack a body of 1200 cavalry with a force of only 300. A fierce fight took place, in which he narrowly escaped with his life ; but fortunately for him, Velasco, thinking that he had to deal with a far larger body of troops, retreated. "A little more, and you would have become my heir," Henry IV afterwards wrote to his sister Catherine. He had run an extremely grave risk. This engagement, which was insignificant as far as the numbers which took part in it were concerned, produced the effect of a great victory. Mayenne, thoroughly discouraged, asked for a truce in order to negotiate, and in Rome, Clement VIII, who had already been shaken by the King's general success in his own country, consented to discuss a reconciliation. D'Ossat and du Perron, in whom Henry IV had great confidence, and whom he had sent to Rome to replace Gondi, conducted the negotiation. The consistory of Cardinals before whom the matter was debated pronounced in favour of the reconciliation. Seven conditions were insisted upon : the absolution granted by the bishops was to be null and void, though the King's subsequent acts were to be valid ; the Prince of Condé was to be brought up in the Catholic

310

religion; the decrees of the Council of Trent were to be published; and all Church property that had been stolen was to be given back. On September 17, 1595, Clement VIII decided to proclaim his decree of absolution; and from that day, French Catholics had no further excuse for refusing allegiance to Henry IV.

Mayenne realized this, and at length offered to treat with him. He demanded three towns as guarantees; the governorship of the Ile de France; the payment of his debts—which were numerous, on account of the expenses of the war; an official declaration that he was innocent of the blood of Henry III, for the King had announced his intention of prosecuting those responsible for the murder of his predecessor; and an acknowledgment that he was negotiating in the name of the League. Henry IV made some objections over the matter of the debts, but he finally gave way on all the points. After the treaty had been signed at Folembray in January, 1596, an interview took place between the King and the Duke in the park of the Château de Montceaux. Henry IV was cordial and charming, and showed his old enemy over the garden, making him walk about quickly for a long time. Mayenne, who was big and fat and afflicted with sciatica, was streaming with perspiration, and suffering agonies. Henry IV noticed it, and whispered in Rosny's ear: "If I lead this fat lump a long enough dance I shall have my revenge without much difficulty for all the ill he has done us; for he will be a dead man." Then turning to Mayenne, he said: "I am walking a little too fast for you; I have worked you too hard. Come now, shake hands, this is the only evil and inconvenience you will ever have to suffer from me."

Joyeuse came to terms on January 24 in return for his appointment as Marshal and Lieutenant of Languedoc. The Duke of Aumale preferred to leave the country. Henry IV welcomed all who came to him with outstretched hand. He was anxious to secure peace at home in order to complete his expulsion of the Spaniards.

The latter held their ground. They had taken Calais and Saint-Quentin. On March 10, 1597, the alarming news arrived that they had suddenly pushed forward and surprised Amiens, sending soldiers disguised as peasants to seize one of the gates, and had installed a force of 5000 infantry and 700 cavalry in that town. With the enemy masters of the course of the Somme, Paris lay open to attack. At every epoch in French history news of this sort had filled the Parisians with consternation. Everybody, and more particularly Henry IV himself, was deeply perturbed. He sprang on his horse and departed forthwith for Amiens, summoning to his support the ban and rear-ban of the country. The siege which he undertook lasted for six months, and cost eight millions, which had to be raised by means of lamentable expedients. But at last, on September 25, 1597, the town surrendered. The success was as brilliant as the check had been mortifying. Henry IV seized the opportunity to endeavour to end the war with this victory, and the Papal Legate offered his mediation, which the King accepted. **Peace of Vervins, 1598.** Peace was discussed and negotiations conducted at Vervins from February to May, 1598. On May 5 a treaty was signed. Spain, completely tired out, consented to give back all she had won, with the exception of Cambray, which she kept. On September 15 in the same year Philip II died, calm and impassive as ever, slowly consumed by a lingering disease at the age of seventy-one. His ambition had been greater than his resources, and its frustration in France had been as complete as its aims had been extravagant. All cause for fear from the direction of Madrid was now at an end.

There still remained two or three districts in France in which the fire had not been extinguished, and these Henry IV hastened to pacify. Amongst them was Brittany, where the Duke of Mercœur, the brother of Queen Louise of Vaudémont and brother-in-law of Henry III, was maintaining his independence, declaring that in default of a direct heir to Anne of Brittany he considered that as he had married an heiress he had a right to claim the succession. But the King of Spain alleged an even stronger claim to the Duchy, and Henry IV accordingly sent troops who captured Dinan. Mercœur gave way, and it was arranged that the King of France should pay his debts, and that one of Henry IV's natural sons, César, Duke of Vendôme, a child of four, should marry Mercœur's six-year-

312

old daughter and become Duke of Brittany. And thus this matter was arranged.

But there was yet another—the question of the Duke of Savoy, who ever since the time when he had tried to turn the troubles of the League to account in order to snatch some French territory, had remained in a state of war. The Duke, Charles Emmanuel, an ambitious, quarrelsome and deceitful prince, had cast a covetous eye upon Dauphiny and the Marquisate of Saluces. Lesdiguières had prevented him from seizing the former province, and Charles Emmanuel had consoled himself with the second. Henry IV informed him that he would allow him to keep Saluces on condition that he gave up Bresse, Bugey, and Valromey, at that time in the possession of Savoy. As the Duke vouchsafed no reply, Henry IV collected 30,000 men in 1600, marched on Chambéry, and after a short and brilliant campaign concluded a peace on his own terms. By this peace France definitively acquired Bresse, Bugey, Valromey, and the district of Gex.

And now at last all trouble with enemies abroad and armed foes at home was at an end. Slowly, step by step, with ad-**End of the** mirable patience, tenacity of purpose, and steadi-**war.** ness, Henry IV had succeeded in pacifying his kingdom. It had required time and flexibility, but now his end had been attained. Only half his task, however, was accomplished. Now that all swords had been sheathed, the work of repairing the harm they had done remained to be carried out, or at all events the restoration of some sort of order and the consolidation of a peace which was still precarious after so many years of war and violence. The country had yet to be induced to take up or return quietly to the ordinary daily occupations of an industrious people secure from alarms. Henry IV applied himself resolutely to this task, in which he was powerfully supported by his friend and companion-in-arms, a Huguenot noble who consecrated all his talents and energies to his King—Monsieur de Rosny, Duke of Sully.

A man of about the same age as Henry IV, devoted and steadfast, Rosny combined a sure judgment and a clear mind **Sully.** with an extraordinary capacity for work. As an administrator he was unsurpassed ; always busy, going through

papers, allowing nothing to escape his attention, he directed
business with inexorable severity. He was a rough diamond, a
big fierce man, with a bald forehead, a long beard and steely
glance, who lived all by himself in the Arsenal in an austerely
furnished room adorned with portraits of Luther and Calvin.
He never ceased working, received people with intolerable
rudeness, without getting up or asking them to be seated, and
constantly refused to do as he was asked. "He is a beast,"
said one ambassador; "a groom" added another; "an
animal" declared a third. But he rendered the King invaluable
services, more especially in the domain of finance.

These finances were in a terrible state of confusion. The
one thing which seemed clear to Henry IV was that he had
a great many debts and never any money. "I am reduced
to such straits," he wrote one day to Rosny, "that I have
scarcely a horse on which I can ride into battle, nor a complete
suit of armour to my back; my shirts are in rags, my doublets
out at elbows, my pots are often empty, and for two days past
I have been dining and supping with one or other of my friends."
In contrast to his own penury, he saw with surprise "that the
treasurers of his finances kept dainty and well-served boards,
and that their houses were full of wealth and luxury." Robbery
and brigandage were not the sole explanation of this anomaly.
There were causes accounting for it connected with the financial
organization of the period, by virtue of which the King had
pledged all his revenues and was left without a penny, whilst
in the meantime the taxes were collected under the ordinary
advantageous conditions enjoyed by the financiers. Determined as he said "to cut off Dame Peculation's arms and
legs," the King turned to his rugged friend, Monsieur de Rosny,
though the latter did not know much about finance. After
the death of Superintendent d'O in 1594, Henry IV replaced
his office by a financial committee of nine, and in 1596 he
appointed Monsieur de Rosny a member of this board. Eager
to set to work, Rosny suggested making a rigorous examination into the whole financial administration of the country,
and set out in person to inspect the districts of four receivers-
general that very year. He was terrifying; he hustled the
receivers, asked to see title-deeds, registers and receipts. He

examined leases, and—if we are to believe his *Economies royales*, which, is, it must be remembered, a written apologia, to be accepted with caution—on his own responsibility he cancelled doubtful claims, dismissed agents, cut down expenditure which he regarded as unnecessary, and, when he had accomplished this, brought back, still according to his own account, a surplus of 500,000 crowns, sufficient to fill seventy waggons. It was a large sum. There was a general outcry. His colleagues exclaimed that he did not understand what he was doing, and accused him of wholesale pillage, declaring that the money must be returned and that he had acted like an impetuous soldier rather than a qualified financier. There was some truth in these assertions. In order to form a clear notion of what was required, Henry IV convoked an assembly of Notables at Rouen in November, 1596, not daring to summon the States-General, which would have been too dangerous.

These Notables were eighty in number. They were elected by the provinces, and consisted of nine ecclesiastics, nineteen **Assembly of** nobles, and fifty-two members of the third estate. **Notables, 1596.** At the opening of the session Henry IV made a celebrated speech, full of good sense and of witty French vivacity : " You know to your own cost," he said, " as I do to mine, that when God called me to the throne, I found France not only half ruined but almost lost altogether to the French nation. . . . I have not summoned you, as my predecessors used to do, to make you approve my desires. I have summoned you to ask your advice, which I wish to believe and to follow ; in short, to place myself in your hands for guidance, a course rarely palatable to Kings, greybeards, and victors. Yet the ardent love I bear my subjects, and the great longing I feel to add two fair titles to my name—those of liberator and restorer of this State—make all this easy and honourable in my eyes." The Chancellor then proceeded to state the financial situation. It was simple enough—quantities of debts. Sully said 296 million pounds—and no credit. The gross receipts were twenty-three million pounds per annum, of which the provincial administration absorbed sixteen millions as necessary expenditure, leaving the rest—the absolutely inadequate sum of seven millions—to the Government for central expenses. The

Notables were of opinion that the existing taxes might be raised without having recourse to loans or the creation of new offices to be put up for sale—there were too many of these already. According to the details of offers that had already been made, there would be a revenue of thirty millions, fifteen of which would suffice for the provincial administration, and fifteen for the central government. Sully maintains that the Notables went even further, and demanded that a council named the advisory council should be nominated by themselves to control the expenditure of at least the fifteen millions devoted to the provinces ; and that Henry IV agreed to the appointment of this council because he considered it would strengthen the credit of the State and put a somewhat stricter check upon the administrators of the revenue. But the truth of this statement has been disputed.

Little by little Henry IV allowed himself to be won over by Rosny's rigorous notions. He was himself, as a matter of fact, naturally somewhat inclined to be avaricious. He ended by establishing a sort of financial superintendency, a post which Rosny seems to have filled in 1598, and the official title of which was bestowed upon him in 1601. In 1599 the new superintendent took up his quarters at the Arsenal, and in addition to this office, was also made Superintendent of Artillery, Public Buildings, and Fortifications. An extremely hard working man, he wished to undertake all he could, both out of zeal for the public good and from a desire to apply his precise and splenetic methods in as many directions as possible.

To make the taxes bring in as much as could be raised with little incidental expense ; to institute rigid economies ; **Sully's policy.** to pay off most of the debts or diminish them by every kind of contrivance ; and, finally, to put money aside, was the programme that Rosny traced out for himself. He conceived no new ideas in financial matters, he merely utilized methods already existing. It is incorrect to say that the keeping of public accounts at this period was in an embryonic condition, and that any individual connected with them could enrich himself at his leisure in the dark jungle of taxation. There were regulations, the observance of which was controlled by the Court of the Exchequer more strictly

316

INTERNAL PEACE. HENRY IV

than is generally imagined. As a matter of fact, if we leave
out of the reckoning the bad returns of the *taille*, it was
owing to a thousand and one decisions which were correct
enough, but ruinous in their results, that the money produced
by the taxes found its way into the pockets of clever agents.
The taxes, like the aids, were farmed out separately on relatively
low terms. Rosny sold them by auction to a single tax-farmer,
Monsieur Jean de Moisset, for a much more advantageous sum ;
and in the same way he increased the amount paid by the five
great farmers-general. In cases where a given annual sum was
due to a man, he had hitherto simply been exempted from the
payment of some State claim upon him, and this exempted
claim always represented a far larger sum than the one to which
he had a right. Rosny had these alienated dues restored to
the State. There were quantities of them, and the property
of the Crown had been dismembered by this process. The
persons concerned, who were chiefly great nobles, remonstrated ;
but the surly minister took no notice and merely told them that
they would be paid in a different way. The debts, above all,
were overwhelming. On every side money was owing to all
manner of people both at home and abroad, for Henry IV had
inherited liabilities incurred by the kings his predecessors during
the civil wars. To the Duke of Tuscany alone a sum of 1,100,000
crowns was owing, and the Grand-Duke, in default of payment,
had seized the Chateau d'If opposite Marseilles, as security,
a humiliation to which Henry IV had been obliged to submit.
Arrangements were made whereby these debts were to be paid
off in regular yearly instalments. In the case of the King's own
subjects Rosny made use of more expeditious methods. Amongst
other liabilities, sixty millions of arrears in interest on state
securities were due. The minister declared that as the titles
of these creditors were not very clear, he wished to revise them.
He then lowered the interest from $8\frac{1}{3}$ per cent .to $6\frac{1}{4}$ per cent.
An outcry was immediately raised that he was acting arbitrarily
and that the State was bankrupt ; whereupon Henry IV,
threatened by an insurrection among the investors, was obliged
to ask Rosny to be less drastic. This, however, did not prevent
the latter from reducing the royal debts by 100 millions of
capital. By a series of similar measures, and above all by

317

opposing largesse of any sort, and by severe economy in expenditure, a method which the minister called "wonderful housekeeping," the Government in the end not only succeeded in balancing its budget, but put aside enough money to stock the Arsenal with provisions for war, and placed a surplus of thirteen millions in the Bastille.

When once the financial difficulties had been overcome, Henry IV and Rosny, who had been made Duke of Sully in Agriculture.   1606, set to work to ameliorate the condition of the people. The importance of the reforms they carried out in the domain of agriculture, commerce, and public works must not be exaggerated. Their chief merit lay in the fact that they put an end to war, and allowed the people to work in peace. Sully said, "Husbandry and the care of cattle are the two udders of France." But, as a matter of fact, he did not do much to alter the conditions of agriculture. In 1595 Henry IV decreed that agricultural implements and live-stock could not be seized in payment of debt ; in so doing, however, he merely revived ancient ordinances which were destined to be re-enacted again after his day. The peasantry owed twenty millions in arrears for taille, and in 1600 the King cancelled this sum, a sacrifice for which he has been praised, but which was inspired, amongst other considerations, by the fact that he would never have been able to recover the money. Between 1597 and 1609, Henry IV lowered the taille from twenty to fourteen millions, for which he deserves greater credit ; and he accepted the offers made by the Dutch to drain certain marsh lands. His predecessors and successors, however, did the same. Above all he studied Olivier de Serres' book, *Le Théâtre d'Agriculture*, which was published during his reign and had a great success. This book taught scientific methods and suggested new objects of cultivation such as the mulberry. Naturally easy and cordial, Henry IV took a delight in talking to the peasants. He loved them, and would have liked to see each of them with " a fowl in his pot on Sundays."

In the domain of commerce, Henry IV encouraged a political economist of interesting ideas, a certain Barthélemy de Laffémas, Commerce.   to whom he lent a willing ear and whom he made Controller-General of Trade. Laffémas asserted that a country should endeavour to be self-supporting, that it should produce all the manufactured goods it requires, and not import them from abroad. It was on his advice, that after the cultivation of the mulberry had become widespread, the Government promoted the establishment of factories for silk-spinning and the manufacture of silks and cloths of gold and silver ; and encouraged and protected the creation of glass and crystal works, carpet factories, wrought leather work and the weaving of fine Flanders linen. The importation of all similar wares was prohibited. This was an attempt at a policy of protection before the time of Colbert. A Board of Trade established at Paris, in the Palais, examined any proposals submitted to it by private individuals, and either recommended them to the King or rejected them.

In connexion with public works, Rosny, who was made Chief Inspector in 1599, improved the roads, began the paving Public works. of the highways round Paris—a work which Louis XIII subsequently continued—and planted great elms along them which for a long time afterwards were called by his name. He conceived a plan for the construction of canals, notably those which were to join the Loire and the Seine—the Briare Canal—the building of which he undertook, and the Atlantic with the Mediterranean—the Canal du Midi in Languedoc—the idea of which he worked out. In a general way he helped to restore the ravages caused by the civil wars—broken bridges and fallen walls. To make good all that had been destroyed, however, time was required, even during the next reign. All these works are evidences of good administration.

Under Henry IV attempts were made at colonization and transatlantic commerce. An East India company was created in Colonization. 1604 ; and settlements were made in Canada about the same time by des Monts and Champlain, enterprises which were repeated in 1608 because the first efforts had been failures. Champlain was eventually to found Quebec, conquer the Red Indians, and explore the great lakes. The Government of Henry IV granted these persons the privileges and the letters patent for which they asked, as did his successors, and as his predecessors would have done in like circumstances.

In the domain of the moral and religious interests of the

country the work accomplished by Henry IV was much greater.
Religious policy of Henry IV. Owing to diverse circumstances, it showed a very different degree of brilliance, duration, and scope. The problem was to induce Catholics and Protestants to live side by side in a spirit of mutual toleration, and Henry IV laid the foundations of a policy destined to last nearly a century.

At the request of the ardent Catholics, the King allowed the Jesuits to return in 1603. The Huguenots and the magistrates were opposed to this, objecting that the order belonged to the League and was Ultramontane and Spanish. Henry IV wittily replied that the Jesuits had only to be allowed to return to France in order to become French; that if they had belonged to the League, so had many others; that, taking it all in all, he preferred to have them as friends rather than enemies; and that he meant to be master. In spite of the remonstrances of the Parliament, the Jesuits, on taking an oath of fealty, were allowed to return. Their colleges were re-opened, and Henry IV even founded a new one—the Collège de la Flèche.

With regard to the Protestants a statute was absolutely necessary. It is true that the struggle which had lasted for thirty years spreading from town to town by means of sudden attacks, surprises, and massacres in the open country, had ceased, but the uneasiness among the Huguenots was universal. What was to be their lot? The Edict of Poitiers was, it is true, operative. But if the King were to die and another monarch less well disposed towards them were to succeed to the throne, what would become of them? They thought of choosing a leader, but Henry IV forbade them to do so. In 1594 they elected representatives, who met together, divided up France into nine circles, and organized these circles into a kind of republic; they then discussed the advisability of taking up arms. This angered Henry IV, but eventually, on the advice of the moderates headed by du Plessis Mornay, they asked the King to make their position secure by means of a clear and decisive edict. Henry IV hastened to grant their request, and
The Edict of Nantes, 1598. on April 13, 1598, he published the edict which was to bear in history the famous name of the Edict of Nantes. In ninety-five general articles and fifty-six special

clauses, Henry IV decided that the Protestants were to enjoy full and entire liberty of conscience. They were to have the right of practising their religion at two places in every bailiwick, with the exception of Paris and the large towns, where services were to be held outside the gates—in the case of Paris at Charenton. They were to be eligible for all offices ; they were to have a special chamber called the Edict Chamber in every Parliament, in which Huguenot cases were to be tried. They were to be allowed to hold synods—the Parliaments stipulated that these synods should only be held by special permission, and with certain prescribed formalities. For a period of eight years the King was to leave over 200 towns in the hands of the Protestants as security for his word and was to maintain the garrisons in these places. And finally, an unexpected favour, he was to pay the salaries of the Protestant ministers and subsidize Protestant colleges. This was the Edict of Poitiers over again with added advantages, and it had the merit of consecrating toleration in the eyes of Europe at a time when no country, Catholic or Protestant, practised that virtue. It had the further merit of lasting for eighty-seven years, when it was revoked by an act of Louis XIV which caused great excitement, and brought the political prudence of Henry IV into even stronger relief. It was not carried without violent opposition on the part of the Catholics, who protested against the privileges by which their adversaries were practically re-warded ; and on the part of the Parliaments, which pleaded that the laws were violated by the articles of the edict. But Henry IV stood his ground. He had the magistrates summoned to him. " I pray you, register the edict," he said to them. " What I have done, I have done in the interests of peace, which I have succeeded in establishing abroad and now wish to establish within my kingdom. You owe me obedience. . . . I have scaled the walls of cities and can easily scale barricades. Do not take your stand on the Catholic religion. I love it better than you do. I am more Catholic than you. I am the eldest son of the Church, which none of you are or can ever be. You are mistaken if you imagine you stand well with the Pope. I am on far better terms with him than you are. Once let me take it in hand, and I will have you all declared heretics for refusing to obey me." His speech was admirable in its brief and natural vivacity, full of sense and reason. Parliament gave way.

We see the opposition with which Henry IV met in the passing of his best measures. It is a mistake to imagine that he was popular during his lifetime. Popularity only came to him after his death. Throughout his reign his contemporaries were above all alive to his faults—among those with which he has been most severely reproached, were his avarice and his forgetfulness of services rendered him. He was also greatly blamed for his disorderly life, for the general discontent and the complaints that were everywhere rife. And, indeed, it must be confessed that his private existence gave some ground for the bitter remarks of the people he scandalized.

Henry IV had no children by Margaret of Valois and was separated from her. After several other intrigues he fell in
Gabrielle d'Estrées. love with Gabrielle d'Estrées, a lovely young girl of twenty, fair, sweet, and graceful. For a long time, distressed at having no direct heir, he had been considering the possibility of having his marriage with Margaret of Valois annulled, and marrying again. His ministers and friends urged him to do so ; and Margaret, who was of an easy disposition, gave her consent. But when Henry IV thereupon suggested that he should marry Gabrielle d'Estrées, whom he had created Marchioness of Beaufort, lovable and amiable though Gabrielle may have been, the disconcerting idea called forth universal protest. The King of France owed a very different marriage to the dignity of his position. The Pope informed him that he would never consent to annul his first marriage for the realization of such a project. The ministers and Margaret herself were violently opposed to it. At this juncture Gabrielle d'Estrées died very suddenly in Paris, on April 10, 1599, at the age of twenty-five. Poison was hinted at, but she probably merely succumbed to puerperal convulsions in giving birth to a still-born child. Her disappearance from the horizon simplified matters. For some time past, ever since 1592, the project of a marriage between Henry IV and Marie de' Medici, the niece of the Grand Duke of Tuscany, had been discussed. In the eyes of the ministers this alliance had, among other advantages, the fact that her dowry would serve to pay all,

or part of the debts which the King of France had contracted to the masters of Florence during the last civil wars. The death of Gabrielle allowed the negotiations for this match to be renewed. Henry IV, however, swiftly fell a victim to a new **Henriette** passion, inspired by Henriette d'Entraigues, after-**d'Entraigues.** wards Marquise de Verneuil. He was morbidly susceptible to women's charms. Henriette was a tall young woman, slim, elegant, and beautifully made, but arrogant, bad-tempered, essentially common, mercenary, and heartless. She extracted a written promise of marriage from Henry IV. Meanwhile, however, the negotiations with the Tuscan Court had been concluded, and Henry IV's marriage with Margaret of Valois annulled; with the result that the union with Marie de' Medici, a woman of eight-and-twenty, rather stout, robustly healthy, and not very intelligent, was celebrated at Florence and Lyons in 1600. In September, 1601, the Dauphin, after-wards Louis XIII, was born at Fontainebleau. Henry IV still continued to see Henriette d'Entraigues. The passion for her which tormented him caused much unhappiness in his domestic life, and came near to producing extraordinary complications. For Henriette, on the grounds that she had the King's written word, conceived the notion of having his marriage with Marie de' Medici annulled in order to bring about her own. To attain her ends, her family, whose members were unscrupulous people, organized a conspiracy which aimed at nothing less than killing Henry IV, and, with the help of England and Spain, proclaiming as King of France a son of Madame de Verneuil by Henry. When the plot was dis-covered the persons concerned were arrested, tried, and con-demned; but Henry IV, with excessive weakness, pardoned them all. The famous promise of marriage was given up, and the King's passion revived once more. The public was indig-nant, shocked and disapproving.

But there were yet other reasons for their discontent. Henry IV was reproached with having been too free with his pardons, of having paid overmuch to his enemies and heaped too many favours on their heads whilst neglecting his friends. His support of Sully, who was universally detested, was un-popular; and complaints were made that he kept the nobility at a distance and listened only to his ministers, middle-class bureaucrats, such as Bellièvre, Cheverny and Villeroy. Catholics and Protestants were alike uneasy, both sides suspicious of the King's sincerity towards them. The public peace, however, was not destined to be troubled. Only one outbreak occurred—the affair of the Duke of Biron.

The son of an old Marshal, and himself a good and courageous general who had received thirty-three wounds during his various **The case of** campaigns, a companion in arms and a friend **Biron, 1602.** of the King, who had twice saved his life, Charles de Gontaut-Biron was a big swarthy man, with deep-set eyes, and a dull glance ; he was ambitious, arrogant, and of no great intelligence. Henry IV had made him Admiral, Marshal, Governor of Burgundy, and a Duke and Peer of the realm, all before the age of thirty-eight. But Biron was not content, and considered that he had not been sufficiently rewarded. He gambled, lost, and incurred enormous debts. The Archduke of the Netherlands and the Duke of Savoy, with whom he had established relations, invited his confidence and listened to his grievances. The Duke of Savoy offered him his sister in marriage together with 200,000 crowns, hoping to turn him into an instrument which he could use. He even discussed the possibility of making him the ruler of Burgundy and Franche Comté which had become independent, and completely turned his head. Henry IV intercepted a suspicious correspondence between them and demanded an explanation. As no satisfactory one was forthcoming, he insisted, having made up his mind to pardon the culprit if he would only confess his double-dealing. Biron, however, remained stubbornly silent and treated the matter with a high hand. The King, accordingly, had him arrested at Fontainebleau and put in the Bastille, where he was tried and condemned to death. He was executed on July 31, 1602. Henry IV had determined to make an example of him.

The end of Henry IV's life was sad, darkened as it was by domestic quarrels rising out of his intrigue with Madame de **Proposed cam-** Verneuil, the distrust of his subjects, and fears **paign in** of all sorts. Great dreams have been attributed **Germany.** to him. Sully maintains that he conceived the idea of forming Europe into a sort of United States consisting of fifteen states—six hereditary monarchies, six elective monarchies, and three federated republics. But the authenticity of this great design has been contested. His attention was chiefly concentrated upon Spain, with whom he foresaw that war would break out again before long. A chance circumstance caused him to renew the conflict. A certain Rhenish Duke, William of Juliers, Cleves, and Berg, died on March 25, 1609, leaving no heir. Numerous competitors for the position presented themselves, and in the meanwhile the Emperor declared that he would sequester the property, with the intention of keeping it himself. Henry IV, determined not to allow the Imperial house to install itself at Juliers, formed an alliance with about ten German Princes in order to secure the Duchy in dispute to the Elector of Brandenburg and the Count of Neuburg. This meant war. The King of France collected an army of 35,000 men and decided to march for the frontier on May 19, 1610. About this very time, however, he fell madly in love, though he was a grey-beard of fifty, with the young wife of the Prince of Condé, Charlotte de Montmorency, who was only fifteen. Annoyed by this infatuation, the Prince of Condé had taken his wife away to Brussels. It has been asserted, though the fact was never proved, that the King's desire to get back this young lady and avenge himself on the Archdukes, who were keeping her in Belgium, had some connexion with his decision to enter upon the campaign.

Before setting out, Henry IV had Marie de' Medici, who was to be Regent in his absence, crowned at Saint-Denis on May 13. But for a long time past he had been constantly besieged by dark presentiments. With his mind full of the discontent and the smothered hostility with which he felt himself surrounded, he would frequently remain lost in thought, seated on a low chair fingering his spectacle-case. Then he would suddenly get up and exclaim, "Good God, I shall die if I stay in this town! They will kill me!" His face was frequently clouded with sadness and he kept repeating to his intimate friends: "You are happier than I," and wishing he were dead. He would add: "When I am gone they will see what I was worth!"

On May 14, at about four o'clock in the afternoon he drove

out to pay a visit to Monsieur de Sully at the Arsenal. He **Murder of** went without an escort; attended only by a few **Henry IV, 1610.**lords-in-waiting, he took his seat in his carriage. At the corner of the Rue de la Ferronnerie and the Rue Saint Honoré, his coach was stopped by a block in the traffic. A man named Ravaillac sprang upon the wheel, and as Henry IV was reading a letter, he stabbed him twice in the breast with a knife, piercing his heart and lung. The King fell back without a sound. Death was almost instantaneous. The curtains of the carriage were drawn and the body brought back to the Louvre. The assassin was a madman and had no accomplices.

Henry IV was right: his people were soon to learn his worth. From one end of France to the other, even in the poorest country hovel, unexampled sorrow and stupefaction reigned supreme. "There is not one amongst us," wrote Bossuet sixty-five years later, "who cannot remember a father or a grandfather describing not only the astonishment, the horror, and the indignation which so sudden and execrable a blow naturally provoked, but the sense of desolation, such as children feel who have lost a good father." No King of France was ever so deeply regretted, and when he was dead his subjects appreciated the qualities of this monarch, who was the most **Appreciation** charming, the most witty, and the most truly **of Henry IV.** French of all the old Kings. They reminded each other of his smiling courtesy, his gentleness and perfect manners. The nobles recalled his jovial familiarity with them, so free, so full of good temper and fellowship; his indomitable spirits and gaiety. But at the same time all remembered that he knew how to be a King, master of himself and others, to whom there was no reply; and how he could assume this character in the twinkling of an eye if necessary, with sovereign impetuosity and pride, knowing how to play the part of a great lord at the proper time, if he liked, and capable of wearing the crown of France with the proud dignity befitting a great kingdom. He was every inch a King and "the poor were intoxicated with love for their sovereign!" Henry IV rendered two invaluable services to his country. He gave peace to his kingdom after thirty years of civil war, and he taught it the meaning of toleration. "France is deeply indebted to me," he wrote on one occasion, " for I work hard for her ! " The country, after his death, and later posterity, ratified this touching statement.

SOURCES. D'Aubigné, *Histoire Universelle*, ed. de Ruble, 1887 ; Palma Cayet, *Chronologie novennaire* and *Chronologie septennaire*, ed. Michaud and Poujoulat ; Henri IV, *Lettres missives*, ed. Berger de Xivrey, 1843 ; Sully, *Économies royales*, ed. Michaud and Poujoulat ; L'Estoile, *Mémoires-Journaux*, ed. G. Brunet, 1875 ; du Plessis-Mornay, *Mémoires et correspondance*, 1824 ; *Mémoires de la Ligue*, 1758 ; Bassompierre, *Mémoires*, ed. Chanterac, 1870 ; *Mémoires d'État de Villeroy*, 1665 ; Cheverny, *Mémoires*, ed. Michaud and Poujoulat ; Cl. Groulart, *Mémoires*, same publishers ; de Thou, *Histoire universelle*, 1734 ; *Journal d'un curé ligueur*, ed. E. de Barthélemy, 1886 ; *Journal du siège de Paris en 1590*, ed. Franklin, 1876 ; *Procès-verbaux des États-Généraux de 1593*, ed. A. Bernard, 1842 ; H. de Laurens, *Discours et rapport véritable de la conférence (de Suresnes)*, 1593 ; *Satyre Menippée*, ed. C. Read, 1876 ; Cardinal d'Ossat, *Lettres*, 1708 ; Desjardins, *Négociations diplomatiques de la France avec la Toscane*, 1875.

WORKS. Poirson, *Histoire du règne de Henri IV*, 1865 ; H. de la Ferrière, *Henri IV, le roi, l'amoureux*, 1890 ; J. B. Lagrèze, *Henri IV, vie privée*, 1885 ; E. Jung, *Henri IV écrivain*, 1855 ; Comte de Saint-Poncy, *Histoire de Marguerite de Valois*, 1887 ; B. Zeller, *Henri IV et Marie de Médicis*, 1877 ; Louis Batiffol, *La vie intime d'une reine de France au XVII siècle (Marie de Médicis)*, 1906 ; C. Dufayard, *Le connétable de Lesdiguières*, 1892 ; G. Fagniez, *L'Économie sociale de la France sous Henri IV*, 1897 ; N. Valois, *Le conseil de raison*, 1885 ; C. Pfister, *Les Économies royales de Sully et le grand dessein*, 1894 ; J. Loiseleur, *Problèmes historiques, mort de Gabrielle d'Estrées*, 1873 ; A. Douarche, *L'Université de Paris et les Jésuites*, 1888 ; Élie Benoist, *Histoire de l'Édit de Nantes*, 1693 ; A. Lods, *L'Édit de Nantes devant le Parlement de Paris*, 1899 ; Anquez, *Histoire des assemblées politiques des réformés de France*, 1859 ; and *Henri IV et l'Allemagne*, 1887 ; Nouaillac, *Villeroy, secrétaire d'État*, 1909 ; C. de la Roncière, *Histoire de la marine française*, vol. iv, 1910.

CHAPTER IX

CIVILIZATION UNDER THE LAST VALOIS

Part played by the Valois in the Renaissance movement ; their
luxury ; influence of Catherine de' Medici. The Court ceremonial ;
the ordinance of 1585. Sumptuousness of the Court ; costumes,
works of art ; inventory of Catherine de' Medici's house. The great
lords imitate the Queen Mother. Characteristics of the art of the
time ; the study of antiquity facilitated by means of printing ;
French taste ; the dogmatic regulation of canons of taste. The
Renaissance ; learned men, historians, publicists, jurisconsults ;
the poets, Ronsard and the Pléiade ; the *Académie du Palais* ; the
Independents : Noël du Faïl, Montaigne, Ambroise Paré, and
Palissy. The arts : architecture ; the architects : Androuet du
Cerceau, Pierre Lescot and the Louvre, Philibert Delorme and the
Tuileries, Jean Bullant and Écouen ; sculpture, Jean Goujon and
Germain Pilon ; painting ; drawings, Clouet, Corneille de Lyon ;
tapestry, enamels, stained glass ; music, Goudimel.

NOTWITHSTANDING the troubles of the civil wars and
the drama of disorder and bloodshed enacted throughout the kingdom, the second half of the sixteenth
century in France was marked by a wonderful brilliance in
the domain of learning, art, and letters. The general condition of the country did not arrest the development of men of brilliant talents—nay, these were
actually bound together by a universal tendency,
a sort of fashion, which gave to the Renaissance
proper in France a peculiar value of its own. It
was more or less due to chance that this remarkable period in
French civilization coincided with the reigns of Henry II and his
sons. The monarchs of the sixteenth century exercised very
little influence upon the literary and artistic movement of their
time. Henry II took no interest in literature ; and though
Charles IX wrote verses, patronised Ronsard, and was interested
in the Pléiade, though Henry III welcomed Henri Estienne and
328

*Part played
by the Valois
in the Renais-
sance Move-
ment.*

furnished subjects for debate at the *Académie du Palais,* it cannot be maintained that, but for them, the talents of the artists of their century would have been very different. It was by another means that they took their unique place in the general movement of civilization during their epoch : they loved luxury and display and they were responsible for much building.

Few Courts have left in history reminiscences of greater magnificence than the Court of the Valois. Festivals, balls, tapestries, jewels, dresses, scintillating stuffs, velvets and brocades all mingled together in a somewhat confused picture full of warm tones and gorgeous colour. Court functions at every epoch, in the fourteenth as well as the fifteenth centuries, and more particularly under Francis I, had always been marked by a studied display of artistic luxury, both in the dress of the courtiers and in the setting arranged for festivities. But the last of the Valois carried this luxury to its utmost extreme.

It was their mother, Catherine de' Medici, who endowed them with this taste. She was rich and she was Italian, a **Influence of** daughter of that Florentine House of Medici **Catherine de'** which adored beautiful things and, in collecting **Medici on** them, was governed by taste as well as love of **Court life.** display. Following in her footsteps, her sons loved every kind of elegance. Catherine indulged in it partly from political motives. She wished, by means of external splendour, to restore to the Crown that prestige, of which circumstance and the absence of moral power were depriving it. " Your Court," she wrote to Charles IX, " must acquire the dignity and decorum I formerly found there." In addition to a studied refinement in its appointments and costumes, the Queen Mother introduced, as an indispensable feature, that elegance of behaviour which is termed etiquette ; and her sons, Henry III above all, fulfilled her wishes even beyond her hopes. Together with a consummate taste in dress and jewellery, the organization of the æsthetics of Court ceremonial is the most signal contribution made by the sons of Henry II to the artistic evolution of the sixteenth century.

If they did not create, they at all events considerably developed that atmosphere of perpetual display in which a King of France was destined to live from the moment he awoke in the morning to the time that he fell asleep at night, a solemn and meticulous existence which Louis XIV alone was capable of observing scrupulously. Catherine de' Medici outlined it in a letter written to Charles IX : the King was to get up at a particular hour ; admit the nobility into his bedroom " whilst he put on his shirt, and his clothes were brought in ; " after this the council, and at ten o'clock mass, to which the King was to go in procession escorted by his guards, and surrounded by the Court ; at eleven o'clock dinner, the courtiers to be in attendance standing ; then twice a week audiences, after which the King was to be free " to study or to be alone," but only until three o'clock ; at three o'clock a walk or a ride with the Court ; supper in the evening with the royal family, and twice a week after supper, a ball ; in short the King was to be constantly on show, for that pleased the nobility ; he was not to allow them out of sight, was to amuse them, and above all to insist that due respect was always shown. Catherine assured her son that this was how the Court was conducted in the time of Francis I.

But Henry III went even further. He aimed at isolating the person of the King ever more and more from the rest of

Ceremonial ordinance of 1585. humanity, with the object of inspiring greater respect ; and on January 1, 1585, he issued an edict, a grand ordinance " to keep each man within the bounds of honour and respect due to his Majesty." From this time forward no one was to approach the King either inside or outside the palace without first being summoned by him to do so ; in the royal presence hats were to be removed, and no one was allowed to sit down or walk about the room or touch any object whatsoever. Strict rules were made regulating the movements of those about the King's person, together with lists of those who were privileged to approach him, entitled " The order that the King would have observed in his Court and the fashion in which he would be honoured, accompanied, and served." At the levée, in the morning, lists of those who were to be allowed to penetrate into the various rooms of the royal suite of apartments—the antechamber, the cabinet, the state-room, and the King's bed-chamber, were made out in writing. They noted many complicated grades and the ushers

330

were strict in seeing that each man's rights were respected. During the King's toilet the water for him to wash with was fetched with great ceremony, and the broth for his breakfast was brought with equal ceremony. A detailed paragraph designated those who were to be allowed to offer the King a table-napkin or a piece of bread. The etiquette of the meals was all arranged, and it was known who might be present to look on, and who had the right of handing the table-napkin. The persons present were forbidden to speak to the King, except on an extremely lofty plane and on subjects calculated to edify the audience. If necessary, barriers separated His Majesty and his Swiss Guards from the rest of the room. When the King went out, the favoured persons who were allowed to follow on foot, on horseback or in carriages, were all appointed beforehand. Audiences were no less minutely regulated. They took place twice a week, on Mondays and Wednesdays in the afternoon, when the King, seated in his " chair of state," received the person admitted, who was instructed to stand at a distance and invited to be brief," in order not to weary His Majesty." The ordinance even settled the days on which balls were to be held—on Sundays and Thursdays after supper ; princes, lords and gentlemen were expected to attend these entertainments. These recurrent balls were an innovation introduced by the Valois, and explain the fact that in the royal castles of the sixteenth century special large " ball rooms " were built—as at Saint-Germain-en-Laye and Fontainebleau —whilst hitherto there had only been ordinary " state rooms." The enactments of this royal protocol, which were thus made inflexible, were observed with more or less precision at the end of the sixteenth and the beginning of the seventeenth century: Henry III himself carried them out very incompletely, and Henry IV extremely badly, for his free and easy manners and wit were ill adapted to show and ostentation. Louis XIII, whose tastes were modest, also paid little attention to them. But Louis XIV's care not to miss a single detail and even to add to them, was destined later on to exemplify their spectacular dignity as well as their tyrannical constraint.

In this setting, the movements of which were regulated by royal mechanism, was displayed all the exaggerated luxury of

young princes who were extremely elegant, extremely rich—
or at least thought themselves so—and extremely extrava-
Splendour gant. They invented fashions in dress, fashions
under the which were considered ridiculous by the wise
last Valois. men of the time, and were above all very costly
and extraordinarily changeable. Willy-nilly the nobles and
courtiers were obliged to follow them, and there was a regular
pageant of magnificent costumes in silks and velvets of every
colour, fine furs, and gold and silver embroidery, the whole
covered, in the case of men as well as of women, with quantities
of jewels representing ridiculous fortunes. At the marriage
of Henry of Béarn, in 1572, the Duke of Anjou, wrote the
Venetian Giovanni Michiel, wore in his cap thirty-two pearls
of twelve carats each, for which he had paid a sum of 23,000
crowns ; whilst the King's dress, including his jewels, was worth
500,000 or 600,000 crowns. In the circle about the princes each
man vied with his neighbour in the number and value of those
elegant costumes of the period, graceful and capricious, if not
comfortable in form. "A courtier," said Lippomano, "is not
considered rich unless he has between twenty-five and thirty
costumes of various styles and can put on a different dress every
day." Foreigners noticed with astonishment the contrast
presented by this unreasonable extravagance and the misery
and want prevalent in a country ruined by civil wars and
covered with shattered buildings. But careless, frivolous and
pleasure-loving, the young nobles who surrounded Catherine
de' Medici's sons thought nothing of these things, and gave
themselves up to the full enjoyment of luxurious
masquerading.

Together with brilliance in dress, the Valois introduced
another fashion : beauty in the internal decorations of houses
—tapestries, carved wood, curtains, carpets and ornaments.
An inventory made on the death of Catherine de' Medici of all
her possessions has been published. This inventory gives us
some idea of what in the sixteenth century were the private
surroundings of a Queen, whom de Thou calls *femina superbi
luxus*, "a woman of superb luxury." It is true that she was
one of those who spent money right royally in order to surround
herself with objects of value, and that in spite of the great

fortune she inherited as the daughter of a Florentine banker, she died deeply in debt.

The mansion which she inhabited in Paris and which she had had built for her, occupied the site of the present Bourse de Commerce. It was afterwards called the **Inventory of Catherine de' Medici's palace.** *Hôtel de Soissons;* but the building is no longer in existence. All the walls were hung with tapestry—Flemish or French tapestry, Beauvais tapestry, *verdures* and subject-pieces, such as the history of Hannibal, which covered a huge tapestry of twelve pieces made to adorn the great hall of the mansion ; the tale of Vulcan ; armorial bearings and mottoes. They were frequently changed in order to vary the aspect of the rooms, and those that were not in use were put away in attics. Altogether the Queen possessed 129 tapestries. Sometimes, in the place of tapestry, the walls were hung with stamped leather, with backgrounds of various colours, orange, black, green, red or blue, picked out with gold and silver. Of these there were 134 pieces. Forty-four Oriental carpets were destined to cover the floors. Many of the rooms in the mansion were panelled with carved wood in which small pictures, enamels, or Venetian mirrors were set for decoration. One cabinet, called the Mirror Cabinet, contained 119 mirrors inserted in this way ; whilst another, the Enamel Cabinet, was adorned with seventy-one Limoges enamels, thirty-nine of which represented various subjects and were oval in shape, while thirty-two, about a foot high, were portraits of princes, lords, and ladies. In addition to these, Catherine de' Medici, possessed some 259 enamels of all kinds, an extremely rich collection. The furniture was in keeping with this sumptuous setting. Beneath ceilings panelled in carved wood picked out with gold, stood huge four-post beds, enclosed by white damask curtains with gold valances, adorned with gold trimmings and embroideries. The bed of the Queen, who, as a widow always wore mourning, was hung with black velvet embroidered with pearls and had jet or ebony posts adorned with silver ; the seats and " chairs of state " or armchairs, were of ebony inlaid with ivory ; the candelabra were of jet, and the tables were covered with black velvet embroidered in white. Elsewhere there were white guipures mounted on black satin, stuffs of gold and silver, embroidered crapes, crimson satins and cloth of gold. And in the midst of all this sumptuous decoration there were collections of objects of all kinds, the smallest of which were worth large sums, Catherine de' Medici had 476 pictures including 341 portraits ; some of these, it is true, were small works meant to be set in the panelling. They are interesting and agreeable mementoes now, owing to their life-like expression and the correctness of the costumes depicted ; a few of them are still preserved in the Louvre and at Versailles. In her private cabinet she had twenty *genre* pictures, landscapes, &c. Next in importance to the pictures was the porcelain. Catherine had 141 pieces of Palissy ware, dishes and bowls. The tables and cabinets were loaded with artistic ornaments, a certain number of which have been preserved in the Galerie d'Apollon, and give us an opportunity of appreciating their elegance of form and their finished workmanship—ewers, goblets, flagons, gondolas of carved rock crystal or *pietra dura* mounted on enamelled gold stands, Chinese lacquers, pieces of ivory, mother-of-pearl, and coral, artistic bindings, bronzes, busts, antique medals, fans, and Venetian glass. All the latest and rarest treasures of the most enlightened taste of the day were to be found in her possession. There was nothing precious, even to books and manuscripts, of which she did not covet a valuable collection. She left 4500 volumes and 776 ancient manuscripts, bearing witness, not to her erudition—the manuscripts were in Latin and treated of austere subjects, and she never read them—but to her eclecticism. We have said nothing of her jewels and her gold and silver plate.

Important as her collections were, however, they were not out of all proportion to those belonging to her contemporaries. The inventories made on the deaths of some of the nobility reveal the same tendencies. Madame de Sainte-Aulaire had forty-five tapestries in her house, and the Guises had seventy-seven in the Château de Joinville alone. Not every collector had as much Palissy ware as Catherine de' Medici ; but they all had pictures, enamels, and crystal, and above all, those embroideries on silk or velvet backgrounds which, although they are now faded, give us an idea of the rich hangings of the period. It was by their encouragement of these luxurious arts that the princes and grandees of the time contributed, in some degree, to their development. But, in other respects, they did not, any more than the Kings, exercise any very great influence over the artistic movement of the second half of the sixteenth century.

This very important movement is marked by several distinct characteristics : its claim not to be empirical as in the **Characteristics** preceding age, but on the contrary, erudite, and **of the art of** to seek its source in a knowledge of antiquity ; **the period.** the circumstance, that notwithstanding this, it remained French and unconsciously followed closely the tradition of the epoch that had gone before, while improving it ; the relative unity of all artistic manifestations of the time by reason of this twofold aspiration ; and lastly, the realization of the dignity of art, resulting in the fact that architects and poets no longer regarded themselves as mere craftsmen, but as creators and scholars of a high order. This was the beginning of the true French Renaissance, in contradistinction to the first Renaissance, which may be said to have ended about 1550 ; because by that date, the best representatives of the age in which individual talents, more or less isolated, coincided with the maintenance of a French tradition carried on ever since the Middle Ages, had disappeared, or were about to disappear. For Marot died in 1544, Rabelais about 1553, and Margaret of Navarre in 1549.

The increase, owing to the invention of printing, in the editions of ancient authors, both Latin and Greek, made the **The study of** study of antiquity extraordinarly fashionable in **the ancients.** the sixteenth century. This movement, gradually inaugurated during the Middle Ages, had gathered strength ever since the beginning of the sixteenth century. It was generally admitted that to be learned was to possess a title to glory, and that it was impossible to be learned without having a thorough knowledge of ancient literature. The ancients had said the last word on morality, law, and art. It was the fashion to swear only by them. Had not the Reformation found its first and its best representatives among the learned men who were familiar with classical philology, and able to refer triumphantly to the original texts ? In imitation of the ancients, it was laid down as an axiom that definite methods and rules are necessary in every branch of study. What was a language that had no grammar, no syntax, and no orthography ? Hence, for instance, arose the idea of fixing the language and eliminating everything superfluous, all errors of taste and lack of restraint, and of suppressing all that was disorderly in the literary and linguistic medley, which was the legacy of the Middle Ages. In addition to this, the daily increasing development of printing-works and the growing output of books published in French gradually led to the idea of unifying grammatical and orthographical forms, so that all books might be uniformly readable. And thus ideas of rule and measure in imitation of the ancients came into existence, ideas which were destined to characterize the whole artistic and literary movement of the second half of the sixteenth century. In 1549 the book which formulated the new doctrine was published—Joachim du Bellay's *Défense et Illustration de la Langue Françoise*. Whereas hitherto it had

Du Bellay's "Défense de la Langue françoise." been regarded as necessary, and for a long time to come, was still to be so regarded, that scientific works should be written in Latin, on account of the nobility of that language, and also in order that the learned men of all countries might be able to understand each other, du Bellay urged his compatriots to write in French. In this he was doubtless influenced by the Protestants, who conducted their services entirely in the vulgar tongue, and following the example set by Calvin in publishing his *Institution Chrétienne* in French, refused to employ a language that was not accessible to all. But on the other hand, du Bellay insisted that the French language should be made a suitable instrument, that it should be purified and enriched, if necessary, by learned philological creations of words which it lacked, and, above all, be endowed with style. In order to realize these aims, it was only necessary, he continued, to turn to the ancients and study their rules. He called upon his countrymen to renounce all the inventions of the Middle Ages, which were inadequate and ugly, ballads, rondeaux, and virelays, to return solely to the ancient tradition illustrated by Horace and Virgil in their odes and epics, and to establish a French prosody, a French syntax, and a French style. Du Bellay's ideas had an enormous success, and were adopted by the Pléiade. They were productive of three results : an imitation which grew closer every day, till it amounted almost to plagiarism, of the ancients ; the bestowing of a more and more rigorous classical education on the rising generation ; and a contempt for the so-called barbarous works of the Middle Ages ; all of which resulted in the artificial productions of an erudite literature which was in no sense popular, but on the contrary, aristocratic.

And, indeed, the imitation of antiquity became the prevailing fashion. Mythology invaded literature and art till it **The classical** encumbered them. The gods and goddesses of **obsession.** Olympus were to be found everywhere, and nymphs figured *ad infinitum* in poetry and bas-reliefs. Every speech invoked the heroes of the ancient world, and there was no historical personage for whom a parallel was not found in the pages of Plutarch. The good side of this fashion was to be found in the fact that instead of losing themselves in mazes of glossaries and commentary, as preceding ages had done, people made a direct study of the texts themselves. But classical works assumed an unparalleled importance and value. The smallest particle in a classic sentence was weighed and balanced as though it had the unique significance of some judicial formula. The fashion became a superstition.

From that time forward it was assumed that outside the productions of antiquity no creation of the human mind deserved the effort of study. The writers of the sixteenth century were the first to suffer from this narrow theory ; for they were afterwards neglected, if not actually despised, by succeeding generations. With the exception of Queen Margaret of Valois (whose book-shelves contained their works) no cultivated person in the seventeenth and eighteenth centuries who formed a " library " thought it essential to include the French Renaissance writers in it. And even the Bibliothèque Royale itself, the present Bibliothèque Nationale, was not so poor in any department as in that devoted to French authors of the sixteenth century. This tendency which is known as " Classicism " weighed heavily upon the development of the French genius after the sixteenth century. Rome was regarded as a school sufficient for all needs. Hence the prolonged indifference to everything that was not Roman, to the original, free, and spontaneous literature of the Middle Ages and of Anglo-Saxon countries, Shakespeare, for instance ; and the contempt for scientific and political speculations, in so far, at least, as their application to practical and industrial life was concerned. It led to the acquisition and development of valuable qualities of propriety, taste, and restraint, but was detrimental to independent, varied, and vital inspiration. In the State it conduced to the realization of Roman uniformity under the absolutism of Louis XIV, which perfectly expressed the juridical idea of the *princeps romanus ;* and the classical standard ended by destroying those communal and provincial institutions characteristic of the Middle Ages, which present such a curious spectacle of freedom and autonomy.

Contempt for the Middle Ages was indeed one of the dogmas that the new school professed most eagerly. Apparently this negative attitude was the very origin of its being. The school had been formed with the object of making war, and "a fine war" [wrote Pasquier] "against ignorance." Ignorance meant the Middle Ages, "the ancient barbarism." All that they had produced in the domain of literature was mere "spicery" according to du Bellay. A "better age" had been inaugurated—the epoch which aimed at bringing things "to perfection." And thus, in contradistinction to the artists of the preceding period, who had endeavoured, each in his own sphere, to do the best they could in accordance with their personal tastes and tendencies, their temperaments and fancies, it was now maintained that an ideal existed destined to be common to all, a theory of beauty brought to light again from the ancient world, a canon. The promulgators of the new theories were dogmatists who became exclusive.

Of this they were fully aware. They also realized that their learned and reasoned efforts could never result in the production of works fit for the public at large—that is to say, popular ; but that they were condemned to remain select and to a certain degree isolated. They accepted this aristocratic position and gloried in it. But in spite of their pretensions, they were not the exclusive creators of the movement they represented. They belonged to a sequence and were the links in a chain. Before their time, the humanists, who had sought in Latin writers models of fine language which they imitated, had, in a certain sense, pointed out the road to them. Italian influence has also been mentioned, that of the Italian banking colony at Lyons, and that of the Italians attracted to France by Catherine de' Medici. But, as a matter of fact, this alleged influence is not easy to trace, and it is admitted that it cannot have lasted long. And, above all, the Classicists owed more than they thought to tradition. In short, as is the case with every fashion, the conditions leading to the development of this movement are shrouded in obscurity and its evolution had its root in various general causes.

The proof of this lies in the fact that the first representatives of this second Renaissance were of diverse origin, and sprang **The French** from widely different conditions and localities. **Renaissance.** Whilst Ronsard, du Bellay and du Bartas belonged to the nobility, and Montaigne and Pasquier to the middle classes, many were of extremely modest, not to say vulgar extraction. Henri Estienne was a printer's workman. The members of the Pléiade lived in Paris; but Antoine de Baïf, Pontus de Thyard, Louise Labé and her group inhabited Lyons, in the vicinity of their printer, Jean de Tournes; whilst Muret and Vauquelin de la Fresnaye belonged to Poitiers. In the domain of art the provinces were as brilliant as Paris.

If we acknowledge the " resurrection " of antiquity as the basis of the Renaissance, pride of place must logically be given to the learned men and philosophers; for it was they who endowed others with the elements of their doctrines or the means for formulating them. The first in this order is the learned printer Henri Estienne—the son of the no less learned **Henri** printer Robert Estienne—who edited so many **Estienne.** of the works of ancient Greek and Latin authors, and above all, compiled a Greek dictionary, the *Thesaurus græcæ linguæ*, the prototype of modern lexicons. He was a clever, precocious man, extremely gifted but terribly bad-tempered. After having studied deeply and worked hard, he had been obliged to flee to Geneva on account of his Protestant ideas. He returned, however, to the Court of Henry III, and was kindly welcomed by that monarch. After numerous troubles brought upon him by his hot temper, he died a ruined, or an almost ruined man, at Lyons in 1598. Henri Estienne's work was very considerable. He published the works of nearly all the Greek writers, translated Pindar and Theocritus into Latin, edited the whole of Plato, and produced first editions of Appian and Anacreon. His publications furnished ample material for study to the philologists.

One of these, a certain Jacques Amyot, wished to make Greek literature in particular accessible to the public by means **Jacques** of translations into French. Amyot was born **Amyot.** at Melun of humble parentage in 1513, but had a brilliant career. He entered the Church, afterwards becoming Professor of Greek and Latin in the university of Bourges, where he attracted attention by his translation of the *Loves of Theagenes and Charicles* by Heliodorus, and of *Daphnis and Chloe* by Longus. He was subsequently made tutor to Henry II's sons, who, when they came to the throne, overwhelmed him with honours, making him Bishop of Auxerre, Grand Chaplain of France, and Commander of the Order of the Holy Ghost. He was supple, but his astuteness failed him before his death ; for he ended his days in great unpopularity in 1593 by reason of his friendship for Henry III. His translation of Plutarch's works is celebrated, and had a great success, both on account of the subject matter and the charming simplicity of its naïve style. This translation did more than a good many editions of ancient writers to make the heroes of antiquity familiar figures. Every private library for the next two hundred years gave Amyot's Plutarch a place of honour.

The accurate methods employed by the philologists in the production and translation of classical texts were also applied **Étienne** to the study of history by the historians, the chief **Pasquier.** of whom was the worthy Étienne Pasquier, a lawyer by profession, born in Paris in 1529. He was a great jurisconsult, whose name was in everybody's mouth, owing to his conduct of many important suits—the case of the University against the Jesuits, for instance. He was a member of the States-General in 1588, and lived in honourable seclusion from 1604 to 1615, when he died. In his *Recherches de la France,* the first volume of which appeared in 1561, the second in 1565, and the eight others at the beginning of the seventeenth century, he made an attempt to reconstruct the history of France by means of direct reference to documents, and the original accounts given by contemporary authors.

Following Pasquier's example, publicists also began to manifest a similar tendency. Jean Bodin, born at Angers in **The publicists.** 1530, was a bad lawyer and a heavy writer, though he was rich in traditional ideas. He was attached to the household of the Duke of Anjou, who had him appointed Grand Master of the Woods and Waters, and afterwards to the Court of Henry IV. In 1560 he published his *Méthode pour étudier l'histoire,* followed in 1576 by his voluminous work *De La République* (literally *De la Chose Publique*) the aim of which was to prove by means of a careful study of the past, that the French monarchy must be in no sense absolute or tyrannical, but moderate and limited. His big book is very confused.

Another publicist, François Hotman, was a Calvinist (1524–1590) and the son of a parliamentary judge. He was a learned professor and an aggressive controversialist who just escaped being compromised by the Conspiracy of Amboise, and finally left France after the Massacre of Saint Bartholomew. In the following year (1573) he published his great work *Franco Gallia, sive tractatus de regimine regum Galliæ et de jure successionis,* in which he, too, returning to the study of the ancient documents of France, tried to prove that the monarchy should be elective and not hereditary, and that, in any case, its authority should be held in check by the regular convocation of the States-General.

After history and political theory, law in its turn felt the effects of the new tendencies—Roman law as represented by **Jurisconsults.** Jacques Cujas, and Common Law as represented by Charles du Moulin. Cujas, who was born at Toulouse in 1522, and was a wandering Professor of Law who taught almost everywhere—at Cahors, Bourges, Valencia, Turin, Paris, and again at Bourges, where he died in 1590—had an unrivalled knowledge of Roman Law. Students flocked to his lectures in order to hear his illuminating commentaries on the old law texts, which he explained by referring to the testimony of contemporary writers, thus placing each law and each jurisconsult in the proper period. He was an admirable Greek scholar and wrote pure Latin. His *Commentaires du Corpus Juris civilis*, his critical editions of Justinian and Ulpian are monumental works, and his name was a venerable authority in the legal world under the old régime.

A jurist less celebrated to-day, but who once enjoyed almost as great a reputation in the legal world, was Charles **Charles du** du Moulin, a native of Paris, born in 1500. He **Moulin.** was of noble descent and possessed a strong and well ordered intellect. He was a Protestant, however, and his religion caused him much misfortune. He was cast into prison, but managed to escape to Germany, where he became a Professor at Tübingen. He subsequently returned to France, and was again cast into prison for having published in 1564, his *Conseil sur le fait du Concile de Trente*, which was regarded as impertinent. He died in 1566. He was not a good speaker and took up the profession of a consulting lawyer. His great work, the *Commentaires sur la Coutume de Paris*, is a weighty publication in which he explains, with valuable historical illustrations, those innumerable Common Law enactments upon which present French law is partly based. He was the authority *par excellence* on Common Law, and was at once jurist, historian, philosopher and well-informed scholar. His work was continued by Guy Coquille and Antoine Loisel.

The learned world had set the example, and, following in its footsteps, literature too prided itself upon returning to antiquity. In this the poets took the lead.

The sixteenth century was rich in poets. Étienne Pasquier talks of "the great flotilla of poets produced in the reign of **The Poets.** Henry II." Many of these have been completely forgotten, and even among those whose names have survived, not one has left a collection of works of such sustained beauty as have certain seventeenth-century writers. Whether their preoccupation with classical antiquity marred or benefited their productions is a delicate question. One thing at all events seems certain, and that is that the sixteenth-century authors are most pleasing when they give free play to qualities of simplicity, natural charm, and spontaneous emotional grace, limpid qualities which seem essentially French. Two different currents can be distinguished in their work—the inspiration derived from antique learning, and the continuation of French traditions with the characteristics of the national temperament. The two currents appear side by side, whilst in certain isolated authors, as we shall see, the second gained the upper hand. Such conflict was inevitable between an education imposed from without and the traditional instinct of a race asserting itself.

The first group of poets to attract attention appeared in Lyons—a city which was at that time an important centre, the point of contact between France and Italy, Switzerland, and Germany. Two names belonging to this group have come down to us—those of Maurice Scève and Louise Labé, who in a tentative and incomplete way foreshadowed the ideas of the Pléiade. But in trying to be classical, Maurice Scève, a worthy and learned alderman, became unintelligible, and his chief work, consisting of 449 decastich verses, *Délie, objet de la plus haute vertu*, is a mere exercise in pedantic subtlety. More spontaneous, however, was the work of Louise Labé, *la Belle Cordière*, as she was called (1526–1566) who, after a strange career in her youth, during which she dressed up as a boy and took part in the siege of Perpignan under the name of Captain Louis, settled down to a sober married life with a merchant of Lyons named Perrin. She wrote sonnets and elegies modelled on the Greek, the passionate accents of which are not always devoid of sincerity. She occupies a position superior to that of Scève and her contemporaries called her Sappho.

But in discussing the poetry of the sixteenth century the mind dwells especially on a much more illustrious group, which **The Pléiade.** received the name of the Pléiade. This was a band of seven authors of unequal merit, who synthesized the poetical movement of the sixteenth century. The original founders who banded themselves together about 1550 were fewer than seven. They called themselves the Brigade, and it was only when they reached their symbolic number in 1556 that they adopted the name Pléiade. The members were Ronsard, du Bellay, Baïf, Belleau, Pontus de Thyard, Jodelle and Daurat. Daurat, who was a Hellenist and never wrote in

French, seems at one time to have been the soul of the enterprise—and what an enterprise! "The renewal of poetical themes, the transformation of style, the reconstitution of the language!" Their pretensions might have appeared ridiculous had not partial success ennobled their overweening ambitions. Two of them were really gifted, Joachim du Bellay and Ronsard.

Du Bellay who was a priest and Canon of Notre Dame de Paris (1524–1560) was obviously marked out by his *Défense et Illustration de la Langue françoise*, clearly a work of the new school, to be a member of the Pléiade. He was a native of Anjou, with delicate health and a lively imagination, who, after travelling about Italy from 1553 to 1557, settled down in Paris. His *Poésies françoises* and his two books of sonnets, *Olive* and *Regrets*, are applications of the system of imitating antiquity. But he is not always happy in his imitations, which are sometimes clumsy and obscure. When, however, he gives free rein to his native spirit, which is natural, charming, sweet, and graceful, and follows the true old French tradition, he is excellent—an exquisite poet.

> Quand reverrai-je, hélas ! de mon pauvre village
> Fumer la cheminée, et en quelle saison
> Reverrai-je le clos de ma pauvre maison ?
> Plus me plaît le séjour qu'ont bati mes aïeux
> Que des palais romains le front audacieux . . .
> Plus que le marbre dur me plaît l'ardoise fine
> Et plus que l'air romain, la douceur angevine.*

More gifted than Du Bellay was Ronsard, the greatest poet of the Renaissance, and one of the best writers of the French language. Pierre de Ronsard was of noble birth and was born in 1524 in the Château de la Poissonnière in Vendôme. In his youth he took part in Court life and was sent on political missions abroad. But in 1540 he became deaf and retired from the world to write verses. In this he found his vocation and

*When shall I look upon the smoke that curls
Above my village chimneys, and behold
The little field about my humble house ? . . .
More fair to me my father's dwelling seems
Than the proud fronts of Roman palaces . . .
Than this enduring marble the grey slate,
Than Roman air the sweet breath of Anjou.

he became the undisputed chief of the Pléiade. " He made an end of the ugly, vulgar, insipid, stupid, and badly rhymed poetry that had existed before," says Brantôme, " and created the well-turned verse of to-day." His first *Odes* appeared in 1550 together with a collection of sonnets called *Amours*. In 1556 he published some *Hymnes* and a continuation of his *Amours*. The first edition of his works was dated 1560. They form a large collection, running to eight volumes in the modern Blanchemain edition, and contain elegies, epithalamia, eclogues and the beginning of an epic poem. The French Kings overwhelmed him with honours ; he became famous, and had numerous abbeys conferred upon him. After having taken an active part in the conflict against the Protestants he died in peace, though somewhat isolated and remote, in 1585. He, too, in addition to his classical pretensions possessed the best French qualities : brilliance, diversity, and a delicate and melancholy gift of harmony, now graceful, now violent, now exquisite, now passionate. But when he tried to imitate the ancients he became enigmatical and pedantic. His mythology is wearisome and his ideas obscure. He rendered great services to literature by the discovery of varied rhythms, the purification of a somewhat hybrid language, and by the association of all that was noble in classical thought with the French spirit. He was a true poet.

These two together, Ronsard and du Bellay, were the leaders of a whole school of poetry, the influence of which was **Ronsard and** still felt in the reign of Henry IV. Writers like **du Bellay.** Philip Desportes, and Vauquelin de la Fresnaye, were amongst their rivals, as well as Guillaume de Salluste, Seigneur du Bartas, a native of Gascony, who was born near Auch (1544–1590). He was a soldier, who was sent on various diplomatic missions to England and Denmark, and was killed at Ivry. A fervent and mystical Huguenot, he wrote a poem on the story of creation which had a great success.

In imitation of the bards of Hellas, Ronsard and his followers conceived the idea of having their poems sung. Hence arose **The Academie** the project of an association of poets and **du Palais.** musicians ; a plan which was carried out in 1570 and developed into an academy called the Académie du Palais.

The French Kings took a great interest in this institution, more especially Charles IX, who declared himself its patron, and granted it certain privileges. It grew and gradually admitted all kinds of members to its ranks, writers, men of the world, and women such as Madame de Retz and Madame de Lignerolles, Its members delivered addresses, to which Henry III came to listen, and for which he himself suggested subjects. At one time this body assumed the name of L'Académie Française, and was a prototype of the society founded by Richelieu. It accentuated and confirmed the aristocratic and restricted character of the whole literary movement of the Renaissance.

But against this aristocratic attitude in literature, protestations were raised in the name of the genius of the race. Du Bellay's *Défense* was attacked by the *Quintil Horatian*, a work attributed to Barthélemy Aneau. "If anyone, by good fortune, takes a pleasure in my pastimes," wrote Sibilet in his preface to the *Iphigenia*, "I do not so much envy him his joy as to be anxious to defend the communication of my diversions, in order to reserve them for a group of half a dozen reputed princes of our language." Independent writers sprang up here and there, who allowed their talents free play, and carried on the traditions of the individualistic authors of the first half of the century, with all the richness of a luxuriant and disorderly style, and a pleasant roving imagination. Yet even these were not untouched by the mania for classical learning so characteristic of the period.

Amongst them was Noël du Faïl, a magistrate in the Parliament of Rennes, a worthy Breton gentleman, born about Noël du Faïl. 1520. He travelled about, studying at Paris, Angers, Blois, Bourges, and Avignon. In 1547 he published under the pseudonym of Léon Ladulfi his *Propos Rustiques*, and in 1548 his *Baliverneries* or *Contes nouveaux d'Eutrapel*. He retired from public life in 1585 and died in 1591. "Our ancestors," he said, "did not speak as rhetorically as we do, but they spoke better, and their language was clearer and more intelligible than ours." His rustic tales, which are full of simplicity and good-natured wit, bear testimony in the exquisite pictures they draw of rural life to a charming feeling for nature, and revive the tradition of the old French story-tellers. If he lacks the power of Rabelais, he has the same free spirit and something of his rollicking gaiety and realism. He had a good knowledge of the ancient writers, which he displays in his work.

But the chief of all is Montaigne, the famous Michel de Montaigne, a native of Périgord, who was born in 1533 and **Montaigne.** died in 1592. He was the son of a well-to-do merchant, and, after having been a counsellor in the Parliament of Bordeaux, gave up his legal career in 1570 to live a country life on his paternal estate. This, however, did not prevent him from travelling in Germany, Switzerland, and Italy ; from holding the office of Mayor of Bordeaux from 1581 to 1585, an office in which he did not give proof of any very remarkable civic virtue ; or from accepting the title of Gentleman of the Bedchamber to Henry III. In 1580, when he was forty-seven, he published two volumes of his essays ; a third appeared in 1588. It is a unique work in which the philosophical author calmly discourses about life in his library on the second floor of the Château de Montaigne, where, from the top of a hill six miles from Libourne, he overlooks the Lidoire, a tributary of the Dordogne. Free from all worldly care, independent and tranquil, he judges men and things with a lenient scepticism. He is of the lineage described above, resembling Rabelais in his easy good-humour, his love of nature and that smiling indulgence which is a species of doubt and indifference, admirably expressed by a flowing, supple style. He too was deeply versed in ancient literature, and filled his works with classical quotations and allusions.

We must also mention Pierre La Ramée, the latinized version of whose name was Ramus. He was born of poor parents in **Ramus.** Vermandois about 1515, and worked as a servant in the Collège de Navarre. He managed to educate himself, and subsequently became a professor. He dared to attack Aristotle, who from the Middle Ages onwards had been regarded as the great authority, maintaining that many of the works ascribed to him were spurious, that the remainder were open to doubt, and that the commentators were misleading. The University took him sharply to task. He ended by being appointed a professor at the Collège de France, where his instruction was of a lucid and original type. He taught a little of everything—grammar, rhetoric, mathematics, and philosophy. Calvinism proved his undoing; he was killed in the Massacre of Saint Bartholomew. He was a jealously independent spirit.

Ambroise Paré (1517–1590) was also a man of unusual gifts, a celebrated surgeon, who knew neither Latin nor Greek, but made **Ambroise Paré.** a way for himself through the Hôtel-Dieu in Paris. He belonged to a family who lived in very modest circumstances near Laval, and he followed the French armies on campaign as a doctor. On the pretext that the little Latin he had been able to acquire was abominable, the faculty only granted him his doctor's degree in 1554. As an operating surgeon, however, his skill amounted to genius. He bravely wrote treatises on anatomy and surgery in French, which laid him open to hostile attacks. He was the founder of French surgery.

Bernard Palissy also was ignorant of Greek and Latin. He was a *savant* as well as a great artist, a working man of the **Palissy.** south of France, a native of Agenais. He adopted the calling of geometrical surveyor, and settled at Saintonge, becoming a convert to Protestantism. The story of his eagerness to discover the secret of Italian enamelled earthenware and of his success is well known. His dishes, "his rustic crocks" as he called them, covered with iridescent enamel which gives the effects of lapis-lazuli, agate, and precious stones in the form of lizards, crayfish, and animals of all sorts, and later on, scenes containing human figures, were his chief titles to fame. Endowed with an inquiring intelligence and an open mind, he read translations of Pliny and studied and taught natural science. In 1563 he published his *Traité des sels divers et de l'agriculture*, and in 1580 his *L'art de terre, de la nature, des eaux et fontaines, des métaux, des terres, la Recepte véritable*, and his *Discours véritables*, which give proof of a scientific spirit extremely advanced for his time and almost proclaim him a precursor of scientific agriculture. He died in obscurity—a prisoner, it is said, on account of his religious opinions.

Thus we see that the study of antiquity was imposed even upon the independents of the second half of the sixteenth century, those who refused to accept the severe discipline to which Ronsard and his followers submitted, but remained faithful to the joyous tradition of their country, its spontaneity and abundance. These two characteristics are even more strongly manifested in the domain of the arts.

The art which shone with the greatest brilliance during the second half of the sixteenth century was architecture. **Architecture.** When we think of the works of the Renaissance we evoke more especially the beautiful buildings of that period, with their necessary accompaniments of graceful and varied sculptural decorations. Whereas before this time the architect, in the strict sense of the word, did not exist, and there were merely master-masons who, in collaboration with the owner, built structures which were raised bit by bit, without much concern about their final effect, and in any case, not on any preconceived symmetrical plan ; from the time of Henry II onwards there came into being a class of theorists and scientific men who laid down principles and prescribed rules. Architects arose, artists who designed a carefully proportioned whole, put a complete work of art upon paper before beginning to build, and moreover, conceived great and exceedingly complicated plans. French architecture at once attained an incomparable degree of beauty. And the initial cause of this evolution was once again the influence of antiquity.

Two Italians, Alberti and Serlio, the former belonging to the fifteenth and the latter to the sixteenth century, had discovered Vitruvius, the Roman architect who lived in the time of Cæsar and Augustus, and his learned book *De architecturâ*. The passion for the study of antiquity fired builders as well as the rest. Serlio's *Book of Architecture* was published in French in 1545, whilst in 1547, the first translation of Vitruvius appeared ; the Roman buildings that still remained standing in Italy served as commentaries to the text. After studying the principles, builders crossed the Alps, and examined these, measured and drew them ; and then, on their return to France, published works in which they demonstrated the theory of the art. Jean Bullant's *Règle d'Architecture* appeared in 1564, and Philibert Delorme's *Architecture* in 1567. In the name of classical authorities, these new theorists formulated the ideas governing their manual craft, raising it to the dignity of a

349

reasoned art ; and those who had been hitherto obscure and empirical mechanics developed into architects—persons of a much higher social standing. Like poetry in the hands of the Pléiade, architecture became learned, and like the Pléiade, the new artists were full of disdain for the " Gothic " style of the Middle Ages. According to Philbert Delorme it was out of date, " barbarous " and had been abandoned by " all who had an inkling of real architecture." And yet they owed more to it than they knew. But less aristocratic than the poets belonging to Ronsard's circle, they consented to work for everybody, and not merely for a chosen few.

Practically speaking, the lesson taught by antiquity to French architects was not so much a sense of proportion—for all the good builders of the past, inspired by some innate, obscure, and exquisite feeling, had always displayed, in their most varied structures an admirable taste for artistic proportions—but a sense of classical symmetry. They studied the Greek orders and became acquainted with the calculations involved in the elements of antique architecture, such as columns and pilasters, pediments and metopes. They learnt all the shades of difference between Ionic, Corinthian, Tuscan and composite capitals, and they circulated among themselves drawings of Greek and Roman temples, all of which led them to feel the need of importing into their structural conceptions a regard for perfect equilibrium between the various parts and an exact correspondence in every particular. A discipline was now established. One of the most famous names among these theorists was that of Jacques Androuet, called du Cerceau.

With the exception of the mediocre church at Montargis, there are few buildings for which du Cerceau is known to have been responsible. The chief of a dynasty of architects who Androuet du worked on as late as the first thirty years of the Cerceau. seventeenth century, he was above all a writer. His *Livre d'Architecture*, and his other engraved works won him considerable fame from his own day onwards. He was born in 1512 and travelled a great deal in Italy, paying a visit to Rome and making drawings of the buildings there from 1530 to 1540. He began to publish his collections in 1545 and died in 1584. His books, in which he gives designs for building, offer a curious

350

medley of the combined influences of antiquity, the Italian Renaissance—which had long preceded the French Renaissance in its application of principles borrowed from Greece and Rome, adapting them, however, to Italian taste, conditions, and manner of life—French tradition, and a personal idiosyncrasy, which is occasionally bizarre and unpractical. The point which is particularly interesting in connexion with him is the persistence of French tradition revealed in some of his plans, which recall Louis XII's Château at Blois, and in the square plan of his mansions, based upon fifteenth-century models—the square plan which was destined to become so popular in the sixteenth and seventeenth centuries.

For as a fact, in spite of the influence of antiquity, the genius of the French nation remained true to itself ; and the proofs of this loyalty are to be found throughout the sixteenth century. The Blois of Louis XII, with its high roofs, its harmonious combination of brick and stone, its lofty chimney stacks, regular windows, and bold general effect, is reflected in the great châteaux of the Renaissance : Ancy-le-Franc, Folembray, Valery and Villers-Cotterets. The square plan, so typically French, is common to Charleval, Anet, Écouen, Bury and Saint-Maur, as well as to Ancy-le-Franc, Villers-Cotterets and Verneuil. If a seventeenth-century mansion, such as the Château de Pont in Champagne, be compared with late fifteenth- and early sixteenth-century buildings in France, such as Blois and Amboise, and with classical or Italian Renaissance buildings, their connexion with the French style of the end of the Middle Ages is at once apparent. The decoration alone shows that foreign models have been studied. In cases where the building allows of developments in the way of sculptural decoration, antique or Italian influence is found embodied in classical elements, such as Greek orders, columns, pilasters, ovoli, bucrania, &c. Mythological subjects especially abound and pagan inspiration predominates. But even here the existence of this tradition in France does not date merely from 1550 and the publication of Vitruvius ; it is anterior to this and its beginnings are lost in obscurity. We shall prove this by making a brief survey of artists and their works.

The French tradition in architecture.

These artists had the good fortune to live during an epoch when the conditions of existence rendered the confined life spent in the sombre fortresses of the fifteenth century distasteful, and when every one was replacing the frowning walls of defence characteristic of the Gothic period by the light, open façades of the new country seats. People built extensively, princes, princesses, and illustrious ladies setting the example, and spending their money freely. Catherine de' Medici was responsible for the Tuileries ; Diane de Poitiers for Anet and Chenonceaux ; and Constable Montmorency for Écouen. But the man who set the example—and the finest example—was the King when he rebuilt the Louvre.

The Renaissance château supersedes the feudal castle.

When the Emperor Charles V passed through France in 1539, Francis I, it is said, felt humiliated at being able to show him as a royal palace only the forbidding fortress of Philip Augustus, slightly improved by King Charles V, of which the Louvre at that time consisted. He made up his mind to have it pulled down and replaced by an airy, symmetrical, and agreeable edifice. It was the brilliant royal victor of Marignano who initiated the architectural art of the second half of the sixteenth century. He enlisted the services of a man of talent named **Pierre Lescot.** Pierre Lescot. Born in 1510, this Pierre Lescot was a priest, the son of a procurator-royal in the Court of Aids. He had a veritable genius for architecture and had been a draughtsman from his childhood onwards. He was extremely learned and also very rich. Amply provided with good posts, for he was made Chaplain-in-Ordinary to the King, Abbot of Clermont in the diocese of Laval, Canon of Notre-Dame de Paris, and Seigneur of Clagny at Versailles, he practised architecture for love of the art—it was the passion of his life. Francis I recognized his worth, and on August 2, 1546, as we know from the letters-patent which are still in existence, he asked him " to build and construct in our castle of the Louvre a large block of dwelling-rooms on the site of the present great hall "— that is to say, that part of the Louvre now occupied by the Hall of the Caryatides and the Salle Lacaze above it. We see that Francis I's idea was somewhat restricted, and it is not known how much work Lescot carried out during the reign of

352

that monarch; probably very little. But Henry II extended
Henry II's   his favour to the architect; and on April 14, 1547,
Louvre.   as soon as he succeeded to the throne, he confirmed the order given by his father. Lescot, however, proposed to Henry II—who accepted his suggestions—a plan of
construction conceived on a far grander scale, which was afterwards carried out, at least in so far as the dimensions were
concerned. The architect set to work and remained attached
to the Louvre till the day of his death in 1578. He enjoyed
a privileged position, being entirely independent of the Superintendent of Public Buildings, making his own arrangements
with the workmen, contractors, and artists, and directing everything alone. He continued his work until 1568, when, owing
to political events, building operations were suspended for ten
years. They were begun again in 1580–1581 under the direction
of Baptiste Androuet du Cerceau. Henry II was responsible
for the west wing of the Louvre, that is to say the part containing the Hall of the Caryatides, and also the corner pavilion
on the side facing the Seine (the Pavillon du Roi) and the first
block of the south wing at right angles to it along the quay.
Charles IX continued this wing as far as about the middle of the
present façade; and this was all that was done during the sixteenth century round the square court of the Louvre. After a
peaceful life, during which he was extolled by his contemporaries,
beloved by the poets, particularly by Ronsard who sang his
glory, and by the men of letters whose society he frequented,
Pierre Lescot died in September, 1578, in his little house in the
cloisters of Notre-Dame, to which his position as canon entitled
him, and was buried in one of the cathedral chapels. He does
not seem to have built or desired to build much beyond the
Louvre.

Lescot may be regarded as the earliest of the great French
architects, and by singular good fortune, it fell to him to design
not only the greatest of French palaces, but also the most
magnificent ever built in France. It is obvious that he was
not responsible for much of the later work. The part that may
certainly be attributed to him is the idea of the great square
court, and the western façades in that court.

Few buildings give an impression of more consummate

beauty than Pierre Lescot's façade of the Louvre overlooking the court. No other building has attained such a happy perfection of harmonious proportion, elegance, nobility, balance, delicate taste, and exact fitness in the details contributing to the general effect. It is neither Greek, Roman, nor Italian, but absolutely French. The decorative sculpture is calculated to support and emphasize the lines of the architecture, and is neither too inconspicuous nor too aggressive, but singularly right and harmonious. The external façade is simpler and is built on to the old and enormously thick wall of the Louvre of Philip Augustus, which was preserved. It rose above the moat, and with its comparatively unornamented windows, high roofs and chimney-stacks, bears a strong resemblance to the traditional French style found at Ancy-le-Franc—which is said to be a little earlier than the Louvre—and at Amboise. The new features introduced on the internal façade of the Louvre, for which Lescot, it is constantly asserted, found his inspiration in classical or Italian models, are the engaged Corinthian columns supporting semicircular arches separated by niches for statues. It is true that these details are frequently found in Italian Renaissance buildings, but in France Lescot merely applied principles that were already well known, and had been slowly penetrating into the country for some years past. The semicircular arches had previously been used in the Château de Madrid, whilst engaged Corinthian pilasters, niches for statues, and friezes were already in existence at Blois and even, as regards certain of these details, at Amboise. Ancy-le-Franc, moreover, is such a striking example of the application of the same principles that, unless we are to accuse him of plagiarism, we may suppose that Lescot was the architect in this case also. In short, Lescot made use of elements to which the French were already accustomed; his originality consists in skilful, remarkable architectural effect. Tradition, learning, and inspiration were all combined in his case and guided by an **Charles IX's additions to the Louvre.** unfailing artistic instinct. The whole school of French architecture of the period turned to the same sources of inspiration. In 1566 Charles IX had the ground floor of the small gallery built—the Galerie d'Apollon—and the lower storey of the great gallery on the river

354

side ; these buildings, though they may not perhaps have been designed by Lescot, preserved the same decorative qualities as the rest of the Louvre. In 1572 the work was stopped by the Massacre of Saint Bartholomew ; but Henry IV continued it once more on his return to Paris in 1594. He carried the gallery along the river as far as the Tuileries, and added to it an entresol or mezzanine, and a first storey, which he made into a great gallery similar to the additional storey he built over the smaller gallery. His architects, even if they did not follow Lescot's designs, were at all events governed by the same ideas.

The other great architects of the second half of the sixteenth century, though very different in character to Lescot, yet present us with the same fundamental features. After Lescot one of the most celebrated was Philibert Delorme.

He too was a priest, and was born in the Lyons district about 1515. He was the son of a master of the works, and
Philibert travelled in Italy where he made a great many
Delorme. drawings. On his return to France, Cardinal du Bellay took an interest in him, and commissioned him to build the Château de Saint-Maur, which attracted much attention. In 1548 Diane de Poitiers entrusted him with the building of Anet, a sumptuous mansion to which Delorme devoted his whole genius, looking upon it as his masterpiece. Of the great square of buildings that he raised, barely one wing and the chapel are still in existence. Henry II was greatly interested in Anet, and took a fancy to the architect, whom he appointed "counsellor and architect to the King," and Superintendent of Buildings—in order to ensure for him the obedience of contractors—and Chaplain-in-Ordinary. He also made him a royal treasurer, and overwhelmed him with abbeys—the Abbeys of Saint Barthélemy-lès-Noyon, of Ivry in the diocese of Évreux, and of Saint Serge-lès-Angers, and nominated him like Lescot, a Canon of Paris. In 1564 Catherine de' Medici asked him to construct the palace she was planning to have built at a short distance from the Louvre—the Tuileries. Ever since the death of Henry II she had disliked Les Tournelles, and had been looking out for some other place of abode. Delorme made a colossal plan for her—a rectangular structure 269 metres wide

and 166 metres deep, containing five inner courts and various amphitheatres. Catherine, however, was destined only to raise a part of the half of the façade which faced west, and a stable. Delorme died in 1570 without having finished even that portion of his façade, and Jean Bullant, who took his place, substituted his own ideas for those of his predecessor. In 1572, after the Massacre of Saint Bartholomew, his work too was stopped.

Philibert Delorme was responsible for numerous buildings. A great many of his works are unknown to us, and those which are acknowledged to be his, have either been destroyed or very much modified. But he published a *Traité d'Architecture* and a work entitled *Nouvelles inventions pour bien bâtir*, which enable us to form some appreciation of his character. He was a learned man, a mathematician who took a delight in difficult problems and their solution by means of calculations. He made a great advance in the technique of his art, more especially in stereotomy or the cutting of stone. But in his case science proved detrimental to inspiration. When he tried to be majestic he became heavy. He did not possess Pierre Lescot's purity of style nor the more advanced science of Jean Bullant. His laboured calculations are too obvious. When he gives free play to his imagination, as he does in some of the designs in his book on architecture, he produces odd results—an artificial mixture of classical, Italian, and French art. The chapel he built at Anet is almost Italian in style, and the front of this building, which has been preserved in the École des Beaux Arts, in Paris, and consists of three storeys, each of a different order, Doric, Ionic, and Corinthian, passing from the heaviest to the most slender form of construction, is an example of his mathematical methods. The tomb of Francis I at Saint-Denis, however, which was designed by him, and is a sort of Roman triumphal arch of three divisions, supporting the kneeling figures of the King and Queen, whilst below lie the two princes sculptured with an almost Gothic realism, and surrounded by equally realistic battle scenes, is a harmonious and graceful monument. Philibert Delorme had a very violent temper, and notwithstanding the fact that he was a canon, his morality was of a somewhat dubious quality. He quarrelled with a great many people and after the death of Henry II, even fell into disgrace from which he was rescued by the favour of Catherine de' Medici.

His successor, Jean Bullant, was born at Écouen in 1510. It was indeed a brilliant generation which first saw the light **Jean Bullant.** between 1510 and 1515, and included so many illustrious names. Like all the rest, he paid his visit to Rome and Italy, which now formed the indispensable apprenticeship for every artistic career. On his return to Écouen, the Constable, Anne de Montmorency, who lived there, attached him to his service. When the Constable was in disgrace, he conceived the idea of rebuilding his castle and charged the young architect with the task. The construction of Écouen, which is still standing, made · Jean Bullant's reputation. Montmorency, who returned to favour during the reign of Henry II, brought his architect to Court, and recommended him to the King; and it was through the Constable's influence that Bullant was appointed Controller of Crown Buildings in 1557. Like Delorme he subsequently seems to have suffered an eclipse. He was, perhaps, disgraced. At all events he went into retirement, when he seized the opportunity to publish two books —his *Recueil d'horlogiographie* in 1561 and his *Règle generale d'architecture* in 1568. The latter work proves that Bullant was a learned mathematician, who studied all the elements of his art, and especially the Greek orders, columns and capitals, in accordance with precise calculations and on scientific principles. He was almost more of an engineer than an architect, and might have said with Philibert Delorme that he was " fascinated by those beautiful inventions that may be discovered by means of mathematics." He studied Vitruvius thoroughly, and was certainly influenced by antiquity, if it be really true that on one of the façades of Écouen he reproduced an arrangement of the Temple of Jupiter Stator at Rome. In 1570, on the death of Philibert Delorme, Catherine de' Medici took him into her service and commissioned him to carry on the building of the Tuileries. But he finished only one pavilion in it and did not do any further work on the palace. He died in the same year as Lescot. His name is exceedingly well known, though his work is meagre enough. He is best known to us by his books. Of the three architects whom we have just been considering, Bullant was the most learned, whilst Lescot was the greatest artist.

Learning and tradition, the two associated terms which we have just discussed in connexion with architecture, are also **Sculpture.**   to be found as conjoined elements in other manifestations of that sixteenth century which was so highly endowed with a sense of the beautiful. Let us now note their effect upon sculpture, a branch of art which may be summed up in two names : Jean Goujon and Germain Pilon.

There are few artists so famous as Jean Goujon about whose lives so little is known. He is believed to have been a **Jean Goujon.**   native of Normandy, though there is no proof of this fact. The accounts of the Cathedral of Rouen, in which his name is mentioned for the first time in 1540–1541, in connexion with the columns supporting the organ in the church of Saint Maclou, which were made by him, as well as the doors of that building, describe him modestly as a " stone-cutter and mason." He carved the statue on the tomb of Georges d'Amboise in Rouen Cathedral. In 1543 we find him in Paris carving the rood-screen of Saint-Germain-l'Auxerrois under the directions of Pierre Lescot. From that moment he leapt into fame. The *Epitome* of Vitruvius which was printed at Toulouse in 1556, calls him a " sculptor of great repute," and Ronsard mentions him in his verses. He was called upon to collaborate in all the great works of the period. Jean Bullant employed him at Écouen in 1544 ; Philibert Delorme at Anet in 1553, and Pierre Lescot on the Fountain of the Holy Innocents and above all at the Louvre from 1550 onwards. He was a prodigious worker, but a great many of his productions have disappeared. The date of his death is unknown. It probably took place about 1565, and not during the Massacre of Saint Bartholomew, for it is by no means certain that he was a Protestant. The sculptural works by him which still survive are very remarkable : The *Diana* from the Château d'Anet, now in the Louvre, the Fountain of the Holy Innocents, the sculptures of the Louvre palace on Pierre Lescot's façade, the vaulting of Henry II's staircase and the Caryatides in the great hall of that name. These Caryatides, which were modelled more or less on descriptions in Vitruvius, and the rich store

358

of mythology, which provides the subjects of his works, gods and goddesses, fauns, nymphs, dolphins, tritons and naiads, prove that Goujon was certainly a pupil of antiquity, though it is probable that he may have gone to antiquity by way of the Italian Renaissance. But how truly French he is in his grace, his delicacy, his discreet and sterling elegance ! Faithful to truth rather than to realism, he fashioned the women of his day, who are at once recognizable, and upon whom he bestowed the supple lines so characteristic of his genius. Lescot probably played some part in designing the sculptural decoration of the façade of the Louvre, but Goujon's share in it was nevertheless considerable, and reveals a nice instinct for ornamentation by means of sculpture, the consummate tact and taste of the great artist, and his skill in adapting himself to certain prescribed conditions in order to produce a harmonious whole.

Germain Pilon remained more frankly true to realistic traditions. He was a Parisian workman and was born in 1535. **Germain Pilon.** His talent placed him above all rivalry. He was the favourite sculptor of Charles IX, who gave him a studio in the Hôtel de Nesle. Commissions poured in upon him and Catherine de' Medici in particular secured his services for the Valois chapel, a large round building with two tiers of columns, which, in imitation of the Medici chapel in Florence, the Queen built against the south transept of the church of Saint-Denis, as a sanctuary for the tombs of the Valois. It was never finished, however, and has since been pulled down. It was a building almost purely Italian in style, in the construction of which Lescot, Bullant, and du Cerceau all took part under various conditions. Pilon was entrusted with the tomb of Henry II, which is still in existence, and for which, between the years of 1565 and 1583, he certainly made the kneeling figures of the King and Queen, clad in their royal robes, the recumbent bodies of the deceased, and the four bronze figures at the corners of the monument, Faith, Temperance, Prudence, and Justice, allegorical representations in the antique manner. But, turning from this, how consummate is the realism with which he portrays the dead bodies of the princes, how crude and relentless is the rendering, yet how skilful and artistic ; with what precision too, with what strict and minute observance of truth is the modelling of the royal costume carried out ! If in the famous Three Graces made by him for the shrine designed to contain the heart of Henry III, the idealism so dear to Greece and the Italian Renaissance is more apparent, the statues of Birague and his wife carved for their tomb reveal, on the contrary, the sense of life in all its vigour. And what shall we say of the busts, and more especially the medallions, by Germain Pilon, representing all the Valois Kings, marvels of admirable precision, of startling vitality, and of elegant art. He was one of the most remarkable artists France has produced.

A man who is far less well known, but deserves greater recognition than he has received is Pierre Bontemps, who carved the bas-reliefs on the tomb of Francis I at Saint Denis, a work **Pierre** which is excellent in every respect, and in which **Bontemps.** the correctness of detail in the battle-scenes, the costumes, the movements and gestures is consummate in its realism, though it is not in the somewhat brutal style of the Middle Ages, but has a supple and orderly ease and freedom. Pierre Bontemps is neither Roman nor Italian. Almost nothing was known about him until Monsieur M. Roy discovered some references to his work.

If sculpture is well represented in the second half of the sixteenth century—and we have not even mentioned the **Painting.** infinite number of decorative details, bas-reliefs, &c., which are to be found on all the buildings, revealing the talent of more than one unknown artist—painting on the other hand makes but a scanty show. Whether because few were produced or because many were destroyed, France is very poor in pictures of this period. Those that survive are not signed. But such as they are, they are closely allied to the chalk drawings of the period, which on the other hand, are extremely numerous, and are chiefly portraits, unfortunately also unsigned. A few names of artists are recorded—the two Jean Cousins, for example. But the majority of the works attributed to them are by no means indubitable, and, as a matter of fact, almost nothing is known about them. The **The Clouets.** most famous of all was François Clouet surnamed Janet. François Clouet was probably born about 1520 and died in 1572. He was the son of Jean Clouet, painter to

360

Francis I. He had a great vogue, received the honorary title of groom of the chamber to the King, and was attached to the courts of Henry II, Francis II and Charles IX. He made numerous portraits of these monarchs as well as of other members of the royal family, and the lords and great men of the realm. A considerable number of chalk drawings by him have been preserved, more especially those carried out in three colours. It is true that he founded a school—or that he followed a fashion ; for chalk drawings of this kind and period are very numerous. It is not easy to say which of these are to be attributed to him and which to his imitators. These portraits are remarkable for sincerity and accuracy. They are very French, often charming in their vivacity, and sometimes extraordinarily forcible. Their simplicity and realism would link them with the old Gothic school did not a certain fine sobriety and discreet elegance temper all that was uncouth in the old style.

To this school belongs Corneille de Lyon, who also drew portraits of the same type as Clouet. But his works are even **Corneille de Lyon.** more difficult to identify, although experts believe they can distinguish the difference in style between the two. The qualities they possess, however, are identical, and are common to all the artists who produced portraits of this nature. They form an unrivalled gallery, both from the point of view of portraiture and of art, and illustrate the history of the sixteenth century in a manner which few other centuries can parallel.

It would be interesting to have more information than we actually possess about an art that flourished in the sixteenth **Tapestry.** century, the art of tapestry-making. We have already seen how indispensable Catherine de' Medici and other great personages considered it, to have not only numerous but exceedingly beautiful specimens of tapestry in their houses. The walls were covered with these tapestries, which were frequently changed in order to vary the look of the rooms. They were chiefly foreign products woven for the most part in Flanders, at Brussels, Valenciennes, Tournay, Ghent and Bruges. Francis I made numerous purchases in these districts and bought amongst others, a " grand history of Scipio " consisting of twenty-two pieces. It cost 40,000 livres and Catherine de' Medici had it brought in 1565 to the Conferences at Bayonne, where it was much admired. These Flemish hangings depicted either subjects reproduced from Italian works of art, such as the pictures of Giulio Romano and Raphael, or scenes from real life such as hunting-parties, landscapes, and battles of the day. The making of tapestry, which was an extremely prosperous industry in France during the fourteenth and fifteenth centuries, was less so at the beginning of the sixteenth. The Kings tried to revive it. Francis I had a factory installed at Fontainebleau, and Henry II followed his example in Paris. It was in this Parisian factory that the famous tapestry belonging to Catherine de' Medici, called the Artemis tapestry, was woven about 1570. There was also a factory at Tours. The French sixteenth-century tapestries are extremely decorative, and are conspicuous for their variety of tones blended into a harmonious whole, as well as for their great wealth of colour; their mythological subjects, gods and goddesses, classical stories with chariots and temples, and borders displaying arabesques in the Italian style, their realistic subjects, balls of the period, receptions, fêtes, pastoral scenes, and hunting-parties containing fairly faithful portraits, also show the influence of the two-fold inspiration that dominated the art of the period.

The enamel work of the sixteenth century won a greater reputation. Limoges was the centre of production for these **Enamels.** famous and beautiful works of art, of which France has preserved a fair number of specimens. This town possessed a class of skilful and tasteful craftsmen, who carried on the profession from father to son—the Courteys, the Reymonds, and the Pénicauds. The best known of them all was Léonard Limousin, upon whom the Kings conferred the title of groom of the chamber and of " painter-in-ordinary and enameller to the King." The Galerie d'Apollon in the Louvre exhibits samples of his work, enamels of a truly admirable purity and evenness of tone. In this case again, we find the customary dual range of subjects—mythological and classical scenes, heroes from Plutarch, and Olympian deities against backgrounds borrowed from Roman buildings, side by side

362

with contemporary portraits of historical personages and others. The latter are less supple than those of Clouet and of his school, and less vital, though they are treated with a realistic attention to correct detail. About one hundred and thirty enamel portraits of his contemporaries by Léonard Limousin are still in existence.

A great deal of stained glass was made during the Renaissance in France, much of which has been preserved. It is **Stained glass.** regarded as inferior to that produced in preceding periods by reason of its profusion of details and figures, which from the distance gives an impression of confusion, and the predominance or too frequent use of white, which blurs and confuses the general effect. These stained glass windows, however, when taken in detail, are remarkable for the beauty of their gradations of colour, their varied and exact drawing, and their great wealth of tones, which are more numerous than before, though, given the style, this is not necessarily a sign of progress. Some of the colours too are extremely beautiful. The subjects are either religious when used in churches, or, as in the case of the set of grisaille windows at Écouen representing the story of Psyche from designs by Michael Coxcie, they show the influence of prevalent fashion.

And finally, in this all too rapid sketch of the arts under the House of Valois, some mention must be made of music. The **Music.** people of the sixteenth century were extremely fond of music and employed it in every form, both grave and gay—the church music of the Catholics, the psalm tunes of the Protestants, the dance and ballet tunes of Court festivities, and the songs of the people. The Pléiade, as we have seen, considered that poetry would gain by being associated with music, and the Académie du Palais was founded with the object of organising this association. Marot made a verse translation of the Psalms in order that they might be set to music. Under the influence of Catherine de' Medici, who gave regular concerts several times a week, her sons, and more especially Charles IX, developed a liking for music. Their favourite form of the art was dance-music. They danced a great deal, in ironic contrast with the tragic nature of the times in which they lived. These sixteenth-century dances, the pavane and other slow and stately measures, in which the couples had to perform the various evolutions with grace, suppleness, and elegance, constituted a delicate art which required distinction in the execution. The music for them was by turns soft and slow or fast and lively—varied, in short. A certain refined form of dancing—the ballet—had a great vogue at the end of the sixteenth century—a vogue which lasted on into the next century. Attempts had already been made in Italy to produce pastoral plays the text of which was interspersed with songs. The ballet is a sort of opera representing a certain theme developed by a series of scenes that are sung, acted, or danced. The most celebrated of these ballets was the one produced by Balthazard Beaujoyeux in 1581, in honour of the marriage of the Duke of Joyeuse, and called " The Queen's Comic Ballet." From this time forward the French Kings of the end of the sixteenth and the beginning of the seventeenth century had a ballet performed every Shrove-tide, an extremely complicated, gorgeous, and expensive entertainment.

Balthazard Beaujoyeux was an Italian whose real name was Baldassarini ; but he lived for a long time in France. **Goudimel.** As a matter of fact, the great French musicians of the sixteenth century were to a certain extent foreigners. Orlando de Lassus and Willaert were Flemish, whilst Goudimel was a native of Franche-Comté, a province which at that time was Spanish. He may, however, be regarded as a Frenchman, and he was certainly a very great musician. He was a Protestant, or suspected of Protestantism, for he was killed at Lyons during the Massacre of Saint Bartholomew in 1572. He had lived in Rome and had kept a school there which produced Palestrina. His masses, motets, and psalm tunes— it was he who wrote the chants for Marot's verses—are remarkable for the purity of their harmony. But in the domain of church music the transformation was destined to come from Italy and the genius of Palestrina, whose Mass of Pope Marcellus dates from 1565. Fugue and counterpoint were the two great elements in the method of this new school ; whilst the writers of songs, like Costeley and Orlando de Lassus, remained true to free and spontaneous inspiration with its original and varied forms. And thus in music as in all the

364

other arts of the sixteenth century we find a constant dualism —learned and studied forms side by side with the free and natural play of instinctive talent.

SOURCES. *Lettres de Catherine de Médicis*, ed. La Ferrière and Baguenault de Puchesse ; de Thou, *Histoire universelle*, 1734 ; Et. Pasquier, *Recherches de la France*, 1561 ; Brantôme, *Œuvres completes*, ed. Lalanne ; Tommaseo, *Relations des ambassadeurs vénitiens*, 1838 ; Alberi, *Relazioni degli ambasciatori Veneti al senato*, 1839 ; A. du Cerceau, *Les plus excellens bastimens de France*, 1576 ; *Les toilettes d'Eléonore d'Autriche* (in *Revue des Sociétés savantes des départements*, 1876) ; de Montégut, *Inventaire des bijoux de Jeanne de Bourdeille dame de Sainte-Aulaire en 1595*, 1881 ; E. Bonnafé, *Inventaire des meubles de Catherine de Medicis en 1589*, 1874 ; *Lettres et devis de Philibert Delorme relatifs à la construction du château de Chenonceaux*, by Chevalier, 1864.

WORKS. H. Lemonnier, *Les origines de l'art classique en France au XVIᵉ siècle* (in *Revue universitaire*, 1895) ; Petit de Julleville, *Histoire de la langue et de la littérature françaises*, vol. iii, 1897 ; Darmesteter and Hatzfeld, *Le XVI siècle en France*, 1883 ; E. Bourciez, *Les moeurs polies et la littérature de cour sous Henri II*, 1886 ; E. Frémy, *L'Académie des derniers Valois*, 1887 ; Glasson, *Histoire du droit et des institutions de la France*, vol. viii, 1903 ; Palustre, *L'Architecture de la Renaissance*, 1860 ; and *La Renaissance en France*, 1879–1885 ; Geymüller, *Geschichte der Baukunst der Renaissance in Frankreich*, 1896 ; A. Berty, *Les grands architects de la Renaissance*, 1860 ; and *Topographie historique du vieux Paris, le Louvre et les Tuileries*, 1866 ; Louis Batiffol, *Le Louvre et les plans de Lescot* (*Gazette des Beaux-Arts*, 1910) ; F. Bournon, *Blois, Chambord et les châteaux du Blésois*, 1908 ; Gonse, *La Sculpture française depuis le XIVᵉ siècle*, 1895 ; H. Bouchot, *Les Clouet et Corneille de Lyon*, 1892 ; E. Moreau-Nélaton, *Les Clouet, peintres officiels des rois de France*, 1908 ; and *Les frères du Monstier, peintres de la reine Catherine de Médicis*, 1908 ; J. Guiffrey, *Histoire de la tapisserie*, 1886 ; L. Boudry and E. Lachenaud *Léonard Limousin*, 1897 ; O. Merson, *Les Vitraux*, 1889 ; H. Expert, *Les maîtres musiciens de la Renaissance française*, 1894 ; E. Lavisse, *Histoire de France* (the chapters on the Renaissance written by H. Lemonnier) ; M. Roy, *Le sculpteur Pierre Bontemps*, 1911 ; and, *Les deux Jean Cousin*, 1909.

CHAPTER X

THE KINGDOM OF FRANCE ABOUT 1600

Impression of prosperity produced by France upon foreign visitors. The kingdom had no written constitution but only traditional customs. The theory of the absolute power of the King. The dense and complex growth of national administration, according to Figon. The people surrounding the King : the King's councils, the Chancellor of France, the Superintendent of Finances, the Secretaries of State. The countless multitude of royal officials in the provinces. Judicial officers : the Grand Council, the Parliaments, bailiffs and seneschals, presidial courts, inferior royal judges and seignorial judges ; special jurisdictions. The finance officials ; system of raising the taxes ; Savings Department (*L'Épargne*) in Paris : the financial division of France into generalities, elections and parishes ; the finance agents ; the numerous and complicated taxes paid by the people ; the budget of 1600. The expenditure ; strictness with which the public accounts were kept ; the Exchequer Court. The administration ; governors of provinces and local governors. Municipalities. The Army and Navy ; the French people in 1600 and their three Estates—the Clergy, the Nobility, and the Third Estate.

THE France of the reign of Henry IV was, as far as extent of domain was concerned, pretty much the same as the France of to-day, save that its somewhat sinuous frontier line left in the hands of foreigners Artois, Cambrésis, the Duchy of Bar, Lorraine—with the exception tion of the enclaves of Metz, Toul and Verdun, of prosperity and the small territory surrounding these places produced by —the whole of Franche-Comté, Savoy, the county France on of Nice, Comtat-Venaissin and Roussillon. In foreign spite of the turmoil of the civil wars and the visitors. results they left behind them, she impressed strangers who visited the country as a "rich and powerful" land. She had a large population, the exact figures of which, however,

366

are not known. Michel Suriano estimated the inhabitants of Paris at 500,000; Davila at 800,000. Travellers remarked that the number of densely populated towns was very large, and that the villages were close together and contained a considerable number of inhabitants. " The multitude of people is everywhere so great," wrote a certain visitor to France, " and the towns and country places so well populated, that the ground is constantly under cultivation, and every trade and mechanical art is well supplied." And, indeed, if the books of a country scrivener or notary of the end of the sixteenth century are consulted, the certificates of the various transactions show that the land was most minutely parcelled out and apportioned. There was scarcely a single " working tradesman " or " manual labourer " who did not possess his own plot of ground and enclosure, together with a house of two or three gables thatched or tiled, a courtyard, a little back garden and a certain amount of arable land, an acre, a rood or two. He paid quit-rent, ground-rent, and mutation fines, all signs of the feudal tenure of his land and proofs that it was held in fief or from a lord of the manor. But, apart from this, a peasant owned and cultivated his property in precisely the same way as the French peasant of to-day. He worked hard and was thrifty, and thus managed to live easily enough.

Travellers such as Erpenius, Jodocus Sincerus, Scamberg, Abraham Golnitz, Goffridus Hegenitius and others, have described the things that constituted the wealth of France. Palma Cayet before them had already pointed out that the country abounded in " corn, wine, oil, fruit, vegetables, and wood, in addition to a vast and luxuriant supply of food for cattle and horses." Corn was produced in sufficient quantities to allow of its exportation. Except in Brittany, Normandy and Picardy, which were cider-drinking provinces, wine was produced throughout the country. The vintages of Argenteuil and Suresnes, though they did not rise much above mediocrity, were known to the Parisians. The wines, however, that were most appreciated were the white wines of Anjou, of Graves at Bordeaux, of Gaillac and of Rabastens; red Burgundy, quantities of which were sent to Paris; and muscatel from Frontignan, which was a special favourite. The export of wine to England and Germany was a great source of revenue, as was also the export of salt. The salt of Languedoc and Saintonge was famous, and Flemish and Dutch boats used to embark cargoes of it all along the coasts of Provence and Poitou. Provence and Languedoc produced hemp, flax, and oil, Berry fine wool, as did also Normandy, where excellent cloth was made. The fruit grown in the southern provinces, and especially in Provence, was famous, though not so celebrated as woad, a plant used for dyeing, which formed the wealth more especially of Languedoc. As many as 200,000 bales of woad were exported annually from Bordeaux. The cultivation of silkworms and mulberries became extensive from the time of Henry IV onwards. Almost everywhere pasturage was fat and good, and large stocks of cattle were reared. Horse breeding was also carried on throughout the kingdom, though the horses were not so strong as those produced in Germany, and heavy cart and carriage horses used to be imported from that country. Mules from Auvergne and Gévaudan were sold to Spain. Milk, butter, and cheese were articles of daily consumption. Louis XIII was fond of Pont l'Évêque cheese, and the officers of his Swiss guard introduced him to the " little Swiss " cheeses. Capons, chickens, and fowls of all kinds filled the poultry-yards. There was not a peasant who did not possess " his pig-sty " or a wood that did not abound in " hares, rabbits, partridges and field-fares " for the sportsmen. Slate was quarried in Anjou and marble in Languedoc ; there were iron mines in Auvergne, coal in the south, and mineral water at Pougues, Val, Vichy, and Balaruc. Trade was extremely brisk. In short France was one of the first countries in Europe to exploit all the elements of agricultural and mineral wealth she possessed, and produced earlier than the rest the average density of population corresponding to her public fortune. She was rich; " the sources of her wealth," said one traveller, " are inexhaustible."

For the government and administration of this great and hard-working country, there was no written constitution or theoretical organization. There were merely traditional ideas, old established institutions, and habits and customs so strong that they were called laws. The central idea of this

368

political constitution based upon " custom," was that of the " absolute sovereign " power of the King.

"Our public state of France," wrote a certain jurist at the beginning of the seventeenth century, "is royal, inasmuch The King's as in the foremost place stands the King, the absolute power. sole sovereign lord, at the head of all." "The King," said another, " is the chief, the source and foundation of all justice and government; " which means that in the person of the King alone all judicial and administrative power was vested, with the result that anyone in the kingdom exercising a part of one or other of his functions, did so merely as a delegate or representative of the monarch, who could resume his rights at any moment. This was the legal theory in its simplest form. But in practice, as it was impossible for the King to do everything and be everywhere at once, he delegated the charge of acting for him to agents whom he appointed to the various functions or "offices," and who were accordingly called, not functionaries but " officers "—" the officers of the King," as they were termed. Five attributes of his power, however, the King never delegated to anyone. These were: the making of laws, the creation of new offices, decisions of peace and war, the right of being the final judge in all judicial matters, and the privilege of coining money. Anybody who dared to encroach upon the King's prerogative in these matters was guilty of high treason. The King made the laws. The inferior authorities could frame regulations "to meet minor contingencies," as the King was not in a position to take cognizance of local details. But these regulations were regarded as provisional "under the good pleasure of his Majesty," and were valid only within the jurisdiction of the authority who promulgated them. In everything and for everything the King was supreme and decided as he thought fit. "For this is our good will and pleasure " was the formula he used in the name of the right conferred upon him by God.

This theory of the royal power did not escape vigorous attacks during the civil wars of the sixteenth century; first, in practice by the revolutionaries; secondly, in law by the theorists. After the Massacre of Saint Bartholomew, the

2 A

question was raised as to whether obedience was due to a King who had become a tyrant. The position of heir-presumptive to the throne enjoyed by the Protestant King Henry of Navarre, raised the problem as to whether the country had not the right to choose another sovereign by means of the States-General, and consequently whether this assembly were not superior to the King. This latter idea was not new. It had been brought forward by the Cabochiens under Charles VI, and also at the meeting of the States in 1484. In refusing to obey the King, first the Protestants and then the Leaguers had given it great strength and actuality. It seemed to be admitted that the kingship was originally based upon the will of the people, and that if a monarch abused his rights he could be deprived of them. From this observation on particular cases it was easy to pass to the very principle of royalty itself, and certain publicists made a vigorous attack upon the monarchical idea. How could millions of men, exclaimed La Boétie, consent to submit, "to one single mannikin, frequently the most cowardly and effeminate person of the nation!" "Even the animals," he continued, "if men did not deliberately ignore their cry, called out to them: 'Long live liberty!'" The movement, however, was premature. For, in reality, under the spell of the wit and ability, the good humour, firmness, prudence and skill of Henry IV, public opinion grew calmer, and settled down at the end of the century into the traditional channels. The theory of royal authority was as clearly defined in 1600 as it had ever been, and in the writings of jurists and the minds of contemporaries, the King remained the supreme pinnacle and keystone of the social organism.

At all events this was so in theory, though in practice it was different. Under Henry IV the absolute rule of the King was held in check by a large agglomeration of passive forces : regularly constituted bodies, traditional rules, old established customs, provincial or municipal privileges, administrative usages, all of them extremely ancient institutions, that had gained strength during the preceding political anarchy, and had they not been broken by Richelieu and Louis XIV with the tacit concurrence of public opinion, would have ensured a general régime of great variety and vitality.

370

We are leaving the States-General out of account. Henry IV, who mistrusted them, refrained from convoking them. Legally **The States-General.** the representatives of the three Estates of the realm —the Clergy, the Nobility, and the third Estate, who were elected at the command of the provosts and *viguiers** on the promulgation of a royal edict of convocation sent to the Parliaments and transmitted by the bailiffs and seneschals, and thence to the provosts—only met for the purpose of presenting their grievances to the King in the form of written memoranda. They had, however, developed other pretensions, which were too menacing. Nor do we refer to the vague and oft-repeated appeal to the "fundamental laws of the realm," implying a restriction of the " full power and authority of the King." Upon strict scrutiny these words point only to three or four uncertain traditions—the so-called Salic Law, reduced to the limitation of the succession to the throne to male heirs only ; the inalienability of the kingdom ; and the injunction that the King must be a Catholic. It was by trammels other than these that the absolute power of the Crown was limited, " by reason of the imbecility of the counsel, government, and prudence of a single man," as the jurist La Roche-Flavin said. His book, incidentally, was condemned. This same La Roche-Flavin, in his *Treize livres des Parlements de France,* explains that the Parliaments were instituted " in the form of senates to maintain law and justice in full force " and that, " no edicts or ordinances were valid or had the right to demand obedience, or rather to be regarded as edicts or ordinances at all, unless they were ratified by the sovereign courts and by the free deliberations of the same." If a royal edict were unseemly, remonstrances must be addressed to the King until he consented to withdraw it. And thus in common with many other magistrates, La Roche-Flavin wished to make the Parliaments play the predominant part in the constitution. But if as a matter of fact remonstrance and opposition on the part of these bodies succeeded on more than one occasion in checking the omnipotence of the Crown, Henry IV found means, more especially in the registration of the Edict of Nantes, to impose his decision

* A judge who in Provence and Languedoc performed the duties fulfilled by a provost in other provinces. (Tr.)

and to vindicate his strict right to be supreme. The will of the King was law and his word a decree. The Parliaments, by condemning La Roche's book, implicitly condemned the theories it contained. There is no sort of principle to be found in the public law of the time implying that "the monarchy of France was not absolute." If it was absolute only in theory, this was due to the fact that passive forces were in practice more powerful than the law. These forces were represented by the entire organization of the kingdom, its central, judicial, financial, provincial and local institutions.

Charles de Figon, wishing to give some idea of the organization of France in his day, placed on the title-page of his book Figon's symbol *Discours des offices de France,* which was published of the tree. in 1579, the picture of a great tree springing from the soil. This represents the King rising aloft by means of the trunk, which is the Chancellor; dividing off into two main branches, the Parliament and the Court of the Exchequer; and then into other smaller ones—the treasurers of the country, heads of the finance departments, the Court of Aids, the Mint, the finance stewards—and the whole once more subdivided and shooting out tiny branches which are interlaced and interwoven and grafted one upon the other, the total giving a complete picture of a bushy and complicated tree. The simile is a fairly accurate one. For during the course of centuries the various institutions of France sprang up in this way, without any preconceived order, in accordance with the necessities and demands of the moment, each branch developing on its own account from a simple bud, some of them withering up to a certain extent but never altogether disappearing, the whole sprouting in picturesque confusion involving perpetual conflicts as to scope and functions.

In the King's immediate neighbourhood were his Majesty's councils, calculated to make the soil about his roots more firm State Councils. and stable. These furnish the first check upon his absolutism. The King decided nothing without asking the "advice of our Council." This was a sensible restriction, inasmuch as affairs of State were so weighty that the King needed all the enlightenment to be gained from men of experience. The King, it is true, had the power to over-rule the advice of his Council, more especially with regard to decisions he had really at heart, but during the course of each day he would refer to it for guidance. In so many cases, the old administrators, who had a fundamental knowledge of the state and its concerns—men like Villeroy, Brulart, and Bellièvre—were capable of supplying just and reasonable appreciations. Who were the members of the King's chief Council? In theory it was composed of princes of the blood, cardinals, dukes, grand officers of the Crown and Secretaries of State—a crowd of people. But in practice only those men were commanded to attend in whose judgment the King had confidence, the men who administered the affairs of State—the Chancellor, the Superintendent of Finance, and the Secretaries of State. The King summoned them to his cabinet in the morning, or] at] any other time of day, when he would have the letters he had received read aloud and discuss them with his advisers, listening to their opinions, and deciding upon the replies to be sent. And frequently enough he merely assented to some solution proposed by them. This was the Council of State, the King's real Council, the one that controlled the national policy. In addition to this there was another which dealt with minor questions connected with the administration, such as appeals to the King, who was the supreme judge in the realm, matters of dispute and details which could only be settled by the so-called decree of the Council. And indeed, although the right of judgment was delegated to the Parliaments and inferior magistrates, the King reserved to himself the power of resuming his privilege should the necessity arise; and this Council, called the Privy Council of State, exercised this function on his behalf, chiefly, however, in administrative concerns and matters of dispute. The members of this Council, in which all the persons belonging to the first Council, in addition to the controllers and stewards of the finances and other officials, to the number of thirty-three, according to an enactment of 1585, had the right to sit—as a matter of fact they never attended in such numbers—met almost every day round a " table covered with purple velvet." Their decisions, which were settled by a majority of votes, were submitted to the King. Disputes in connexion with financial matters were treated separately, as they were numerous enough to require a special Council. This third Council, called the Finance Council, sat on Tuesdays, Thursdays, and Saturdays, from six to half-past nine in the morning, and was composed of the Chancellor, certain Secretaries of State, and the finance stewards. Their duties consisted in granting to the towns leave to raise taxes in their own jurisdiction, in regulating assignments for special expenditure, and in dealing with financial requisitions addressed to the King. The register of the enactments of this council have been preserved.

What was the counterpart at this period of what we now know as the ministries ? Of all the branches existing in the administration of to-day two only were organized at this time—Justice and Finance, the recognized and official heads of which were respectively the Chancellor of France and the Superintendent of Finance.

Justice and Finance.

No important enactment made by the King of France was valid unless it was sealed with the seal of State. The Chancellor alone possessed the seals and sealed with his own hands — an exceptional prerogative. Traditional custom forbade his dismissal. The King might send him away from Court, but he could not deprive him of his title. " A temporary Keeper of the Seals " had to take his place. A great personage, clad in a robe of crimson velvet with huge sleeves lined with red satin and a silk sash of the same colour, the Chancellor was the natural head of all the judicial bodies in the kingdom. He was assisted by Masters of Requests to whom the charge of drawing up reports upon matters that had been submitted to the royal Council was confided. The post filled by these Masters of Requests, upon whom extraordinary commissions as stewards in the provinces were conferred later was " a fine office with extensive powers." The Chancellor was the corner-stone of the whole administration of the country, for various reasons rising out of a confusion of judicial and administrative powers.

The Chancellor.

The Superintendent of Finance was supreme in the control of the public finances. He was supported by financial stewards, men who were learned in the science of finance, and had under his orders a

The Superintendent of Finance.

374

host of agents who were scattered throughout the country for the purpose of the collection, centralization, and despatch of the money raised by the taxes.

Next to the Chancellor and the Superintendent of Finance, came the Secretaries of State. It is necessary to understand Secretaries of their position at this period, which was at once State. modest and important. In the fourteenth century the King had three secretaries whose duty it was to receive and answer his correspondence. When, at the end of the fifteenth century, one of these " royal secretaries " chanced to be Florimond Robertet, an experienced man of great intelligence, well versed in affairs of State, Charles VIII learnt to appreciate his advice, and Louis XII and Francis I retained the services of so valuable a helper. And thus the office was virtually created. Under Henry II there were four secretaries whose functions this monarch defined by an edict of September 14, 1547. They examined the correspondence and " dispatched " affairs of state. In order to avoid confusion, they divided France into four quarters, and each dealt with the questions connected with the provinces in his division and the foreign countries adjoining them. Thus one had Normandy and Picardy together with England and Flanders ; the second Provence, Languedoc, Guyenne and Brittany together with Spain ; the third, Champagne and Burgundy with Germany, Switzerland and Savoy ; and the fourth, Dauphiny and Lyons with Rome, Venice, and the Levant. The four departments were not equal in importance. Henry III considered it advantageous to centralize foreign affairs generally in the hands of one of the four, and matters connected with war in the hands of another. This was the object of the Edict of Blois of January 1, 1549. Here we have the modern ministerial system in embryo. Matters were still in this condition in 1600. Louis XIII's regulations of 1619, and above all of 1626, had to come before the centralization of foreign affairs and of questions of war was definitely completed, and even after this the secretaries concerned still continued to take cognizance of all that affected their quarter of the country These " Secretaries of State and Command," as they were called, were often men of the middle classes, who earned a salary of 50,000 francs a year in the exercise of their functions. They had a beautiful uniform—a cloak of violet velvet slashed to the bottom of the right side and lined with crimson taffetas, and a black velvet cap. To all appearance merely ordinary scribes, they were in reality, next to the Chancellor, the most important personages in the kingdom. They drew up the memoranda and instructions for the ambassadors, and the credentials of the provincial Governors, and informed everybody of the King's will and the decisions of the Council of State. There was not a single government secret which they did not share. Every public letter dictated by the King had to be endorsed by them in order to be valid, and this even went so far that their signature alone was of importance, and the King's autograph was in the end imitated by some copyist. And thus we find them on the high road to that omnipotence to which such violent exception was taken in the eighteenth century. They had a few clerks under them, but possessed no office, archives, or public building.

Such are the rough outlines of the central government. To the above offices must be added those of the Constable and the Admiral. But as these functions were more or less restricted to the army and the navy, we will return to them later on. The government played but a small part in the King's large Court, which existed chiefly for the sovereign's personal service. By the side of the crowd of gorgeous functionaries who surrounded his Majesty—the Grand Master of the Household, the Lord High Chamberlain, the First Lord of the Bedchamber, the Chief Butler, the Chief Pantler, the Chief Cupbearer, the Master of the Horse, the Master of the Hounds, the Master of the Robes, &c., with their subordinates and others, numbering altogether in 1601, 1041 persons and in 1589, 1725—the counsellors and Secretaries of State, and even the Chancellor himself, shine with less brilliance, and seem colourless and circumspect creatures. But they toiled industriously, and beneath them laboured the huge army of royal officials in the provinces.

And just as the Chancellor was the most important of the **The Magistrature.** ministers, so too the most numerous and powerful of the officials were the magistrates.

It amounted almost to a principle of public law under the old régime that all judicial authority should carry with it certain administrative powers, and that all administrative offices should entail certain judicial functions ; a mixture and confusion of powers which a certain seventeenth-century jurist explained by saying : " The magistracy stands above everything, because the aim and end of the public administration includes within itself the aims and ends of all the others." Hence it came about that in France there were almost as many judges as royal officials, and heaven knows that they were numerous enough, " there being no State in the world that hath so many officials of all kinds as the kingdom of France ! " Any private individual who possessed the smallest manor had a right of high, medium, or petty jurisdiction within it. The tiniest village which to-day might boast a single functionary in the person of a modest teacher, possessed at this period a royal or manorial provost, his assessor, a representative of the Procurator-General, and an usher or sergeant. From the King, the supreme magistrate of the realm, whose fundamental office was represented by the *main de justice*, down to the smallest feudal bailiff, France was covered with an endless net-work of jurisdictions which formed the real state organization for the maintenance of public order.

In the olden days the first Capet Kings used to dispense justice in person ; Saint Louis, for example, at Vincennes seated **Justice under** at the foot of a tree. The increase of public **the early** business, however, put an end to this patriarchal **Capets.** custom, and the council of clerks, who helped the King, constituted themselves into a regular judicial court— the Parliament, which became free and independent. The King, however, still reserved to himself the right of judging certain cases. The second small body of clerks and jurists which he formed about him in order that they might explain these cases to him, in their turn also constituted a new court, deatched themselves from the King, and formed an organization of their own, becoming the Grand Council. We have already **The Grand** seen how, even after this, the King reserved to **Council.** himself the right of participation in certain trials which were brought before the Council of State. Thus the various branches of judicial administration gradually sprouted from the royal trunk. Compared with those of the Parliaments, the functions of the Grand Council were somewhat uncertain. The four presidents and the various counsellors belonging to it took cognizance more especially of the differences that arose between the principal jurisdictions of the kingdom, those which were called the sovereign courts by reason of their " ends and limits." They also took cognizance of certain appeals determined by an edict of Henry II of September, 1567 ; of " conflicting decrees ; " and above all, of matters connected with archbishoprics, bishoprics, and abbeys. Notwithstanding its high sounding title the Grand Council played a minor part, the Parliaments having seized on every function of importance in this connexion.

A country visitor coming to Paris for the first time must certainly have felt moved when, in the Rue de la Barillerie, **The Parliaments.** he passed through the somewhat low arched door leading, in front of the Sainte Chapelle, into the Cour de Mai, round which rose the various buildings of the Palace belonging to the ancient Parliament of Paris. His emotion must have redoubled when after crossing the great hall of the procurators—the Salle des Pas perdus, an old building with double Gothic aisles, dating from the time of Saint Louis, adorned with statues of the French Kings in carved wood—he entered the Grand Court, and, on some day of solemn audience, gazed upon the two hundred magistrates of the chief sovereign tribunal in the realm, clad in their red robes, an illustrious and imposing assembly filled with a consciousness of its own dignity and rights, and at once respected and feared by the subjects whose lives and goods it held in its power, as well as by the King to whose will it opposed, under the archaic and impersonal form of rigid decrees, the formidable mass of law, justice, and tradition. As compared with the seven other Parliaments, those of Toulouse, Bordeaux, Rouen, Aix, Grenoble, Dijon, and Rennes, the Parliament of Paris was the most illustrious and most ancient. Toulouse, which ranked next to Paris in age and importance, consisted of about a hundred magistrates.

The two hundred magistrates of Paris only met at a general assembly for cases of extreme importance " the greatest and most weighty affairs concerning the State and the public weal," the ratification of edicts, the reception of magistrates, mercurial sessions, the drawing up of ordinances, and debates on the affairs of the kingdom. For although the Parliaments had orginally been created for the administration of justice alone, " it is nevertheless recorded in the registers that they frequently interfered in matters of state, of war, and of finance, either owing to the absence, indisposition or minority of the Kings of France, or by royal permission, or when business brooked of no delay. For the hearing of ordinary cases the magistrates were divided into several separate courts—first, the Grand Court, which was the kernel of the whole assembly ; then five Courts of Enquiry, which heard appeals made from the decisions of inferior judges to the jurisdiction of the Parliament ; here " judging " counsellors listened to " reporting " counsellors and returned the final verdicts ; and two Courts of Requests, each composed of two presidents and eight counsellors, which examined the petitions laid before Parliament, sent back some to the inferior magistrates, dealt with the trivial ones, and reserved for the Courts of Enquiry those that were of sufficient importance. In addition there was a Criminal Court, called La Tournelle, which had jurisdiction over criminal offences, and consisted of two presidents, eight counsellors from the Grand Court, and two from each of the Courts of Enquiry, the whole body of officials being changed every three months " inasmuch as the duty of constantly passing sentence of death and condemning men impairs the natural kindness of the judges and renders them to a certain extent cruel and inhuman." Lastly, during the legal vacations, there was a Vacation Court consisting of a judge and thirteen counsellors, which tried criminal causes and settled minor cases. To these must be added the Edict Court, founded by Henry III in 1576, which took cognizance of matters of dispute between Protestants and Catholics, and which, in the Parliament of Paris, was composed of two Presidents and sixteen counsellors, eight being Catholics and eight Huguenots. All the Parliaments of the country were organized on a similar plan, with fewer courts containing fewer magistrates. Toulouse had only two courts, a Court of Enquiry and a Court of Requests. The Edict Courts sat in a different place from the Parliament—in the case of Toulouse at Castres.

What cases fell within and what without the jurisdiction of the parliaments ? This is a complex question, the answers **Jurisdiction** to which are somewhat indefinite and arbitrary. **of the** In the first place the parliaments might claim **Parliaments.** to take cognizance of all cases connected with important personages—dukes and peers of the realm, princes, prelates, chapters, lords of the manor and townships and all who had the right to be heard before it in virtue of a special privilege called the privilege of *committimus ;* " also of all cases of great weight and importance connected with affairs of state,"— matters concerning the universities, navigation, and in general all appeals from the decisions of inferior tribunals. The limita- tions were vague enough, and the parliaments did very much as they pleased and were more or less masters of the situation. Hence their formidable prestige and the respectful fear they inspired. Let us examine the magistrates somewhat more closely.

The chief of these was the First President, a personage, who filled as important a position in his own province as did **Constitution** the Chancellor in the kingdom; " *Monsieur le* **of the** *premier,*" as he was called, or " *Messire So-and-* **Parliaments.** *so* " when he was a knight, that is to say of noble birth. At the end of the sixteenth century, however, all the First Presidents considered themselves knights *ex officio.* The First President was the head of the Parliament ; he presided over the Grand Court, and also had the right to preside over any of the others. He alone enjoyed the privilege of being allowed to come from his own house to the audience-chamber in his red robes ; the counsellors and other presidents had to dress at the Palace. He represented the King in the loftiest of all his functions : the administration of justice. Hence he took precedence of the governor or lieutenant-general of a province, and, except in church, even of archbishops and bishops. Any great personage, save a prince of the blood, who arrived in a parliamentary town, even the Constable himself, had to pay his first visit to him. At Toulouse, on the death of a First President, all the church bells of the parishes were rung, and the Cardaillac, the great bell in the cathedral of Saint-Étienne, was tolled, an honour otherwise reserved for an Archbishop. He

380

was so high a dignitary that if the governor of a province and his lieutenant-general chanced to be absent, he took their place "considering himself lieutenant-general to the King within the jurisdiction of his court." He also interfered in military and financial matters. Moreover, during the civil wars, he rendered great services in the south by maintaining or re-establishing public order, taking military measures for defence, and safe-guarding the country for the King. He was nominated by the King, who could transfer him wherever he chose, and appoint a President of Paris First President of Aix, or promote a First President of Toulouse to the equivalent post in Paris. All the parliaments of France were supposed to constitute a single corporate whole.

After the First President came the Presidents who wore black velvet caps (*presidents à mortier*) and presided over the various minor courts, and the Counsellors, who were also august personages and surrounded by a quasi-religious prestige. In the exercise of his office the person of a magistrate was sacred and inviolable. His function was so lofty that it ennobled both him and his descendants. He enjoyed all the privileges of the nobility, and was exempt from the payment of the taille and other dues, and from having soldiers billeted upon him in time of war. He could not be dismissed from office, his salary could not be attached, and, in case of misdemeanour, he could be judged only by the full body of the parliament assembled with all its courts. He alone of all royal officials wore the red robe "scarlet and crimson being the colours and vestments proper to the King." Among the counsellors were ecclesiastics called clerical counsellors—the others being lay counsellors—whose number was fixed by the ordinances : forty in Paris, ten at Toulouse, eight at Rennes, and six in the other Parliaments. If they overstepped these numbers, "letters of laïsation" (meaning laïcisation) were obtained from the King, in order to revert to the regulation number. To these clerics were confided more especially ecclesiastical, religious, and sacred cases, in order that they might defend the rights and privileges of the Church, and instruct the lay magistrates upon details connected with the ecclesiastical estate.

Lastly came "the Parquet" (the Bar): the Procurator-

General, the Advocates-General and "the King's men," all of whom at royal audiences occupied the centre of the floor of the Grand Court, kneeling on the floor (*parquet*), whence their name. In accordance with the edict of May, 1586, each Parliament had one Procurator-General, two Advocates-General, and in addition sixteen Vice-Procurators-General in Paris, ten at Toulouse and Bordeaux, and six everywhere else. As representatives of the King, the Parquet defended the royal interests if they were at stake in any trial, and on behalf of the public weal opposed the oppression of the weak by the strong, protecting the former. They prosecuted in criminal trials and gave opinions in private cases. They were, in short, a species of "neutral puisne judges, the hands on the balance that inclines correctly towards the side to which the weight of reason carries the judgment." They ranked lower than the counsellors, and did not attend the general meetings of the chambers, though they enjoyed the privileges of the court. The King relied upon them to inform him if any violation of the edicts took place in the Parliaments.

Similar privileges were enjoyed by the registrars—the civil registrar and the criminal registrar, who farmed their registers, which belonged to the King's estate, wore the red robe, and attended audiences seated and with their heads covered. Their duty consisted in transcribing judgments in their registers, and forwarding them with the assistance of court-clerks and "bag-keepers," "well-drilled people and honest creatures, steady, decorous and reliable."

How were the magistrates appointed ? Roughly speaking, in order to be a counsellor it was necessary for a man to have been an advocate for four years, and to have taken his degree ; whilst to be eligible for the presidency he must have been a counsellor for six years. An enquiry was made into the religious convictions, and the life and morals of the candidates, no man being eligible who was either "deaf, dumb, blind, raving mad, lame, humpbacked, rheumatic, gouty, a Jew, a peasant, deformed or clip-eared." Magistrates' seats were sold just as lawyer's practices are sold to-day. On condition of paying into the royal exchequer a certain annual tax called the *paulette* (after Monsieur Paulet, who invented the system) the King authorized the judges to sell their offices for ready money to anybody they pleased. Thus all judicial grades in France became hereditary and venal. How different from the days when the King himself appointed the magistrates upon the recommendation of the Parliaments, when these magistrates after taking the oath, elected their Presidents from among the counsellors, and the counsellors from the lawyers at the bar! The sale of offices was gradually introduced from the time of Francis I onwards, and the King had no power to dismiss judges unless they failed in the payment of their annual tax. The result was, that seats were handed down in families from father to son, and men often entered the Parliament too young or remained when they were too old. In order to maintain discipline and tradition, dignity of bearing and professional pride in assemblies over-secure in their tenure of office, there existed an institution resembling the Chapters of monasteries—the mercurial Court. A session which was held originally every Tuesday (*Mercredi*)—whence the title mercurial —afterwards once a month, and under Henry IV once a year, the mercurial treated " of the faults of officers of the court, their infringements of the ordinances and customs of the Palace," and dealt out exhortations, advice, and threats. It was at these mercurial sessions that the judges were requested to be punctual in their attendance ; to go to Mass every day ; to be upright, sober, and decent in their behaviour ; secret in business ; to converse only upon lofty and never upon frivolous subjects ; to avoid any familiarity with the parties in suits, and to refuse gifts or invitations to dinner from them ; to set an example of good conduct, that is to say not to hunt, dance or play cards, not to use scent, wear wigs or dye their hair, and not to laugh. " It is impossible," declared La Roche-Flavin, " to find a perfect magistrate."

Let us examine them as they march past in order of rank, two and two, the Presidents at the head, preceded by the ushers carrying rods and the registrars, and followed by the Parquet, the ushers, the advocates and the procurators, all majestic in their red robes. Their costume was the old royal costume of the thirteenth century—a scarlet robe, a long red cloak, lined with ermine, or some white fur with black stripes or spots, " the said cloak thrown open over the shoulders so as to show the said fur ; " and on their heads the flat round velvet cap, adorned in the case of the Presidents, with gold —the *mortiers* which we see worn by the Kings on thirteenth-century seals. They took their seats solemnly in the Grand Court on high benches—for ordinary sessions they would wear only black and sit on low seats. In Paris the setting of this august assembly consisted of a wainscoted chamber decorated with red and gold beneath a gilded ceiling with pendentives, dating from the time of Louis XII, the walls hung with tapestry and the windows filled with stained glass, the whole sprinkled with golden fleurs-de-lis. In a corner to the left would stand the King's empty seat, consisting of great cushions of blue velvet spangled with gold fleurs-de-lis under a canopy of cloth of gold embroidered with porcupines (this too dated from the reign of Louis XII). When the King was present for the registration of some edict at what was called a *lit de justice*, the magistrates would keep silence, because in the presence of the sovereign their power, as his delegates, was suspended. To the right of the King's seat was the bench belonging to the lords temporal of the realm ; on the left that assigned to the lords spiritual ; beneath it, the presidential bench ; and, lastly, the counsellors sat in tiers on the three other sides. Ordinary meetings were held in the morning from eight to ten o'clock. The Parliament of Paris was the only one to hold a session in the afternoon (the *relevée* as it was called) from two to five o'clock. After the evidence had been given and the pleading finished, the judges decided the case by a majority, each one expressing his opinion by order of seniority. He who agreed with the person preceding him merely said " *idem* " (ditto) or " raised his cap " whence arose the expression " cap option " (*opiner du bonnet*). The Parliament had an annual vacation from Holy Cross Day, September 14, to the day after the Feast of Saint Martin, November 12, a well-earned repose from arduous labours for which the magistrates were but poorly paid. Their fixed salaries were low, and they had in addition the fees fixed by the presidents in each case for the reporting counsellors, which the litigants had to pay.

Lastly, as the indisputable adjuncts to every court there

was the "innumerable host" of lawyers, "enough to make
Lawyers. several regiments or even a small army,"
divided up into listeners—the modern " juniors"—pleaders
and consulting counsels—our " leaders "—" the triple palisade of
the garden of justice," " leaves, flowers, and fruit," " bud, sprig,
and perfect branch." They were recommended to speak
" briefly and to the point," to be " pertinent and short." This
advice was ill-observed. Next came the terrible crowd of
attorneys, " the feet of the Parliament," but " breeders of
law-suits." No one, from King to peasant, could do without
them ; for no defence was legal unless it were " heard by an
attorney." What a litigious crew they were ! But for them,
" there would have been extremely few law-suits." They
lived by litigation and abused it. Last of all came the horde
of ushers, criers, and others, who kept order during the hearing
of cases, and executed sentences, made distraints, notified
judgments and presented writs—a vast and swarming black
multitude !

Under the Parliaments was the old-established inferior
jurisdiction of the bailiffs and seneschals in the provinces. The
Bailiffs and kingdom was divided into governments, and the
Seneschals. governments into districts, called bailiwicks in
the north and seneschalships in the south. The bailiff or seneschal was a judge representing the King. The origin of this
office is lost in the shades of time. At one period he had
been the King's only officer, exercising administrative, judicial,
and military functions. But in course of time all these attributes were taken from him by degrees. He had to be of noble
birth and was therefore a " short-robed " judge. To help
him in the administration of justice, and even to act as his
substitute if necessary, he had a civil lieutenant called " a
long-robed judge," who was a true magistrate, and a criminal
lieutenant for dealing with crimes and misdemeanours. Appeal
could be made from their verdicts to the Parliaments. Finally,
in order to relieve these courts and the Parliaments, Henry II
created, in 1551, an intermediate tribunal called the Presidial
Presidial Court. One of these was allotted to each bailiff
Courts. or seneschal throughout the domain and to
" the best towns," and was composed of six judges of the

same rank as those belonging to the bailiff's tribunal, and a red-robed President. But its jurisdiction was wider, a Presidial Court being the final court for all civil cases to the amount of 1000 pounds. The institution of a court which curtailed expenses and long journeys was a boon for parties to a suit.

Under the bailiffs or seneschals, there were scattered throughout the towns and boroughs a number of inferior royal judges **Inferior royal** who, according to the district, were called pro- **judges.** vosts, *viguiers,* lords of the manor or viscounts. They also had jurisdiction over civil and criminal cases, but only those of minor importance. Their chief function, however, was to hear appeals from the decisions of the manorial judges ; for, below them, there was yet another stratum of magistrates. Every individual fief-holder, who had a right of high, medium, and petty jurisdiction, had a provost who judged civil and criminal cases, a survival from early feudal times when the lord of the manor exercised full sovereign rights in his own demesne. A perpetual struggle, however, was carried on between these petty private magistrates of the villages and the royal judges in the neighbourhood, who invented all manner of trifling pretexts to destroy the judicial power of individuals, and make the exercise of their rights impossible.

And thus from one end of the country to the other, France was covered with a network of judges. In addition to the **Special** ones already enumerated, there were all kinds **jurisdictions.** of special jurisdictions. Military matters, desertions, crimes committed by soldiers, and malversation in the administration of regimental funds, were under the jurisdiction of the Marshalsea. Naval affairs, navigation, fishing rights and prizes were controlled by the Admiralty. All offences connected with woods and waters were referred to the Master of the Woods and Waters. This official had under his command a separate Master for each province who had an escort of captains, gamekeepers, and verderers. In Paris these three jurisdictions were called the Marble Table. Parisian cases were judged by the Provost of Paris, or at all events by his lieutenant, who sat in the Châtelet (the Provost was in the position of bailiff of Paris). All crimes that could be committed at the King's Court were dealt with by a special department called the Provostship of the Royal Residence; the Provost of the Royal Residence, like a bailiff, having under him two lieutenants, and, in addition, fifty archers who acted as police within the radius of six miles of the Court when it was travelling about. And lastly, over and above all this, the Parliaments sent commissions from time to time to "the most distant provinces" to exercise exceptional judicial powers under the name of "Great Days." Even now we have made no mention of the municipal police courts. Every institution that enjoyed the smallest particle of authority in France administered justice. And, on the other hand, all the courts, on the pretext of having police jurisdiction, passed administrative regulations which they enforced on pain of penalty. The universal confusion between the law and the administration resulted in a vast unwieldy machine which acted automatically throughout the country, the King being powerless to control it. Combined with the claim made by the Parliaments to the effect that no royal edict should be held valid that had not been registered by themselves, this power was in a position to oppose an exasperating force of inertia to the sovereign's will. The King had no hold over it even through legislation, as the judgments of the whole of this judicial world were based upon Roman Law, canon law, common law, usages and customs, "uses and observances" and equity, and took but small account of edicts and ordinances. Thus, in spite of all "his plenary powers and royal authority," the King was paralyzed throughout his kingdom by the huge growth of a judicial organization, throwing out minute yet almost independent roots, that adhered to the soil and became passively immovable. He was no less tightly fettered by the second branch of the administration, which was equally minute in its organization—the financial department.

If the administration of justice for the preservation of public order has always been regarded as the first necessity of the **Finance and Taxation.** State, the raising of money for maintenance has been looked upon as the second. Men of this period made ingenious comparisons between the State and the human body, likening finance to the nervous system. From

Paris to the smallest villages, a whole hierarchy extended whose business it was to collect the taxes.

The headquarters of the system in the immediate environment of the King was the central office of the Exchequer called **L'Épargne.** *l'Épargne* (literally Savings Department) containing the Receiver-General's office and the Treasury of *l'Épargne*, and administered by Treasurers called *Trésoriers de l'Épargne*. It was to these headquarters that the royal receivers, when they had paid everything that had to be settled upon the spot, sent any surplus. Wooden coffers secured by double locks, the keys of which were confided to the safekeeping of various officials, had once existed in the Louvre for storing this money. But, about 1600, when all the money was spent before it could reach them, these coffers became useless. Sully, however, after eight years of economical government, was able to place in the treasury tower of the Bastille 13,000,000 pounds, which were secured in 8000 sacks, 270 barrels and 4 coffers.

Every year under the direction of the Superintendent of Finance the Treasurers of *l'Épargne* drew up a "rough estimate" **The financial** of the sums required for the following year—the **divisions** modern "draft budget." This "estimate" **of France.** revised by the Council of Finance and signed by the King, then had to be provided for. France was cut up for financial purposes into a certain number of special divisions, called "generalities," from the old expression "Receiver-General of finances" which became shortened to "General of Finances." There were in 1607, twenty-one generalities in the country, of which sixteen were large. Their order of importance, based on the magnitude of their returns, was as follows—Rouen, Poitiers, Tours, Limoges, Paris, Caen, Orleans, Riom, Bordeaux, Lyons, Moulins, Bourges, Amiens, Châlons, Soissons, and Grenoble. The Council of Finance divided the taxes to be raised between all the generalities in proportion to the resources of each one, as shown by the "special estimates" sent in advance to Paris by the financial agents attached to the generalities. The generalities in their turn were divided into smaller sections called elections, a word reminiscent of the time when the tax-assessors were elected by the people. This, however, was prior to the reign of Louis XI, after which the office was in the gift of the King, or was even hereditary. The election was subdivided into parishes. France, under Henry IV, contained 149 elections and 23,159 parishes in the sixteen generalities enumerated above.

At the head of each generality there was a " general office " consisting of about ten officials called " treasurers of France " and " generals of finance," and numbering altogether throughout the kingdom 197 treasurers. It was their business to draw up every year and send to Paris the " rough estimates " or budgets for their respective generalities. They were helped by a receiver-general of finance, who centralized the surplus money collected from the minor centres. They distributed the burden of taxation over the various elections. For three months of the year each of them in turn rode round to inspect their district, examining the accounts of the inferior agents, looking into cases of malversation, abuses, and mistakes. They had the power of suspending accountants and temporarily filling their places. Reports of their " tours of inspection " were forwarded to Paris.

In each election likewise there was " an office " consisting of eight or ten agents called " the elect " (élus): " Monsieur l'élu." For the 149 elections, there were 1340 representatives, who distributed the burden of taxation over the parishes, and were helped by a local receiver of finances, whose duty it was to centralize the sums raised by the taxation of the parishes. We now come to the parishes, which formed the lowest rung in the administrative ladder. The representatives distributed the claims during the fortnight following the receipt of the "commission." This they did "with equity, justice and impartiality," after having informed themselves of the resources of each parish by means of the tours which they too made every year with the object of finding out the means of the inhabitants through cross-questioning the chief men in the villages. The results of these investigations were recorded in the written reports. On Sunday, at sermon time at High Mass, the priest announced the arrival of the document prescribing the amount of taxation to be raised in the parish. After Mass or Vespers, the men assembled in the church, and, if the parish were taxed at less than 300 crowns of grand taille, appointed two of themselves, and if at more than this amount, four, to "assess"

Assessors and collectors. the taxes and collect them. These were the collectors, the "assessors" of the parishes. The assessment made by these officials was of course not acquiesced in by the taxpayer without objection or recrimination, which was called "repudiating the assessment" of the taxes. Recourse was then had to the "elect" who settled without appeal any claim not above one crown. The document arranging the amount to be demanded from the contributors, *les cotisés* as they were called, was drawn up by the collectors—if they could not write a clerk helped them—and signed by the "elect." The collectors then went round from door to door demanding the money, "crossing" (striking out) the names of those who paid up, and "endorsing" them (putting their names on the back), thus making themselves responsible for the amount collected, which they despatched untouched to the local receivers of the election. The collector's task was a hard one, troublesome and unpleasant, and involving endless responsibility and worry. But everybody had to take his turn at it.

Such was the fiscal organization of these sixteen generalities which were called the generalities of the election districts. Besides them there were districts called the State districts, which consisted of five generalities : Nantes, Toulouse, Montpellier, Dijon and Aix. Here the distribution was made by States elected by the provinces—provincial assemblies which were the relics of local liberty and independence, and were destined to disappear. The States discussed with the King the amount they considered it possible to raise for him, placing him in a pitiable position of dependence. The inferior divisions in these places were called by various names. Brittany had seventeen local receiver's offices called hearth-tax receiver's offices, because the taxes were levied on fires. At Toulouse and Montpellier the eleven receiver's offices were called dioceses, and were confused with these. In Burgundy and Provence there were no local receiver's offices, but only a general receiver's office. The collecting of the taxes in the lower strata was organized in the way that has already been described.

But of what did this taxation consist ; what were the

contributions that the subjects of Henry IV had to pay ; and what were the resources the King of France had at his disposal ? They were infinite, complicated, and difficult to specify. As a matter of fact, he lived by all manner of expedients, and raised money from every possible source.

In the first place he had the revenues belonging to the royal demesne, the King's revenues as a landowner and his **Numerous and complicated taxes paid by the people.** revenues as a feudal lord—farms, corn, wine, poultry, quit-rents, rents, fifths and twenty-fifths, landcheaps or fines of alienation, waifs, escheats, fines, confiscations, seals, tabellionage, &c., from which in 1600 he derived a net income of 89,307 pounds. In addition to this, there were two kinds of taxes ; those raised directly by the King's agents, which we should call direct taxes ; those raised by means of tax-farmers and various receiving offices ; and, finally what was known as " extraordinary moneys." The first two kinds, the direct taxes and those which were centralized by the royal officials, consisted essentially of the taille. This was the levy the organization of which we have **The Taille.** just been discussing. The taille was a real tax, that is to say a property tax paid on all land, even the royal estates. This was the system in Provence and Languedoc. Or it might be personal, that is to say, a percentage on his possessions paid by every non-privileged person. Or else it might be mixed, a combination of the two systems. The King's Council accordingly settled in advance the sum that the taille throughout the country ought to bring in. This sum was distributed over the various generalities by means of warrants addressed to the treasurers-general. If the sum thus obtained were insufficient, or the returns were not high enough, the King would decide to raise a supplement called an extraordinary levy or " grand levy." The net receipts from the taille in 1600 was 10,843,544 pounds of which 893,545 pounds came from the State districts, and the rest from the election districts. As may be imagined, the returns were bad, for the taxpayers were grudging. It was in vain that the parish collectors, who had the right to make settlements every three months, were persecuted by the local receivers, and the local receivers by the general receivers, who had to pay in the assignments; the collection of dues was by no means always easy.

After the taille, which formed the chief revenue of the State, the farming out of general and special taxes was the second source of supply. These were revenues which were sold to the highest bidder for a particular number of years, varying in different instances. The tax-farmer paid a fixed sum every year and collected the taxes at his own risk and peril. There were some thirty taxes that were farmed out in this way, such as the gabelle or tax on the sale of salt ; the aids: taxes on provisions and merchandize sold in the country ; taxes on imports, our modern customs; tolls; and taxes on cards, tarots, &c. In 1600 the farmed taxes brought in 3,000,000 pounds to the royal exchequer. Like the receivers the tax-farmers paid such expenses as they were authorized to meet out of their receipts and sent the surplus from their farming to *l'Épargne* every three months.

There were other sources of revenue, such, for instance, as the *taillon* or lesser taille. When the distribution of the **The Budget** taille had been made, a supplement was added **of 1600.** " arranged on the same basis and at a halfpenny in the pound," a sort of additional centime. From the *taillon* 590,238 pounds were raised in 1600. It was devoted exclusively to expenditure in connexion with the maintenance of the army, and never entered *l'Épargne*. Then there were the "incidental dues" such as the tax called the *paulette* on magistrates, temporary levies on various concerns, the total from which added another 1,644,046 pounds ; and the gifts from the clergy, who paid no taxes, but instead made voluntary contributions to the Exchequer.

Altogether the net receipts for the year 1600, which were forwarded to the King in Paris, amounted to the total sum of 16,208,823 pounds. This sum was insufficient to meet the expenses, and it was necessary to have recourse to other means, and to raise what was known as "extraordinary moneys" by the creation of new offices, fiscal inventions and ingenious subtleties in the accounts, which produced another 4,333,994 pounds, thus making the grand total for that year 20,542,817 pounds.

How was this money spent ? It was spent in two ways.

KINGDOM OF FRANCE ABOUT 1600

In the first place all State expenses in the provinces, the wages
State of royal officials, the upkeep of the royal estates,
expenditure. repairs, legal costs, &c., were paid upon the
spot. Unlike the modern system of account-keeping, particular
expenses were calculated on the basis of particular receipts;
the receiver paid the money, carefully keeping the budget,
bills, receipts, and registers, the whole signed and initialled.
There were a host of receivers : receivers of incidental moneys,
receivers of the salt magazines, receivers of the farmed taxes.
They all forwarded any surplus to the general receiver's office
of the generality, together with explanatory memoranda, sending
the exact amount of cash they had received. After a certain
period of grace, if they failed to remit their "balance," they
were fined or obliged to pay interest on the sums they kept
at the rate of 8⅓ per cent. The Receiver-General, in his turn,
forwarded every three months to *l'Épargne* any surplus he had
after expenses had been met. He sent the money in sealed
bags, carried by a clerk, with a memorandum describing the
sums despatched, the kinds of coin, the day of dispatch, the
number of waggons filled, the whole addressed to the Superintendent of Finance ; and, at the end of the year he gave the
Court of the Exchequer a duplicate of his accounts.

Thus it was by means of the surplus sent from the provinces
that the central government was carried on. It was calculated
that the Court and the provinces ought to divide the general
receipts of the State equally between them. The government,
of course, decided beforehand the amount to be kept by the
provinces. Each generality received instructions approved by
the King "with details and particulars for each election " of
all the various sums to be paid out and the net amount that
ought to be handed over to His Majesty. As a matter of fact the
net returns to His Majesty varied very considerably, according
as to whether the receipts from the taxes were good or bad.

In 1600, the maintenance of the Court alone cost 2,368,899
Strictness with pounds, for it was "necessary to make conspicuous
which the and shining, as is only seemly, the splendour and
public Accounts majesty of the household of the King and of his
were kept. suite." The money was administered by means
of a strict system of accounts, separate receivers and

393

treasurers being appointed to each department of the household. There was a spencer to deal with expenditure on food, a " steward " of the Royal wardrobe, one receiver for the stables and another for the household officials. Everything was paid in accordance with statements, receipts, registers and lists. The budget of the expenditure of the central government included, in addition to this, some twenty items such as 1,812 787 pounds for pensions ; 243,322 pounds for the royal guards ; 1,038,000 pounds a year for the Swiss companies ; 201,666 pounds for embassy expenses ; 478,727 pounds for fortifications ; 558,352 pounds for building ; 7,067,685 pounds in interest on Crown debts, an exceedingly heavy not to say crushing charge ; for ordinary and extraordinary war expenses—our modern army budget—4,946,363 pounds. There were war treasurers in ordinary who allotted the money from this budget to the various paymasters of the companies. The treasurer of *l'Épargne* paid nothing except on receipt of statements, bills, and orders signed by the King, sealed with the Great Seal and supervised by a financial steward, all of which transactions were afterwards revised by the Court of the Exchequer.

For there was an extremely strict Court of the Exchequer before which sheaves of documents with technical names had to

Exchequer Court. be laid—notes of hand called *debentur,* certificates called *servivi,* &c. This Court, which was the second great administrative body in the kingdom, consisted of several offices ; the head office, with ten presidents and sixty-two chief accountants ; two offices which balanced the accounts ; a corrector's office which drew up reports of the closed accounts for the Court of the Exchequer ; and a fourth office, called the auditor's office, which drew up reports on the accounts waiting to be closed—not to mention the Procurator-General and the Advocate-General. All these officials were engaged in sifting the public accounts, lodging protests, raising opposition, and coming down for the slightest deficit upon the receivers and treasurers, who trembled before them. This Court had to read and ratify the edicts, the ordinances concerning finance, exemptions, privileges, and abatements, and passed measures discharging the responsible officials of their liabilities, failing which their private property could be attached. In practice its jurisdiction was very far from being nominal; it was effective and rigorous, and the financial agents were constantly having trouble with it, whilst above all the King himself was not free to do as he pleased.

Besides the Court of the Exchequer, there was the Court of Aids, which had two presidents and two chambers, each **Court of Aids** containing twenty-six counsellors, a procurator-**and Mint.** general and two advocates-general. It decided the cases arising from the collection of the taxes, the refusals to pay, the appeals against fines, and disputed contracts with tax-farmers. And, lastly, the Court of the Mint, with four presidents, and twenty masters or general counsellors, which took cognizance of all disputes arising in connexion with the coinage of money, and, as an extension of this duty, all cases related to the trade and industry in precious metals.

And thus at the end of the sixteenth century the legal and financial administration of the country had been organized with great precision and even minuteness, through the channel of traditional institutions slowly built up through the ages, and preserved, extended, and made more complex with time (the system of public accounts was stricter than is generally believed even in the thirteenth century), but preserved intact once the ferment of the civil wars was over and the inevitable disorder arising from temporarily disorganized machinery. The administration properly so called, that is to say the direct administrative work of the central power in the provinces was much more embryonic, owing to the survival of strong municipal rights and liberties which were scrupulously respected.

For the purposes of administration France was divided into fourteen governments, at the head of which great nobles **Administration.** were placed as governors. They had lieutenants-**Governors.** general, former counsellors of the sovereign courts, to help them and take their places when, as frequently occurred, they were absent from their province. The governor's only duties were to maintain the public peace and, in the words of an ordinance of 1579, " to keep his district in safety, guard it against ravages, visit the fortresses," and to inform the King if any event of importance occurred. The governor was in fact merely a military chief who kept watch and ward over his province. He was not allowed to interfere in the administration of justice, except for the purpose of supporting judges in the execution of sentences. He was responsible for the garrisons and their maintenance, for the fortification of strongholds and their supply of ammunition. Under his direct orders local governors or captains fulfilled similar duties in many of the towns, and in the forts and citadels of the kingdom, more particularly on the frontier. In short the governor was more of a military official than anything else. He was frequently a duke, peer, or grand baron of the realm. He represented the King, and his authority, which was the highest in the province, surrounded him with the halo of the royal power of which he was the delegate, whilst at the same time he held in his hands the material force necessary to support this prestige.

At one time, the active agent under the governor was the bailiff or seneschal. His duty also was to safeguard the **Governor's** public peace, and he too was a kind of military **Executive.** official, though more of a "national guard." " By riding round on tours of inspection he saw to it that justice was rightly and duly administered." He had, moreover, been a captain or lieutenant of men-at-arms, and was a person of noble birth appointed by the King from a list of candidates sent by the governor. His "long-robed" lieutenants relieved him of the judicial part of his functions, so that the only duty remaining to him was to keep watch and ward and, when the country was in danger, to convoke the ban and rear-ban.

For the practical maintenance of peace in the "country-side, villages and unfortified towns" the "tranquillity and safety **Police.** of honest folks," there was the Marshalsea, composed of the provosts of the Marshals of France, general and local, supported by lieutenants and archers. They composed the public body charged with the duty of arresting "robbers, murderers, loiterers on the high roads, idlers, vagabonds, and other persons without means of subsistence or domicile" and conveying them to the prisons of the bailiwick or of the presidial court—the duty of the modern corps of gendarmes (constabulary). In Paris the police consisted of 240 archers— of whom thirty-two were mounted—belonging to the Knight of the Watch, and commanded by four lieutenants with the help of commissaries—the former examining commissaries of the Châtelet, who eventually developed into police superintendents. By an edict of June, 1586, there were about forty commissaries in Paris, four in parliamentary towns, two in places which were the seat of a presidial court, and one for all districts under the jurisdiction of a bailiff or a provost.

Thus the administration exercised the functions of a police force more than anything else. This was due to the fact that **Municipalities.** the towns, boroughs, and parishes still retained a great deal of local authority. The municipalities varied considerably in their organization owing to differences of origin, tradition, and custom. Paris, for instance, had a Provost of the Merchants instead of a Mayor, four aldermen, who held office for two years, and twenty-six counsellors; whilst each of the sixteen quarters of the city had at its head a *quartenier* with *cinquanteniers* and *dizeniers* under them, and a complete municipal guard. At Bordeaux there was a Mayor and six *jurats;* at Périgueux a Mayor and six consuls; at Poitiers a Mayor, twenty-five aldermen and a council of seventy-five citizens; in one place there were *maieurs,** in a second, such as Toulouse, *capitouls,* and in others *jurés,* consuls, and town syndics. Elected in various ways by the inhabitants, frequently for one year only, these municipal officers looked after the town police, the cleaning of the streets, and the repair of the ramparts. They saw to the closing of the gates in the evening and the ringing of the curfew, ascertained that the town was well stocked with provisions, that artisans performed their work conscientiously, and that the weights and measures were correct. The funds for carrying on the administration were obtained from the municipal taxes, and when it was necessary to undertake public works the officials asked the Council of State to pass a decree authorizing them to raise a fresh levy. In many places the municipal authorities administered justice— forming a tribunal of police or of justices of the peace. Appeal could be made from their verdicts to the inferior royal judges. An interesting spectacle is afforded by these large and small towns, boroughs, and villages, discussing and arranging their

* A name given to mayors in the Middle Ages. (Tr.)

own affairs, sedately and peacefully, like prudent people who had attained to years of discretion. The life lived in them was varied and picturesque. But occasionally, even at this period, when complications arose, or it was temporarily necessary to secure strict unity of action, the government sent Masters of Requests to the frontier provinces with " extraordinary commissions " to take up the provisional administration " of justice, police, and finance." These were the Intendants (stewards), the future instruments of the levelling process, of a domineering and withering system of centralization.

The army and the navy remain to be discussed. No standing army or navy worth mentioning existed. The method prevailing at this time was to raise regiments only when troops were required for war. Amongst the class of people who had no homes and few scruples, were to be found those who were ready to enlist for money ; and of these there was always a plentiful supply. But in view of the risk of being kidnapped, to which the Kings of the second half of the sixteenth century had been exposed, the Court became inclined to keep a permanent armed force always on foot. In addition to this, garrisons were required for the fortresses. But above all the staff of great officers was permanent: first, the Constable, who was a grand Crown official, a sort of Generalissimo, who had supreme command of all the forces, even taking precedence of princes of the blood. Under him were the Marshals of France who commanded the army under certain contingencies. Francis I insisted upon having four, but the number varied according to circumstances. Next in rank came the Colonel-General of Infantry, who was a sort of " director of the forces." The regiments were commanded by Field Masters or Marshals. Of the troops, the first permanent unit was the King's guard, a superb body of men with brilliant uniforms—first the four mounted companies of the Lifeguards, with 360 men to a company, each of which was divided into six brigades, making a total of 1440 men and eighty-three officers, all dressed in the royal colours, the colours of the House of Bourbon, blue, white, and red. This was a very old established force dating from the time of Charles VII, Louis XI, and Francis I. Next came the company of light-

The Army and the Navy.

Permanent troops.

398

horse belonging to the royal guard, a body of 200 men created by Henry IV ; and above all the regiment of the French Guards which was formed about 1564 after the attempt to kidnap the King at Montceaux, and consisted of twenty companies, the full complement of which was 500 men to each company. In 1600, however, they had only eighty, a number raised to 300 for the war with Savoy. This was the oldest and most glorious of the infantry regiments. And last of all the Swiss. The regiment of Swiss Guards was only created in 1616 by Louis XIII. Under Henry IV, the King had only one company of Swiss, called the Hundred Swiss, in his bodyguard. This company dated from the time of Louis XII ; its members wore a variegated slashed uniform and were employed in the King's special service.

First among the other permanent troops were the Swiss contingents. Ever since the time of Louis XI the Kings of **Swiss Con-** France had hired mercenaries in the cantons **tingent.** of Switzerland. Some of these companies were recognized and acknowledged by the Helvetian authorities, others were recruited by captains. According to the treaties not more than 16,000 or less than 6000 could be procured in this way. Their Colonel-General was Monsieur de Harlay de Sancy, and they were divided into companies of 200 men, all admirable in their discipline and devotion to the Crown. Beyond these, the only permanent troops were four regiments of infantry from Picardy, Piedmont, Champagne, and Navarre ; a fifth, belonging to Normandy, dated only from 1616 or 1617. The word regiment was used by Monluc and meant a group of companies or ensigns which, in the course of time, thus became stable. After the Peace of Vervins in 1598, Henry IV either disbanded or reformed all the regiments he had at that moment, with the exception of the four just mentioned, which were made up of varying numbers of companies, ten or twelve, containing a nominal contingent of 300 men. As a matter of fact they had not nearly so many. The men were rough soldiers, vigorous and hardy ; but they were scamps and marauders, insolent and insubordinate. Divided, according to the weapon they carried, into pikemen and musketeers, they would march along, the latter surrounding the former, preceded by their fifes and drums, escorted by their officers, captains, lieutenants, and ensigns, their petty officers, sergeants, corporals, and lance-pesades. They were drilled, though they wore no uniform, and were billeted on the inhabitants of the place they were in. When the King wished to raise fresh troops he gave signed commissions to captains, who recruited men to the sound of the drum, offering them earnest-money and payment for their services. The cavalry consisted in the first place of companies of light-horse, the members of which wore helmets and breast-plates, each company containing about fifty " masters." They were quartered in the small towns and frequently changed their garrisons. This body was the light cavalry. Then came the heavy cavalry, consisting of companies called ordnance companies and companies of men-at-arms, each of 100 lancers, raised in time of war by princes, governors, and other authori-ties. The members of this body were men of gentle birth, well mounted and equipped. But there was a tendency to replace them by light horsemen. The cavalry regiments were not created until the reign of Louis XIII. The artillery was even simpler. The Grand Master of the Artillery, Monsieur de Rosny, laid in a store of cannon and casks of ammunition in the Arsenal in Paris. In time of war, people who owned carts were paid so much a day to transport all this ordnance. No special artillery corps existed at this period.

And if the country were suddenly invaded, or some grave and imminent danger threatened, the King had recourse to the **Ban and** old feudal custom of calling out the ban and **rear-ban.** rear-ban, a sort of " general levy." The bailiffs and seneschals convoked all the enfieffed nobility, who had to serve as cavalrymen for three months without payment, and the people of the parishes were summoned to serve as infantry —an inefficacious method which was practically never used.

As for the navy, it was a negligible quantity. There was certainly an Admiral, a personage who had supreme control **The Navy** of everything connected with the sea and the **practically** coast. The Admiral, however, who was a great **non-existent.** Crown official, like Coligny, for instance, was not a sailor. He was a sort of judicial administrator who had jurisdiction in all the maritime towns and dealt with all crimes committed at sea " and on the sea-shore," all matters connected with navigation, fishing, freightage, sales and breaking-up of ships, and insurance policies. He was helped by officers called Admiralty officers, lieutenants-general and local lieutenants, counsellors and procurators. He appointed vice-admirals, superintendents, coast captains and coastguards, and naval captains and controllers. As for the ships they were a sorry affair. During the disastrous years of anarchy, everything had been allowed to go to ruin. There were merely a few galleys on which criminals were sent to row under the command of a general of the galleys. When in 1600, Henry IV wanted a small escort for the ship that bore Marie de' Medici from Florence, he was obliged to borrow vessels from the Knights of Malta and from the Pope.

Such, briefly, were the institutions by means of which France was governed at the end of the sixteenth and the beginning of the seventeenth century. The administration certainly resembled the bushy tree described by Charles de Figon—and even now we have made no mention of the conflict of functions, the tangle of authorities and the disputes and encroachments that occurred. The large principal branches were fairly well defined ; whilst throughout the whole organism there ran a vital sap, which endowed it with an originality differentiating the organization of this period from the automatic mechanism of the uniform institutions of a later date. It is true that there were many inconveniences connected with the old methods, creaking wheels, parts that worked badly or stopped working altogether, duplicate offices, waste, injustice, and violence. But the whole structure possessed colour and picturesqueness, it was extremely solid and above all it was endowed with vitality—a great merit. What was the life of the French people within this frame ?

Socially, the French people were divided into three great **The three** Estates. Every individual had either entered **Estates or** into the ecclesiastical Estate, or he belonged to **Orders.** the Estate of the nobility or that of the commons, called the Third Estate. The political assembly of the representatives of these three estates was called the States-General. A man belonged and necessarily belonged to one or other of these three Estates. The first in order of precedence was the ecclesiastical Estate.

In 1600 the clergy constituted a vast body forming, so to speak, a State within a State. It was a skilfully organized **The Clergy.** hierarchy. Its enormous revenues made it independent. It had its own judges, with special tribunals rising from the lowest to the highest grades—diocesan courts, metropolitan courts, appeals to Rome, &c., which the State was forced to recognize. These tribunals took cognizance of every sort of case, provided clerics were involved. It had its own legislation, the canon law, which it alone could modify. It paid no taxes and was liable to none of the charges, such as having soldiers billeted upon its members, to which ordinary subjects were exposed. It formed a complete close society, which was respectful to the King, but outside his sphere of power, although, as a matter of fact, he endeavoured to get some sort of control over it by appointing the Bishops and Abbots, an extraordinary right conferred upon him by the Concordat. For a long time the Church even tried to go beyond the bounds of its purely ecclesiastical jurisdiction, and, as late as the reign of Henry IV, its judges claimed the right, to the exclusion of the lay magistrates, of dealing with all questions connected with separations, annulments of marriages, and divorce, on the pretext that matters concerning the sacraments were at issue. But the officers of the Crown resisted this demand, and entered upon a struggle to restrict the privileges of the Church and force the clerics to enter as ordinary subjects within the sphere of the common law. It was destined to be a long conflict lasting for centuries.

The staff of the Church at the beginning of the seventeenth century was extremely numerous. There were so many ecclesiastics in France that there were not nearly enough posts for all of them, although the number of situations available was very considerable. In the 136 archiepiscopal or episcopal dioceses into which the kingdom was divided—large ones like Rouen, including several modern departments, and tiny ones like Saint-Papoul containing barely one canton—there were about 40,000 titular priests. These were helped in their duties by an equal number of clerics who were called vicars, chaplains, or confessors, or lived as best they could, making a total of 80,000. The cathedral chapters were composed on an average of sixty canons. Together with those forming college chapters the number of canons amounted to 19,000, whilst the number of commendatory, that is to say, secular, abbots and priors, was 5000. They were all provided with prebends. The poorest of them all were the country clergy. A priest could be the titular priest of several cures, that is to say, he could enjoy the revenues of several posts at once. In the places he did not visit his duties were performed by a vicar, to whom he paid a small fixed salary, so small indeed, that in order to eke out a livelihood the latter was obliged to increase his incidental charges and demand payment for the administration of the sacraments, even the sacrament of penitence. But in addition to these, there was a whole host of unattached priests, who, not finding posts, were obliged to work for their living. They prepared wax, sowed corn, did carpentry and carried out commissions. They were given the courtesy title of "*messires*" but were as badly treated as if they had been common workmen. The religious services were very long everywhere. In Normandy, in the little country churches, the Sunday services would be as follows : Matins, the first High Mass called the Mass of Our Lady, frequently with an obit—the foundations of obits were innumerable ; this was followed by the parochial High Mass—the High Mass with a sermon—when the officiating priest gave out all the notices on administrative and other matters. In the afternoon came Vespers and often a procession. Benediction did not exist at this time. The task of preaching, even in country districts, was left to the religious orders.

The number of monks and nuns was equally great. Under Henry IV people complained bitterly that there were too many **Religious** of them, too many orders and convents, and above **Orders.** all, too many "mendicants." There were the "old mendicants" the Carmelites, the Augustinians, the Jacobins, and the Greyfriars, who numbered 13,500. They went about preaching in country places and got their living by begging from door to door ; they were said to collect from 1,200,000 to 1,300,000 pounds a year. These friars made some return for the money they collected, inasmuch as they preached the Gospel in rural districts. But those who went by the title of the " reformed Franciscans " the Recollets, the Capuchins and the Picpus,* numbering some 21,000, preached much less and begged much more—collecting, it was estimated, almost 8,000,000 pounds a year. They were perpetually building and seemed to irritate the people ; for, according to a contemporary writer, in order to beg they were continually visiting country houses one after the other, and the inmates were obliged to receive them out of charity and give them money. " No one could be more importunate ; they fed extremely well wherever they went and only visited the nobility." They were regarded as useless. There were 8000 Benedictines ; 1600 Carthusians ; 900 Cistercians ; 1500 Premonstrants ; 2500 Jesuits ; and others ; the grand total amounting to over 70,000 monks and friars. There were some 80,000 nuns—12,500 nuns of Saint Clare, 3000 Carmelites, 9000 Ursulines, 18,000 Benedictines. As a matter of fact the number of nunneries was countless. So much for the clergy.

From the mighty lord, who was a great personage at Court and owned a sumptuous castle in the country—The Nobility. like the Duke of Épernon's castle at Cardillac, which was practically a royal palace—to the humble country squire perishing of hunger on his poverty-stricken estate, the nobility represented all manner of people of varying fortunes. But they all possessed certain privileges of their rank in common—exemption from taxation, and the right to offer personal service as cavalrymen in time of war in good positions. In the reign of Henry IV they certainly possessed all the virtues and vices characteristic of their kind : carelessness, valour, gaiety, extravagance, familiarity varied by insolence, a capacity for deep devotion, and provocative manners ; they were ready at one moment to embrace a man and at the next to fight a duel with him. They were charming,

* These were the members of the third religious order of Saint Francis of Assisi. They derived their name from their headquarters in the *Rue Picpus*, in Paris. (Tr.)

brilliant and terrible people. They may be divided into two categories : those who went to Court, and those who never left their estates in the country.

To the first category belonged the highest of the nobility, " princes and barons." They were rich and grew even more wealthy through the patronage of the King, who made them governors of provinces, ambassadors or Court officials, such as Masters of the Horse, Grand Cupbearers, &c. They made a great show and were surrounded by a suite of followers who lived upon their bounty and gathered up the crumbs that fell from their tables. They kept open house, had great mansions in Paris, and fine castles in the country. They were in their way potentates, and considered themselves more or less the masters, as became abundantly clear during the minority of Louis XIII. After them came the whole crowd of nobles who tried to make their way by securing posts at Court. By dint of perseverance they might be made pantlers, equerries, or gentlemen-in-waiting ; even then they were only on duty for three months in the year and obtained extremely modest salaries. But there was always the chance of finding some opportunity for putting themselves forward ! Unfortunately for them, Court life, even for three months out of the twelve, was ruinous. To live up to his rank a man had so many expenses in the way of dress, horses, food, and servants, that moderate patrimonies were exhausted in the process. Fashions were constantly changing in accordance with the demands of extravagant luxury, and unless he wished to be a laughing-stock, a courtier was obliged to follow them. " The amount spent by the nobility on clothes," says la Noue, " is enormous and excessive." And, indeed, the fact which particularly struck strangers about these Court nobles was that they ended in poverty, in spite of the gambling at cards and at dice in which they indulged in the hope of replenishing their purses. " If wars have brought us four ounces of poverty," observes la Noue, " our follies are responsible for twelve ; " and according to him these follies consisted of unnecessary expenditure on clothes, food, furniture, and buildings.

How much calmer was the lot of those who remained in the country ! " Their simple secluded life in their castles," says

Suriano, "entailed neither great expense, liveries, rich clothes, valuable horses nor banquets." And the number of these lesser nobles who lived on their own estates was very large ; France was full of them. Under Henry IV, courtiers were a mere handful by comparison with the nobles scattered all over the country in their manors and little châteaux. There they lived the dignified lives befitting their rank, but simply and quietly, side by side with the villagers in whose interests they shared, speaking the same dialect and playing the same games, cultivating their land and visiting each other on horseback ; for they travelled about a great deal in the neighbourhood of their property. Olivier de Serres, in his *Théâtre d'Agriculture* gives them good advice on the subject of suitable buildings and furniture, and the stocking of their houses with everything necessary for their rural existence. But nothing can give a Diary of the better idea of their manner of life than a perusal Sieur de of the entertaining diary written by one of them Gouberville. —the Sieur de Gouberville, Seigneur of Mesnil-au-Val, a small parish of the Cotentin near Cherbourg in the Val-de-Saire. Monsieur de Gouberville was an old bachelor who inhabited his manor, surrounded by some fourteen to eighteen "serving-men and chambermaids," people of the neighbourhood, all living together and eating at the same table. He used to beat them, but also nursed them devotedly when they were ill. For wages he paid them the price of a bushel of corn a day, and, in addition, one suit of clothes a year and their shoes. His own dress was serviceable though not lacking in elegance. He wore a fine linen ruff trimmed with lace, hose made of velvet, drugget or satin ; false trunk-hose—riding-breeches—of tan leather. His doublets were made of red cloth and his coats and cloaks were black. He wore felt or velvet hats, leather capes in wet weather and boots that he had made at home by a journeyman bootmaker. In the great hall of his manor, which also served as a kitchen, in front of the huge chimney with its high mantelpiece, where trunks of trees were burnt, he took his meals seated at one end of the massive table with his people round him eating off pewter dishes. His chief article of diet was meat, butcher's meat, plenty of fowls, not much venison, except in pasties ; hares, rabbits from the warren,

406

sea fish in abundance—the beach was a stone's throw from his door—no fruit, and very few vegetables. He drank cider and cultivated twenty-nine, whilst knowing as many as forty, different varieties of apple-trees. When he wanted wine he bought it in the town—claret or Bordeaux, Burgundy, Anjou, and Orleans. His house was lighted by candles. By way of amusement he played dice, backgammon, or cards at home ; or he would go and watch the people of the parish playing skittles and bowls, and the old French games of *croche* and *soule* or wrestling. He hunted and had plenty of dogs ; he knew how to handle a musket and a pistol, and how to use goshawks and ferrets. He was not much of a reader and at most had *Amadis de Gaule*, a fashionable novel of the day, read aloud to him during the winter evenings in the chimney-corner. His chief occupation was the cultivation of his fields in which he grew wheat, oats, and barley. He visited them every day and watched his people at work, unless it " poured the whole day " when he remained " at home." When he wanted to gather in his harvest, in his capacity as lord of the manor, he had all his tenants, from whom he had a right to demand forced labour, summoned " by monitory " at sermon time during High Mass. On the appointed day they all arrived to the number of some fifty to seventy men and women. They worked gaily, and in the evening there was a huge supper at the manor, after which they danced until a late hour of the night. By way of cattle, Monsieur de Gouberville had a number of horses, oxen, and cows, " horned cattle," and pigs. But they all wandered about pretty freely in the forests, and their owner was very vague as to their numbers. When he wanted to catch any of them he had to organize battues and summon everybody in the district to take part in them. Taking it all in all, he led a somewhat rough life, but one that was healthy and invigorating and very similar to that of the peasants round him, attached to the soil and socially speaking, firmly rooted in it.

This calm and solid stability was also characteristic of the Third Estate. It is true that the civil wars darkened the horizon and aroused lively passions ; but once the danger was past, the people all went back to their work, obliterated the traces of the conflict, and re-established the peaceful appearance of the countryside once more. Foreigners visiting France

The Third Estate or plebeians. at the end of the sixteenth and the beginning of the seventeenth century were chiefly struck by the fact that the masses seemed hardworking and thrifty and, by their clothes which were usually "seemly and decent," showed that they were comfortably off. "They are very particular about their food and their dress," one of these travellers remarked. These visitors did not, however, shut their eyes to their faults, but considered the members of the lower classes at this time gamblers and rakes, who swore and took the name of God in vain, and were "hasty and hot-tempered" and above all frivolous, with that incurable frivolity which made Charles V declare: "They are wise without seeming so." Finally they were ardent to the point of exaggeration in their religious feelings, either for or against a given point of view. In the eyes of strangers, the artisans and peasants appeared somewhat coarse and brutal, at all events on occasion. But they rendered justice to their good qualities. "It is generally noticeable," they remarked, "that the people of France are everywhere good." They were respectful towards the great, the nobles, and the officers of justice and of finance; they were full of kind attention and courtesy towards strangers; hospitable; and deferential to women, to whom they allowed a great deal of freedom. The women, it was observed, for their part, were pious and thrifty; they went to Mass every day and spent the whole of Sunday in church attending Low Mass, High Mass, sermon, and vespers. The utmost that Lippomano had to say against them was that their thrift verged upon avarice.

As for morals in general, Brantôme's scandalous stories must not be taken too literally. He was a scandalmonger,

Morals. only too ready to collect doubtful versions of adventures or tales more or less founded on fact, and circulated as jokes or funny stories. The members of the middle classes, as well as many of the noble families, could furnish endless examples of irreproachable conduct and domestic virtue. The names of the women who became notorious in connexion with Henry IV have been handed down to us; whilst nothing is said about all those who, like the beautiful and sagacious

Madame de Guercheville or Madame de Sainte-Beuve, repulsed his overtures. Nevertheless, it must be confessed that in comparison with modern tastes and standards there was a certain lack of delicacy at this period. Monsieur de Gouberville, for instance, had among his servants some illegitimate brothers of his own, whom he may perhaps have treated slightly differently to the rest, but the distinction was scarcely noticeable. He used also frequently to go to Russy near Bayeux to visit a certain uncle, who was a worthy ecclesiastic, living on the revenues of cures in which, as a matter of fact, he never resided. Now this good priest presented his nephew with little cousins whose mother was only a servant, a circumstance which does not seem to have shocked the Sire of Mesnil-au-Val, any more than the country at large was shocked at the spectacle of Henry IV bringing up his children by Marie de' Medici, Gabrielle d'Estrées, and the Marquise de Verneuil altogether pell-mell at Saint Germain-en-Laye. Public opinion was less strict on such matters than it is to-day, both with regard to conduct and language. For the things that were said, written, or read in the circle of young ladies of good family, who superintended the education of the Dauphin of France and of his brothers and sisters at Saint-Germain, would never be tolerated in any modest or well-behaved family to-day, especially before children. The Diary of Jean Héroard, Louis XIII's doctor when he was a child, gives us plenty of information on this subject. The people of this age were more free and easy than we are, or we have become more scrupulous.

The Third Estate included the magistrates, the merchants, all classes of citizens, artisans, the masses in the towns, and the country folk.

Noël de Faïl, a counsellor in the Parliament of Rennes, has described the life of the peasantry in the sixteenth century in his tales, which abound in fun and good humour. **The sixteenth-century peasant.** The rough work in the fields was very much the same as it is to-day, neither more wretched nor less hard and monotonous. Only the merry-making on Sundays seems to have been more frankly whole-hearted. On the weekly day of rest the young people, after having been to church, might be seen practising archery, playing at prisoner's base, jumping, and racing, whilst the old men would look on as they sat chatting under the village trees. Then to the sound of a rebec, a hautboy, or a flute, the young people would begin to dance, and their elders, remembering their own exploits of former days, would get up mechanically and " beat time with their feet," to the tune they knew so well. After this they would carouse in the tavern when glasses would be clinked (*dringuer* or *trinquer* from the German *trinken*) to the singing of songs. They did not drink brandy, which was a rare and extremely expensive drug, and was only sold by the apothecary. These country rustics, like the masses in the towns, dressed roughly during the week, but kept themselves clean and neat on Sundays, and above all, were well fed. Writers boast of " the good nourishment both in food and drink to which the masses were accustomed as they were in no other country." They had four or five meals a day, not much bread and fruit, but, like Monsieur de Gouberville, plenty of meat. In the towns, public cooks and pastrycooks (people who sold meat-pasties) retailed all kinds of ready cooked dishes in abundance. They ate beef and mutton—pork was left for the poorest—lamb, salt fish, salmon, cod, and herrings ; and by way of vegetables, peas, rice, artichokes, and lentils.

The life of the artisans in the towns was extremely circumscribed and strictly regulated, in the sense that there was The sixteenth-century artisan. no such thing as free labour. If a man wished to practise a trade, he had to join the corporation of that trade, go through his apprenticeship and be made a companion, after which he had to produce a masterpiece in order to be admitted to the rank of master, a position to which not many attained and which it was neither easy nor cheap to reach, as the price of the masterships was fixed. The work done was subject to the laws of the corporation and an individual was not free to make anything he chose. But people were used to the system and the workman " had plenty of industry and worked merrily." A great many disputes, tumults, and strikes took place, but, on the whole, the industry which belonged to a particular place or district went on quietly enough. People sometimes grew rich, and it was chiefly the merchants who amassed fortunes.

410

The merchant class was the one that had command of the money, and was accordingly pandered to and fawned upon ; **The Merchant Class.** but the nobility despised this manner of life and would have considered themselves disgraced if they had been obliged to make a living by trade. In the towns the merchants were the highest in rank, they formed the municipalities, and were the notables. But it is curious to observe that they too had such a low opinion of their calling that the greatest wish of their lives was to make their sons royal officials—" functionaries." To amass enough wealth to send their boys to study at the universities—at the University of Paris alone there were 15,000 students—and afterwards to buy them some post was the dream of their ambition. Already the petty nobility who were badly off were trying to make their way into the Parliaments, whilst townsmen's sons aspired to become judges, lawyers, treasurers, tax-collectors, and receivers of all kinds. The Kings raised no objection to this movement, for, as a matter of fact, tradition itself demanded that the posts of Chancellor of France and Secretary of State should be given only to members of the Third Estate—a great privilege !

And thus above or on a par with the merchants we find the whole citizen class of magistrates, men of law, and others, **Magistrates.** dignified and honourable people, excellent parishioners, charitable, steady, in enjoyment of easy circumstances and respected by all. They were conspicuous on account of their correct and quiet dress, and their grave and measured gait. They were good husbands, good fathers, and good Christians. They had a town-house and a country-house where they went for change of air. They were quiet and moderate in their behaviour, worthy people and loyal subjects. It was from their ranks that the " politicians " were recruited. But they could also be merry and gay, and physical exercises were among their principal diversions.

For physical exercises—the last factor common to the whole nation—were universally popular about the year 1600. Nobles, **Love of outdoor games.** burghers, and peasants alike, gave themselves up ardently to all kinds of games that had survived from the Middle Ages. The English, who were surprised

411

by this fashion, copied it, though they considered the French "very immoderate." The most popular sport—from the old French word *desport*, game—was the game of *paume*, which the Englishman Sir Robert Dallington, who visited France in 1597, calls tennis. "It is in greater vogue here," he says, "than in the whole of the rest of Christendom, as is shown by the number of tennis-courts which are to be found everywhere in such numbers that there is not a single borough or town in France that does not possess one or several. At Orleans there are sixty, and in Paris I cannot say how many hundreds. Frenchmen are born with a racquet in their hands." Talking of pall-mall he adds, "I am exceedingly surprised that among all the mad and ridiculous games we have brought over from France we have not introduced this one into England"

There was much that was healthy about the subjects of Henry IV. They lived in one of the roughest and most brutal, **Sterling qualities of the nation as a whole.** though also one of the most original and attractive periods of French history. The bad sides of this epoch which general history reveals, do less than justice to the qualities of honesty, diligence, stability, and regularity possessed by the people.

SOURCES. Dallington, *The View of France*, 1598; 1892; *Deliciæ Galliæ*, 1609; Jodocus Sincerus, *Itinerarium Galliæ*, 1616; G. Hegenitius, *Gallo-Brabanticum*, 1630; Th. Erpenius, *De peregrinatione gallica*, 1631; Abr. Golnitz, *Ulysses Belgico-Gallicus*, 1631; H. Du Boys, *De l'origine et autorité des rois*, 1604; F. Le Jay, *De la dignité des rois et princes souverains*, 1589; P. Constant, *De l'excellence et dignité des rois*, 1598; N. Bergeron, *Police générale du royaume de France*, 1617; C. de Figon, *Discours des États et offices de France*, 1579; J. Hurault, *Des offices d'Estat*, 1588; C. Loyseau, *Cinq livres du droit des offices*, 1613; C. Fauchet, *Origine des dignités et magistrats de France*, 1600; C. Chappuzeau, *Traité des diverses juridictions de France*, 1618; La Roche-Flavin, *Treize livres des Parlements de France*, 1617; Cimber and Donjou, *Archives curieuses de l'histoire de France*, vols. x and xiv; Isambert, *Receuil général des anciennes lois françaises*, vols. xiv and xv; *Traité des finances de France*, 1580; N. Froumanteau, *Le Secret des finances de France*, 1581; *Traité des revenue et dépenses de France en l'année* 1607, in *Revue rétrospective*, vol. iv; J. Hennequin, *Le Guidon général des finances*, 1610; N. Rémond, *Sommaire traité des revenus et dépenses des finances de France*, 1622; *Le nombre des ecclésiastiques de France, celui des religieux et religieuses*, in *Archives Curieuses*, vol. xiv; C. Loyseau, *Traité des seigneuries*, 1608; Nicolas Rapin, *Les Plaisirs d'un gentilhomme champétre*, 1575; Gilles de Gouberville, *Journal*, ed. Beaurepaire and Blagny, 1892–1895; Noël

412

KINGDOM OF FRANCE ABOUT 1600

du Faïl, *Œuvres facétieuses*, ed. Assézat, 1874 ; Jean Héroard, *Journal*, ed. Soulié, 1869.

WORKS. G. Weill, *Les théories sur le pouvoir royal en France pendant les guerres de religion*, 1892 ; N. Valois, *Le conseil du roi aux XIVe, XVe et XVIe siècles* 1889 ; Fauvelet du Toc, *Histoire des secretaires d'État*, 1668 ; J. Joly, *Trois livres des offices de France*, 1638 ; Guyot, *Traité des droits, fonctions . . . en France*, 1786 ; P. Picaut, *Traité des Parlements*, 1679 ; de Bastard d'Estang, *Les Parlements de France*, 1857 ; Mallet, *Comptes rendus de l'administration des finances du royaume de France*, 1789 ; C. de Beaune, *Traité de la Chambre des Comptes*, 1647 ; Le P. Daniel, *Histoire de la milice française*, 1721 ; Fagniez, *L'Économie sociale de la France sous Henri IV*, 1897 ; P. de Vaissière, *Gentilshommes campagnards de l'ancienne France*, 1903.

INDEX

415

INDEX

INDEX

2 D

INDEX

418

INDEX

419

INDEX

INDEX

INDEX

Printed by BALLANTYNE, HANSON AND CO. LTD.
At the Ballantyne Press
LONDON AND EDINBURGH